HOUSING STANDARDISATION AND DESIGN GOVERNANCE

Equitable access to decent housing remains a major global challenge, particularly for lower-income populations reliant on an insufficient supply of subsidised, affordable homes. This is exacerbated by the continued commodification of housing, demographic change, and the increasing time many people now spend at home. Addressing these challenges requires, as this book argues, stronger state intervention, closer cooperation between housing regulators, providers, and occupants, and a more robust evidence base that links housing policy, supply, quality, and design, along with a shift towards more long-term social and environmental housing values.

This book examines how housing design governance and lived experience shape the quality of homes and the wellbeing of residents, analysing the political, economic, social, historical, and environmental drivers of design. Drawing on new and rich comparative data and evidence from England, Chile, China, the Netherlands, Spain, and Switzerland, it explores how contextual standards, cultural norms, social expectations, and regulatory practices influence everyday life and perceptions of subsidised housing.

Combining historical, technical, and social perspectives through a comparative international lens, this interdisciplinary design research offers a multidimensional understanding of housing quality. It provides insights for policymakers, housing providers, and designers, demonstrating how design research and lived experience studies can inform standards and policies to create more inclusive, adaptable, and sustainable homes and neighborhoods, with implications for contemporary housing practice.

Sam Jacoby is Professor of Architectural and Urban Design Research, Research Lead of the School of Architecture, and Director of both the Intergenerational Design Lab and the Laboratory for Design and Machine Learning at the Royal College of Art. His interdisciplinary work focuses on the social impact of design research, spatial strategies, and architecture.

Alvaro Arancibia is an architect trained at the Pontificia Universidad Católica de Chile, with an MPhil in Urban Design and a PhD in Architectural Design from the Architectural Association in London. His work bridges practice and research, focusing on collective housing and urban design in Santiago, Chile. His doctoral thesis received the AA Graduate Prize for Research: Outstanding Work 2015–2016, and between 2022 and 2025 he was co-investigator of the project Housing Standardisation: The Architecture of Regulations and Design Standards. Through his practice, he has won several housing competitions organised by the Chilean Ministry of Housing, including the Mirador Laguna project, completed in 2024. His research and design work have been published internationally and presented at universities in Chile, the United Kingdom, the United States, and Mexico, contributing to debates on housing policy, standards, and typologies.

HOUSING STANDARDISATION AND DESIGN GOVERNANCE

Sam Jacoby and Alvaro Arancibia

Routledge
Taylor & Francis Group
LONDON AND NEW YORK

Designed cover image: Floor plans of homes studied in the Housing Standardisation project. Drawn by Claudia Andrea Chavarría.

First published 2026
by Routledge
4 Park Square, Milton Park, Abingdon, Oxon OX14 4RN

and by Routledge
605 Third Avenue, New York, NY 10158

Routledge is an imprint of the Taylor & Francis Group, an informa business

This work was supported by the UK Arts and Humanities Research Council [AH/W003198/1].

For Product Safety Concerns and Information please contact our EU representative GPSR@taylorandfrancis.com. Taylor & Francis Verlag GmbH, Kaufingerstraße 24, 80331 München, Germany.

British Library Cataloguing-in-Publication Data
A catalogue record for this book is available from the British Library

ISBN: 9781032679167 (hbk)
ISBN: 9781032672533 (pbk)
ISBN: 9781032679204 (ebk)

DOI: 10.4324/9781032679204

Typeset in Times New Roman
by KnowledgeWorks Global Ltd.

CONTENTS

ACKNOWLEDGEMENTS

This book developed through discussions and studies that began in 2019, and it would not have been possible without the generosity of many individuals and organisations who shared their time, expertise, data, and support.

We are deeply grateful to our project team and colleagues – Lucia Alonso Aranda, Seyithan Özer, Consuelo Albornoz Marambio, Claudia Andrea Chavarría, and Robin Roussel – whose dedication, ideas, and collaboration shaped every stage of the research. We also thank our local researchers, Raül Avilla-Royo, Gianna Bottema, Salome Rohner, and Lu Wang, whose local knowledge and thoughtful engagement were essential to the success of this work. Our sincere thanks go to our advisory board members: Professor Peter Bishop, Dr Dhruv Sookhoo, Pablo Jordan, Rupesh Varsani, and Dr Elanor Warwick.

We acknowledge the invaluable support of the housing providers, who facilitated access to study participants and shared their knowledge and data, in particular AMB:IMPSOL (Josep Maria Borrell Bru and Xavier Gracia Marcos), ASIG, Baugenossenschaft Glattal Zürich, Clarion Housing Group (Ayo Allu and Elanor Warwick), de Alliantie (Jaap Darwinkel and Arthur Friederichs), Peabody (Guinevere Dimmock, Robin Palmer, and David Stronge), and Ymere (Denise Koeleveld and Timme Schunselaar). In addition to these representatives, we are also grateful to the many housing experts who kindly agreed to be interviewed: Carlos Araya (Ministry of Housing and Urban Development, Chile), José Astaburuaga and Mario Grandón (Gevecon), Peter Bishop, Patricio Bravo and Gabriel Lagos (Consolida), Philip Boyle, Mónica Bustos (INVI - Universidad de Chile), Cristian Castillo (Alpinku Arquitectos), Jennifer Duyne Barenstein (ETH Wohnforum), Ron Edelaar (EMI Architects), Alex Ely (Mae Architects), Caterina Figuerola and Ibon Bilbao (llindarquitectura), Alejandro Garretón (Isiete), Camilo Lanata and Rodrigo Retamal (Ministry of Housing and Urban Development, Chile), Andrej Mećava and Amanda Rashid (London Borough of Hounslow), Patricio Miranda and Francisco Vergara (Francisco Vergara Arquitectos), Marta Peris and José Manuel Toral (Peris+Toral Arquitectes), Josep Ricart (H Arquitectes), Dhruv Sookhoo, Favio Salguero (Oval), Anna Vergés, Loreto Wahr, and Victor Suazo (TECHO).

We particularly extend our sincere thanks to the study participants and their families in Chile, China, England, the Netherlands, Spain, and Switzerland, who welcomed us into their homes and generously shared their daily lives with us.

We are also grateful to the organisations and individuals who supported our public events: symposia at the Barbican in London (Jon Astbury) and at the Pontificia Universidad Católica de Chile; exhibitions and roundtables at the Asociación de Oficinas de Arquitectos de Chile (Pablo Jordan), the Building Centre in London (Tom Nomico, Sandra Hedblad, and Laura Broderick), the Col·legi d'Arquitectes de Catalunya (Gemma Molas Bernabé and Àngels Isabel Florea Jauset), and AMB:IMPSOL in Barcelona (Josep Maria Borrell Bru and Marta Pérez Franco). We are especially grateful to the Architecture Foundation (Ellis Woodman), which co-organised the London events, and to the many speakers, participants, and audiences who contributed great insight and enthusiasm.

Special thanks are due to Luiza Tatarska, Weronika Pestka, and Przemek Ksiazek (film editing); Diego Hernán Rivera Hechem (exhibition models); Emilio Pérez (website and graphic design); Taz Gray, Luiza Tatarska, and Lucy Last (administrative support); and Tim Flight (manuscript editing). We also thank Hannah Studd, Fran Ford, and the Routledge production team. We are grateful to our home institutions – the Royal College of Art and the Pontificia Universidad Católica de Chile – and especially Adrian Lahoud, Luis Eduardo Bresciani, and Pilar Urrejola for their sustained support of this project.

This project was supported by the Arts and Humanities Research Council [grant number AH/W003198/1]. We further received generous financial support from the Prosit Philosophiae Foundation, the Royal College of Art (Research Development Fund, Strategic Priorities Fund, and Research Impact Development Scheme), the Pontificia Universidad Católica de Chile (Fondo Semilla), AMB:IMPSOL, and the Built Environment Trust.

LIST OF CONTRIBUTORS

Consuelo Albornoz Marambio is an architect with a master's degree in architecture from the Universidad de Chile. She has worked as a teaching assistant at the Universidad de Chile and the Pontificia Universidad Católica, and as a lecturer at the Universidad de las Américas. She was a researcher on the AHRC-funded project Housing Standardisation: The Architecture of Regulations and Design Standards, and has also worked as a research assistant on various studies about housing, modern architecture, and semiotics. She is currently the Executive Director of the Concurso Nacional de Proyectos de Título (National Graduation Project Competition), which showcases the best final-year projects from Chilean architecture schools.

Lucia Alonso Aranda is an architect and researcher based in London. She is currently a researcher at the Royal College of Art, focusing on the relationships between housing, design policy, and wellbeing. From 2022 to 2025, she contributed as a researcher to the UK Arts and Humanities Research Council project "Housing Standardisation: The Architecture of Regulations and Design Standards". She holds a BArch in Architecture and Urbanism from the Universidad Iberoamericana (Mexico City) and an MPhil in Architecture and Urban Design from the Architectural Association (London), funded by FONCA-CONACYT.

Alvaro Arancibia is an architect trained at the Pontificia Universidad Católica de Chile, with an MPhil in Urban Design and a PhD in Architectural Design from the Architectural Association in London. His work bridges practice and research, focusing on collective housing and urban design in Santiago, Chile. His doctoral thesis received the AA Graduate Prize for Research: Outstanding Work 2015–2016, and between 2022 and 2025 he was co-investigator of the project Housing Standardisation: The Architecture of Regulations and Design Standards. Through his practice, he has won several housing competitions organised by the Chilean Ministry of Housing, including the Mirador Laguna project, completed in 2024. His research and design work have been published internationally and presented at universities in Chile, the United Kingdom, the United States, and Mexico, contributing to debates on housing policy, standards, and typologies.

Sam Jacoby is Professor of Architectural and Urban Design Research, Research Lead of the School of Architecture, and Director of both the Intergenerational Design Lab and the Laboratory for Design and Machine Learning at the Royal College of Art. His interdisciplinary work focuses on the social impact of design research, spatial strategies, and architecture.

Seyithan Özer is a Lecturer at the University of Hertfordshire and Arts University Bournemouth. His research explores the construction and systematisation of design knowledge in the built environment, with a particular focus on the making of regulations, policies, manuals, and guidelines and their shaping of architectural practice. He holds a PhD from the Royal College of Art, London.

INTRODUCTION

Housing Standardisation and Design Governance

Sam Jacoby and Alvaro Arancibia

What makes a well-designed home?
How is it defined and realised?

This book explores these questions by examining the relationship between housing design quality and the growing standardisation of housing. While both terms are widely used in housing discourse and practice, their meanings and implications are often unclear. Despite a long history of regulatory efforts to improve housing quality, evolving needs, economic pressures, and shifting political priorities have made both defining and achieving it difficult. For example, while high-quality and well-designed housing is a common policy aim, it is rarely explicitly defined or consistently applied. In architecture, design quality is often presumed rather than evidenced. As a result, housing design quality has remained a vague and contested concept, whose interpretation and value depends on who defines it and in what context (Alonso Aranda & Jacoby, 2023; Jacoby & Alonso Aranda, 2022).

Housing design is increasingly unspecific to a site or development and is instead based on existing, standard house types. This is particularly evident in large-scale affordable housing developments, where cost-efficiency and risk management are prioritised over specificity of design. However, the design and adaptation of these standard house types can vary, depending on the preferences of housebuilders and regulatory context, which are both shaped by cultural expectations and norms (Özer & Jacoby, 2023). Thus, while housing design outcomes are not necessarily optimal design solutions, they often reflect prevailing practices within a housing system or the established conventions of different housing organisations.

To clarify what design quality and standardisation mean in practice, our research was initially framed around three interconnected hypotheses. First, that housing design is extensively standardised, with large developments showing increasing uniformity in design and appearance across sites, regions, and countries. Second, that this design standardisation is closely related to regulatory and market standardisation, particularly at the lower, affordable end of the market, where homes are typically built to meet only the minimum legal and commercial requirements. Third, that subsidised homes are often "designed" more by regulation and performance

DOI: 10.4324/9781032679204-1

standards than by architects – meaning that homes and design quality are less the outcome of design intentions than the result of design governance processes.

To both support and challenge these hypotheses – and to clarify the formation and effects of housing standardisation and design governance – we examined the historical, technical, social, and cultural drivers shaping housing design, along with the lived reality of the homes they produce. In the housing context, design governance broadly refers to the policies, regulations, standards, and decision-making processes that define the quality and adequacy of homes within a specific political, economic, and cultural context. Understanding the interaction of these design drivers and design decisions requires examining the effects of diverse governance structures and cultural norms, which we studied by comparing them across several countries to highlight differences in approach and outcomes.

Homes are arguably the most important spaces in our lives due to their fundamental impact on our quality of life. Therefore, the quality of homes and their design is critical to our health and wellbeing. Yet what constitutes "good" housing design or quality is often subjective and varies greatly between political and cultural contexts. Despite the existential and social importance of the home, there is a significant lack of evidence-based understanding of what average homes look like, what determines their design, and how they are actually used and experienced by residents.

Many key drivers of housing design are also beyond the immediate control of architects and housebuilders, shaped instead by policy frameworks, housing and planning systems, building regulations, voluntary design guidance, and design standards. Together, these form the design governance and the tools available to it, which determine what homes are built and how they are designed (Carmona, 2017). The development, interpretation, and implementation of design governance by policymakers, housebuilders, and designers – and how people live in the homes that result from these processes of negotiation and translation – are critical to understanding housing design quality but have received only limited attention in academic research and public policy debates (White et al., 2024). This is especially important for subsidised housing, where design is often reduced to regulatory compliance.

To study these important but underexplored relationships, we examined housing design governance, including its formal and informal policies, processes, tools, and the diverse actors involved in regulating and shaping housing design. This reflects a wide range of both public and private sector interests as well as the available means to influence the design quality of housing and neighbourhoods.

At the same time, we focused on the realities of recently built subsidised homes across different tenures (social and affordable rent, cooperative, and shared and outright ownership), paying particular attention to their design, layout, and lived experience. Understanding the disconnect between what is planned and how homes are actually used and experienced matters, as this directly affects how housing quality is perceived by residents.

Our studies were guided by the following questions:

- How does design governance shape housing design, and what forms of evidence underpin its processes and decision-making?
- What spatial, technical, and social reasoning or cultural norms inform housing design controls and housing expectations, and how does this shape the standardisation of subsidised housing?
- To what extent is design governance influenced by time, place, and housing systems?
- How are subsidised homes and their design experienced, and what does this tell us about design governance?

To examine these questions, we adopted an international comparison of housing systems, standards, and homes to draw out the contextual and path-dependent nature of design governance, housing supply, and the role of subsidised housing in different housing markets (Özer & Jacoby, 2022). We combined regulatory, spatial, and social data using a mixed-method, multiscalar approach to analyse how housing design quality is conceptualised, regulated, implemented, and experienced (Jacoby & Özer, 2024).

We began the comparison with a study of the historical and regulatory contexts of England and Chile, countries widely known for their neoliberal policy environments and market-driven housing systems (Alonso Aranda, 2024; Arancibia, 2024; Jacoby et al., 2022). Since housing affordability crises are often linked to neoliberal policies, financialisation, and speculation, these two cases offer valuable insight into how these dynamics manifest in design governance and the built form. Standardisation in both countries is also closely linked to the dominance of a small number of large housebuilders, many of whom have their own standard house types and development practices.

We then compared housing systems and design standards through a review of policy, regulatory, and planning documents in six countries: England, Chile, Spain, Switzerland, the Netherlands, and China. These countries represent diverse housing systems, design governance approaches, and subsidised housing models. We specifically analysed the design standards of recently completed subsidised housing projects and their design outcomes, with projects selected to reflect typical local forms of subsidised provision and procurement. For this detailed study of housing standardisation, we focused on a city in each country with known affordability challenges: London, Santiago, Barcelona, Zurich, Amsterdam, and Shenzhen. We also included additional case studies from across England for a more comprehensive national study.

Furthermore, we visited 37 homes in the six chosen cities and across England for an in-depth study of housing realities and the lived experience of residents. This created a detailed cartography of subsidised homes and their residents, with the visual, spatial, and social analysis, including drawings, photographs, 3D interior scans, physical models, drone footage, in-depth interviews, and live-motion tracking over five days using an ultra-wideband, real-time location system. These studies revealed how residents furnish, adapt, and use their homes in ways that often substantially differ from common planning assumptions. Combined with interviews, the empirical findings provide a nuanced insight into how homes are inhabited and perceived in relation to daily routines and spatial preferences – highlighting how standardised housing is appropriated by individuals in diverse cultural and policy contexts.

This book is a detailed study of housing standardisation and the architecture produced by regulations and standards. It interrogates the functions, assumptions, priorities, and effects of design governance approaches. Its aim is to develop a historically grounded and case-study–based account of housing design governance and its context-specific nature, generating new knowledge about how the interaction of spatial, social, and technical reasoning determines the design of housing and defines design values.

It is argued here that housing design quality cannot be understood or improved without paying closer attention to the systems and standards that structure it. This also highlights the common disjunction between how quality is conceived and measured, and how it is actually experienced. If we are to equitably improve housing, we cannot treat it as an abstract or generalisable problem, but must recognise it as a lived and material reality.

The housing crisis is not only a crisis of affordable supply but also a crisis of design, governance, and imagination – fundamentally challenging how we conceptualise and structure the

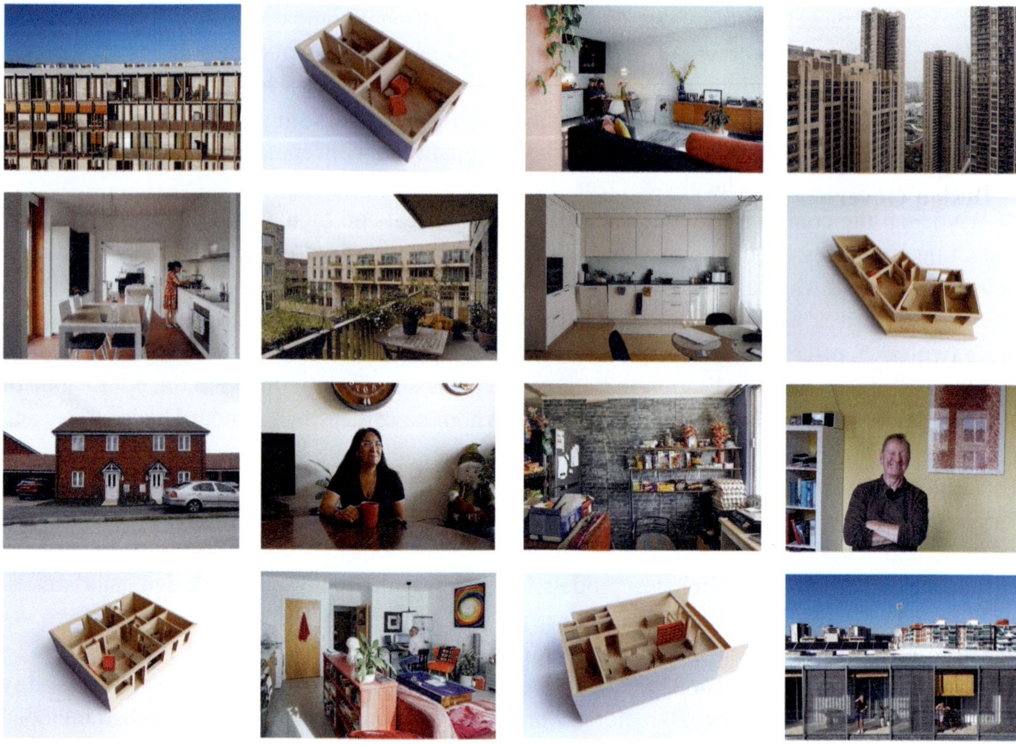

FIGURE 0.1 Housing case studies.

Note: The full project data are available online: https://doi.org/10.60624/nnc8-1557.

spaces of daily life. If we are to develop long-term housing that is more equitable and user-adaptable, we need to fully understand the systems that shape it and the homes they produce or fail to produce.

The book is organised in five sections:

Part 1: Study Contexts

This section sets out the intellectual, political, socio-economic, and cultural contexts of the subsidised housing study and book.

- **Chapter 1: The Design Governance of Subsidised Housing**
  The first chapter introduces the wider framing of the study in relation to design governance, housing standardisation, housing design quality, and the importance of lived experience.
- **Chapter 2: Comparative Housing Design Research**
  This chapter discusses the methodological approach to this comparative housing study, integrating design research.

Part 2: Design Governance Histories

This part provides a historical analysis of design governance in England and Chile, two countries with prominent neoliberal housing policies.

- **Chapter 3: Housing Standards and Standardisation in England: A Historical Study of Design Governance**
  The first chapter of this section traces the evolution of housing standards and typologies in England and their role in shaping design outcomes.
- **Chapter 4: The Evolution of Housing Standards in Chile**
  In a companion chapter, the development of housing regulation and standardisation in Chile under the neoliberal housing model are explored, highlighting key reforms and continuities.

Part 3: Systems and Standards

This section presents a comparative analysis of housing systems and standards in England, Chile, Spain, Switzerland, the Netherlands, and China.

- **Chapter 5: Housing Systems: Subsidised Housing Design and Regulatory Instruments**
  Here, an overview of housing governance, provision, and tenure structures is provided.
- **Chapter 6: Housing Standards: Socio-technical Design Controls**
  In this chapter, a comparison is made between national design standards, spatial requirements, and regulatory frameworks.

Part 4: Homes

Focusing on housing realities through a study of home use and lived experience, this section offers an in-depth analysis of 37 case studies of recently built subsidised homes in England and London, Santiago (Chile), Barcelona (Spain), Zurich (Switzerland), Amsterdam (the Netherlands), and Shenzhen (China).

- **Chapter 7: In-depth Case Study Cartographies**
  This chapter provides an overview of the case studies through photographs, models, maps, and plans.
- **Chapter 8: Home-Use Studies: An Insight into Lived Experiences**
  This chapter examines how residents furnish, adapt, and inhabit their homes, revealing patterns of spatial use and appropriation.
- **Chapter 9: Wellbeing and Housing Quality: Comparative Case Studies in Six Countries**
  Here, detailed studies of selected homes across the six countries are presented, combining architectural, spatial, and ethnographic analysis.

Part 5: Conclusion

- **Chapter 10: Decent Homes: Emerging Bodies of Evidence**
  This final chapter synthesises the findings, reflects on the implications for housing policy and design governance, and proposes directions for future research and practice.

PART I
Study Contexts

1

THE DESIGN GOVERNANCE OF SUBSIDISED HOUSING

Sam Jacoby

Access to "adequate, safe, and affordable housing" is part of UN Sustainable Development Goal 11 and a fundamental human right in a just society. According to UN-Habitat (2023), meeting the projected housing demand for the world's population by 2030 requires the supply of 96,000 new homes per day. In England alone, the estimated housing shortage amounts to around 2.5 million homes (Bidwells, 2024). At the UK Government's current target of 300,000 new homes per year, it would take over a generation for supply to catch up with housing needs by 2061, even without considering the much greater projected housing demand.

The longstanding failure of both policy and the market to deliver enough adequate housing – especially in the social and affordable sector – was widely exposed by the COVID-19 pandemic. While most Europeans already spent more than half their lives at home before the pandemic (World Health Organization, 2013), this has since increased in Britain to an average of 18 hours and 43 minutes per day (IPA, 2023), amplifying the impact of housing and its conditions on health and wellbeing. The pandemic lockdown also exacerbated housing inequalities by changing the way homes are used and the spaces needed, affecting perceptions of home and long-term housing expectations (Alonso Aranda & Jacoby, 2023; Jacoby & Alonso Aranda, 2022). This heightened public awareness of the importance of not only decent but also well-designed and generous homes that meet diverse needs.

Problems with housing cause 39% of private renters in England to feel stressed and anxious, and 22% to become physically unwell (Shelter, 2021). Poor housing conditions contribute significantly to adverse health outcomes and are estimated to cost the National Health Service (NHS) in England £1.4 billion annually in treatment (BRE Group, 2021). This highlights the negative but often preventable impact of substandard housing on issues such as mental health, child development, family relationships, and accidents (Reynolds & Robinson, 2005). There is thus widespread consensus on the central role housing plays in public health, community resilience, placemaking, and social welfare, with better living standards and quality of life closely linked to improved housing conditions. Unsurprisingly, policies therefore call for "high-quality, well-designed, and sustainable" affordable homes (Labour Party, 2024). Yet what this actually means in practice is not always clear, as policymakers, housing professionals, and the public often hold divergent views on what constitutes housing quality and how it should be measured.

DOI: 10.4324/9781032679204-3

Although housing quality debates in architecture commonly focus on issues of design and maintenance, the primary driver is the housing system. Shaped by historical policies and contingencies, regulatory practices, and housing markets, housing systems are defined by housing providers, tenures, target populations, and financing, including subsidies. They reflect political and socio-economic agendas and determine whether housing access is understood as an individual responsibility or a collective right within a welfare system. While the housing system is a key determinant of how and what housing is provided, the role of design-related guidelines, regulatory frameworks, and policy as a barrier or driver to significant improvements in housing quality is frequently overlooked (Özer & Jacoby, 2022). Consequently, the second key driver of housing quality is design governance.

The question of how to define housing quality and its relation to these two drivers requires further study and clarification. In particular, the specific contribution of architectural design to the everyday life of residents, and the tension between the institutionalisation and increasing standardisation of housing versus the diversification of housing needs and uses, have received little attention. As de Certeau (1984) argues, everyday practices tactically reappropriate the rules and norms of institutional strategies, a dynamic that is also evident in how residents use and adapt their homes. In addition, the underlying relationships between spatial, social, and technical reasoning and perceptions of quality in subsidised housing deserve greater examination (Jacoby & Özer, 2024),

With the housing supply and affordability crisis now also widely affecting the middle classes, the focus has shifted from rented post-war "public" housing (once widely available as a form of general welfare provision) and "social" housing (typically limited to the most vulnerable) to a broader category of "affordable" housing that comprises all typical tenures from homeownership to social rent. Whereas in 1979, 31% of English households lived in homes rented from local authorities and private registered providers such as housing associations, this had fallen to just 16% by 2024 (Department for Levelling Up, Housing and Communities [DLUHC], 2025a). New affordable housing supply is no longer only focused on rental but also increasingly on ownership, with social rent homes accounting now for just 16% compared to 33% for shared ownership (Ministry of Housing, Communities and Local Government [MHCLG], 2024).

Thus, social housing has increasingly been absorbed into the wider category of affordable housing, driven by concerns over housing affordability. This has de-emphasised social welfare and social rent provision, redirecting policy toward affordable rent and shared ownership, tenures often aimed at middle-income households. As a result, there is some ambiguity about what counts as "social" or "affordable" housing, and how this shapes the type and quality of provision. These definitions can differ between countries, reflecting prevailing welfare aspirations and economic policies, and can produce very different housing realities.

For instance, the UN-Habitat (2019) defines affordable housing costs as a maximum 30% of a household's net income. It also recognises housing as a human right, which includes security of tenure, access to essential services, affordability, safety, habitability, sufficient space, accessibility, appropriate location, and respect for cultural identity. In contrast to this income-based assessment, according to England's market-based definition, affordable homes are generally let or sold at up to 80% of local market rents or prices (MHCLG, 2024). Unlike the UN's broad commitment to a legal right to housing, the UK's Decent Home Standard is narrowly defined in terms of minimum statutory standards related to health and safety, state of repair, reasonable facilities and services, and thermal comfort (Department for Communities and Local Government

[DCLG], 2006a). These differences emphasise how much housing context and therefore housing access and quality can vary.

Despite major demographic transformations – with 30% of households in England now consisting of a single person, 18% aged 65 and over (Centre for Ageing Better, 2025), and only 14% made up of married couples with dependent children (Office for National Statistics [ONS], 2022) – the traditional nuclear family home is still widely seen as the norm (Alonso Aranda, 2024). Thus, to fully understand the drivers of housing design and perception, it is essential to examine how typical homes relate to design governance, market dynamics, cultural norms, everyday home use, and the assumptions, reasoning, and evidence on which they are based. This multi-layered dynamic is often overlooked by architectural historians and designers alike. However, reproducing past models based on common assumptions and traditional norms exacerbates housing problems, as this prioritises market demand over genuine need.

A more connected and inclusive approach to studying housing histories and realities is therefore needed, one that balances policy and design perspectives with the lived experiences of residents. As design policy, regulations, and standards tend to be abstract and generalised, it is important to compare them to social policy perspectives and the insight that lived experience can provide into commonalities and seemingly marginal yet socially critical needs (McIntosh & Wright, 2018). In fact, everyone is a housing expert: through their substantial lived experience, people develop important collective knowledge that is too often overlooked in policy and design.

There is an abundance of studies of housing from an architectural perspective of design and technological innovation dealing with specific architects, housing sectors, or building typologies. Examples include works such as *Radical Housing* by Dove (2020); *Housing for All* by Andreas, Jung, and Cachola Schmal (2019); *Floor Plan Manual Housing* by Heckmann, Schneider, and Zapel (2017); *Social Housing* by Karakusevic and Batchelor (2017); and *Courtyard Houses* by Pfeifer and Brauneck (2007). But these studies often remain disconnected from those in other disciplines, especially the social sciences, which in turn tend to disregard problems of design. In particular, little attention has been paid to how housing outcomes are a response to a combination of housing systems and design governance that determine the typical design, usability, and lived experience of homes. These issues are widely considered a problem of practice, undeserving of historiographical attention or critical study.

Architectural academia still tends to be focused on traditional historical and theoretical research, disregarding the importance of practice-led or practice-based design research in architecture that, including policy, governance, and evidence-based enquiries, are naturally more impact-driven (Aydemir & Jacoby, 2022). However, practice-led research is essential to a comprehensive analysis of housing determinants and to addressing urgent housing-related social and environmental challenges faced by architecture and society as a whole. Some noteworthy exceptions that deal with aspects of these relationships include *Environmental Health and Housing* by Stewart and Lynch (2018); *Remaking Housing Policy* by Clapham (2019); *Architecture and the Welfare State* by Swenarton, Avermaete, and van den Heuvel (2014); *The Politics of Social Housing in Britain* by Manoochehri (2012); *Building the New Jerusalem* by Swenarton (2008); *Housing Design Quality* by Carmon (2001); and *The English Terraced House* by Muthesius (1982). However, the persistent failure to deliver well-designed homes in the necessary quantity and to subsequently maintain and modernise them calls for a deeper analysis of design governance in relation to housing provision, management, and lived experiences. This analysis is important to not only understand how design quality is defined, governed, and controlled, but also how it ultimately impacts the everyday life of residents.

"Design governance" refers to the formal and informal tools used by government and housing stakeholders to guide design decisions through best practice guides, incentivise design quality through policy or funding and tax benefits, and control design and development outcomes by enforcing compliance with minimum standards (Carmona, et al., 2023; Carmona, 2017). This relies on both statutory and non-statutory frameworks, including planning and housing policies, design codes, building regulations, employer requirements, standards, and best practices. Design governance is influenced by specific jurisdictions and organisational contexts, defined by housing visions, enforcement, and decision-making processes, and typically involves negotiation and collaboration between developers, local authorities, and design consultants, as well as local communities. In broader terms, housing design governance regulates and integrates regulatory regimes, policy, and evidence base, but also negotiation and decision-making processes shaped by social, political, and economic context. While theoretical frameworks for design governance are well-established, empirical research on its current use in practice is lacking (White et al., 2024).

The existing body of work engaging with the regulatory contexts of design is dominated by practice-based technical design guides or policy reviews that deal with questions such as how to implement building regulations, improve building performance, or assess space standards. Typical examples of this approach include the *RIBA Health and Safety Guide* by Bentley-Gockmann (2020); *Healthy Buildings* by Allen and Macomber (2020); *Housing Fit for Purpose* by Stevenson (2019); *The Housing Design Handbook* by Levitt and McCafferty (2018); *One Hundred Years of Housing Space Standards* by Park (2017); *Improving the Design of New Housing* by the Commission for Architecture and the Built Environment (CABE, 2010); and *Design Quality in New Housing* by Cousins (2009). But there remains a paucity of cross-disciplinary design research integrating architectural practice-led and academic housing studies, as well as housing research from other disciplines – especially those concerned with the evidence base for, and effectiveness of, design governance.

Effective design standards and ambitious design values are critical, particularly in the context of significant recent transformations in housing policy, such as the wider adoption of a National Model Design Code or the Labour Party's commitment to build 300,000 new high-quality homes each year in England. Compared to many EU countries, England has weak design and building controls, due to a combination of deregulation, insufficient oversight, poor enforcement of existing regulations, and market-driven decision-making (House of Lords Science and Technology Committee, 2005). Architects in England are also often sidelined from major housing policy and design quality decisions, and have limited leadership or influence on broader sectoral reforms. By revisiting regulatory histories and comparing regulatory systems and housing design, this book aims to contextualise what ambitious design governance might mean historiographically, in current housing practice, and as a lived experience. It also asks what re-engagement is needed by architects to have greater relevance again in housing policy and transformations.

According to the study *Building More, Building Beautiful* by Airey, Scruton, and Wales (2018), 84% of people in the UK believe that well-designed buildings and public spaces improve their quality of life. The UK Government's *Planning for the Future* white paper (MHCLG, 2020b) clarifies this as meaning that architecture's primary value lies in creating "beauty", which it largely defines in terms of traditional design. However, the related report *Living with*

Beauty from the Building Better, Building Beautiful Commission (2020), chaired by Scruton and tasked by the UK Government with creating a pathway for delivering well-designed new homes, criticises architects for failing to understand popular taste and the "empirical connections between built form and well-being", instead designing homes undesired by the public. Even the Royal Institute of British Architects' (RIBA; 2020) *Social Value Toolkit for Architecture* admits that architects are "shockingly ignorant" of how their work impacts others or how to explain its value. Thus, being able to evidence and communicate the social and long-term value of architectural design is an urgent problem for the profession, recognised by both RIBA and the UK Collaborative Centre for Housing Evidence (Samuel, 2018; White et al., 2020).

One reason for the marginalisation of architecture is a significant gap between its aspirational self-image and how it is perceived by others. This is in part due to the discipline's longstanding failure to engage effectively with policymakers, stakeholders, and the public through evidence-based design and research. By the 1980s, much of this work was left to social scientists, who extensively studied housing in relation to the economy, social welfare, public health policy, and user needs (Samuel, 2018). Examples of notable longitudinal housing studies include the Mass Observation Project, established in 1937, a series of regular housing condition surveys conducted by the UK Government's housing department beginning in 1967 (initially the Housing Conditions Survey and since 2008 the annual English Housing Survey), the British Household Panel Survey (1991–2009), and the longitudinal study Understanding Society (since 2009).

The division between architects, social scientists, and policymakers, however, did not always exist. For example, the *Design Bulletins* published by the Ministry of Housing and Local Government (MoHLG) and other government agencies evidence their close collaboration – particularly those from the late 1960s, such as *The Family at Home: A Study of Households in Sheffield* (MoHLG, 1969), which assessed new homes by studying how residents used and perceived them. To reconnect to this tradition of integrated social, design, and housing studies, and to situate it historically, this book includes a historiographical review of design governance, incorporating a detailed analysis of housing policy, regulations, and standards; substantial new qualitative data related to the use and lived experience of the home; and conventional design research focused on housing.

Another important reason for architecture's marginalisation is rooted in a biopolitical history of housing (Foucault, 2007; Rabinow & Rose, 2006). This saw a shift from spatialised governmentality (Jacoby, 2020) – the instrumentalisation of architecture and planning by government to shape subjectivities – to a neoliberal regime in which housing is primarily governed through the market, supported by policies of deregulation and privatisation. The state no longer assumes direct responsibility for housing as a form of public welfare, instead delegating this to private actors. Architects are of limited value to the functioning of this commodified housing system. Symptomatically, the independent New Homes Quality Board, a consumer protection body in the UK tasked with regulating the housing market and quality of new homes, has currently no architect members. Understanding the socio-spatial and governmental transformations behind this requires examining how architecture and design mediate relationships between space, the household, institutional practices, and biotechnical strategies in everyday life (Bray, 2018; Donzelot, 1997).

This book frames this architectural design research enquiry through a study of design governance, using an interdisciplinary lens, including design history and governmentality and housing studies. It examines how design governance, regulation, and socio-cultural norms shape typical housing and lived experience, positioning design governance as a biopolitical technology that standardises housing and everyday life. As part of this analysis, the book specifically explores how a standardisation of housing is informed by policy, regulation, and the market (housing systems); how spatial, social, and technical evidence or cultural expectations define housing quality and design value (housing standards); and how these are perceived and experienced by residents (lived experience of the home).

These studies focus on recently completed subsidised housing, as its various forms are often built at scale, designed to minimum legal standards and market requirements, and with a high level of repetition and standardisation (Figure 1.1). Subsidised housing includes social, public, and affordable housing, supported by subsidies that either assist households (demand-side) or reduce costs for providers and developers (supply-side). It is rented or sold below market rates and involves an allocation process, with eligibility typically including income-based criteria. Due to budgetary constraints, safeguarding minimum standards in subsidised and affordable housing is of particular importance, whereas minimum standards are typically less evident or relevant in other private-sector housing.

This book offers an in-depth analysis of housing in England (rather than the entire UK, as housing policy is a devolved matter and varies across the constituent nations) and, to a lesser extent, in Chile. Both countries are exemplary cases of neoliberal housing systems, which, despite their similarities, operate through different policies and market mechanisms to commodify access to and the right to housing (Jacoby et al., 2022). For instance, Chile provides no social housing and only demand-side subsidies, which support around 56% of new homeownership each year (Rebolledo, 2023). Despite its long public and social housing history, England's supply-side subsidies have now dropped to just 12%, compared to 88% for demand-side subsidies, largely paid in the form of housing benefits, including more than a third for private rent tenants (Gibb, 2024; Stephens et al., 2024). Considering these extensive subsidies and policy interventions in favour of the private sector in both countries, the popular rhetoric of housing

FIGURE 1.1 Studied subsidised housing developments in (a) Santiago, (b) Eastleight, (c) Shenzhen, and (d) Zurich.

neoliberalisation as shorthand for a state retreat from housing responsibilities and financing is overly simplistic.

A particular problem of prioritising market self-regulation is that this results in greater sectoral differences in dwelling size and housing quality, as well as a stigmatisation and residualisation of social housing (Jacoby et al., 2022). In this book, recently completed homes in England and Chile are compared to those in China, the Netherlands, Spain, and Switzerland to study the effects of housing systems and common regulatory and design governance approaches on differences in subsidised housing outcomes.

The book is organised around two comparative frameworks: a historical comparison of design governance and housing supply in England and Chile and an international comparison of current regulation, design practices, and housing outcomes. Both frameworks complement each other in revealing the contextual factors shaping housing controls, design standardisation, and the architecture of regulations and design standards. They also help clarify how design governance is informed by housing systems and policies, and how this evolves over time in response to shifting political, economic, and social priorities or key historical events.

By re-evaluating the relationships between housing governance and design reasoning, the book studies both wider and more specific drivers of design. This offers new insights into what typical homes look like and how their quality is understood in different countries, as well as how new subsidised housing relates to daily home use (Figure 1.2). The study thereby examines how different forms of design governance are informed by socio-spatial, socio-cultural, and socio-technical norms or evidence; how housing is standardised through design controls and functional requirements; and how this relates to the lived experience of residents. By comparing these factors across diverse contexts and histories, the book aims to identify transferable lessons for tackling some of today's housing challenges and for more effectively integrating design practices, policies, governance, and lived experience in the design of future homes.

Housing Design, Its Governance, and Standardisation

Bernard Rudofsky famously claimed in his 1964 exhibition *Architecture Without Architects* at the Museum of Modern Art in New York – and in the accompanying book, subtitled *An Introduction to Non-pedigreed Architecture* – that the vast history of architecture is one of communal design and building, not of formal architecture or architects. Although Rudofsky's (1964) mainly photographic evidence revealed little about the cultural contexts, social values, lived experiences, or material practices sustaining this architecture, these aspects have since received increasing, yet still limited, attention within architectural discourse.

Even two generations after Rudofsky, little has changed: only around 20% of buildings in the developed world are thought to be designed by architects (Davies, 2005). In the United Kingdom, the RIBA estimates that a mere 6% of homes are architect-designed, with less than a quarter of these for public housing projects (RIBA, 2018). This is supported by data showing that fewer than a third of the UK's 25 largest housebuilders employ their own architects (Marrs, 2015). Consequently, housing in general, and subsidised housing in particular, is standardised in design and traditional in construction, with many design decisions made by large housing developers and providers themselves, and often determined by minimum development standards and the goal of maximising profit.

Much housing design in England therefore results from economic decisions and the established practices and preferences of a small number of large housing organisations, with the 10 largest

FIGURE 1.2 *Housing Standardisation: Who Designs Our Homes and How Do We Live?,* exhibition held at The Building Centre, London (November 2024 to January 2025).

housebuilders responsible for 55% of new homes in 2024 (Buckle et al., 2024). This limits diversity in housing supply and design. In addition, with 44% of all new affordable homes delivered by private developers without the support of government grants as part of a planning obligation known as Section 106 agreements (DLUHC, 2024a), this is not part of their core business, and there is often little incentive for developers to deliver good design.

This challenges widely held beliefs about housing design processes and decision-making – as well as the notion of community design evoked by Rudofsky – revealing instead the extent to which both are determined by housing regulations and standards. By extension, this limits what "well-designed" might mean and what is achievable. It highlights the lack of a holistic understanding of design processes and outcomes and raises questions about who ultimately controls and determines them. The financialisation of affordable housing delivery further underscores the need to prioritise the social and political dimensions of housing and its design, if not to reconsider the role of the state in the direct provision of social and rent-controlled homes. To fully understand what informs these dynamics, it is essential to examine the historical trajectories and path dependencies as well as the evolving roles of housing within society.

Arguably, nothing has shaped political subjectivities in modern societies more than housing and its design. The home has historically served as a site where legal, regulatory, economic, pedagogical, and familial systems of social control converge, becoming spatialised within the private domain and establishing a "government through the family" (Donzelot, 1997). This process coincided with the rise of nation-states and their exercise of pastoral power (Foucault, 2007), transforming the social organisation from broader kinship systems to the nuclear family or to non-familial communal and work-based relationships.

Prompted by industrialisation and poor living conditions, Victorian housing reforms were driven by a strong moral belief in the need to improve public health and living standards for the working class. Philanthropic housing companies such as the Peabody Trust and the Society for Improving the Condition of the Labouring Classes understood the housing problem not simply as one of building at scale and low cost, but also as a means of instilling and spatialising social norms and moral values through the design of model dwellings (Gaskell, 1986). These model dwellings therefore contributed to the development of the modern nuclear family home. In this process, housing quality was directly equated with architectural design, and design value was explicitly linked to tangible social and health benefits.

A well-known example of this is the model houses designed for working-class families by the architect Henry Roberts on the occasion of the Great Exhibition of 1851. Fundamental to the morally and physically "hygienic" domesticity it championed was a focus on the nuclear family and its fourfold separation: the functional separation of internal sanitation and ventilation between homes, the social separation of the individual family from lodgers and other outsiders, the spatial separation of domestic functions, and a gender separation, with children of different sexes sleeping in their own bedrooms. This was to promote the productivity of the family – both within and beyond the home – and led to a standardisation and privatisation of family life and housing.

A century later, as demonstrated by post-war mass-housing projects throughout Europe – especially large public housing developments – this model of the single-family dwelling had become the norm. Exemplified by Le Corbusier's (1927/1923) assertion that "a house is a machine for living in", the Modern Movement advocated designing homes that met both the practical and biological needs of the family. This, it argued, necessitated the standardisation of design as well as effective housing standards to ensure that homes and their inhabitants were functional, efficient, productive, and healthy. While this understanding of housing design as reflecting and nurturing morality, health, and economy echoed Victorian beliefs, a fundamental change was the recognition of housing as a right. It was now regarded as a pillar of social welfare and, therefore, a state responsibility. The new public housing was seen as a means to provide social equity, mobility, and economic security (Kemeny, 1995), while fostering social ambitions and collective identities. In England, post-war council housing was thus state-owned, rented, and accessible to a broad cross-section of society. It often consisted of standardised, high-density developments, with many designed and delivered by local authority architects.

However, significant changes in the housing context, such as the extensive marketisation of housing, changes in household demographics, and the impact of the COVID-19 pandemic, have both reinforced and reshaped the socio-economic and welfare function of housing. This includes a shift from social and public to "affordable" housing, an acknowledgment that the problem of housing affordability has expanded from working-class families to working households of different classes more generally. Since the late 1970s, neoliberal economic reforms and housing marketisation have contributed to an almost global shift from government-led housing provision to the privatisation of housing supply and maintenance. As a result, responsibility for social welfare has been increasingly transferred from the state to individual households, with social and economic security becoming dependent on property ownership and inherited wealth (Cooper, 2017). As part of this process, there has been a shift from supply-side to demand-side housing subsidies.

But even with substantial state support, the private sector has persistently failed to deliver sufficient affordable homes, revealing the fundamental structural limitations of market-led housing provision. In England, only around 36% of the new homes needed are built each year, and almost 5% of all households are on local authority waiting lists for social homes (RIBA, 2025; Bramley, 2018). Since the 1980s, the increase of demand-side subsidies has not alleviated housing shortages but instead contributed to a growing affordable housing deficit (Gibb, 2024). The notion that the private sector is more cost-effective and delivers better outcomes than direct investment in the social rent sector, rooted in the deeply ingrained belief in the socio-economic benefits of property ownership, belies the fact that social housing delivers far greater financial and wider economic returns, even in the short term.

Over five years, the UK Government will subsidise private landlords by an estimated £73 billion through Universal Credit and Housing Benefit payments, six times its investment in the Affordable Homes Programme 2021–2026 over the same period (New Economics Foundation, 2024). Annually, the government spends about £30 billion on housing benefits to both public and private landlords – roughly 1.4% of GDP – because at 17%, the social housing stock is insufficient to meet demand (Department for Work and Pensions, 2024; ONS, 2025). By contrast, the Netherlands, where social housing makes up 29% of homes, spends only 0.5% of GDP on housing support (OECD, 2021).

Yet England's 4.2 million social rented homes generate an estimated £77.7 billion annually in economic opportunities and public service savings, delivering a social return of roughly £2.23 for every pound invested (Clifford et al., 2024; RIBA, 2024). By comparison, 4.8 million private rented homes contribute only an estimated £45 billion per year to the UK economy (PricewaterhouseCoopers LLP, 2024). On a per-home basis, social housing creates nearly three times more net economic and social value than private rented homes. Given this inefficient allocation of housing investment, it is unsurprising that the housing crisis remains both perpetual and growing.

The Right-to-Buy scheme under Margaret Thatcher, introduced by the Housing Act 1980, is widely regarded as the landmark policy that marked the demise of public housing. By encouraging the large-scale sale of council homes and housing marketisation, it is considered to be a root cause of the housing supply crisis. However, both public and private housing supply in England had been in decline since the 1960s (Figure 1.3). Compared to many European countries – including the Netherlands, Switzerland, and Spain – the post-war private sector in the UK has a lower average housebuilding rate per capita (Watling & Breach, 2023; Bentley, 2017). This is partly due to the Town and Country Planning Act of 1947 and the Land Compensation Act of 1961, restricting land availability for housing development, and rising land costs, with house prices increasingly detached from average earnings since the 1990s.

While economics and market forces are not the focus of this book, they are nonetheless primary drivers of housing policy, design governance, and supply. For example, as the cost of

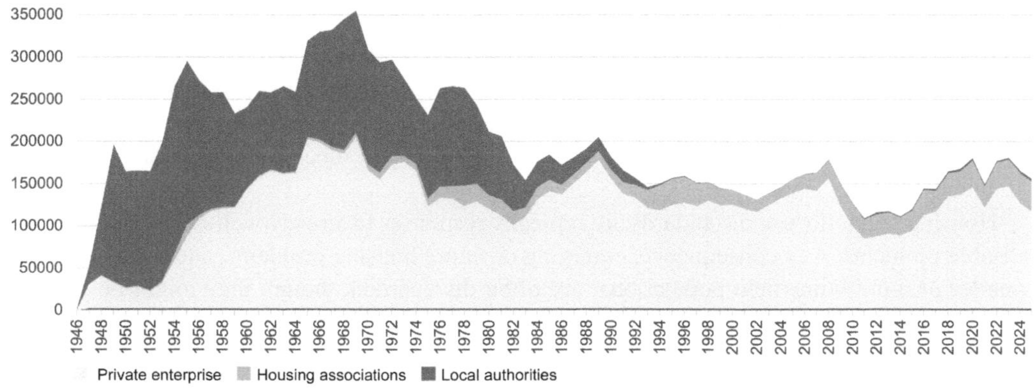

FIGURE 1.3 Housebuilding completions in England by tenure (1946–2024).

Source: DLUHC (2025b).

building a new social rent home in London has risen to an average of over £400,000 and the maximum government grant is £60,000, substantial cross-subsidy and investment is needed by housing associations (Housing, Communities and Local Government Committee, 2018). This has far-reaching implications for the way they operate, the types of housing that can be delivered, and how homes are designed. This study is therefore interested in how these changes in housing practices affect the meaning of "design", particularly in relation to the use of standards and design standardisation. It also examines the influence of design decisions not only on the material form of housing but also on the daily experience of residents. As part of this, the motivations and effectiveness of standards are questioned, to determine whether housing standards improve or merely standardise life.

The term "standard" has attained many connotations of norms and conventions in housing, but it commonly signifies a technically defined minimum specification (Ratcliff, 1952). Quantitative forms of assessment are also prevalent in the Building Regulations – first formally introduced in England in 1965 – and their technical requirements. These assessments typically use metrics that are numerically measurable, such as heat emission, structural load, or minimum dimensions. Nevertheless, the underlying ambitions are often qualitative, related, for example, to improving living standards, health, safety, and environmental protection. Measuring compliance with design standards using minimum performance requirements makes housing quantifiable and encourages standardisation – from building components, elements, and layouts to construction methods – in an effort to reduce risks and costs. However, this deliberately technocratic translation of housing quality often results in a loss of ambition, with these minimum requirements – particularly mandatory regulations – becoming the maximum design and compliance targets by some affordable housing providers.

Whereas regulations are mandatory and apply to all housing, sectoral differences in housing quality are in part due to the application of varying standards. Typically based on best practice, standards are generally more demanding than regulations and are usually voluntary. Their use is therefore often incentivised, for example, by making them a condition of housing grants, or specific to sectors and housing providers. As a result, standards are inconsistently adopted and many homes are "substandard" if compared across sectors or regions. In England, for example, a study by Cromarty and Barton (2022) found that 23% of privately rented homes fail the Decent

Homes Standard, and Özer & Jacoby (2023) reported that 57% of recently completed affordable housing does not meet the current Nationally Described Space Standard. As housing quality is insufficiently regulated, systemic problems persist: analysing 142 large housing developments by volume housebuilders in England, the Place Alliance (2020) concluded that three-quarters should have been refused planning permission for failing to meet National Planning Policy Framework design guidelines.

Housing regulations and standards are typically responses to already well-defined and generalisable problems. As a consequence, emerging or future housing problems, and those affecting smaller or more vulnerable populations, are often disregarded, though they might be in need of greater regulatory support. However, the relationships between qualitative and quantitative aims or assessment, and the balance between higher legal protection of regulations or higher requirements of standards, continually shift along with new housing priorities, changes in design governance, and the technical or social evidence on which they might be based (Park, 2017).

In England, this dynamic tension dates back to at least the Rebuilding of the City of London Act 1667, the first in a series of housing legislation enacted after the Great Fire of London in 1666 to regularise housing construction and quality – which were eventually consolidated by the Building Act 1774. These design standards had a clear typological preference for terraced houses, which were often built speculatively and at scale by developers. For example, this standardisation led to the proliferation of the so-called byelaw terraced house from the late nineteenth century until the early twentieth century, designed to comply with the Public Health Act 1875. As regulation increasingly responded to public health and social concerns in rapidly growing cities, especially the need to manage overcrowding and the spread of diseases, the mid-nineteenth century promoted the single nuclear family home.

The nineteenth-century beliefs in sanitation and morality were increasingly supported by scientific attempts to make new connections between housing, design, human behaviour, and wellbeing. Historical studies, like Charles Booth's social cartography in *Maps Descriptive of London Poverty* (1898–99), demonstrated how social classes and their economic and moral standing could be spatialised by mapping the homes they live in. The *Tudor Walters Report* (1918) instrumentalised this socio–spatial connection by determining the space standards and quality of space needed to improve the life and behaviour of the "lower" classes. Therefore, space standards have become widely accepted literal measurements of housing quality, based on the principle that housing needs can be rationally and universally translated into standard furniture dimensions, anthropometric measurements, circulation areas, and activity zones.

Thus, in preparation for post-war reconstruction, the period from the *Tudor Walters Report* on housing and the Housing Act 1919 to the *Dudley Report* (1944) and Housing Manuals of 1944/1949 was dominated by concerns with the first "scientific" space standards for public housing. This was followed by the *Parker Morris Report* (MoHLG, 1961), *Homes for Today and Tomorrow,* and *Design Bulletin 6: Space in the Home* (MoHLG, 1968a), which based their space-standard calculations on the study of typical daily activities in a family household, the items of furniture and space required for these activities, and a comprehensive collection of evidence gathered through field observations and consultation with housing experts and stakeholders (Palate, 2022). The normative understanding of a family's daily routines and functional requirements has remained the model for establishing not only current space standards, but also evidence-based design policy and housing standardisation. Today, in countries where housing design is controlled beyond building regulations, the majority use some form of space standards, standard items of furniture, and minimum dimensions to safeguard "essential" functional requirements.

But legal status, calculation, and enforcement of design requirements depend on design governance approaches, regulatory differences between subsidised and private housing sectors, and cultural norms. When comparing dwelling and furniture sizes across countries, substantial differences are apparent. For example, minimum space requirements per person range from 7 m^2 in Hong Kong to 22.5 m^2 in parts of Australia (Özer & Jacoby, 2022), while standard furniture dimensions also vary, such as the UK National House Building Council's single-bedroom bed of 0.75×1.9 m compared with the Swedish standard of 0.9×2.1 m (Croydon Council, 2008). There are further differences in the type of furniture and storage provided, as well as in how circulation or activity space is calculated.

These variances are only partially explained by local housing systems and reflect different economic development and socio-cultural housing expectations. For example, twentieth-century housing adapted the nineteenth-century cottage flat in the form of its modern maisonettes, while traditional rooms such as the parlour disappeared – which as a space primarily used for formal gatherings and receiving guests reflected social status. These differences and transformations in housing layout and preferences demonstrate that regulations, standards, and design outcomes, despite their perceived universality, are in continuous flux and conditioned by changing cultural perceptions of space and shifts in home use and social norms (Figure 1.4).

The expected housing standard at a given place and time determines the size and quality of homes. Cultural norms, technological advancements, social status, personal experiences, lifestyle, age, and many other factors make what is deemed "enough" or "good" space a subjective and contextual judgment (Mullins & Murie, 2006; Park, 2017; Ravetz & Turkington, 1995). In England, where homes are primarily described and marketed by the number of bedrooms, and where stating a property's size is not a legal requirement, there is a strong preference for homes with more bedrooms, even if the overall dwelling size is smaller. By contrast, in many other countries, property sales and rentals are directly based on the floor area, with less emphasis placed on the number of rooms (Fig. 1.5). These differences in measuring and valuing property result in different preferred layouts and space distribution. It also means that in England there is less awareness of what dwelling sizes and space standards mean (Jacoby & Alonso Aranda, 2023). Thus, how space standards and design are experienced is subject to expectations and "moral encodings" that both reveal and influence the purpose or function of homes (Gallent et al., 2010; Imrie, 2006). By assuming a normative relationship between space and activity, space standards can limit the flexibility and usability of homes (Goodchild & Furbey, 1986; Madigan & Milner, 1999). In addition, there is a considerable lag between changes in external factors, research, and regulatory controls; for example, space standards continue to be widely based on the functional requirements and social norms of the mid-twentieth-century family.

While in the past public health and behavioural studies had an important influence on housing regulations and design standards, more recently issues of sustainability and long-term housing needs have come to the fore. Examples of this are the technical practice guide Lifetime Home Standards from the 1990s (Habinteg Housing Association, 2011), which is now largely adopted by the Building Regulations in England, or the Code for Sustainable Homes (DCLG, 2006b), which was made mandatory from 2008 to 2010 in an attempt to deliver zero-carbon homes. But standards today rarely prescribe specific design solutions. Instead, standard functional requirements with general design guidance or quantitative performance requirements without reference to a design solution are commonly used. This has resulted in an increasing range of technical

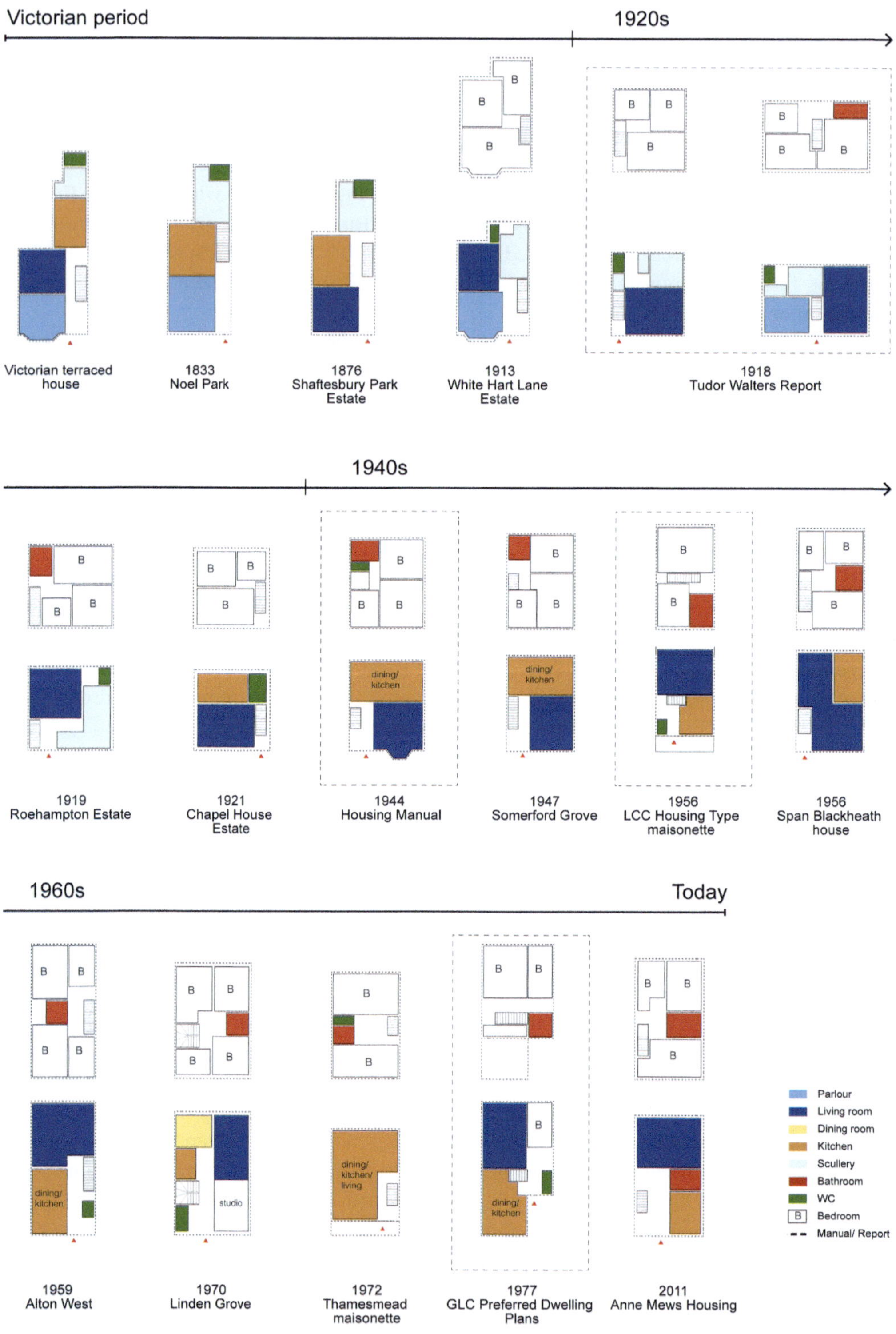

FIGURE 1.4 The changing layout of rooms and functions in two-storey houses and maisonettes in England.

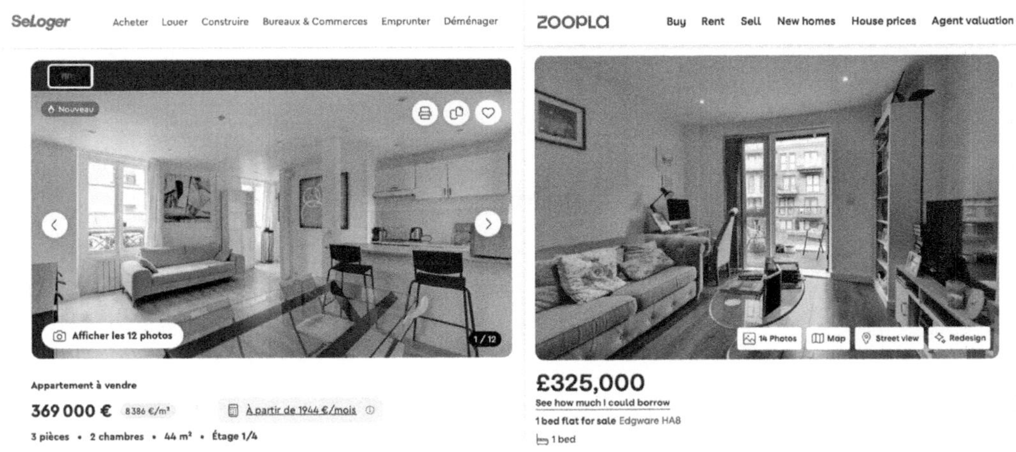

FIGURE 1.5 Typical property online advertisement in France (Paris) and England (London).

and performance-based design standards and policies that, in combination with best-practice design guides, effectively make bespoke architectural design extraneous to affordable housing design (Imrie & Street, 2009).

Today, a growing interest in social and cultural design values highlights a shift from physical to psychological and social wellbeing assessments of the home that are measured through levels of participation or the creation of positive emotions (Samuel, 2018). But the social value attributed to houses as "homes", frequently based on the claim that "high-quality" housing improves health, educational attainment, social mobility, and quality of communities and place, is difficult to measure, especially in respect to architectural design (Reynolds & Robinson, 2005). The RIBA's *Social Value Toolkit* (2020), a response to the Social Value Act 2012, highlights this difficulty by providing performance targets and metrics to quantify social value as a financial return on investment without any specific reference to housing design or its qualitative value.

The problem of architects having to justify the value of design is compounded by the highly contextual nature of how housing design quality, which is understood both through individual lived housing experiences and through nationally shared housing experiences shaped by changing housing expectations and realities. These changes are evident in different design governance approaches, which this book studies through key regulatory instruments, policies, housing commissions and research or technical reports, design or practice guides, and performance metrics that represent different periods of housebuilding or regulatory contexts. This forms the basis of a design research study of typical dwelling designs and housing typologies.

In general, the three main regulatory instruments in use to control dwelling layout and size in the subsidised housing sector are "space standards", "functional requirements", and "standard unit or block types" (Özer & Jacoby, 2022). A common approach is to use space standards that define both overall minimum dwelling sizes and specific room- or function-based requirements, such as minimum dimensions and space for the use of typical furniture such as a bed, wardrobe, dining table, and kitchen units (Figure 1.6). To evaluate the advantages and limitations of typical housing models shaped by these regulatory mechanisms, subsidised housing design, quality, standards, and lived experiences in six countries and cities are compared: London and England, Santiago (Chile), Amsterdam (Netherlands), Barcelona (Spain), Shenzhen (China), and Zurich

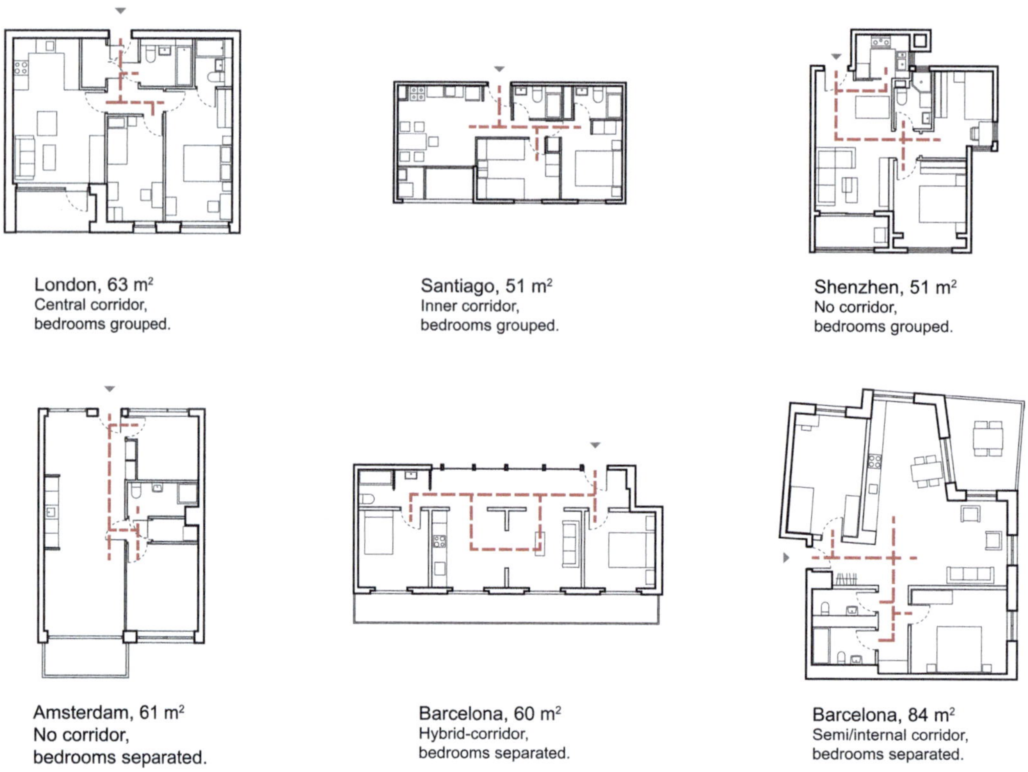

FIGURE 1.6 Two-bedroom flats and common plan organisation.

(Switzerland). These countries represent a range of common design governance approaches, regulatory frameworks, housing markets, and subsidised housing systems.

The role and outcomes of *space standards* in subsidised housing vary widely between countries, reflecting differences in housing regulation and political-economic models (Figure 1.7). Despite a long history of space standards in England, dating back to the *Tudor Walters Report* (1918), they are not mandatory. Nonetheless, they have been widely adopted in the social and affordable housing sectors as a subsidy condition, reflecting England's liberal market economy with a deregulated housing market but substantial state intervention in social and affordable housing supply. This book compares housing in London with the rest of England, as the adoption of space standards and housing outcomes depend on local market dynamics and local authority policy priorities (Özer & Jacoby, 2023). In contrast to England, Chile is a neoliberal market economy without formal social housing that only subsidises homeownership (Jacoby et al., 2022). Housing policy has pushed space standards to a minimum and fully commodified housing delivery, resulting in high long-term housing costs. While Chile has successfully reduced the housing shortage through extensive supply-side subsidies, this has come at the expense of housing quality, which is particularly evident in the capital, Santiago. Spain is another country employing space standards within a housing market primarily oriented towards homeownership. As a mixed capitalist economy, it has the lowest level of social housing provision in Europe. However, there is growing social housing and policy experimentation aimed at improving housing standards and quality, particularly in Barcelona.

In countries where design is regulated through mandatory *functional requirements*, such as Switzerland and the Netherlands, regulatory approaches and housing outcomes can differ significantly. Switzerland, a free market economy, does not provide social housing directly but subsidises accessible housing through private cooperatives. Despite extensive design regulations, its Housing Evaluation System (Wohnungs-Bewertungs-System [WBS]) permits considerable design flexibility, as its user-centred focus includes wide-ranging and finely grained quantitative and qualitative assessment methods. In contrast, the Netherlands, a welfare-state economy, has the largest social rent sector in Europe, accounting for 29% of housing (Centraal Bureau voor de Statistiek, 2024). Interestingly, it is provided by both housing corporations and private landlords and governed by detailed local plans and strict housing policies, with uniform design standards applied across all housing tenures.

China is one of the few countries that still extensively uses standard block and type plans to regulate housing provision. This approach relies on housing prototypes and pilot projects as well as significant design standardisation – from buildings and dwelling units to kitchens, bathrooms, and quality of finishes, typical of countries with high regulatory control at both central and local government levels. China has an emerging large-scale public and affordable rental sector in major Tier 1 cities such as Shenzhen and Guangzhou (Wang & Jacoby, 2023), aiming to address the lack of affordable housing supply following its transition to a mixed socialist market economy and the dismantling of the communist work-unit system that previously offered housing to its urban workers (Jacoby & Cheng, 2020).

There is a surprising lack of comparative housing studies dealing with design, both at national and international levels, and even fewer consider the wider issues of design regulations, market characteristics, and social welfare as connected problems (Özer & Jacoby, 2022; Scanlon et al., 2014). In addition, conventional methodologies in comparative housing studies that analyse social welfare and market classifications cannot sufficiently explain differentiated or specific design outcomes, as they are based on generalisations or abstractions (Hoekstra, 2005). For example, housing in England is often studied without acknowledging substantial differences between London and other regions. At the same time, similar design strategies are used widely across the globe with comparable outcomes, irrespective of regulations and standards. To analyse these differences and similarities requires a more nuanced architectural design research approach that takes into account a range of socio-spatial factors in relation to more generalisable design regulations and specific local contexts and housing design outcomes.

This book and its design research are therefore an attempt to study the various evidence-based understandings, but also the more subjective perceptions, of housing design and quality, thereby reviewing the robustness of past and current evidence and the relevance of architectural design to today's housing problems and debates. While there are many political and economic reasons for the perpetual housing crisis in the UK and beyond, the design guidelines, regulatory frameworks, and policy that have led to aspirational but often ineffective housing standards play an important role in this failure. Housing standards, while typically expressed in quantitative terms, almost always derive from an underlying qualitative ambition to improve living conditions and housing standards. While minimum standards are important to safeguarding essential and expected housing quality, they have often become a targeted maximum instead of a baseline for improvements driven by ambition and innovation. In addition, little seems to have changed in the spatial reasoning and design of housing for a decade, despite fundamental changes in household compositions and demographics.

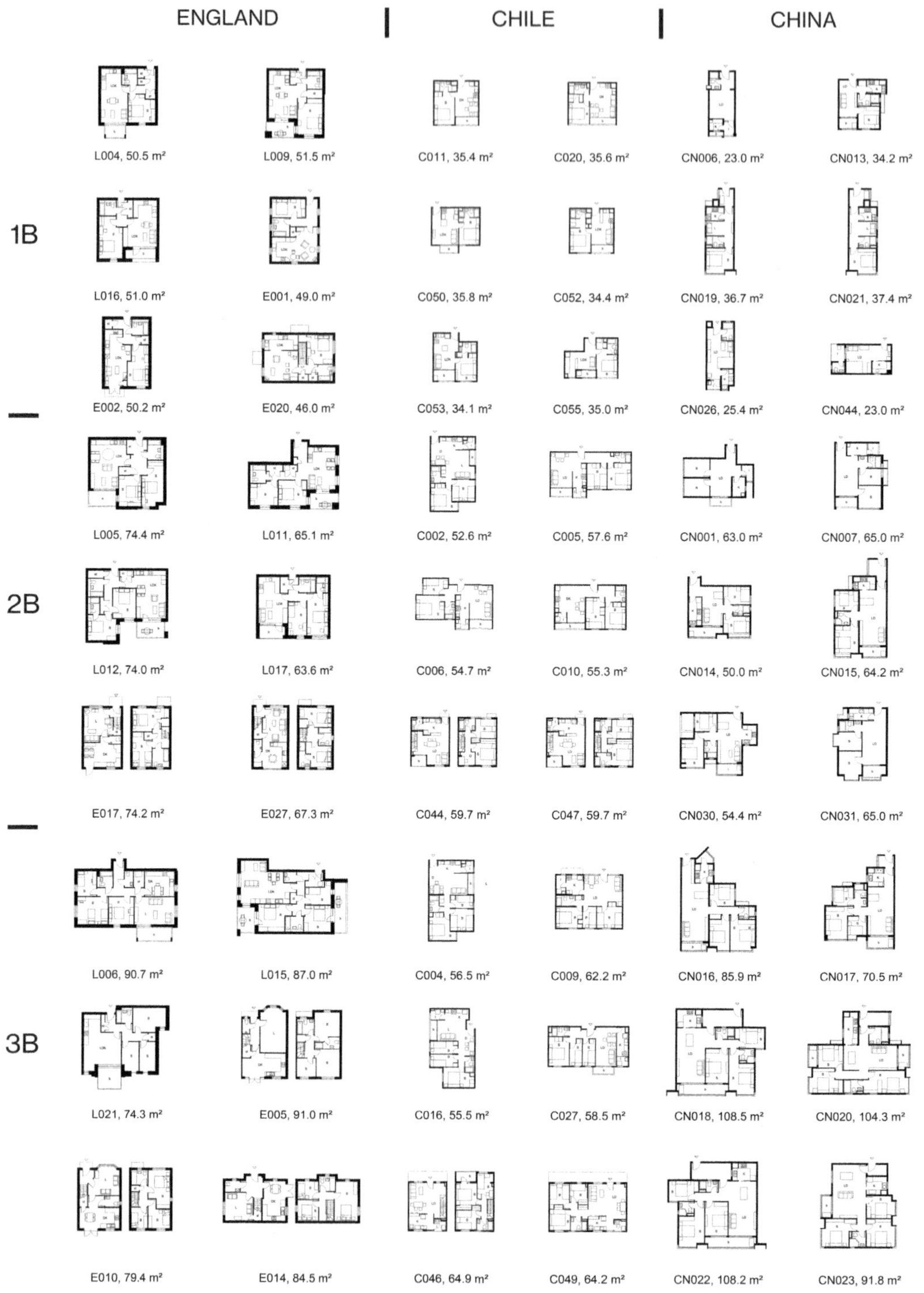

FIGURE 1.7 Housing plans by country and number of bedrooms in the studied sample of subsidised housing projects. *(Continued)*

Note: Full project data are available online: https://doi.org/10.60624/b68t-ae27.

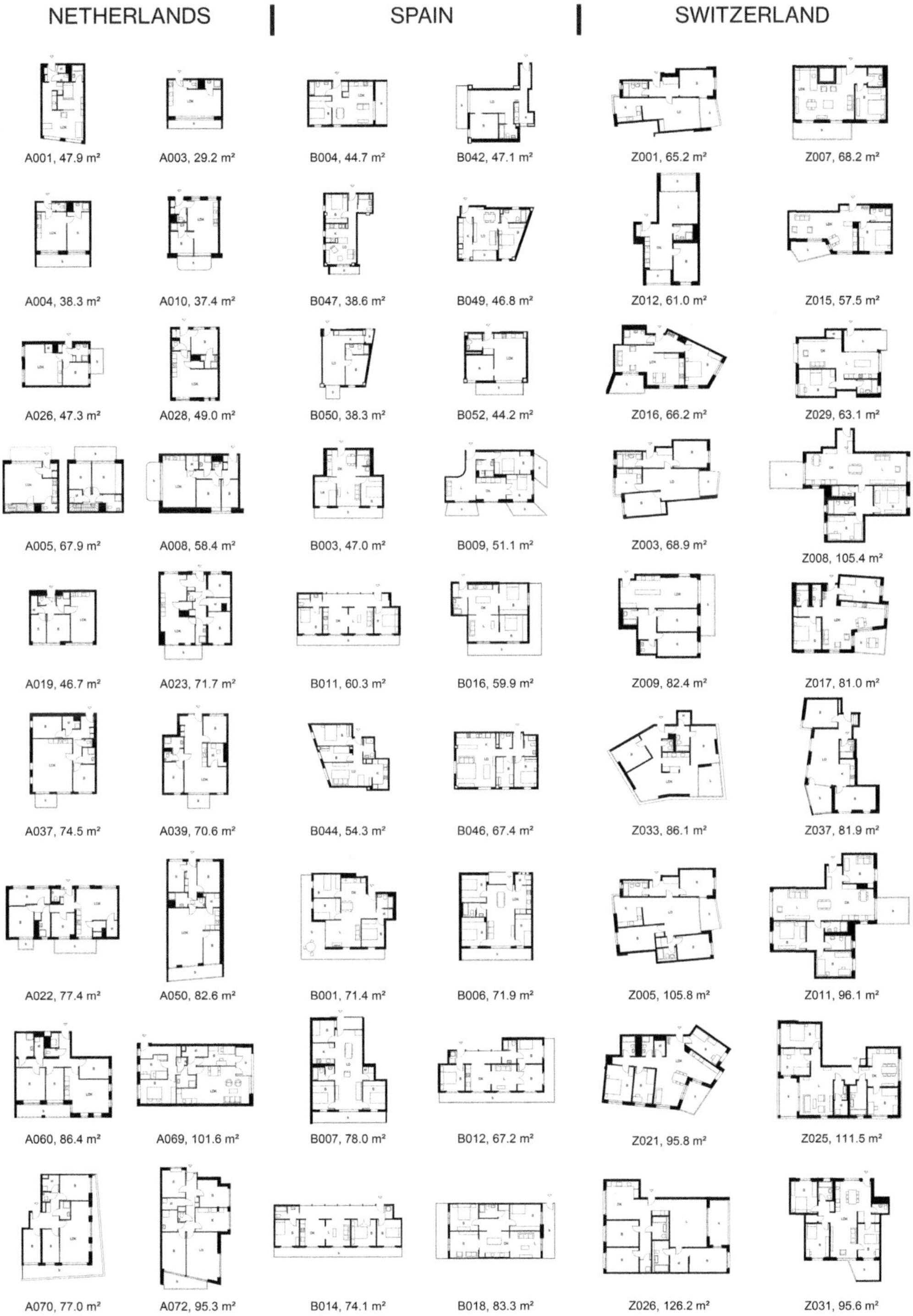

FIGURE 1.7 *(Continued)*

Housing expectations and satisfaction largely depend on what people are used to: cultural norms and social aspirations around housing, past housing experiences, and local housing markets. At the same time, the generalised and standardised approach to regulation and design tends to be most problematic for those who are most in need of protection and support. Therefore, future housing standards and design need to take greater account of lived experiences and social and environmental values, which directly shape both the realities and perceptions of housing and provide evidence of its successes and failures. Achieving this requires not only greater responsibility from the state but also public debate and education to realise greater improvements in living conditions and housing quality.

2

COMPARATIVE HOUSING DESIGN RESEARCH

Seyithan Özer and Sam Jacoby

The provision of subsidised housing is, in many countries, an important pillar of the social welfare system and a socio-economic necessity. It is therefore a commonly used policy instrument to address problems of widespread housing unaffordability and inequality. However, the design, regulation, and implementation of subsidised housing can greatly vary between different national and regional contexts (Özer & Jacoby, 2022). While often motivated by socio-political ambitions and aims – such as providing affordable, accessible, and equitable homes – subsidised housing systems are, in practice, equally shaped by regulatory cultures, technical standards, economic conditions, and socio-spatial practices.

Although housing design is increasingly recognised in housing studies as essential to understanding the ambitions and impacts of housing policies and systems, comparative studies that examine how design is controlled across different countries and jurisdictions remain limited (Karn & Nystrom, 1998; Özer & Jacoby, 2022). Traditional housing comparisons also still predominantly focus on high-level housing attributes, using categories familiar from housing system studies such as tenure structure, housing finance, supply and demand, allocation, regulation, policies, and affordability (Hoekstra, 2010; Scanlon et al., 2014). In particular, there is a need for more longitudinal studies of the historical contingencies and path dependencies of design controls and governance (Alves, 2020), in order to clarify the policy responsiveness of housing systems and the effects of policy on housing design.

As more recent housing studies have argued, current approaches to housing policy are shaped by historical developments, with their comprehensive understanding requiring analytical frameworks that account for both policy legacies and long-term trajectories (Blackwell & Bengtsson, 2021; Blackwell & Kohl, 2018). A similar approach should be applied to the study of design governance, as it is embedded in broader policy and institutional histories. Particularly in Europe, and in countries influenced by European policy models, design governance often reflects long-term policy and regulatory developments. Even in countries where design controls respond to more immediate developmental pressures and use different regulatory instruments, housing

DOI: 10.4324/9781032679204-4

priorities, design outcomes, path dependencies, and institutional layering must be considered (Jenkins & Smith, 2001; Murray & Clapham, 2015).

Design research that is practice-led and focused on architectural design practice and design thinking (Aydemir & Jacoby, 2022; Lawrence, 1983) therefore offers a valuable and complementary analytical framework to study housing design and the control of its quality in greater depth through design governance processes, such as regulatory instruments, technical standards, and socio-spatial reasoning and practices (Lawrence, 1985; Özer & Jacoby, 2022). By examining design regulations, design standards, and spatial layouts, design research can reveal the contextual values, constraints, and policy priorities shaping housing realities, and provide tangible insights into the supply, usability, and quality of homes.

Accordingly, the following chapters in this book provide a historical analysis of how design governance approaches have developed in relation to housing policy trajectories and key historical events shaping housing, and how this relates to the formation of housing systems and formulation of housing standards. Subsequent chapters provide analyses of the current design controls and design practices in six countries with distinct subsidised housing systems. By situating contemporary design practices within their political-economic, social, and institutional contexts, the underlying constraints, rationales, and path-dependent dynamics that shape design regulation and its outcomes can be analysed.

Design Controls

In most countries, meeting basic design standards related to health, safety, and environmental performance is mandatory for all housing developments. These standards typically cover issues such as structural integrity, fire safety, energy consumption, ventilation, sanitation, and space standards, and have prescribed minimum performance requirements. They are commonly enforced through a mixture of national building codes, regulations, and legislation.

In some countries, the same minimum standards apply to all housing sectors – the regulatory approach therefore can be considered as "universal". In others, a "differentiated" approach is taken, with additional or specific standards applied to only certain housing sectors, most commonly the various forms of subsidised housing. These design requirements typically relate to size or function but can also extend to the material quality of homes by specifying fixtures, materials, and finishes. Meeting subsidised housing-specific requirements can be enshrined in law but are more commonly a condition of subsidy programmes and planning agreements. Differentiated regulatory approaches tend to reflect housing policies with a stronger market orientation and deregulation of the private sector, and often result in greater differences between housing sectors in design and quality.

However, regardless of whether design regulation is universal or differentiated, many countries adopt a combination of regulatory approaches and tools to control housing design, including standardised design solutions, mandatory design requirements, and optional best-practice guidelines (Appolloni & D'Alessandro, 2021; Gallent et al., 2010; Pedro & Boueri, 2011). Beyond basic design standards, these cover a wider range of design issues related to the distribution of spaces, their usability, provision of amenities, overcrowding, environmental comfort, and building maintenance.

The formulation of both mandatory and voluntary design standards is often derived from established best practice and influenced by a wide range of housing actors, including government, local authorities, professional bodies, housing providers, and civil society organisations. However, the nature and extent of design controls are not only the outcomes of technical concerns but equally shaped by how housing is locally conceptualised and the particular housing system through which it is delivered. These housing systems, according to housing studies literature, are typically classified based on how private and social rental markets are regulated, existing policy and subsidy frameworks, and prevailing sector size and tenure patterns (Flynn & Montalbano, 2024; Hansson & Lundgren, 2018). Both system-related aspects and wider housing contexts inform whether design controls are applied in a differentiated or universal manner.

In comparative housing studies, two canonical frameworks are commonly used to distinguish housing systems: "dualist" versus "unitary" rental markets (Kemeny, 1995) and "mass" versus "residual" social housing (Harloe, 1995). While these frameworks share similarities, the former focuses on the relationship and governance structure between private and social rental sectors, whereas the latter primarily considers the size and accessibility of the social housing sector. In unitary rental markets, public and private sectors compete within a single market under similar levels of regulation, while mass housing systems feature large-scale, often state-controlled social and public housing available to a wide range of households and income groups. Both models are expected to provide greater housing affordability and accessibility compared to dualist or residual systems. This is because in those housing systems, public and private rental sectors are separated, with the social sector highly regulated and functioning as a "safety net" for the most vulnerable and disadvantaged groups. Consequently, the social housing sector is small and becomes residualised.

However, these 30-year-old classifications of housing systems face growing criticism as they are based on Western European contexts and welfare typologies that are not transferable to emerging or transitioning housing markets. For example, studies on post-Communist countries (Hegedüs et al., 2012), East Asia (Y. P. Wang & Murie, 2011), and Latin America (Murray & Clapham, 2015) all highlight the need for greater region-specific and contextual analytical frameworks for comparative housing studies. In addition, far-reaching housing deregulation and financialisation across Europe over the last four decades have created increasingly varied housing systems that do not conform to traditional binary classifications (Blessing, 2015; Stephens, 2020). As many governments have retreated from direct involvement in public housing provision to reduce public spending and strengthen the private market – particularly by promoting homeownership – the social renting sector has shrunk and diversified into different affordable housing tenures, making traditional welfare typologies less relevant (Aalbers, 2016).

Yet these broad trends have not unfolded uniformly. Studies drawing on historical institutionalist perspectives show that although social housing has generally been pushed to the periphery of the welfare state, the degree and nature of this retreat have varied significantly by country (Blackwell & Bengtsson, 2021; Kadi & Lilius, 2024). This highlights the importance of considering how institutional legacies and policy choices shape housing systems and outcomes. As Stephens (2020) observes, housing systems have diverged despite facing the same pressures of global financialisation. In China, for instance, housing marketisation occurred alongside sustained state control and a growing recent state-led affordable housing provision in large cities (L. Wang & Jacoby, 2023).

Despite their limitations, traditional housing system classifications remain useful for describing subsidised housing by distinguishing between social housing as a "safety net" (dualist), provided within a separate housing sector, and public housing as affordable homes within a common housing sector shared with the private market (unitary). In Western countries, differentiated design controls largely correspond to the dualist rental systems while universal regulatory controls correspond to unitary rental systems.

In many contexts, especially countries with high housing deficits, affordability and increasing the housing supply are commonly prioritised over improving housing quality. As a result, housing evaluations tend to focus on technical metrics such as minimum dwelling size, room functions, occupancy rates, and circulation standards, often without giving sufficient consideration to the long-term usability, flexibility, and lived experience of homes, or how these standards are shaped by or shape housing expectations. This raises important questions about what constitutes adequate housing design standards and who should define them. While technical standards are essential to safeguarding and improving housing quality, they are not universal or neutral, and equal attention should be paid to what complementary or equivalent social standards might be, and how they could inform them.

A prominent example of this socio-technical tension is space standards (Table 2.1). These are widely accepted as a technical standard to measure housing adequacy and usability as well as design quality. Yet to fully understand how space standards abstract housing quality into room dimensions, and how they are developed, interpreted, and applied requires an understanding of historical context and interdisciplinary insights to link social and spatial histories to evolving design practices, governance approaches, and transformations in housing supply and market dynamics. This book is therefore an attempt to consider both the technical dimensions of housing standards and the social dimensions of the lived experience of homes, exploring how this questions long-held beliefs about housing and its design as well as how housing is studied.

The design outcome of subsidised housing is typically controlled through the use of three primary regulatory instruments: (1) minimum dwelling size standards, (2) functional requirements, such as room dimensions and furniture placement, and (3) standardised unit or block plans (Özer & Jacoby, 2022). Although similar in approach, the form and application of these regulatory tools vary by country and historical period, reflecting shifting design governance models, housing market conditions, and policy priorities. For example, countries with large, subsidised housing programmes that rely on the private sector for delivery, such as Colombia, Brazil, and Singapore, combine functional requirements with basic target dwelling sizes to offer greater design flexibility and reduce costs and subsidies.

In practice, regulatory frameworks typically combine minimum dwelling or room standards with either additional functional criteria or typical unit plans. Most design controls therefore include minimum-size standards, usually defined by minimum room dimensions or floor areas, and based either on the number of bedrooms or the maximum number of occupants (bedspaces). The calculation of space standards is also often linked to laws and standards on overcrowding, which take into account the age and sex of household members, or allocation criteria specific to housing providers. Increasingly, dimensional standards also consider demographic change and household transformation by including accessibility requirements and universal design principles.

However, minimum dwelling sizes are often based on assumptions about typical home use and derived from graphic and dimensional studies of standard furniture, the space needed for common domestic activities, anthropometric measurements related to their use, and associated circulation spaces. In this way, dwelling sizes are directly linked to the use and function of a home, with minimum dimensions and floor areas both rationalising and spatialising functional criteria. These are often prescribed through room-based furniture schedules and activity zones for common domestic functions, but sometimes also include provision for possible future home extensions or modifications.

TABLE 2.1 Comparison of housing design control documents and standards.

Country	*Document*	*Sector[1]*	*Min. dwelling area[2]*	*Key functional requirements[2,3]*
Australia[4]	Queensland, Social Housing Design Guideline (2024)	SH	• Studio: 33 m^2 • 1B: 49 m^2 • 2B: 60 m^2 • 3B: 95 m^2	• Furniture schedules and layouts (three dwelling types according to accessibility) • Multi-purpose internal space of min. 1.9 × 2.1 m • External space provision Room specifications • Min. bedroom size: 11 m^2/2.7–3 m. • Min. living room width 3.3 m • Min. ceiling height 2.6 m
	South Australia Housing Authority, House Design Guide (2020)	SH	Rental (min./max/.): • Bedsit: 38–55 m^2 • 1B: 55–65 m^2 • 2B: 65–90 m^2	• Ca. 10 to 15% allowance for vertical circulation
Austria[4]	Bauordnung for Vienna (2023)	SH, PH	• 30 m^2 (flat)	• Flats with two habitable rooms to have separate WC and be convertible for disabled users
Brazil	Minha Casa Minha Vida Programme Specifications (2017)	SH	Min. 2B: • 2B house: 36 m^2 • 2B flat: 39 m^2	• Houses to be extendable without affecting natural light/ventilation of existing spaces • External service area min. 1.8 × 2.4 m Room specifications • Min. room widths: living room 3.3–3.6 m, bedroom 2.4 m, kitchen 1.8 m, bathroom 1.5 m • Min. ceiling height 2.6 m • Furniture schedule for each area
Canada[4]	Vancouver Housing Design and Technical Guidelines (2025)	SH	• Studio: 30–37 m^2 • 1B: 46 m^2 • 2B: 66 m^2 (flats)	• Storage requirement: min. unit width of 3.6 m Room specifications • Min. living room ceiling height 2.4 m • Furniture schedule (kitchen, bathroom)
	British Columbia Housing Design Guidelines and Construction Standards (2019)	SH	• Studio: 33 m^2 • 1B: 46 m^2 • 2B: 66 m^2 (flats)	Room specifications • Min. bedroom sizes: single: 8.5 m^2/2.6m, double 9.3 m^2/2.8 m, twin 11.15 m^2/2.8 m • Furniture schedule (living areas, bedrooms) • Kitchen, bathroom: min. fixtures, appliances, and counter frontages

(*Continued*)

TABLE 2.1 (Continued)

Country	*Document*	*Sector*[1]	*Min. dwelling area*[2]	*Key functional requirements*[2,3]
Chile	Supreme Decree 19 (Social and Territorial Integration Programme)	SH	–	Room specifications • Min. bedroom size: 7 m^2/2.2 m • Furniture schedule (living areas, bedrooms) • Kitchen, bathroom: min. fixtures, appliances, and counter frontages
	Supreme Decree 49 (Solidarity Housing Choice Fund)	SH	–	Room specifications • Min. bedroom size: 2.6 × 2.2 m • Furniture schedule (living areas, bedrooms) • Kitchen, bathroom: min. fixtures, appliances, and counter frontages
China[4]	Beijing Public Rental Housing Design Guidelines (2010)	SH	4 dwelling size categories: • 30 m^2 • 40 m^2 • 50 m^2 • 60 m^2	• Specification of interior standards (12 items including living room, bedroom, kitchen, toilet) Room specifications • Min. kitchen and wet-space sizes for each category
	Shanghai Affordable Housing Design Guidelines (2010)	SH	• 40–50 m^2 (all dwellings)	–
	Shenzhen Public Housing Design Standards (2021)	SH	• 1B: 35–40 m^2 • 2B: 60–70 m^2 • 3B: 80–90 m^2	Room specifications • Min. bedroom sizes: single: 5 m^2, double 9 m^2
		SH	–	Four modular flat types: • 1P/2P: 14.1–14.5 m^2 • 2P/3P: 21.4–22 m^2 • 3P/4P: 30.2–31 m^2 • 4P/5P: 35–36.1 m^2
England	Nationally Described Space Standard (2015)[6]	SH	• 1B/1P: 39 m^2 • 1B/2P: 50 m^2 • 2B/3P: 61 m^2 • 2B/4P: 70 m^2	• Built-in storage areas, provision of wet-spaces Room specifications • Min. bedroom sizes: single: 7.5 m^2/2.15 m, double 11.5 m^2/2.55 m (2.75 m for the first bedroom)

(Continued)

TABLE 2.1 (Continued)

Country	*Document*	*Sector*[1]	*Min. dwelling area*[2]	*Key functional requirements*[2,3]
Finland	Building Regulations (2017)	SH, PH	• 20 m² (dwelling)	Room specifications • Min. habitable room size: 7 m² • Window to floor area ratio: 1:10 • Min. ceiling height 3 m
France	Code of Construction and Housing (2019)	SH, PH	• 14 m²/33 m³ per person (≤4 bed spaces) • 10 m²/23 m³ (>4 bed spaces)	Room specifications • Min. 1 room of 9 m²/20 m³ • Min. ceiling height 1.8 m
Ireland	Design Standards for New Apartments (2018)	SH, PH	• 2P: 45 m² • 3P: 63 m² (dwellings)	• Dual aspect ratios, separate standards for shared accommodation Room specifications • Min. bedroom sizes: single: 7.1 m²/2.1 m, double: 11.4 m²/2.8 m, twin: 13m² /2.8 m • Min. living area sizes: 1B: 23 m²/3.3 m, 2B: 28 m²/3.6 m
Netherlands[4]	Building Regulations (2012)	SH, PH	• 18 m² (dwelling)	Room specifications • Min. one habitable room of 11 m²/3 m • Min. habitable room width: 1.8 m
	The Housing Standard (De Woonstandard, 2024)	SH	• 1B: 24–50 m² • 2B: 50–65 m² • 3B: 65–80 m²	Room specifications • Min. bedroom sizes: single: 3.0 × 1.8 m, double: 3.8 × 2.9 m
Scotland	Building Standards Technical Handbook (2017)	SH, PH	–	• Built-in storage areas • Provision of wet-spaces Room specifications • Min. one bedroom of 12 m²/2.8 m • Furniture schedule and layouts for bedrooms
	The Glasgow Standard (2019)	SH	• 2P: 48.5 m² • 3P: 61 m² (dwellings)	Room specifications • Min. bedroom sizes: Single: 7 m², double: 11.5 m² • Furniture schedule and typical layouts for living area and bedrooms

(*Continued*)

TABLE 2.1 (Continued)

Country	*Document*	*Sector*[1]	*Min. dwelling area*[2]	*Key functional requirements*[2,3]
Singapore	Housing Development Board Documents	SH	–	Six basic flat types: • 2R (Type 1): 36 m² • 2R (Type 2): 45 m² • 3R: 60–65 m² • 4R: 90 m² • 5R: 110 m² • 3Gen (6R): 115 m²
Spain	Decree 13/2010	SH	• <90 m² (general needs home) • <100 m² (accessible) • <120 m² (large families)	–
	Decree on the Minimum Conditions for Habitability (141/2012)	SH, PH	• >36 m²	Room specifications • Min. bedroom sizes: 6 m²/2 m • Min ceiling height 2.5 m
	INCASOL Social Housing Standards (2019)	SH	• 3P: 50 m² • 4P: 60 m² • 5P: 70 m²	Room specifications • Min. bedroom sizes: single: 10 m²/2.6 m, double: 8m²/2.4 m
Sweden	Building Regulations (2019)	SH, PH	–	• Requirements to separate spaces for social contact, sleep and rest, and cooking depending on dwelling size. Room specifications • Min. 1 double bedroom or separable bedspace for dwellings > 55 m² • Min. 1 separable single bedspace in dwellings 35–55 m²
Switzerland	WBS Housing Assessment System (2015)[7]	SH	• 1B: 30–50 m² • 2B: 45–65 m²	• Flexibility, furnishability, and adaptability ratings Room specifications • First bedroom: 14 m², second bedroom: 10 m² (in 2B)
	Supplementary Building Regulations for Zurich (2016)	SH, PH	–	Room specifications • Min. kitchen size: 6 m² (studios: 4 m²) • Min. storage: 8 m² (5 m²: ≤ two-room units)

(Continued)

TABLE 2.1 (Continued)

Country	*Document*	*Sector*[1]	*Min. dwelling area*[2]	*Key functional requirements*[2,3]
USA[4]	NYC Building Code (2023)	SH	–	Room specifications • Min. 1 habitable room of 13.9 m^2 • Min. habitable room area: 7.4 m^2 • Min. habitable room width 2.4 m (other than kitchen), half of bedrooms min. 2.1 m • Min. ceiling height 2.1 m

Notes:

Most countries have regional variations; the table includes one or two examples only.

[1]SH = subsidised housing sector, PH = private housing sector.

[2]Selection only. B = bedrooms, P = persons, R = rooms.

[3]Excludes accessibility, material, technical, and construction specifications.

[4]Country with regional variation in housing design controls.

[5]Hong Kong has a separate housing and planning system under the "One Country, Two Systems" framework.

[6]Applies to all tenures in London, elsewhere only to subsidised housing.

[7]WBS is required for subsidised housing and recommended for private housing.

Table adapted in part from Özer & Jacoby (2022).

In addition to these socio-technical calculations, design governance and standards reflect housing priorities and welfare roles. Subsidised housing serves a wide range of social and economic policy aims, which includes promoting equitable urban development, enhancing social welfare, addressing developmental needs, and contributing to economic stability and growth. The specific priorities and needs have a direct effect on how standards are defined and implemented, enabling greater housing supply or improved quality.

For example, China uses standardised block and typical dwelling plans to regulate design outcomes, as these allow for large-scale, rapid development in a context where affordable housing provision is largely state-led, thus, requiring less formal regulation. In Tier 1 cities like Beijing and Shanghai, affordable housing pilot programmes develop or incorporate standard unit plans as effective design guidance tools alongside target dwelling sizes. Likewise, public housing provision by the Hong Kong Housing Authority relies on standard unit and block plans, which have been regularly updated since the 1950s to improve unit sizes and amenities while adapting to changing household needs, increasing site constraints, and ongoing advances in modular construction (L. Wang et al., 2024). However, whereas affordable housing programmes in mainland China prioritise supply, Hong Kong focuses on Modular Integrated Construction (MiC) to improve build quality.

More specifically related to issues of design in China and especially Hong Kong, typical dwelling plans specify the design of service areas but allow greater flexibility in internal partitioning. However, due to small dwelling sizes and fixed service locations, deviations from standard layouts are limited. While space standards traditionally equate functions to rooms, this relationship is increasingly questioned to provide greater design flexibility, by regulating instead the provision of functional zones that are not room-specific. For example, the Netherlands permits a "free layout" approach, requiring only a notional "living area" that can be arranged across rooms in any combination. Sweden's building regulations and design guides have similarly moved from prescribing specific rooms and their functions to the requirement of accommodating key domestic activities – such as sleeping, resting, cooking, socialising, or eating – without being restricted by fixed room configurations (Vega & Liñán, 2024). Meanwhile, Switzerland's Wohnungs-Bewertungs-System (WBS; Housing Evaluation System), encourages flexible living arrangements with habitable rooms that are function-neutral.

Social Norms

Based on the measurable dimensions of standard furniture layouts, as well as the activity zones and access spaces needed for effective home use, space standards derive from normative ideas about households and their daily routines. These norms still largely rely on twentieth-century household models and continue to be centred on the nuclear, working family, including its social hierarchies and gendered spatial divisions (Alonso Aranda, 2024; Jacoby et al., 2022; Lawrence, 1985). Dwelling layouts can be therefore seen as a materialisation of both technical design controls and social norms.

In Singapore, public housing is reserved for families and designed around the typical life-cycle of a nuclear family. Homes support traditional familial patterns and spatial hierarchies through master bedrooms with an en suite and open-plan living areas with easily separable kitchens. In Colombia, where subsidised housing is primarily provided for ownership, planning regulations require that new family dwellings can accommodate the future addition of at least one bedroom within the existing dwelling footprint, emphasising long-term usability and adaptation to commonly expected changes in family household needs (Wilcox et al., 2024).

The design of homes thus reveals the socio-spatial reasoning underpinning space standards and how the implicit assumptions made about home use inform the organisation and relationship between rooms. Design research hereby provides a lens to examine these dynamic socio-cultural, economic, and political factors that shape actual, physical housing outcomes – important analytical dimensions that traditional housing studies and housing system frameworks often overlook.

To bridge existing gaps between architectural design research and housing studies and social sciences, this book specifically examines the governance of subsidised housing design, the built environment, and everyday housing experiences. Focusing on these interconnected dimensions is essential for design research, and it enriches the theorisation and contextualisation of housing studies by grounding research methodologically and analytically in the everyday realities and practices of housing.

This emphasises the importance of understanding housing problems and systems in tangible terms, such as those offered by the study of housing design and real-life housing conditions, and by using qualitative analysis rather than their abstraction into policies, systems, and standards. This reverses to some extent the common analytical order in traditional housing studies, which privileges a top-down approach starting with the study of systems to explain housing outcomes. Design research, by contrast, focuses on the material outcomes of housing to explain the wider systems that shape them.

Symptomatic of this difference in perspective is that the term "housing outcomes" in housing studies refers to the consequences of housing systems, policies, markets, and practices for households and communities, whereas in design research it refers to the material and experienceable outcomes of housing design processes, decisions, and governance. While in the former, understanding design and built architecture can play a role, it is the explicit focus of the latter, which is directly interested in how the intentions of design relate to the realities of use and how homes perform and are experienced and inhabited.

A comparison of typical dwellings as prescribed by national design standards reveals substantial variation in "standard" dimensions across countries (Table 2.1). For instance, in Hong Kong, the standard unit size for a two-person dwelling ranges between 14.1 m^2 and 22 m^2, while it is 28 m^2 in France, 49 m^2 in Canada, and between 55 and 65 m^2 in Australia. This translates into significant differences in the average minimum space provided per person – from as little as 7 m^2 in Hong Kong to 22.5 m^2 in Australia. Similarly, standards for individual rooms and

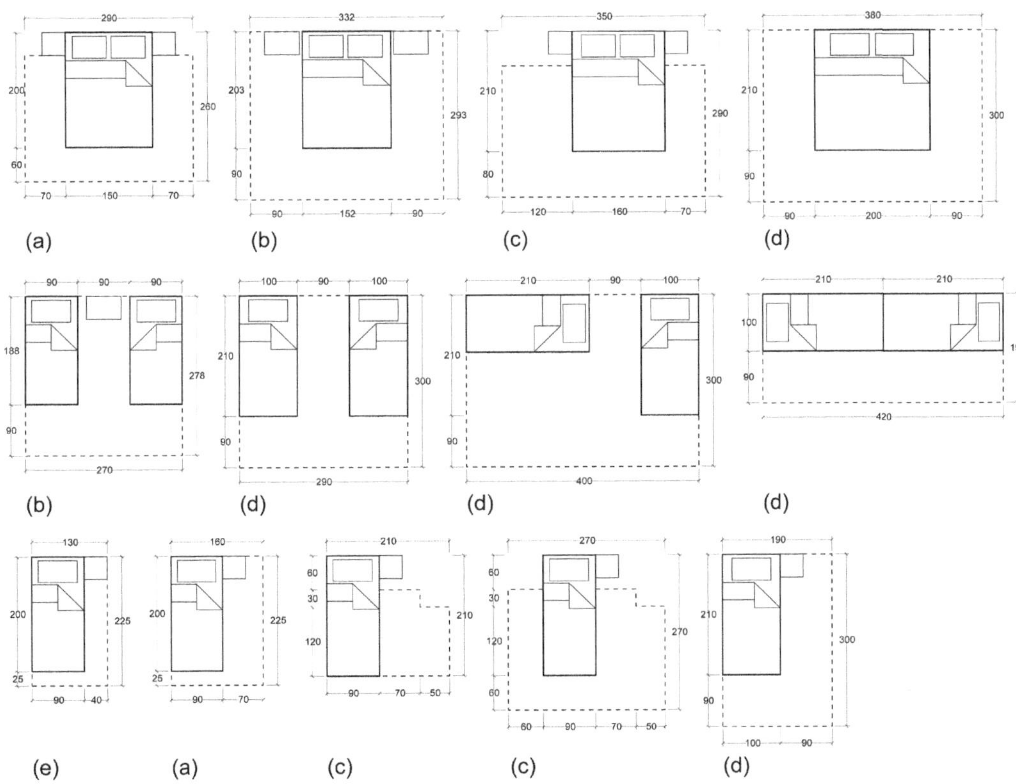

FIGURE 2.1 Space standards and activity zones for bedrooms.

Source: Özer & Jacoby, "The design of subsidized housing" (2022).

Note: Dash indicates activity zone. The dimensions are derived from: (a) Scottish Government, *Building Standards Technical Handbook: Domestic* (2017); (b) Glasgow City Council, *The Glasgow Standard* (2019); (c) SS 839661 T1, Swedish Institute for Standards; (d) Bundesamt für *Wohnungswesen, Housing Assessment System WBS* (2015); (e) Queensland Department of Housing, *Social Housing Design Guideline* (2024).

required activity zones differ considerably, reflecting divergent furniture norms, cultural expectations, and spatial practices. These differences are particularly evident in minimum bedroom sizes (Figure 2.1): the minimum floor area of a double bedroom is as little as 9 m^2 in France and as much as 12 m^2 in Scotland. In addition, minimum activity zones vary, with the *Queensland Social Housing Design Guide* (2017) mandating a 90-cm wide movement zone beside a bed, while the *London Housing Design Guide* (GLA, 2010) requires only 40 cm. These discrepancies in dimensional standards cannot be explained by economic pressures such as land values and development costs alone but, importantly, also reflect differences in socio-cultural norms and expectations related to how space is used, valued, and regulated.

This intrinsic relationship between socio-cultural, political, and economic contexts and housing systems and space standards, as well as their variations across countries due to different policy approaches, market orientation, planning traditions, and welfare models, is increasingly acknowledged in housing studies (Appolloni & D'Alessandro, 2021; Sendi, 2013; Susanto et al., 2020). The contextual nature of the drivers and determinants of housing standards between countries and periods (McNelis, 2016) highlights the need to understand them in relation to historical policy or regulatory trajectories and contingencies as well as in respect to changing conceptualisations and expectations of housing.

Cultural norms and preferences also play an important role in housing design and layout decisions. This is especially legible in subsidised housing and small dwellings built under budgetary constraints, where balancing usable floor area, number of units, and housing quality typically results in designs that are close to or even below minimum permissible dwelling sizes and dimensions. This lack of space limits flexibility, and universal design strategies are often used to maximise usable floor area, but minimum dwelling sizes primarily depend on local market expectations and regulatory requirements. For example, recently completed two-bedroom units in Vancouver, Canada, measure approximately 65 m^2, while comparable social rent units in Scotland are only around 60 m^2.

While in many Western countries separate circulation spaces such as hallways or corridors are the long-established social norm (Evans, 1978), in other regions like East Asia separate circulation zones are often minimised by combining and "overlapping" these with other activity zones within rooms, permitting direct movement between spaces (Figure 2.2). Another design example is the relationship between kitchens and living areas. Whereas in countries like China the preference is to separate these functions to isolate cooking smells and noise, combined kitchen and living rooms are common in many other countries. As Ozaki (2002) argues, cultural interpretations of privacy influence not only the spatial separation between kitchens and living areas but also the placement of bedrooms in relation to other functions and spaces.

These underscores how housing is shaped by cultural priorities that inform domestic activities and the interactions between household members and residents, and how housing design is receptive to socio-cultural norms that affect everyday practices, privacy needs, and spatial household structures. There is, therefore, a need for a greater adoption of a qualitative lens in housing studies (Stephens & Norris, 2014), including ethnographic studies (Wetzstein, 2018), to capture differences in socio-cultural drivers and context.

While this relationship between socio-cultural, political, and economic contexts and housing systems is widely recognised in housing studies and analysed in relation to policy frameworks, planning traditions, market orientations, and welfare models, there remains a lack of connection between this and variations in design outcomes, which offers a more concrete reading of how policy and regulatory frameworks fail or succeed. The drivers behind housing

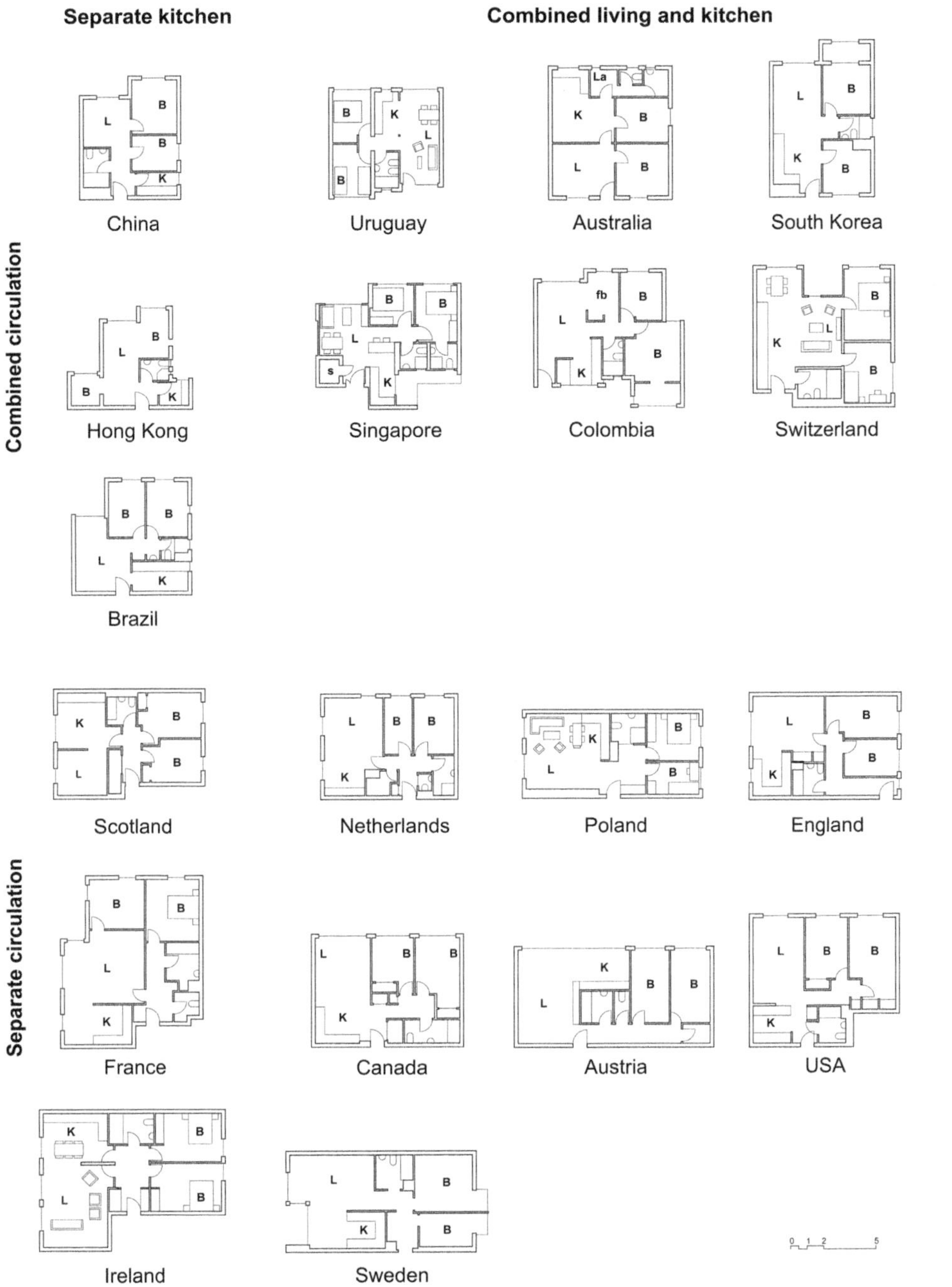

FIGURE 2.2 Typical two-bedroom dwelling plans organised according to different design strategies (separate/combined kitchens or corridors).

Source: Özer & Jacoby (2022).

Note: K, kitchen; L, living room; B, bedroom; la, laundry; s, household shelter; fb, future bedroom; sa, sauna.

Based on public information from local authorities, housing associations, and cooperatives. Size and layout differences reflect efficiency strategies (e.g., combined kitchens/corridors producing smaller dwellings) and varying concepts of home use.

standards vary between countries and time periods, underscoring the need to also understand them within their historical and institutional contexts and within evolving conceptions of housing (McNelis, 2016).

In bringing together historical, technical, and social perspectives, this book offers a comprehensive analysis of subsidised housing design and its governance. By tracing the historical evolution of design governance, examining the technical and spatial reasoning underpinning design standards, and interrogating the lived experiences and perceptions of homes, it highlights how housing outcomes cannot be solely understood as products of policy and economy but must also be seen in relation to cultural norms and spatial and material design.

This integrated design research approach enables a richer comparison of subsidised housing across time and countries, revealing both the contingencies and consistencies that inform its design and function (Table 2.2). By linking regulatory cultures, socio-technical standards, and spatialised social practices, the framework provides a basis for analysing how housing systems evolve, how state interventions translate into housing supply, and how social aims are embedded in design strategies. It encourages multi-scalar studies that can trace the historical contingencies and policy adaptations shaping housing outcomes. In doing so, it situates architectural design research not as a secondary concern but as central to understanding the functionality, meaning, and performance of subsidised housing. This integration of theory, method, and lived experience reinforces the call for a more historically grounded, spatially sensitive, and socially attuned approach to housing studies. The design lens thus contributes not only to the theorisation of housing systems but also to the development of methodologies capable of capturing both universal design principles and their situated application.

TABLE 2.2 Potential interdisciplinary research agenda for comparative subsidised housing studies.

	Context	*Methodology*	*Analysis*
Design governance and standardisation	• Formal and informal policies, regulations, and standards; regulatory instruments and decision-making processes; interactions between public and private actors • Historical path dependencies and evolution of housing aims, conventions, and practices • Variation across housing systems and organisations • Influence of socio-cultural norms on design governance and regulatory approaches • Standardisation as a regulatory and market-driven design process	• Comparative review of regulatory frameworks, policies, and subsidy rules across six countries • Identification of standard house types, adaptations, and design governance processes • Historical analysis of design governance in England and Chile • Longitudinal studies and literature reviews to trace policy and institutional transformations	• Study drivers of regulatory and housing practices • Examine how design governance shapes housing outcomes and quality, and their path dependencies • Assess state interventions, policy choices, and regulatory instruments and their effectiveness • Compare institutional and market roles in housing design and provision

(*Continued*)

TABLE 2.2 (Continued)

	Context	*Methodology*	*Analysis*
Housing standards and spatial reasoning	• Historical evolution of minimum dwelling sizes, functional zoning, and layout principles • Translation of universal principles into local design outcomes; discretionary vs. codified standards • Socio-technical housing norms and links between spatial standards and social aims, usability, and adaptability	• Literature review to analyse historical and socio-cultural influences on codified or discretionary standards and their formulation and implementation • Comparative analyses of housing standards, dwelling layouts, functional distributions, and dimensions, both over time and across regions	• Examine how standards influence dwelling organisation, flexibility, and adaptability • Evaluate layout efficiency, privacy, and long-term usability • Explore cultural and regulatory determinants of spatial reasoning • Identify where standards diverge from social practices and needs
Lived experience and social data	• Everyday lived use of homes vs. planning standards • Socio-cultural norms of daily routines, space use, housing expectations, and social values • Housing quality realities and perceptions	• Qualitative fieldwork in 37 subsidised homes across six countries • Live motion tracking, interviews, user diaries, spatial and visual home documentation • Analysis of furniture placement, room adaptation, spatial appropriation, and household practices	• Study how residents interpret, adapt, and modify domestic spaces • Assess misalignment between regulatory assumptions, technical design, and lived experience • Evaluate design flexibility and adaptability • Inform future design standards and governance approaches
Integration of insights	• Combining historical, technical, and social perspectives • Design research as mediator between policy, standards, cultural norms, and lived experience studies • Multi-scalar approach linking regulatory cultures, socio-technical standards, and spatialised social practices	• Mixed-method comparative analysis • Integration of policy, technical, and social data • Cross-national and longitudinal comparisons • Combined assessment of universal principles and localised applications	• Analyse interactions between governance, standards, cultural norms, and household practices • Evaluate how design mediates policy aims and social outcomes • Identify contingencies and consistencies shaping housing performance • Provide a framework for contextual, historically grounded, and socially attuned housing assessment

Note: Full project data – including participant and stakeholder interviews, in-depth home case studies, and plan and space standard analysis – are available at https://doi.org/10.60624/nnc8-1557.

PART II

Design Governance Histories

3

HOUSING STANDARDS AND STANDARDISATION IN ENGLAND

A Historical Study of Design Governance

Lucia Alonso Aranda and Sam Jacoby

According to the *UN Procurement Practitioners Handbook* (United Nations, 2022), the purpose of standardisation is "to achieve economies of scale, compatibility with other products, facilitation of operation, maintenance, and repair of already purchased goods". Standards typically specify minimum performance requirements to create greater consistency and reliability, which necessitates an agreed-upon method of assessing performance thresholds and compliance. Standards are commonly found in regulatory documents such as legal acts, as well as voluntary best-practice guides, including manuals and reports. A standard thus often defines a performance baseline, but it is sometimes also considered the optimal design solution.

Standardisation refers to the process through which a standard is developed or implemented. Standards can lead to the standardisation of housing design, which requires the creation, implementation, and enforcement of standards. By the turn of the twentieth century, modern industrial production methods increased the rationalisation and standardisation of housing design, including the repetition of standard components, methods, or processes, enabling housebuilders to mitigate risks associated with market volatility and changes in labour, material availability, and development costs (Carmona, 2001).

Standard house types are commonly used by housebuilders to streamline production, reduce costs and time, and maximise profits (Nicol & Hooper, 1999). There are numerous potential risk-related benefits associated with this: first, repetition lowers design costs per unit by reducing fees for architects and designers; second, building standard units reduces training needs for the labour force; third, familiarity with a standard design and process helps limit building defects; and finally, it is easier to obtain statutory approvals for standardised housing, as its compliance with planning and design requirements is already established. Volume housebuilders therefore typically maintain a limited range of house types, modifying them only incrementally when regulatory or market changes demand it (Ball, 1983). While the average lifespan of a standard unit type for private developers is around five years, some have been used for decades – with one developer's house-type reported to be almost identical to designs first introduced in 1955 (Leopold & Bishop, 1983).

DOI: 10.4324/9781032679204-6

While standardisation offers clear benefits, it is also often associated with monotonous design and uninspired housing (Booth, 2003; Goodchild, 2016; Leopold & Bishop, 1983), indifferent to context and lacking a sense of identity and place. There are thus questions about the extent to which construction efficiency translates into housing quality (Payne, 2013), and there are also concerns that the standardisation of house types often results in reduced dwelling floor areas (Goodchild & Karn, 1997). Till and Schneider (2007), in their book *Flexible Housing*, warn that minimum space standards can create "determinate spaces", meaning that "soft spaces" such as circulation areas lose their important flexibility and that functions and behaviour become restricted. They argue that long-term housing requires flexible designs that can accommodate different spatial arrangements and adapt to changing living patterns.

This view is supported by Goodchild and Furbey (1986), who found that the space standards proposed by the Parker Morris Committee in their report *Homes for Today and Tomorrow* (1961) limited changes in furniture layouts and the long-term usability of homes by assuming a fixed relationship between space and activities. In addition, Leopold and Bishop (1983) argue that mass-produced, standardised housing "subverts the traditional role of the architect" and tends to simplify design. This simplification is linked to a decline in traditional building skills, which can prevent housing flexibility and innovation (Adams et al., 2011; Ball, 1983). Emmitt (2013) therefore states that "simplification should not be confused with standardisation", highlighting that standardisation is not always the best or simplest solution.

What these perspectives on housing design highlight is the issue of design governance, and how it is embedded within the wider socio-political, economic, technical, and cultural contexts of housing. Little attention has been paid to how standardisation and design governance collectively influence not only housing typologies and outcomes but also the lived experience of domestic space by determining its use, usability, flexibility, adaptability, and design quality. Housing outcomes are the result of historical and institutional decision-making and processes shaped by social values, political choices, and regulatory frameworks, with the drivers behind housing priorities changing over time. However, this connection between housing regulation and housing design outcomes is frequently dismissed as a problem of practice and therefore often overlooked in historical enquiries.

Yet the formation of housing systems has evolved over time in parallel to changes in housing regulation and design governance in the pursuit of improving housing quality and its changing definitions. To fully understand housing standardisation processes and the meaning by housing quality at different times, it is important to consider the historical contexts of housing design governance, the legislative attitudes and measures that have shaped it, and the changing social ambitions of housing. The following therefore examines key moments in the formation of design governance in England and the establishment of housing design standards.

1189–1774: Prehistory and Emergence of Design Governance

The Building Act 1774 was the first consolidated effort to establish formal and consistent housing standards in England and represented the most comprehensive housing legislation introduced to that date. Essentially a building construction code, it had a considerable impact on the design of Georgian terraced housing (Muthesius, 1982; Rasmussen, 1967; Summerson, 1945). The terraced house was, as Guillery et al. (2004) observed, the outcome of an interplay between "tradition, the profit motive, legislation and fashion". These dynamics shaped the emergence of housing design governance as exemplified by the Building Act, although it was preceded by a series of important earlier efforts to standardise building design and construction.

This prehistory of design governance includes the Assize of Buildings of 1189, the first statutory building control introduced to regulate how solid stone party walls, rainwater gutters, and cesspits were to be designed, and it enshrined rights to light and views into law (Riley, 1863). Later, A Proclamation for Buildings in and About London (1605) by King James I promoted greater design standardisation, stating that new buildings must be constructed in solid materials, brick, or stone, and that "the forefront thereof shall be uniforme in order and forme" (Larkin & Hughes, 1973). In response to the Great Fire of London in 1666, the Rebuilding Act 1667 further enacted minimum requirements for internal room heights, resulting in the uniform height of terraced houses and the development of large, homogenous urban areas (Ley, 2000).

Despite these precedents, the formalisation of housing legislation and design standards is predominantly associated with later moments in regulatory history. Burns and Grebler (1977) identify the Common Lodging Houses Act 1851 (Shaftesbury Act) as one of the first examples of comprehensive housing legislation. According to Booth (2003), the modern system of planning control was only established in 1947, although he also traced it back to earlier Public Health Acts (1848, 1858, 1861, and 1875), which controlled building standards and public health-related issues such as water supply, sewerage, drainage, ventilation, and building structure. In a more recent review of housing space standards, Park (2017) claims that the Parker Morris standards of 1961 created the first modern, evidence-based standards related to housing design.

However, as Cooper (2010) posits, regulations must be understood not only as situated "within particular models of society and governance prevalent at a particular time, but also as taking their shape from the philosophy of governance prevalent at that time". Attitudes towards regulation and design governance in England have changed over time along with wider government policy, from minimal state intervention in the nineteenth century to social reformism in the early twentieth century, and the rise of the welfare state after World War II. According to Chang (1997), the laissez-faire regulatory approach of the past gave way, in the post-war period from 1945 to 1970, to increased state involvement and an "age of regulation", as regulatory regimes began to function more comprehensively and effectively. The late 1970s, however, saw a transitional period leading to extensive deregulation.

Doling (1997) proposes a classification of six strategic policy approaches to housing: non-intervention, exhortation, regulation, taxation, subsidy, and provision. While each approach is distinct, they are in practice often combined in response to different circumstances and needs. With the exception of the non-intervention approach, the state plays a direct role in housing delivery in all others to varying degrees. A common form of state intervention in housing supply is setting minimum standards and promoting their adoption by housing developers, either through voluntary codes of practice or mandatory regulatory frameworks (Spink, 2005).

Since the Building Act 1774, key drivers of housing standardisation have included health and safety, sanitation, social welfare, and profit. Standardisation is evident in the scale of uniform housing built using typologies shaped by changing models of home and land ownership, stylistic and aesthetic preferences, socio-cultural motivations, and major historical transformations in housing need or use. Although housing legislation and regulation often formalise the "best" practice of the time, they have historically also been reactive to major external events, such as post-war reconstruction (Park, 2017). The design of standardised housing is thus often a rational response aimed at minimising risks and lowering construction costs, but it is also informed by social expectations and market appeal. As Muthesius (1982) argues, the standardisation of terraced housing was inevitable, as builders sought the most cost-effective materials and design solutions. However, Leopold and Bishop (1983) further explain that standardised homes "tend to be modified versions of simple traditional house types with an established track record for marketability".

Despite regional variations resulting in different housing typologies and styles, standardisation remains a fundamental characteristic of housing, especially in terraced housing. For example, the urban mews is predominantly found in London and sometimes in Brighton, while back-to-back houses are more common in northern cities such as Leeds. Yet the adaptability and variety of standardised terraced housing have made it popular and encouraged its dominance across England.

~1715–1830: Georgian Period – Terraced Housing, Building Codes, and Speculative Development

In the seventeenth and eighteenth centuries, successive building regulations and construction codes resulted in an increasing standardisation of housing and building elements, partly driven by the need to make buildings safer but also aiming to reduce development risks and construction costs. In southern England, including London after the Great Fire, solid brickwork was used for much of the housing following the London Act 1667 (Ley, 2000).

The Georgian era (1714–1830) saw the introduction of new standards and regulations that established rights for, and reduced risks to, building owners and freeholders, improving building performance, preventing fire spread, and promoting what would become the dominant Georgian style (Booth, 2003). The profit-seeking, speculative builders who largely developed the Georgian terraced house welcomed the savings offered by standardising architectural and structural building elements. This was reinforced by government-issued housing regulations, with the standardisation of plans and building processes becoming a major driver of the proliferation of terraced housing (Muthesius, 1982).

Speculative housing developments during the Georgian period were a response to population growth, especially in London, where the most densely populated suburbs were larger than in other English cities throughout the eighteenth century (Guillery et al., 2004). According to Summerson (1945), it was "the beginning of that system of speculation by hereditary landlords which brought half of London into being". In many parts of the city, land was owned by large estates held in family trusts for generations. While these estates usually laid out streets and sewers before developments took place, investment and construction were undertaken by speculative builders, with landowners retaining the freehold and low-risk returns in perpetuity.

The main developer would agree on a development plan with the landowner and could then sublease individual plots to smaller developers – often tradesmen such as master builders, bricklayers, or carpenters – in return for a peppercorn rent, typically for two years, enabling them to build and sell a house at a profit or collect rent (Marshall et al., 2013). The executing developer organised the various building trades during construction, with designs commonly based on widely available pattern books. While the main developers benefitted from ground rent paid by the leaseholders, they had to pay the freeholding landowners their dues from it. Building leases were initially issued for as little as 33 years, but by the end of the Georgian era, leaseholds were typically granted for a period of 99 years. By 1800, it was common to sell properties with finished interiors, whereas previously only the building shell or "carcass" was sold to leaseholders.

During this building boom, regulations such as the Building Act 1774 were introduced to establish general building standards and a legal framework for enforcement, with the aim of improving construction quality and reducing risks from fire spread and other building hazards. The act therefore covered issues ranging from building materials, foundation and party wall structure, fire compartmentation, and building escape routes to party wall disputes (Figure 3.1). For example, the use of timber ornamentation or other flammable exterior materials was restricted, as they were a common cause of fire spread between buildings.

The growing awareness and management of building-related risks, including financial risks, led to greater formalisation and standardisation of the building industry, as evidenced by the Building Act 1774, which recognised the increasing influence of banks and insurance companies

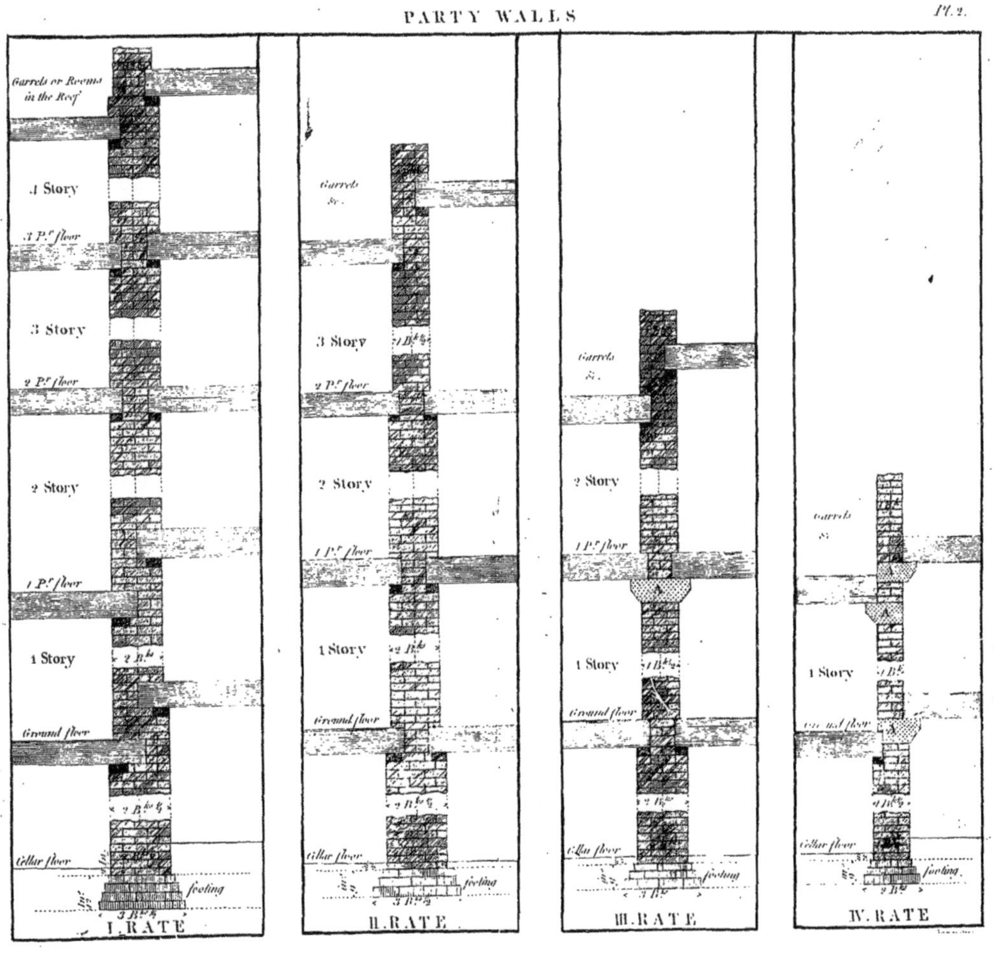

FIGURE 3.1 Party walls showing the different construction details of terraced houses according to four rates of the Building Act of 1774.

Source: John Matthews, *An Abstract of the Act of Parliament made in the Fourteenth Year of his Present Majesty King George III* (1774).

on decisions related to construction (Dutta, 2014). Some provisions regarding insurance and liability still remain partly in effect today.

Just as risk management became a major driver of development decisions, taxation increasingly influenced housing design and production by incentivising greater standardisation and regulation. The Building Act 1774 thus classified buildings into seven "rates" for taxation, four of which applied to dwelling houses (Figure 3.2). Each rate corresponded to different party wall specifications and maximum ground floor areas and building heights, with tax levels based on these factors alongside property value. This encouraged designs within the upper limits of lower rate brackets to minimise costs and taxes, Consequently, building two- or three-room houses within the fourth rate was more profitable than taller tenements taxed at the third rate. This led to the proliferation of long, narrow Georgian terraced houses, often built by speculative developers using standard designs from pattern books. The act thus effectively discouraged design experimentation (Summerson, 1945) and instead promoted standardised and optimised layouts.

The act was enforced by district surveyors, appointed by magistrates to assess building rates and make decisions on estate developments. However, district surveyors had limited powers because there was no government system for the proper enforcement of regulations (Booth, 2003). Thus, until the mid-nineteenth century, they mainly represented the interests of freeholders. Nevertheless, this system set a precedent for the future government-led enforcement of design and building controls that are common today (Booth, 2003).

The taxation system was highly effective in regulating building materials. For example, the brick tax imposed in 1784, levied according to the number of bricks used, forced brickmakers to produce larger bricks and encouraged greater use of timber, with the government later setting a maximum brick size of 150 in^3. When the brick tax was abolished in 1850, many brickmakers had already invested in machine-made bricks, making a return to smaller sizes uneconomical (Lucas, 1997). Just as the introduction of these taxes during the eighteenth century led to significant changes in the building industry and housing design, their subsequent withdrawal had a similar profound effect. For instance, after the repeal of the Window Tax in 1851 – originally introduced in 1696 and responsible for houses with few windows – the bay window emerged as a prominent feature and has become characteristic of the traditional British home.

Regulation, financial risk management, and taxation were formative in creating a market-driven housing supply dominated by speculative development. They also profoundly impacted housing design, particularly through prolific pattern books that were frequently used by developers, craftsmen, master builders, and architects alike, and which therefore played a vital role in translating regulations into design. Pattern books were both educational and practical, providing standard construction details and methods for measuring building quantities, which became increasingly scientific after the Building Act 1774. Widely consulted by builders, they offered guidance on how to maximise saleable floor area and profit by making construction more cost-effective and reducing potential mistakes and risks in the use of materials and labour estimation. Pattern books thus promoted the extensive adoption of standardised structural, architectural, and decorative elements (Guillery et al., 2004; Stewart, 2009; Summerson, 1945). This standardisation enabled builders to meet rising housing demand and made the terraced house the most successful housing model in England (Brown & Steadman, 1987).

Generic floor plans in pattern books were successful because they were flexible enough to permit necessary adaptations to different site constraints, required building heights, and stylistic preferences. Popular pattern books included Halfpenny's *The Modern Builders Assistant* (1757), the Society of Architects' *The Builders Magazine* (1779), Langley's *The Builders Complete*

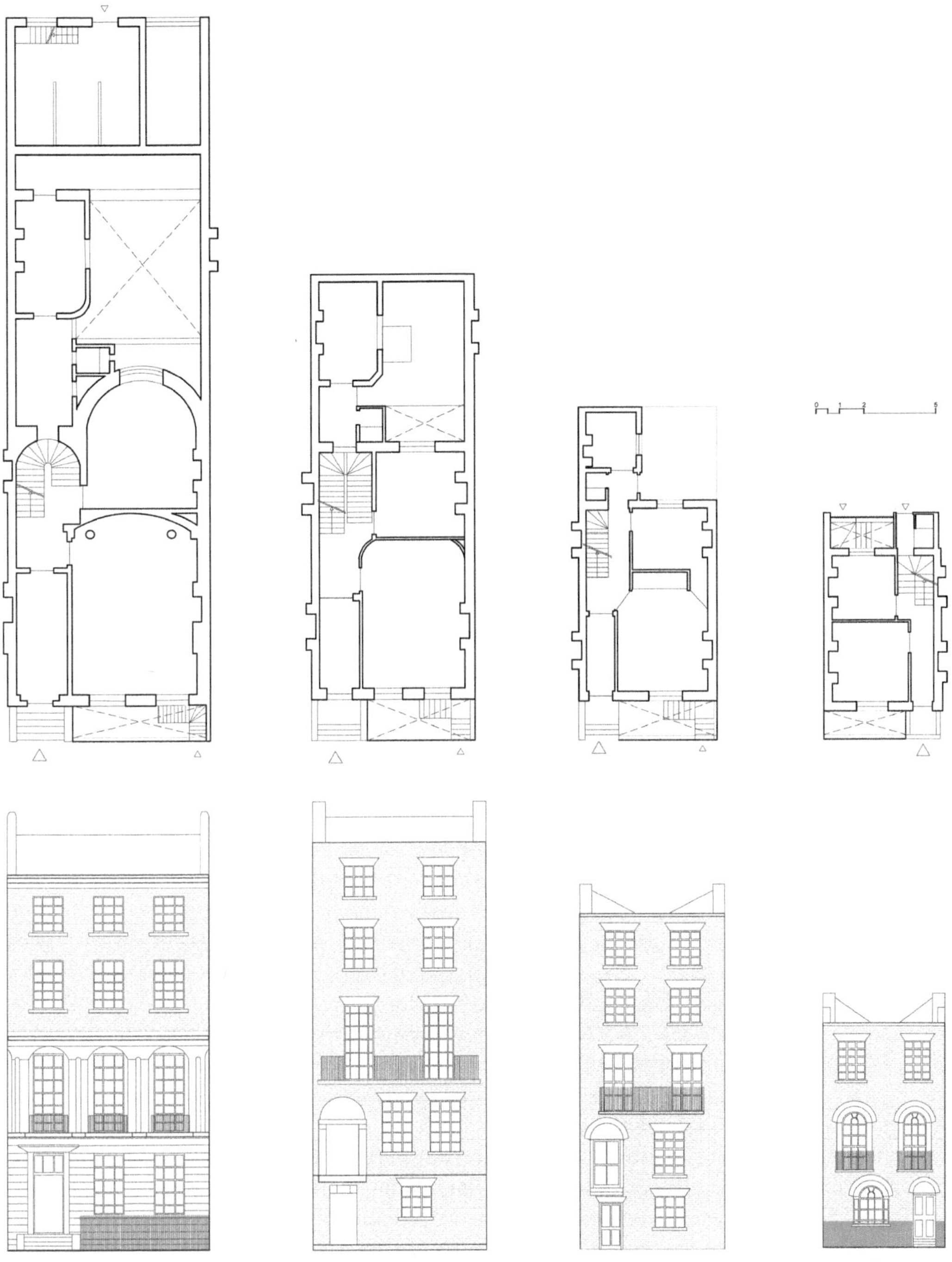

FIGURE 3.2 Elevation and ground-floor plan of terraced houses according to their four rates defined by the Building Act 1774.

Source: Redrawn by Gianna Bottema from Peter Nicholson, *The Builder's and Workman's New Director* (1834).

Assistant (1790), Pain's *Pain's British Palladio* (1793), and Nicholson's *The Builder's & Workman's New Director* (1834). These design manuals helped not only to standardise plans and building quantities, but also the ornamental mouldings commonly used in early Georgian architecture to cover structural joints and transitions between building planes, making them more affordable and creating greater, if minor, stylistic expression. Practice manuals also showed how to simplify complex geometries, otherwise only achievable in high-end housing, such as converting a parabolic curve into x- and y-coordinate points joined by straight lines (Nicholson, 1852), enabling both design standardisation and further stylistic differentiation.

The production of practice manuals for architects and builders in England arguably first began in 1715 with two seminal publications: *Vitruvius Britannicus, or, The British architect: Containing the plans, elevations, and sections of the regular buildings, both publick and private, in Great Britain; with variety of new designs* by Colen Campbell (1715), meant as a record of the best classical buildings built in England at the time, and a new edition of Andrea Palladio's *Four Books of Architecture* published by Giacomo Leoni (1715). Inspired by this, a long list of books compiled by and for craftsmen was published within the following ten years (Summerson, 1945).

A particularly prolific writer of practice manuals was Peter Nicholson, whose books explained to builders how to meet new regulatory requirements in great detail. They exemplified the growing interest in detailed building technology, as indicated by extensive subtitles such as: *An Architectural Dictionary, Containing a Correct Nomenclature and Derivation of the Terms Employed by Architects, Builders, and Workmen. Exhibiting, in a Perspicuous Point of View, the Theory and Practice of the Various Branches of Architecture, in Carpentry, Joinery, Masonry, Bricklaying, and Their Dependence on Each Other; The Science Necessary to Understand; And the Lives of the Principal Architects. The Whole Forming a Complete Guide to the Science of Architecture and the Art of Building* (1812, 1819), and *The New Practical Builder, and Workman's Companion: Containing a Full Display and Elucidation of the Most Recent and Skilful Methods, Pursued by Architects and Artificers, in the Various Departments of Carpentry, Joinery, Bricklaying, Masonry, Slating, Plumbing, Painting, Glazing, Plastering, &C. &C.: Including, Also, New Treatises on Geometry, Theoretical and Practical, Trigonometry, Conic Sections, Perspective, Shadows, and Elevations; A Summary of the Art of Building; Copious Accounts of Building Materials, Strength of Timber, Cements, &C.; A Description of the Tools Used by the Different Workmen; An Extensive Glossary of the Technical Terms Peculiar to Each Department; And the Theory and Practice of the Five Orders, as Employed in Decorative Architecture* (1823).

The new construction-related publications covered a great variety of content, ranging from manuals for carpenters to sales brochures for mass-produced building components marketed by manufacturers. Notable examples of these technical guides for craftsmen include Batty Langley's *The City and Country Builder's and Workman's Treasury of Designs* (1740) and Isaak Ware's *Complete Body of Architecture* (1756).

As the eighteenth century progressed, architects also increasingly published pattern books to gain recognition and secure new commissions (Emmitt, 2013). By then, these books had become platforms to showcase talent and disseminate new decorative styles, house types, and lifestyles (Figure 3.3). Initially aimed at builders and developers, pattern books increasingly began to target clients, tradesmen, and wider public audiences as publishing became more affordable towards the end of the eighteenth century. These books therefore included rich illustrations of villas, smaller houses, and cottages that were no longer solely intended for a professional readership. Today, pattern books are still used in England, for example, by housing associations to document, develop, and implement their commonly used standardised house types and development standards.

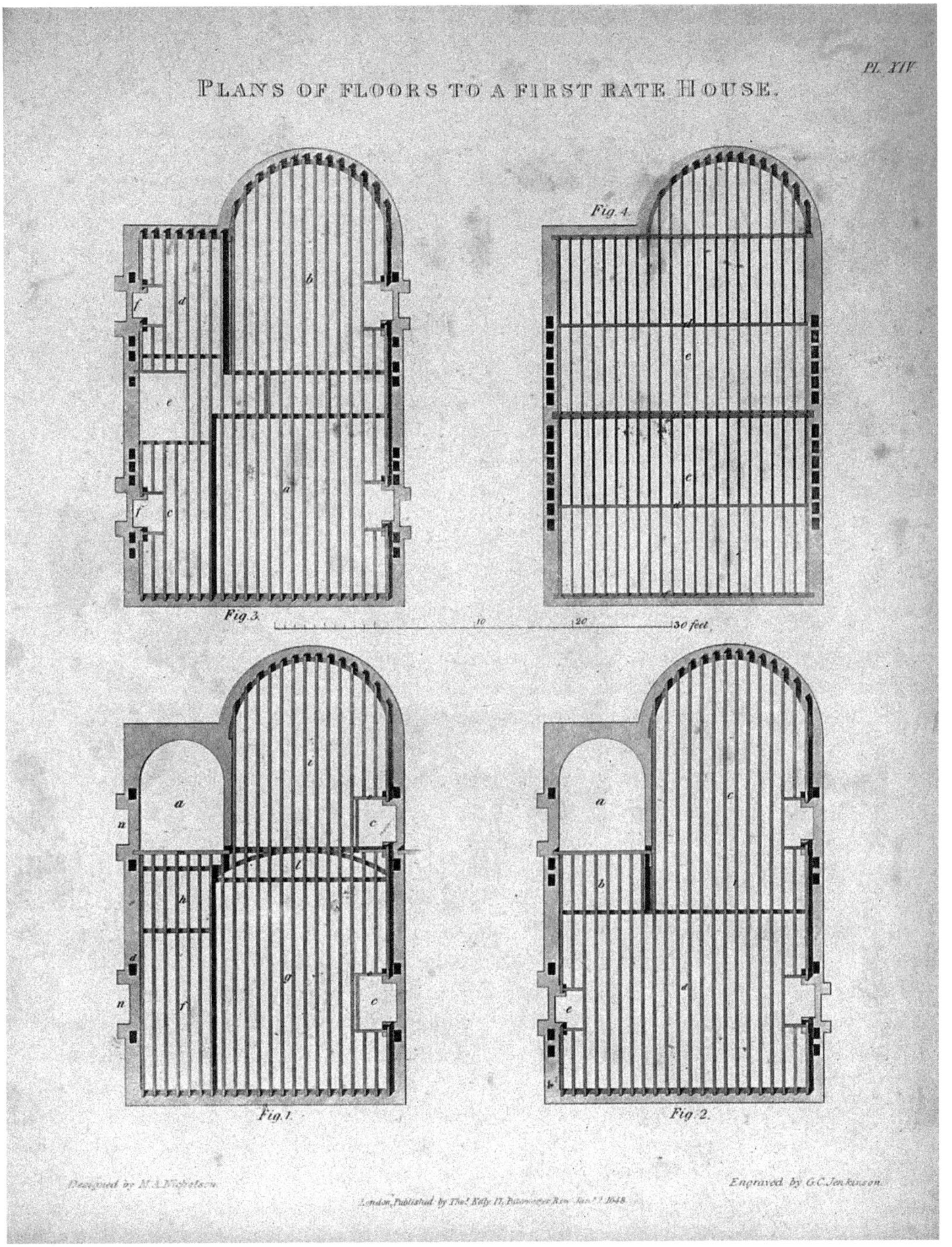

FIGURE 3.3 Floor plans of a first-rate house showing the floor joist layout.

Source: Peter Nicholson, *The Builder's and Workman's New Director* (1834).

Balancing Flexibility and Efficiency

The proliferation of Georgian terraced houses was not only attributable to the popularity of pattern books but also coincided with advances in technology and building materials. For example, improved manufacturing processes lowered the cost of glass, allowing windows to be made larger to provide cross-ventilation and natural light from only the front and back elevations, with sash windows increasingly prefabricated (Wall, 2016). While the Victorians found the Georgian style promoted by the Building Act 1774 to be so monotonous and restrained that they referred to it as the "Black Act" (Summerson, 1945), housing in London in the eighteenth century was, in fact, stylistically diverse and included mixed vernacular styles. However, these houses have often not survived, whereas the large, uniform Georgian houses for the wealthy continue to define the image of London (Guillery et al., 2004).

Despite their significant impact, the provisions of the Building Act 1774 failed to address the growing housing crisis caused by rising urban migration, unregulated growth, and a housing shortage. As a building construction code, the act lacked broader consideration of housing and development standards, such as the design of drainage, sanitary facilities, or ventilation. The rapid expansion of suburban working-class housing was thus largely left to the unregulated market and speculative builders, who built small, terraced housing at scale.

1830–1890: Victorian Period – Sanitary Reform, Building Byelaws, and Philanthropic Housing

Acknowledging the limitations of Georgian housing regulations, the Victorian period paid increasing attention to the connection between poor sanitation, substandard housing, and public health. Scientific studies using surveys and mappings increasingly informed sanitary reforms and new housing regulation, as early Victorian statistics revealed a direct link between housing conditions and high mortality rates. In the context of mid-nineteenth-century cholera epidemics, Edwin Chadwick (1842) in his influential *Report on the Sanitary Conditions of the Labouring Poor* provided the first statistical evidence of how social and spatial inequalities translated into negative health outcomes and unsanitary conditions. In response, England passed a series of sanitary measures, such as the Public Health Act 1848, which established the Central Board of Health to oversee national sanitation policy – including sewage, clean water supply, and paving – along with local boards of health tasked with its implementation at the municipal level.

Despite this increasingly evidence-based policymaking, sanitary problems were often still framed in moral terms. For example, Chadwick highlighted the moral costs of slum housing, asserting that poor health and hopelessness led to recklessness, drunkenness, and a lack of forethought. Similarly, Charles Booth (1889), in his *Life and Labour of the People in London*, used poverty maps to document poor housing conditions, classifying poverty and directly linking it to a lack of morality and greater criminality (Figure 3.4). Both Chadwick and Booth, despite their scientific interests, reinforced the widely held Victorian belief that social reform could be achieved by improving individuals rather than society at large (Bulmer, 2015). Aligned with this attitude, policy interventions began to focus on the impact they could have on individual families.

Housing and its design became pressing issues in the nineteenth century, resulting in a greater rationalisation of housing regulation. At the same time, the laissez-faire policy approach of nineteenth-century England introduced new stakeholders to housing and its governance. The Building Act 1774 was insufficient to address unsanitary housing conditions, overcrowding, and the growth of slums caused by industrialisation and a rapid increase in the urban population and

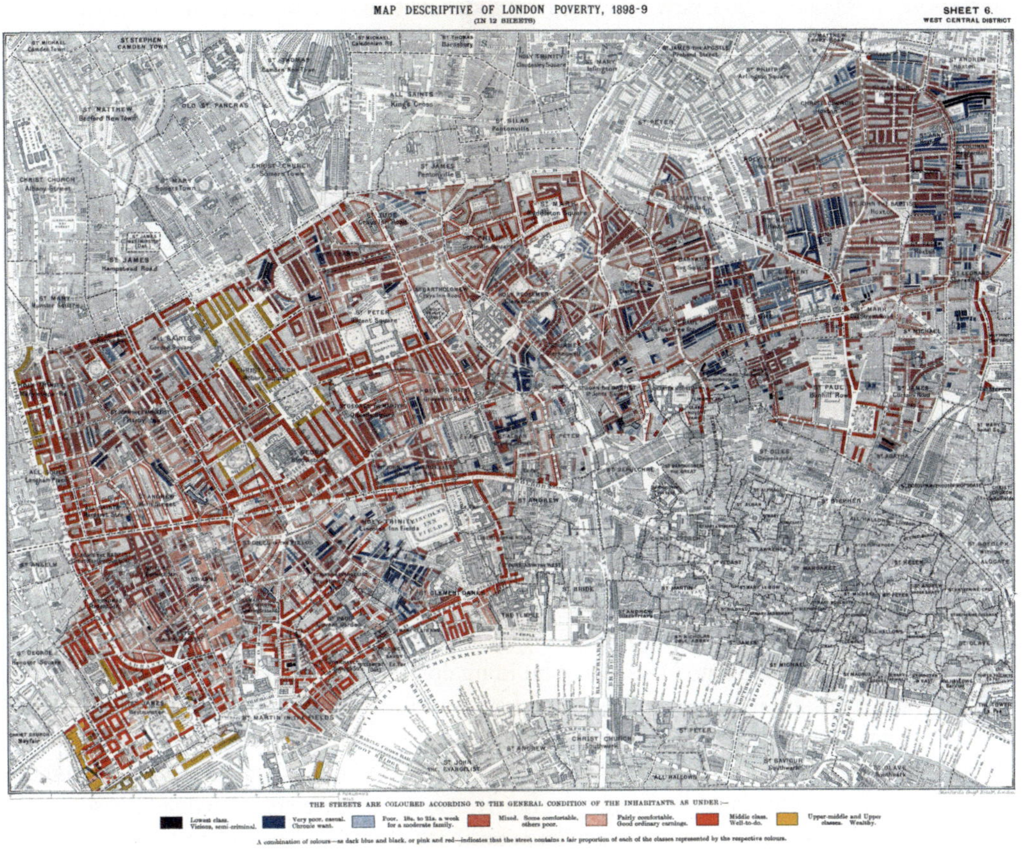

FIGURE 3.4 London poverty maps: West and Central District.

Source: Charles Booth, *Life and Labour of the People in London* (1898–1899).

migration. New regulations were urgently needed, with Parliament approving over 400 Local Improvement Acts dealing with sanitary control and building regulations between 1800 and 1845. Cities also introduced local building standards to address these issues. For example, the Bristol Building Act of 1840 and the Liverpool Building Act of 1842 both improved housing quality, regulated building materials, and addressed sanitation problems.

The strengthening of local government represented a significant political and regulatory advance that enabled the successful adoption of local housing byelaws and thus greater housing design control. This was made possible by the Municipal Corporations Act 1835, which created new municipal boroughs and reformed local government structure. It established elected and accountable councils that acted in the public interest, with the improvement of housing conditions seen as a key focus. The subsequent Metropolitan Building Act 1844 further established the District Surveyor Association to ensure consistency in byelaws, enforcement, and housing practices.

Driven by concerns over public health and social order, the government's approach to housing regulation was, however, not yet intended to support a greater responsibility for housing provision (Lund, 2017. It was therefore left to philanthropic housing trusts that emerged in the 1840s to respond to the urgent need to build homes at scale for the working classes (Malpass &

Murie, 1987). As part of this, new housing standards had to be established, which was achieved less through central regulations and more through exemplary cases such as the "model dwellings" promoted by housing philanthropists and reformers (Clifford & Ferm, 2021). Regulation was decentralised, although local "model byelaws" introduced, for the first time, an integrated approach to building control, urban design, and public health.

These byelaws shaped the design of streets and buildings, and functioned much like local plans today, providing a development framework that local authorities could adopt or adapt to their needs. Central government oversight was still relatively light, achieved primarily through the approval of byelaws and the control of local boards of health by the Local Government Act Office, established in 1858 as a sub-department of the Home Office. However, the Public Health Act 1875 subsequently replaced the local boards of health with local sanitation authorities, making councils directly responsible for housing and infrastructure improvements to enhance public health. The act thereby consolidated 22 previous acts, recognising the importance of consistent minimum standards in creating a healthy built environment.

Yet frequent changes and additions to housing legislation made enforcement and monitoring difficult in practice, especially with administration remaining fragmented across vestries, parishes, and councils. This failure to effectively regulate building standards and address poor sanitation is often attributed to prevailing laissez-faire attitudes, strong property rights protection, a profit focus, and increased housing costs due to new byelaws (Rodger, 1995). The lack of standardised byelaws across regions and varying specifications for building materials and components further exacerbated increasing building costs (Ley, 1990).

There was still significant inconsistency in the use of regulatory instruments, resulting in different housing outcomes across England. Some councils relied on improvement acts – private acts of Parliament passed locally to undertake urban projects such as road paving and street lighting – instead of adopting byelaws. For example, in Liverpool, building acts remained the sole regulatory framework to enforce building standards until 1864, while surrounding councils adopted building byelaws and implemented the Local Government Act 1858. This allowed these councils to legally prevent the construction of high-density back-to-back houses favoured by speculative builders, which Liverpool could not do until it aligned its regulatory approach. At the same time, back-to-back houses were banned in London through the Metropolitan Act 1844, which required a minimum 14 m^2 backyard – not including outdoor toilets (Harrison, 2017). Thus, significant regional differences in building control, enforcement, and housing quality persisted.

Although byelaws were an important step towards improving housing design, they faced considerable objections. For instance, rural authorities experiencing less urgency for building control complained that the byelaws stipulated by the Local Government Act 1894 were based on urban conditions irrelevant to them. In response, the Local Government Board drafted new byelaws for rural areas. Byelaws also often reflected common practices rather than technological advancements or best practice. For example, they did little to encourage the adoption of newer building technologies, such as thermal insulation and damp-proof courses. Although Portland cement was increasingly used in construction due to its strength and low cost, it was not approved for concrete footings until 1912 (Ley, 1990).

At the same time, a lack of technical specificity could render byelaws ineffective. For instance, in Bath, an 1866 byelaw for air ventilation required the upper part of casement windows to open, but it did not specify a minimum opening size to guarantee sufficient airflow. This led to an amendment two years later, regulating the opening size relative to the size of the room (Ley, 1990). Byelaws sometimes also conflicted with traditional construction methods and materials, leading local developers to simply ignore them. For example, in Sheffield, the model byelaw for fire prevention required party walls to extend beyond the roofline to form parapet walls, but builders preferred to bed roof tiles in cement mortar directly on top of party walls, following established local practice (Ley, 2000). A conservative building industry often viewed new construction techniques or material innovations as unnecessary risks, thus delaying their inclusion in byelaws.

Encompassing regulations found in various building acts, town improvement clauses, and metropolitan building acts, byelaws were intended to create greater regulatory uniformity and responsiveness. Supporting this, the Local Government Board and the Royal Institute of British Architects (RIBA) created a set of model requirements, including 94 byelaws dealing with design issues ranging from street widths, foundations, wall sizes, and building heights to open space provisions (Ley, 2000). Issued in 1877, this model set served as a basic construction code for developers and helped local authorities to standardise byelaws. Although it responded to the need for a greater alignment of regulatory approaches, it also started to recognise the need for a stronger regulatory culture in the building sector, which emerged with philanthropic housing companies.

Philanthropic model dwelling companies, such as the East End Dwellings Company and Peabody Trust, developed inner-city, multi-storey tenement blocks and cottage flats. Meanwhile, other companies, primarily the Artizans, Labourers & General Dwellings Company, built suburban cottages for workers along existing railway lines (Figure 3.5). Although largely London-centric, companies such as Newcastle-upon-Tyne's Improved Industrial Dwellings Company provided housing beyond the capital. Many of these companies operated on the basis of a socially motivated form of housing investment, also known as "five per cent philanthropy", with private investors expecting a modest return of around 5% while supporting the construction of working-class homes (Tarn, 1973).

The layout of the tenement blocks was influenced by Henry Roberts' Model Houses for Four Families, commissioned by the Society for Improving the Conditions of the Labouring Classes for the Great Exhibition of 1851 (Figure 3.6). These self-contained flats provided running water and natural ventilation, a division of functions with separate kitchen and living areas, and separate bedrooms for parents and children of different sexes (Chey, 2017). With these projects motivated less by profit than by bettering society and housing conditions for the poor, a strong moral ethos drove these efforts to improve housing standards through voluntary, civil action, an attitude that still exists in England and its approach to design governance.

The standardised layout of tenements reflected the pragmatism of Victorian philanthropy and represented "a new conception of urban and social order" (Davidovici, 2017). While the corridor historically emerged as a spatial device to segregate functions and social classes in traditional enfilade building layouts (Evans, 1997), model dwellings focused their socio-spatial order on the nuclear family itself. Byelaws further extended regulation to the "unbuilt" space between buildings, such as street width and the space at the rear of each house, emphasising the importance of not only "sanitising" the interior of the home but also the external environment. Thus, regulation of the domestic sphere encompassed that of homes and their neighbourhoods. For Victorian reformers, the many entries and exits to slums and the indiscriminate use or sharing of domestic rooms by people of different ages and sexes, for example, represented a moral disorder that had to be eradicated through social, public health, and housing reforms.

However, the multi-storey tenement housing built by philanthropic societies and industrial companies only benefitted a small portion of Victorian working-class families, with the vast majority living in housing developed by small speculative builders (Mitchell, 1988). Houses in multiple occupation were common, resulting in their growing subdivision into separate flats. As

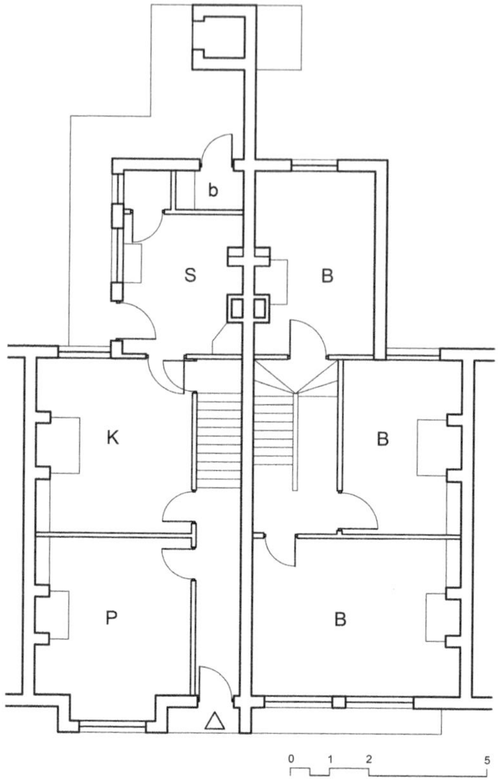

FIGURE 3.5 Ground and first floor plan, third-class terraced house, built by the Artizans, Labourers & General Dwellings Company, Noel Park (1833).

Source: Redrawn by the authors. *Key*: B, bedroom; P, parlour; K, kitchen; S, scullery; b, bathroom.

Lord Shaftesbury claimed, adapting houses into flats was "the only way in which they would be able to provide for the great mass of the population of London". However, Banister Fletcher (1871) at the same time criticised speculative builders for knowing only "one form of plan which they have never varied". To address this, Fletcher proposed better designs to adapt single-family homes into flats, each with its own scullery and toilet (Figure 3.7).

Another common housing typology for the growing working-class population in industrial cities such as Birmingham, Manchester, Nottingham, and Leeds were back-to-back terraced houses, popular from the late eighteenth century to the early twentieth century (Figure 3.8). Unlike houses with both a front and a back door, back-to-back houses had shared rear walls and only a front door and windows, and thus only a single aspect. They therefore lacked cross ventilation or an outdoor space and had poor natural lighting. In comparison, the more skilled urban worker often lived in a so-called "two-up, two-down" – a small, terraced house with two main rooms on the ground floor, two bedrooms above, and a garden to the rear. Until the Public Health Act 1875, both housing types shared a water supply and toilet between several households.

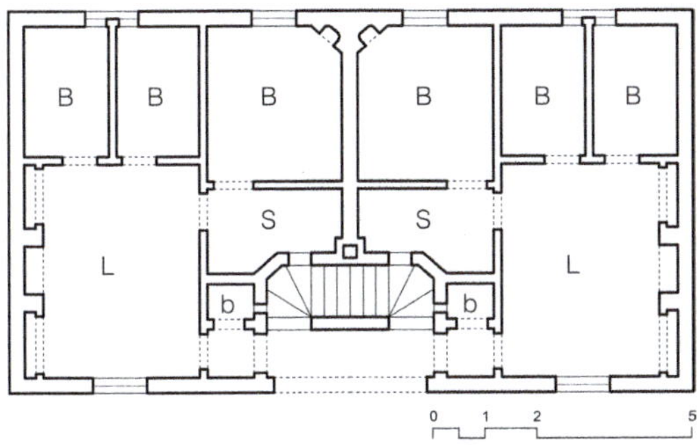

FIGURE 3.6 Model Houses for Four Families by Henry Roberts for the Society for Improving the Conditions of the Working Classes (1850).

Source: Plan redrawn by the authors from Roberts (1950). *Key*: B, bedroom; L, living room; S, scullery; b, bathroom.

The Victorian suburb, built near new railway stations by philanthropic housing companies and speculative builders, was originally targeted at the working classes and made possible by the growing separation of home from work and by improved, more affordable public transport following the Cheap Trains Act 1864 (Mitchell, 1988). However, it soon also became popular with middle-class families fleeing inner cities for a quitter lifestyle. New commercial suburbs,

FIGURE 3.7 Model plans for adaptation of existing dwelling houses for letting in flats.

Source: Banister Fletcher, *Model Houses for the Industrial Classes* (1871).

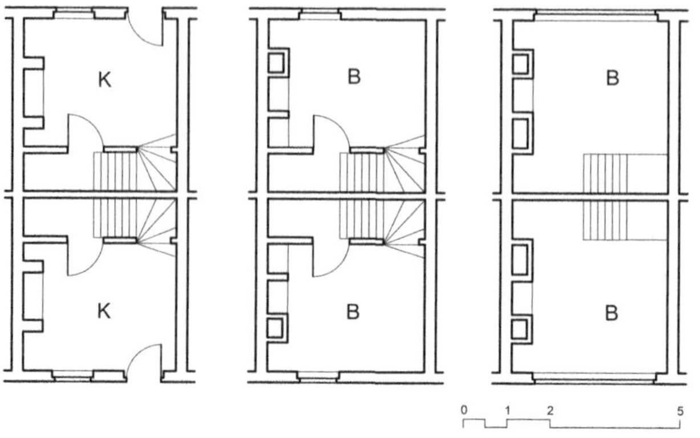

FIGURE 3.8 Typical example of a three-storey back-to-back house built in Nottingham between 1784 and 1830.

Source: Drawn by the authors.

Key: B, bedroom; K, kitchen.

created in the early twentieth century by train companies such as the Metropolitan Railway, reflected this trend when marketing their developments near railway stations with easy access to central London as "Metro-land in the countryside".

Uniform in appearance and standardised in layout, suburban developments typically comprised small two-storey terraced houses with front gardens but no basements or parlours. So-called cottage flats (also known as maisonettes, tenement flats, or half-houses) became increasingly popular, providing homes for workers unable to afford higher rents for traditional family homes but who preferred living in houses rather than tenements (Thom, 2017). Initially more common in the north of England, each cottage flat occupied one floor of a two-storey building and had a separate ground-floor entrance door. Two entrances were paired and mirrored, with four flats and two houses forming a discrete unit appearing as a row of terraced houses or sometimes a pair of semi-detached houses.

By 1900, construction byelaws were widely criticised by both builders and housing reformers. Reformers condemned them for failing to prevent speculative developers from building slums with low-quality housing, severe overcrowding, and poor sanitation. Builders viewed the byelaws as too restrictive, focusing primarily on public health and less on housing and building problems. Both groups nonetheless agreed that byelaws imposed unnecessary costs and made housing a high-risk investment (Booth, 2003). In addition, taxes on building materials commonly represented almost a third of new housing development costs (Burnett, 1986). Although private developers continued to build houses, these regulatory and financial pressures led to the growing recognition that the state should play a more active role in housing provision. Consequently, by the end of the nineteenth century, a major shift in housing policy and supply occurred, when local authorities began to directly intervene in housing supply.

Until the twentieth century, precedents for municipal housing were limited to a few projects for workers in St. Martin's Cottages Liverpool (1869), Birmingham (1889), and London (1900) (Steffel, 1976). While the Common Lodging Houses Act 1851 (Shaftesbury Act) and the Housing of the Working Classes Act 1885 set enforceable health and sanitary standards, the subsequent Housing of the Working Classes Act 1890 focused directly and for the first time on housing supply. It gave local authorities the power to clear slums and build the first council homes by introducing the option of compulsory purchase of land and access to financing. This change in policy was driven by a fundamental shift in how the state saw the role of housing and its own social responsibility, with the shifting emphasis from public health to housing itself marking an important transition in the history of social welfare and housing, and also in design governance. The number of homes built by London's local authorities soon began to exceed that of philanthropic companies, with work on the first council housing in London's Boundary Estate starting in 1890.

1890–1939: Early Twentieth-Century Housing – Nuclear Family Homes, Standardisation, and State Intervention

From 1890, speculative suburban housing in London was often built without the traditional rear closet wing, due to the relocation of sculleries and toilets inside the home, smaller household sizes, wider frontages to increase natural sunlight and ventilation, and the desire to enlarge gardens. In addition, the Arts and Crafts and Garden City movements created new preferences in housing layouts, which began to influence the internal arrangements of working-class homes (Ravetz & Turkington, 2013).

Generally, houses were becoming smaller but wider than before, with the narrowest measuring only 5.2 m in width (Figure 3.9). The internal staircase in a wider but shorter hall could therefore be placed closer to the entrance, leaving more space for the kitchen at the back of the house, reflecting changing socio-economic considerations and preferences. The new terraced houses were usually built in groups of four or six, with private gardens to the front and back.

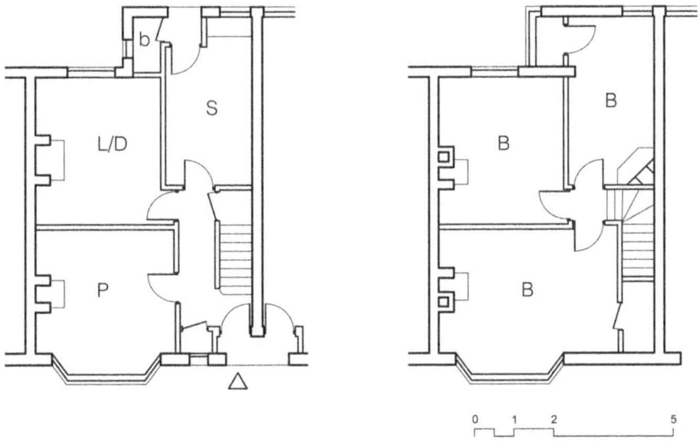

FIGURE 3.9 Ground- and first-floor plan of a three-bedroom cottage built by London County Council, White Hart Lane Estate, Tottenham (1913).

Source: Drawn by the authors.

Key: B, bedroom; L/D, living-dining room; P, parlour; S, scullery; b, bathroom.

By the end of World War I, Victorian working-class terraced housing had become widely associated with slums and overcrowding; in cities like London, houses were often sublet, with two or three families sharing the rent. In fact, in 1911, 40% of families in London shared a house (Muthesius, 1982). The new, smaller terraced houses that had become popular were just over half the size of previous terraced houses with a rear extension but were intended for the sole use of one family. This change in occupancy created new social, spatial, and technical housing standards.

From the turn of the twentieth century up to World War II, the standardisation of homes was driven by efforts to improve building and cost efficiencies, technological advances overcoming material shortages, and speculative housebuilders seeking to maximise profits. During World War I, the growth of ammunition factories and war-related industries had also led to a rising demand for temporary housing to accommodate munitions factory workers, which had to be built quickly and at a low cost. For example, Well Hall Estate (now the Progress Estate) was built in 1915 in Woolwich as a garden suburb to house the workers of the Royal Arsenal. This new type of state-provided home was an early demonstration of housing rationalisation and standardisation that anticipated both post-war housing challenges and solutions.

Building on this, the Tudor Walters Committee published, at the end of World War I in November 1918, *The Report of the Committee Appointed to Consider Questions of Building Construction in Connection with the Provision of Dwellings for the Working Classes* (*Tudor Walters Report*). It proposed solutions to the anticipated post-war housing, material, and skilled labour force shortages (Greenhalgh, 1990). Faced with a housing crisis at the end of World War I, standardisation of housing design became paramount to mass-producing housing effectively using industrial prefabrication methods and skills honed during the war.

As thousands of soldiers returned home, Prime Minister Lloyd George famously promised that the government would build "homes fit for heroes". Delivering on this promise required a paradigm shift, recognising that traditional construction methods could not meet the scale and speed needed for the expected post-war housing programme. Thus, developing standardised dwelling layouts and construction methods was essential, as demonstrated by the *Tudor Walters Report* (Tudor Walters Committee, 1918).

The report proposed efficient and economical layouts for single-family homes. It recommended shorter terraces with wider frontages for better natural ventilation and sunlight, but also, importantly, to accommodate a bathroom separate from the scullery to improve hygiene and a third upstairs bedroom to reduce overcrowding. This concern with overcrowding was subsequently reinforced by the Housing Act 1935, which introduced minimum space standards per person. Contributing to an ongoing debate and design experimentation over the ideal width and depth of a standard home, the report warned against the common narrow-fronted houses with rear extensions, arguing that they failed to provide adequately for the daily life of a modern family (Figure 3.10). The report thus highlighted the needs of the nuclear family, which would become a driving concern of housing development, design, and regulation in England (Alonso Aranda, 2024).

Compared to Victorian byelaws, the standards for post-war housing recommended by the *Tudor Walters Report* were revolutionary and "a major innovation" in social policy (Burnett, 1986). Previously, the design, space, and layout of homes were only considered important insofar as they related to public health and building safety, whereas the report specifically focused

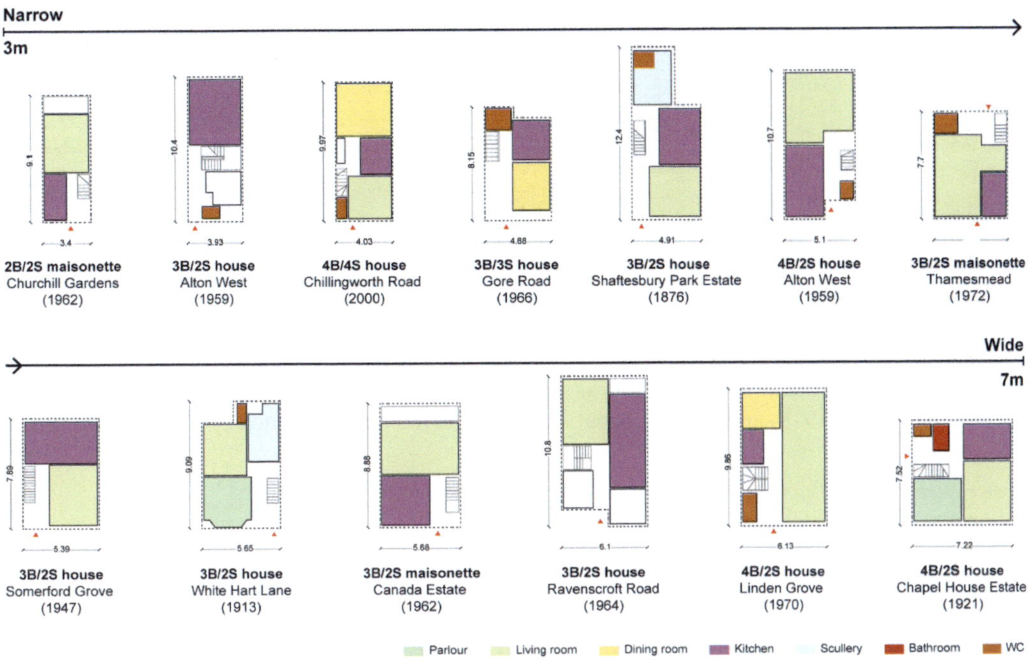

FIGURE 3.10 Comparison of houses and maisonettes according to width and internal organisation.

on housing quality and design. It emphasised the importance of regulating the size of dwellings, good proportions, and town and site planning aspects such as street width and layout, orientation, and density to create high-quality homes and neighbourhoods. However, despite promoting greater regulations, it also acknowledged that previous rules had hindered construction innovation.

The *Tudor Walters Report* argued that, by simplifying design and reducing variations that were more expensive in manufacture and maintenance, good design and standardisation would produce better housing at lower cost. At the same time, it recognised the possible limitations of plans becoming "too stereotyped", advocating for a balanced approach to standardisation that would not prevent "the introduction of radical improvement". The proposed standard housing layouts for two-storey cottages could be arranged in small groups of four or six houses, with different roof shapes and exterior decoration as preferred by builders or residents, offering sufficient variety to meet different needs and tastes (Figure 3.11). The minimum recommended provision for a home was a living room, scullery, larder, three bedrooms on the second floor, and a bathroom. The inclusion of a traditional parlour was only recommended where extra rent could be charged to cover higher construction costs (Table 3.1).

The *Tudor Walters Report* and its attitude to design and regulation embraced the ideas of "scientific management" developed by Frederick Taylor (1911) in the late nineteenth century. It anticipated the later popularisation of these scientific principles in design processes by the Modern Movement and seminal design guides such as the *Architectural*

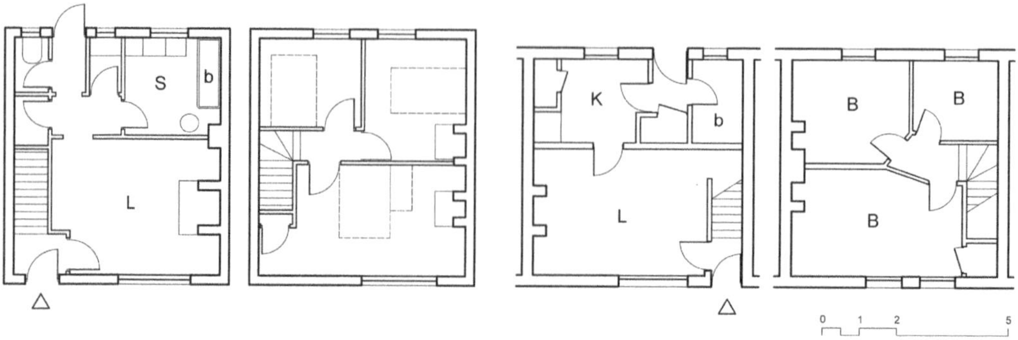

FIGURE 3.11 Comparison of three-bed, two-storey houses: (left) type plan in the *Tudor Walters Report* (1918) and (right) Chapel House Estate in Poplar designed by the Office of Works (1921).

Source: Tudor Walters Report (1918) and British History Online. Redrawn by the authors.

Key: B, bedroom; L, living room; K, kitchen; b, bathroom.

Graphic Standards for Architects, Engineers, Decorators, Builders and Draftsmen (1932) by Charles George Ramsey and Harold Reeve Sleeper, and *Bauentwurfslehre* (Architect's Data) by Ernst Neufert (1936). The report further affirmed that the housing shortage could be resolved through economies of scale and the use of new materials and standardised methods of production.

Given a post-war shortage of traditional building materials and skills, a technical subcommittee within the Tudor Walters Committee was tasked with finding new suitable construction methods and materials. Existing methods were considered too expensive, and necessary building materials were scarce. Similarly, the Department of Scientific and Industrial Research formed a new Building Materials Research Committee (BMRC) in 1917 – which later became the Building Research Station in 1921, a precursor to today's Building Research Establishment (BRE). This was the first research organisation dedicated to building science, with Raymond Unwin acting as its chairperson. Unwin had gained valuable experience heading the housing

TABLE 3.1 Provision of space and rooms according to dwelling type

	House with parlour	*House without parlour*
Parlour	11.2 m²	–
Living room	16.7 m²	16.7 m²
Scullery	7.4 m²	7.4 m²
Larder	2.2 m²	2.2 m²
Bedroom 1	14.9 m²	13.9 m²
Bedroom 2	11.2 m²	9.3 m²
Bedroom 3	10.2 m²	6 m²

Source: Based on the *Tudor Walters Report* (1918).

design team at the Ministry of Munitions during World War I, tasked with providing temporary housing for munitions factory workers.

The *Tudor Walters Report* was in significant parts based on the work of its technical subcommittees, which formed part of the Housing (Building Construction) Committee and focused on materials and supplies, construction, organisation and labour, and plans. It specifically made recommendations on how to use stone, brick, and timber in construction, combined with new materials such as concrete, steel, aluminum, and rubber. For example, it detailed how to use standard concrete beams and in-situ floors to reduce timber use due to material shortages. It also developed new construction and building standards, advising which building components could be manufactured off-site (such as doors, windows, and stairs) or on-site (concrete lintels, partition slabs, and walling). As part of this, the properties and performance of factory-made components were studied with the aim of standardising production (Lynch, 2010). The standardisation of building materials and their design was thus an important driver of new construction and housing standards.

The Housing and Town Planning Act 1919 (Addison Act) formally adopted many recommendations of the *Tudor Walters Report*. It made local councils directly responsible for supplying affordable homes for rent, with costs recovered through central government contributions, local taxes, and rental income. This council housing delivery model would essentially remain unchanged for the next 50 years. However, the impact of the *Tudor Walters Report* went beyond merely creating a housing manual, and was formative to "the theory and practice of low-cost housing design" (Swenarton, 2008). According to Park (2017), it was furthermore "an extremely important step in the evolution of housing standards – perhaps the first time that housing quality was formally acknowledged to be a matter of national importance".

Following the Addison Act, local authorities widely adopted the layouts and designs published in the associated *Manual on the Preparation of State-aided Housing Schemes* in 1919. Although they had little experience as housing developers or landlords, local authorities had gained valuable experience planning and implementing public health measures. With the aid of design guides such as the *Tudor Walters Report*, they were therefore seen by the government as more reliable than private or philanthropic organisations in achieving housing targets (Burdon, 2017). The year 1919 also saw the formation of the Ministry of Health, which absorbed the Local Government Board and centralised responsibility for housing policy and regulation. This centralization was important for greater national regulatory alignment, as a separate housing department, the Ministry of Local Government and Housing, not created until 1951. However, the design standards demanded by the *Tudor Walters Report* and the Addison Act were also considered major contributors to rising housing costs. The resulting high rents made new homes ultimately unaffordable for the very working-class families they were intended for. In response, by 1921, the Ministry of Health instructed local authorities that the previous minimum requirements set by the Addison Act were to be treated as maximum housing standards, in order to reduce construction and rental costs (Hobhouse, 1994).

Before the Addison Act of 1919, local authorities supported the provision of only about 2% of new homes. The Act created the first public housing programme, starting in 1919, and introduced a new process of direct state intervention (Bowley, 1947), which required borough councils to build public housing. While successful, it did not meet its ambitious target, with only 213,800 of the planned 500,000 homes completed within three years of programme. Nevertheless, from 1919 to 1923, the number of subsidised new homes grew to over 60%, with private builders incentivised by the Housing (Additional Powers) Act 1919 to meet new housing standards (Bowley, 1947). They received a subsidy of £130 for rented and £160 for sold dwellings if the homes complied with the new standards (Spink, 2005).

While this led to greater consistency in the design standards of both private and public housing, private homeowners often preferred more ornate finishes to differentiate their homes from rented social housing (Punter & Carmona, 1997), highlighting the influence of sociocultural associations and stigma on aesthetic and housing design preferences. However, as in 1918, less than a quarter of homes in England were owner-occupied; new homes were primarily built for letting, whether social or private. Although this provided increasing housing security to social housing tenants, rental tenures gave residents only limited or no control over changes to their homes, making it difficult to adapt them to their needs – a continuing problem in today's rental housing.

Another important influence on new council housing design was the Modern Movement, although its impact differed from that on mainland Europe. While it prioritised efficient housing design and economies of scale, in England it was also greatly shaped by the Garden City movement, whose rural ideals, as Greenhalgh (1990) notes, influenced the emergence of a new social order and national identity in the 1920s. While the Modern Movement embraced industrial production and standardisation, English design continued to reference traditional housing typologies such as cottage flats and terraced houses. New publications such as *Houses We Live In* (Ministry of Health, 1939) sought to define a new modern housing agenda based on rational design, functional layouts, and cost efficiency, favouring simple rectangular plans with minimal decoration.

Influenced by the principles of the Modern Movement, design experimentation and standardisation changed how people lived in their urban homes (Turner, 2015). The first mass housing developments in England were completed in the 1930s, intended to deliver a new model for housing (Urban, 2011). A prominent example is Kensal House (1938), a development of 68 worker apartments designed by Maxwell Fry and Elizabeth Denby for the Gas, Light, and Coke Company in London (Figure 3.12). Responding to the debate on *Existenzminimum* in mainland Europe, room sizes were made to directly correspond to their intended function (Heynen & Baydar, 2005). Kitchens were dimensioned to accommodate equipment and layouts identified as necessary through optimisation and efficiency studies by Margarete Schütte-Lihotzky for her Frankfurt Kitchen.

In a radical departure from previous housing models, multi-storey living began to gain acceptance. By 1930, privately developed blocks of flats for the middle classes in London had become a popular form of investment (Ravetz, 1974). Flats were advertised as economical and promising a modern lifestyle by charities, housing reformers, and industries such as gas companies, which had a significant impact on home design, particularly in the layout of kitchens and bathrooms due to innovations in the design of services and appliances (Figure 3.11). The design of flats was transformed from tenement blocks to multi-storey housing with shared amenities such as open spaces, lifts, and on-site facilities. The Housing Act 1930 (Greenwood Act) and its housing policies, standards, and subsidies focused not only on traditional and low-rise housing typologies, but also on medium- and low-rise blocks of flats (Hobhouse, 1994).

The Housing Act 1935, defined by Park (2017) as the "next important milestone" in housing legislation after the Addison Act of 1919, addressed the still widespread problem of overcrowding. The introduction of the first overcrowding standards responded to key concerns about the

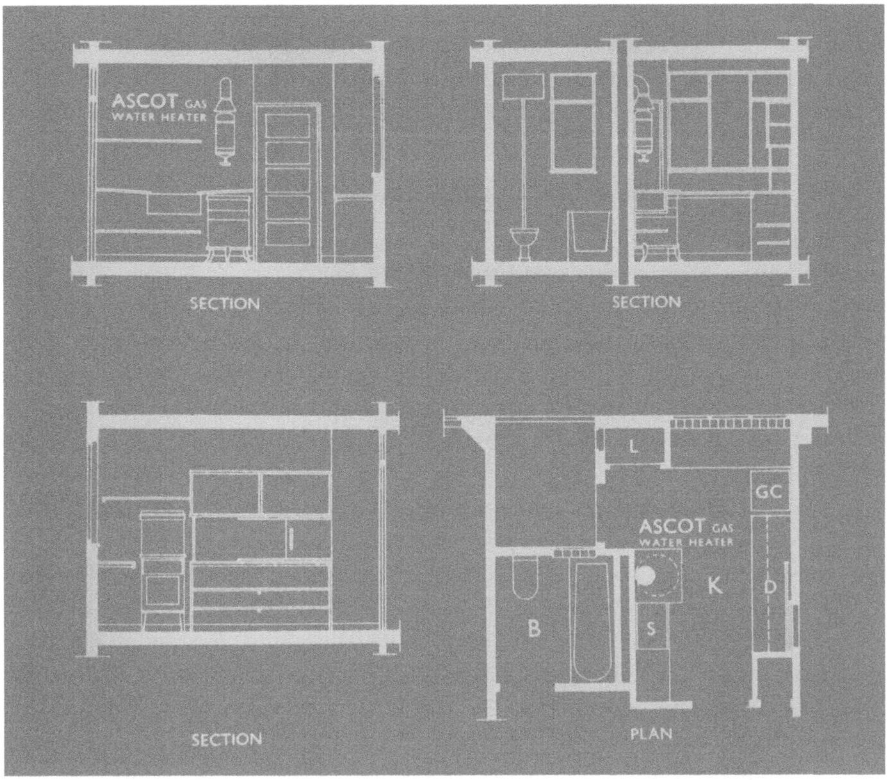

(a)

(b)

FIGURE 3.12 Kensal House, section and plan of kitchen and services (a) and photograph of kitchen (b).

Source: Flats: Municipal and Private Enterprise (Friedman, 1938).

suitability, quality, and adequacy of existing homes. The standards defined overcrowding as two or more unmarried people of the opposite sex aged over 10 sleeping in the same habitable room (including kitchens) and regulated the maximum number of residents per dwelling based on available bed spaces – a definition still in use today.

1945–1980: Post-World War II Housing and Evidence-Based Standards

In the aftermath of World War II, England was extensively damaged by bombing and, once again, faced a severe housing crisis and shortages of materials and labour. This prompted a comprehensive review of construction methods and housing standards. In response to homes lost during the war, the Housing (Temporary Accommodation) Act 1944 committed to providing housing for every family in need and completing the unfinished pre-war slum clearance project. The act facilitated the construction of prefabricated temporary homes, introduced rent controls to curb building price inflation, subsidised privately built homes, and counteracted cost increases in building materials.

Housing associations, charitable organisations, and social science researchers played an important role in shaping post-war housing policies by contributing to key government-led studies on design, construction, and planning, such as the County of London Plan (1943), the *Dudley Report* (1944), the Housing Manuals of 1944 and 1949, and the later *Parker Morris Report* (1961). Over the next three decades, a series of essential design and planning manuals guided developers and designers. According to Clifford (2021), post-war standards reflected "a belief in scientific rationality in their development and social democracy in their application", positioning the state as the primary provider of housing.

As evident from the *Tudor Walters Report* and later government-commissioned housing reports, policymakers sought evidence from a broad range of experts, third-sector organisations, and professional bodies involved in the design, delivery, and use of homes. While approached from the perspective of technical and functional requirements, these reports started to consider the lived experience of those using the homes. From the late 1930s, housing policymakers also grew increasingly interested in public opinion and how to influence or change it. Consequently, council estate tenants were recognised as individual subjects with specific needs, as "clients" or "users", rather than just passive recipients of government support (Hollow, 2014). Thus, during the post-war reconstruction in the 1940s, social surveys, opinion polls, public exhibitions, brochures, and publications were widely used to consult with the public.

One noteworthy example is the County of London Plan (Abercrombie Plan) of 1943, which proposed the neighbourhood unit as a planning solution to rationalise developments. Each unit was designed to accommodate up to 10,000 residents at varying densities and with different housing typologies and community facilities (Figure 3.13). Initially exhibited at County Hall in 1943, the exhibition's popularity led to its display being moved to the Royal Academy in Piccadilly. The large-scale diagrams were less intended to communicate specifics than to symbolically convey a new scientific approach to town planning (Amati, 2022; Wakeman, 2016). This shift in public engagement marked an important change in post-war town planning practice and the increasing involvement of the public in design governance processes.

As part of the government's post-war reconstruction efforts, in 1942 the Ministry of Health established a new housing sub-committee chaired by Lord Dudley, the Design of Dwellings

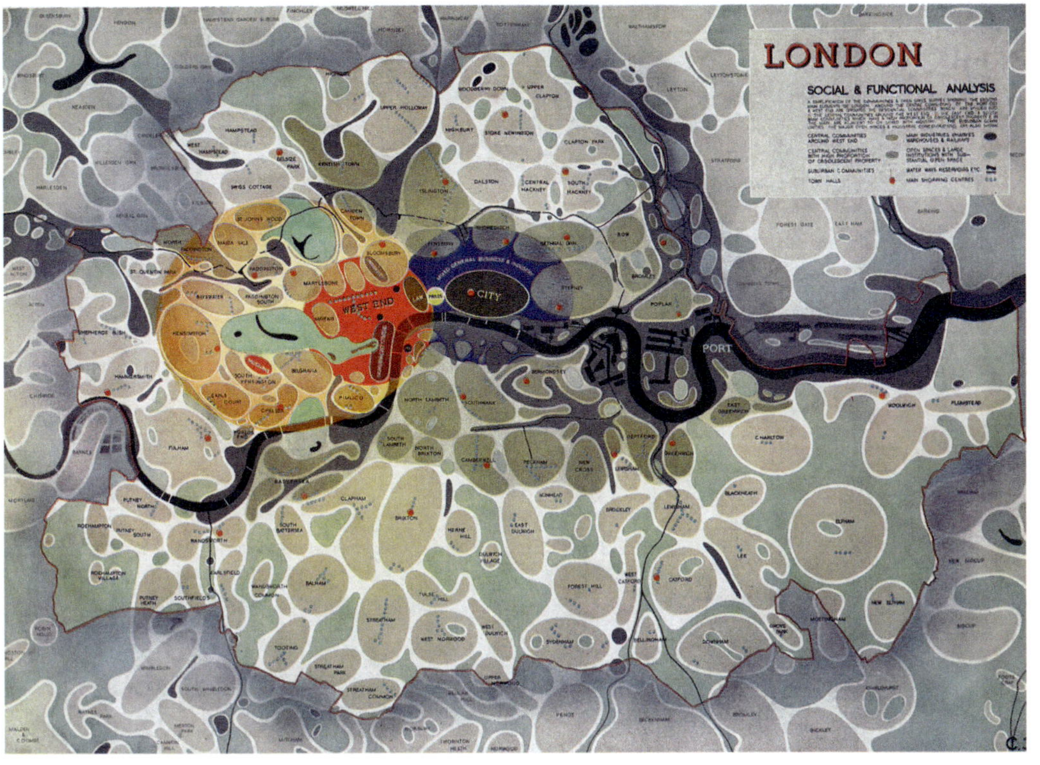

FIGURE 3.13 London: Social and Functional Analysis.

Source: Forshaw & Abercrombie, *County of London Plan* (1943).

Committee (Dudley Committee), to consolidate evidence for housing policy, sector improvements, and housing supply. The 18-member committee worked closely with women's organisations and other voluntary groups to incorporate their lived experiences and insights as evidence underpinning their review of housing standards initially introduced by the *Tudor Walters Report*.

Design of Dwellings (the *Dudley Report*) was published in 1944 by the Dudley Committee in an attempt to modernise building solutions, construction methods, and living conditions. It proposed layouts for two-storey homes with separate kitchens and dining rooms instead of their traditional combination into a kitchen-diner (Figure 3.14). The report also supported the idea of a standard neighbourhood unit to create more self-contained communities while fostering interactions between different social classes. These neighbourhood units were envisioned as mixed-use developments with urban fabrics and characters distinct from both previous models of suburban and isolated cottage estates and urban tenement blocks (Bullock, 2002).

Just as the *Tudor Walters Report* influenced the Addison Act of 1919, the *Dudley Report* shaped the *Housing Manual 1944*. The manual provided recommended housing layouts to achieve its minimum room sizes with adequate circulation spaces, especially for two- and

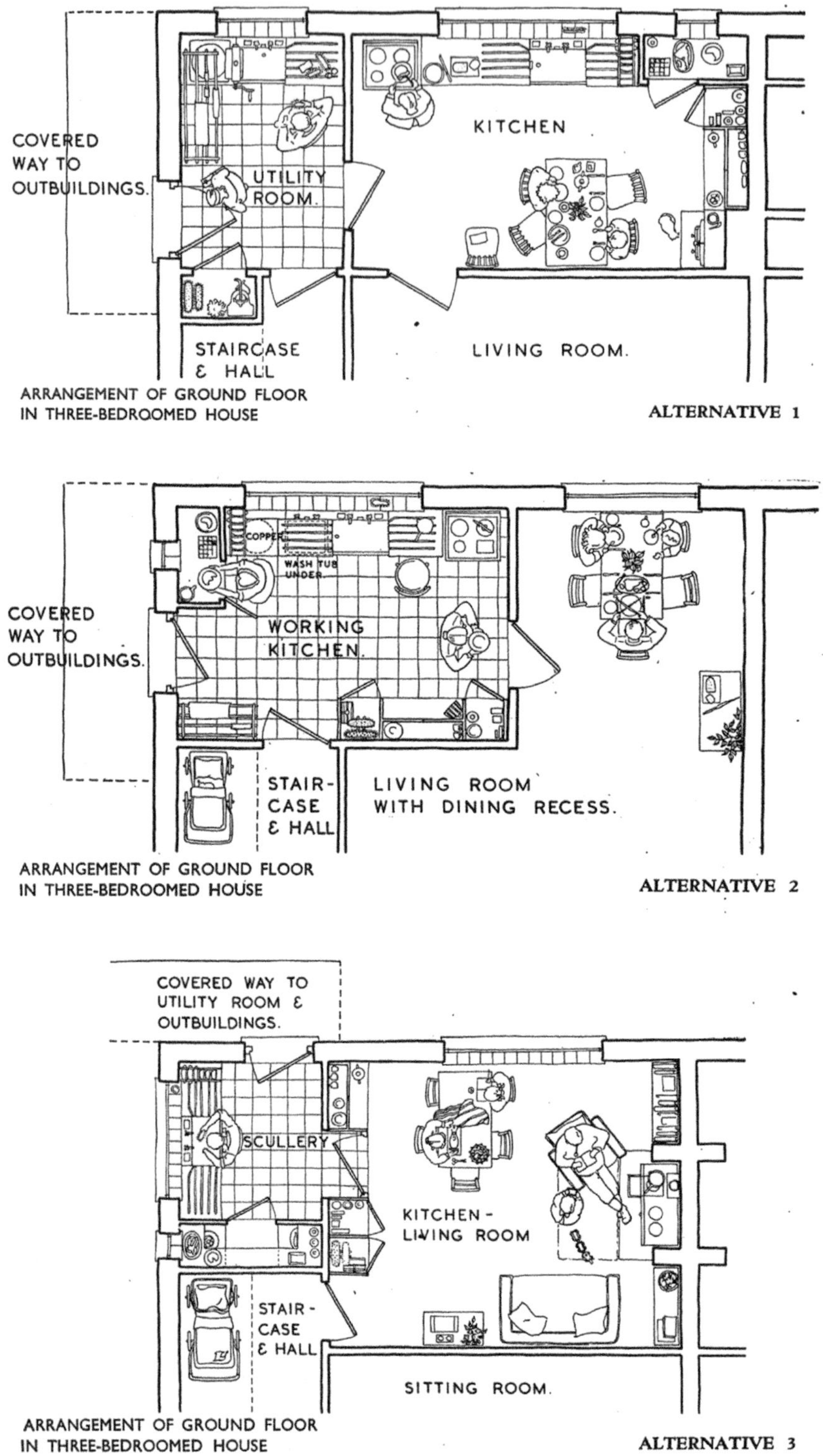

FIGURE 3.14 Alternative kitchen, dining, and living arrangements.

Source: Adapted from Ministry of Housing and Local Government (Dudley Committee), *Design of Dwellings* (1944).

TABLE 3.2 Space standards according to house type, based on *Housing Manual 1944*

House type	*Room(s)*	*Floor area (m^2)*
A – Kitchen-living room house	Kitchen-living room	16.7–18.6
	Kitchen-living room (where separate sitting room is provided)	15.8–16.7
	Sitting room (if provided)	10.2–11.2
	Scullery-wash house	6.0–7.4
	Scullery only	3.3–4.2
	Wash house only	3.3–4.2
B – Working kitchen house	Living room (no separate dining space)	16.7–18.6
	Living room and dining space	18.8–22.8
	Working kitchen	8.4–9.3
C – Dining kitchen house	Living room	14.9–16.7
	Dining kitchen	10.2–11.6
	Wash house	3.3–4.2
All house types	First bedroom	12.5–14.0
	Other double bedroom	10.2–11.2
	Single bedroom	6.5–7.4

three-bedroom homes for younger families. It also advocated greater building efficiency through new construction methods and materials (Park, 2017). However, due to inflation and enhanced housing standards resulting in a 25% cost increase, council homes built in the 1940s were significantly more expensive than those from the 1930s. In the 1940s, the average dwelling size increased to 92.9 m^2 from 74.3 m^2 in 1939 (Manoochehri, 2012), indicating a significant and rapid increase in the size of smaller homes (Table 3.2; Figure 3.15).

The subsequent *Housing Manual 1949* addressed the urgency of a more diverse housing strategy that considered the different needs of single households, young families, the elderly, and people with disabilities, as well as their implications for minimum room and dwelling sizes. It also provided plans for semi-detached and terraced houses for both rural and urban locations (Table 3.3).

The *Housing Manual 1949* was later supplemented by design guides such as *Technical Appendices* (1951), *Housing for Special Purposes* (1951), and *Houses: 2nd Supplement* (1952) and *3rd Supplement* (1953). These guides incorporated many post-war housing improvements, including immersion heaters, bathrooms with toilets, lifts, and internal staircases and corridors replacing external deck access. Considering economic constraints, the supplements tried to help housing authorities overcome limited construction materials and labour and increase density to save on land costs. Based on research by the British Standards Institute and the Building Research Station, the technical appendices of the *Housing Manual 1949* established function-related standards for developers and architects, analogous to performance requirements commonly used in current building regulations.

While the *Dudley Report* and the 1944 and 1949 *Housing Manuals* encouraged the construction of flats and maisonettes, the housing type most frequently illustrated in the reports, manuals, and subsequent publications was still the house. Later publications such as *Housing Type Plans* (1956) and *Flats and Houses* (1958) broadened this to include type plans for flats and

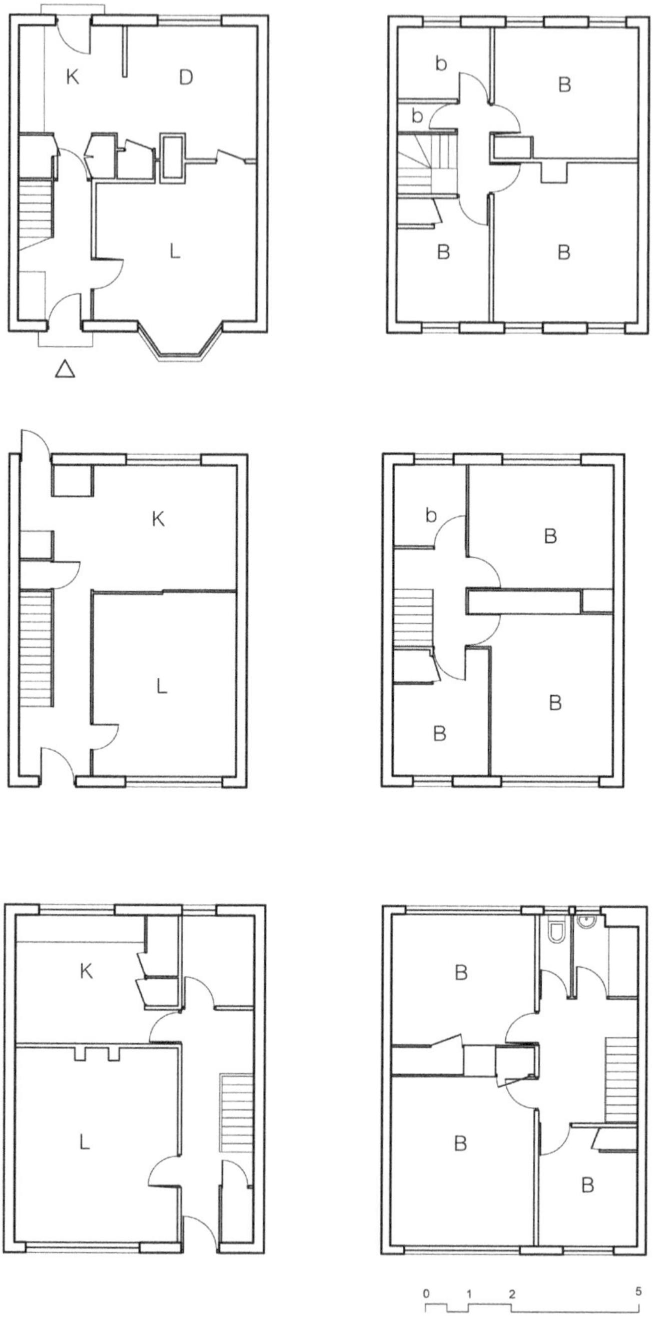

FIGURE 3.15 Comparison of three-bed, two-storey houses: (top) house type from the *Housing Manual* (1944), (middle) Somerford Grove designed by Frederick Gibberd (1947), and (bottom) London County Council house type.

Sources: Housing Manual (1949), *Architectural Review* (1949), *Housing Type Plans* (1956). Redrawn by the authors.

Key: B, bedroom; L, living room; K, kitchen; D, dining room; b, bathroom.

TABLE 3.3 Space standards for a two-storey house or maisonette

No. of bedrooms	*No. of persons*	*Internal floor area (m²)*
2	4	69.7–74.3
3	5	83.6–88.3
3	6	91.1–95.7
4	6	92.9–101.3
4	7	102.2–109.2

Source: Based on *Housing Manual* (1949).

maisonettes, demonstrating a growing acceptance of mixed-use developments and high-density blocks of flats as solutions to England's housing shortage.

In higher-density, larger estates, point blocks were often combined with low-rise terraced houses and blocks of maisonettes. To increase density without having to provide lifts, a requirement introduced by the *Dudley Report* for accessing dwellings more than three storeys high, mid-rise three- to five-storey blocks were designed with maisonette entrances at or below the third storey, above flats or garages (Figure 3.16). Tower blocks only became popular after a lift subsidy was introduced in 1946, reducing installation costs.

Both "point block" and "slab block" types were effective in achieving higher densities and lowering building costs through industrialised steel frame and precast concrete panel construction, which enabled greater standardisation and replication across projects. The *Dudley Report* specifically examined Y- and H-shaped standard plans for tower blocks and their advantages in providing better natural light compared to the more common closed courtyard or semi-courtyard layouts in earlier Modernist estates (Figure 3.17).

Following the *Dudley Report*, major housing reviews occurred again during the 1960s, coinciding with the creation of new administrative bodies and the publication of several influential housing design guides. The Housing Act 1964, for example, established the Housing

FIGURE 3.16 Maisonette type plan.

Source: London County Council, *Housing Type Plan* (1956). Redrawn by the authors. *Key*: B, bedroom; L, living room; K, kitchen; b, bathroom.

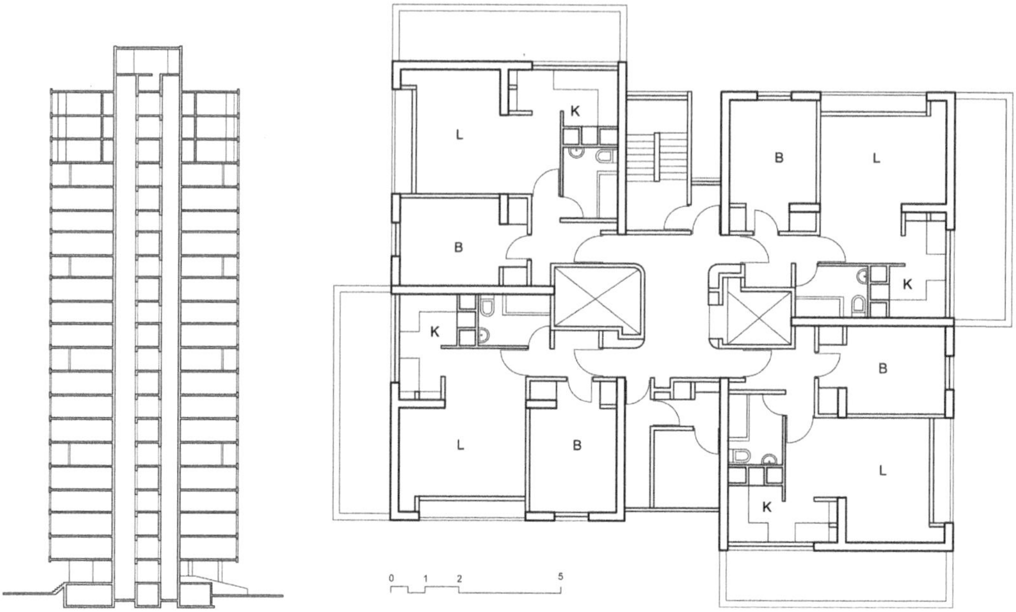

FIGURE 3.17 Section and floor plan of a typical H-shaped tower block on the Canada Estate, designed by the London County Council's Architects Department (1962).

Source: Crawford (1975). Redrawn by the authors.

Key: B, bedroom; L, living room; K, kitchen.

Corporation, a regulatory body overseeing housing associations and funding allocation for new housing projects. The London Government Act 1963 led to the formation of the Greater London Council (GLC) in 1965, unifying London's governance by consolidating 28 metropolitan boroughs into 12 and adding new outer urban areas, resulting in a total of 32 London boroughs.

Central to this period of housing progress was the publication of *Homes for Today and Tomorrow* (*Parker Morris Report*) in 1961, commissioned by the Ministry of Housing and Local Government and prepared by the Parker Morris Committee under the Central Housing Advisory Committee. The committee, comprising planners, architects, surveyors, doctors, engineers, and local housing officials, collected and analysed diverse data from 1959 to 1961 through surveys, visits to over 600 homes built since World War II, and a review of written and oral evidence from over 80 organisations and many individuals. Evidence was also submitted by the public sector, including 76 local authorities, but also housing experts (RIBA, Housing Centre Trust) and health professionals (Royal Society of Health) as well as housing charities (Guinness Trust), women's associations, housebuilders, and commercial bodies such as the Furniture Development Council and British Refrigeration Association. The committee was therefore explicitly interested in qualitative data on the everyday use of homes, and how spatial planning and design could support domestic activities and needs.

Based on this research, the *Parker Morris Report* recommended minimum housing standards, including overall unit sizes for various dwelling types (Table 3.4). While acknowledging

TABLE 3.4 Space standards according to dwelling types

Dwelling type	*1 person*	*2 person*	*3 person*	*4 person*	*5 person*	*6 person*
3-storey house	–	–	–	–	93.8	97.5
2-storey house (centre terrace)	–	–	–	74.3	84.5	92
2-storey house (semi/end terrace)	–	–	–	71.5	81.8	92
Maisonette	–	–	–	71.5	81.8	92
Flat	29.7	44.6	56.7	69.7	79	86.4
Single-storey house	29.7	44.6	56.7	66.8	75.2	83.6
Storage						
Houses	2.8	3.5	4.1	4.6	4.6	4.6
Flats and maisonettes	0.7 (1.8)	0.9 (1.8)	1.1 (1.8)	1.4 (1.8)	1.4 (1.8)	1.4 (1.8)

Source: Based on the *Parker Morris Report* (1961).

Note: Storage for flats and maisonettes shows additional external storage in parentheses.

potential cost increases due to the proposed higher standards, it argued that they were necessary to improve housing quality and eliminate substandard homes. The standards emphasised room dimensions and floor areas alongside the usability of spaces, as well as the importance of designing homes to accommodate diverse family activities and evolving use over time and by different household compositions. As households increasingly owned modern household appliances (vacuum cleaners, refrigerators, washing machines, and other electrical goods), more space was needed to store and install them. By 1969, the *Parker Morris Report*'s space standards became compulsory for all new council housing until their abolition in 1980 (Figure 3.18).

The *Parker Morris Report*'s standards and integration of technological advancements and social data on lived experiences had a profound influence on post-war housing design guidance and became embedded into several key design bulletins and manuals issued by various government

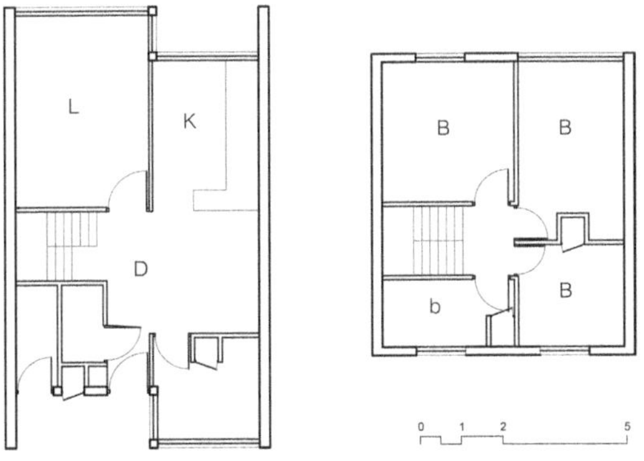

FIGURE 3.18 Ground- and first-floor plan of a three-bedroom, two-storey house on Ravenscroft Road, West Ham, designed to Parker Morris standards by Cleeve Barr, Research and Development Group, Ministry of Housing and Local Government (1964).

Source: Crawford, (1975). Redrawn by the authors. *Key*: B, bedroom; L, living room; K, kitchen; b, bathroom.

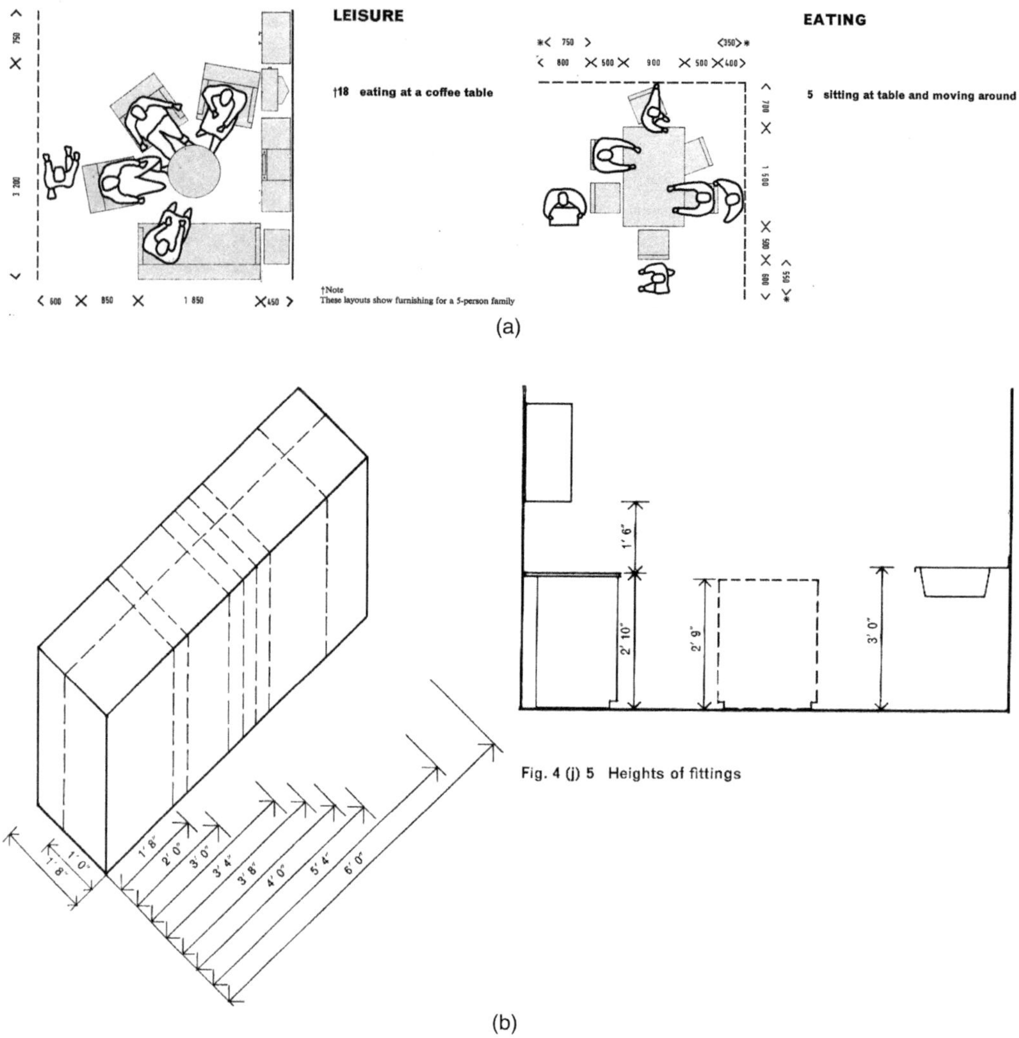

FIGURE 3.19 Typical space requirements and furniture dimensions (a: leisure and eating; b: standard kitchen dimensions).

Sources: Design Bulletin 6: Space in the Home (1968) and *Design Bulletin 8: Dimensions and Components for Housing* (1963).

agencies to improve design and construction practices. For example, *Design Bulletin 8: Dimensions and Components for Housing – With Special Reference to Industrial Building* (1963) recommended the standardisation of housing components and dimensions based on typical housing needs (Figure 3.19). The bulletin targeted manufacturers, architects, and the building industry, highlighting the benefits of standardisation, such as the easier production of components, greater consistency in quality, reduced production costs through mechanisation, and improved product availability – all contributing to more accurate cost control. Similarly, the National Building Agency's design bulletin *Generic Plans: Two and Three Storey Houses* (1965) provided a series of new standardised housing plans, with dimensions informed by industrial construction methods and the practicalities of component production.

However, perhaps the most seminal design guide was the Ministry of Housing's *Design Bulletin 6: Space in the Home – Metric Edition* (1968), which was written as a supplement to the *Homes for Today and Tomorrow* (1961) report. The need to update the recommendations of the *Parker Morris Report* following the UK's official adoption of the metric system in 1972 provided *Design Bulletin 6* with an opportunity to develop and instrumentalise the design principles and evidence-based approach promoted by the report. The bulletin translated domestic routines and changing home-use patterns into recommended room dimensions, standard furniture layouts, and circulation spaces, using anthropometric data to ensure that homes could support both typical day-to-day activities and adapt to changing household needs (Figure 3.18).

This approach of combining social and design studies in both the establishment of new design standards, as in the *Parker Morris Report,* and the assessment of recently built homes starting in the 1960s through post-occupancy evaluations, signalled both a radical departure from the previous focus on technology and economic construction but also a logical development of the human-centric design focus and ethos evident in the new council housing. Examples of these post-occupancy evaluations by the Ministry of Housing and Local Government are *Design Bulletin 11: Old People's Flatlets at Stevenage: An Account of the Project with an Appraisal* (1966), *Design Bulletin 2: Grouped Flats for Old People: A Sociological Study – Metric Edition* (1968b), *Design Bulletin 14: House Planning: A Guide to User Needs* (1968c), and *Design Bulletin 17: The Family at Home: A Study of Households in Sheffield* (1969). They illustrate the wide range of socio-spatial concerns at the heart of the Design Bulletin series, often conducted by both social scientists and architects.

These social studies built on a tradition of longitudinal and ethnographic research, such as the Mass Observation Project, which was first established in 1937 and remains active today, although it was suspended from the early 1950s to 1981. An important focus of the project was on how people used and experienced their homes, including domestic routines and the gendered division of space. The growing socio-spatial studies also reflected a sector-wide interest in user feedback, as evidenced by the RIBA's first edition of the *Plan of Work* (1963), which included a section on post-occupancy evaluation, requiring the review of completed buildings by architects to understand performance and user experience (Bordass & Leaman, 2005).

This focus on domestic life and the lived experience of residents was also part of a growing effort by the government to comprehensively collect housing data to inform its policy decisions. This included the Housing Conditions Survey, first conducted in 1967 to systematically evaluate the physical condition, amenities, and occupancy of the housing stock in England – today known as the English Housing Survey. It assessed whether homes were unfit under the Housing Act 1957 by considering their state of repair and the presence of four basic amenities – an indoor WC, fixed bath or shower, wash hand basin, and hot and cold water – and recorded key housing characteristics such as dwelling type, age, tenure, number of rooms, multi-occupation, gross rateable value, and the condition of the surrounding environment. Along with the gathering of new evidence, housing standards and their definition, assessment, and communication continuously evolved.

More than a decade after the publication of the *Parker Morris Report*, the Greater London Council's Department of Architecture and Civic Design released *Preferred Dwelling Plans* (1977), offering 38 updated standard housing layouts reflecting changed housing demand and practice. The guide aimed to reduce wasteful, duplicated design work by combining structural standardisation with flexible interior layouts that met the Parker Morris standards. Internal elements such as kitchens, bathrooms, and staircases were all standardised, with working drawings included for housebuilders. The intention of the standardised plans was not to replace the architect but to streamline early stages of planning so architects could "spend more time on the architectural treatment of the exterior of the dwelling" (Greater London Council, 1977).

In this period of intense focus on housing, government-led housing supply peaked in 1968 with 420,000 new council homes built in England alone (Woodman & Greeves, 2008). To achieve this, changes in housing density and construction were implemented, such as the prefabrication and use of new materials like concrete, permitting the fast erection of tall buildings. However, dissatisfaction with the post-war reconstruction programme and public opposition to tower blocks grew as housing began to deteriorate because of high long-term maintenance costs and issues with new building materials, exposing significant problems in housing quality (Turner, 2015). The inhumane scale and density of tower blocks were also criticised for causing social isolation, especially among families with children. When a gas explosion in 1968 caused the partial collapse of the newly built Ronan Point in London, a prefabricated 22-storey tower block, killing four people, calls for changes in housing policy and supply intensified.

1980–Present: Neoliberal Housing Policy and Housing Deregulation

In contrast to the substantial government expenditure and regulation of housing between 1945 and 1970, when Britain's local authorities collectively built 3.7 million new homes (Merrett, 1979), the 1980s ushered in far-reaching changes in housing policy that favoured a free market and its self-regulation. This neoliberal policy shift returned to laissez-faire housing traditions and resulted in reduced direct government intervention and spending on housing, alongside the privatisation of housing supply and management. The move from state-led to private development, which began in the 1970s, also generated new market demands that altered the methods of standardisation and mass production (Tallon, 2020).

In England, neoliberal housing policy emerged through the government's withdrawal from direct housing provision, exemplified by the Right to Buy Act of 1980, which privatised council housing and promoted market-led delivery. Yet this transition has not resulted in the government ceasing major market interventions, as it continues to heavily subsidise private housing provision and regulate housing quality through a wide range of policies and standards (Jacoby et al., 2022). However, supply-side subsidies have shifted towards demand-side subsidies, with the UK government still spending around £30 billion annually on housing benefits alone (Department for Work and Pensions, 2024), similar to the budget for transport. English neoliberal housing policy is hybrid rather than absolute, relying on active state intervention and design governance to balance market imperatives and social obligation to ensure that housing supply is decent and affordable.

Following the Housing Act 1974, private, non-profit housing associations began receiving substantial public funding. By 1980, housing associations owned and managed over 400,000 homes in England (National Housing Federation, n.d.). The Housing Act of 1980, introduced by Margaret Thatcher's government, gave council tenants with a minimum three-year history of tenancy the right to buy their homes at significant discounts of 30–50% below market value. Those unable to purchase their homes were given the option to transfer ownership to private landlords or housing associations. While many councils transferred their housing stock to housing associations to reduce public expenditure and liability, there was also a marked decrease in new council housing supply, and funding regulations prioritised cost efficiency over housing quality (Park, 2017).

Housing associations became the primary providers of what had now effectively become "social housing" for individuals with special needs or vulnerabilities not served by the market, contrasting with the more widely accessible public or council housing of previous decades. This change towards social housing supply also introduced new design standards; for example, the Design and Contract Criteria (1983) by the Housing Corporation, the national affordable housing agency in England that represented and funded social housing until 2008. This replaced the Parker Morris standards, which had been mandatory for publicly funded housing until 1980. As part of regulatory efforts to prevent overcrowding, the Housing Act 1985 also set limits on the number of people allowed to officially sleep in a room, which included both bedrooms and living rooms (Table 3.5).

The housing sector subsequently underwent substantial structural changes in design governance, including extensive deregulation. Whereas homes were predominantly built by local developers in the post-war period, by the 1970s, most private housing was delivered by a small number of large-volume housebuilders operating regionally or nationally (Carmona, 2001; Hooper & Nicol, 2000). In 1998, of the 20,000 housebuilders registered with the National House Building Council (NHBC), the largest 10 were responsible for 35% of the UK housing output and 40 accounted for 60% (Birkbeck, 1999). Furthermore, in the absence of recommended or mandatory space standards, the use of proprietary standardised house designs by developers increased from 1990, signalling a return to "model" dwellings. Notably, 90% of the largest housebuilders, especially those building over 2,000 units per annum, extensively use standard house types (Nicol & Hooper, 1999).

By the early 1990s, deregulation had led to a noticeable decrease in the size of new homes in both the private and public housing sectors. A comparison of affordable homes completed

TABLE 3.5 Space standard for overcrowding based on the Housing Act 1985

No. of rooms	*No. of people*
1	2
2	3
3	5
4	7.5
5 or more	2 for each room
Floor area of room (m^2)	*No. of people*
4.65–6.5	0.5
6.5–8.36	1
8.36–10.22	1.5
10.22	2

Note: Counts all habitable rooms. Children aged 1–10 count as half a unit; children under 1 are excluded.

in 1991–1992 by housing associations and the private sector showed that housing was now 5–15% below the Parker Morris standards in size, with more than half of the projects with lower standards built by housing associations (Karn & Sheridan, 1994). Homeownership expanded rapidly throughout the 1980s, but the housing market crashed in the early 1990s, marked by interest rates nearing 15% and a record 75,500 repossessions in 1991 (McMullan et al., 2021). Consequently, the term "affordable housing" emerged in the late 1990s in response to widespread issues caused by rising property prices and rents in a free housing market characterised by insufficient private-sector supply and management of social housing.

At the same time, widespread usability problems in small homes led to a reassessment and partial reintroduction of more regulated housing standards. For example, the Joseph Rowntree Foundation and the Habinteg Housing Association developed the Lifetime Home Standards in 1991, based on 16 design criteria to make homes more adaptable to different lifestyles at minimal cost, raising awareness of housing needs for people with disabilities and an ageing population. In 1999, parts of these design standards were adopted by the *Building Regulations, Approved Document M: Access to and Use of Buildings, Volume 1: Dwellings*. Meanwhile, the Housing Corporation replaced its Design and Contract Criteria (1983) with the Scheme Development Standards (SDS) in 1993 for subsidised housing, defining minimum housing standards in relation to furniture schedules, circulation spaces, relationships between rooms, and noise transmission. Parallel to this, the Housing Corporation updated its funding allocation based on the Total Cost Indicators (1993) approach, which considered land and property costs.

In 1997, the Housing Quality Indicators (HQIs) were introduced to quantify housing standards and provide a new tool for assessing housing schemes based on both cost and quality criteria (Housing Corporation, 1999). To further safeguard housing quality, the National Housing Federation published *Standards and Quality in Development: A Good Practice Guide* (Drury, 1998), differentiating between "essential" and "desirable" housing design criteria. While not mandatory, this guide was effectively used as a funding eligibility assessment tool, with its good practice standards therefore widely adopted by housing associations (Park, 2017). Housing developers also often equate adopting standards with questions of "buildability", design standardisation, and project viability, as less variation reduces their organisational challenges and risk, while increasing profitability and quality control (Carmona, 2001; Leopold & Bishop, 1983). Consequently, most housebuilders have their own standard house types and development standards as tried and tested development and design models. Even where it is not directly enforced by regulations, the standardisation of housing continues to be driven by organisation-level, and often economic, motivations.

Since the mid-2000s, environmental and sustainability standards have become key considerations in new housing developments, following the government's introduction of the Code for Sustainable Homes (2006). Developed by the Building Research Establishment (BRE), the code rated homes from Level 1 to 6, with the required energy efficiency exceeding that required by the building regulations. Although largely voluntary, it was mandatory for housing funded by the Homes and Communities Agency (HCA) or where the code had been adopted in local plans by local authorities. The code aimed to deliver zero-carbon homes by 2016 (Department for Communities and Local Government, 2007). In 2008, the government also created the Zero Carbon Hub, promoting new energy efficiency standards and improved thermal performance through low-carbon technologies and energy-efficient materials, minimum energy efficiency standards for heating and cooling, and a 70% reduction in regulated energy use emissions

(M'Sirdi et al., 2012). However, the Code for Sustainable Homes was withdrawn in 2015 and replaced by the voluntary Home Quality Mark, also developed by BRE, intended to guide consumer decisions when renting or buying homes. Some aspects of the Code for Sustainable Homes were later incorporated into building regulations, such as energy performance requirements equivalent to its Level 4.

In 2008, the HCA was established, merging English Partnerships and the investment functions of the Housing Corporation. It was tasked with funding affordable housing and supporting the delivery of sustainable communities in England. Between 2011 and 2015, the HCA implemented the Affordable Homes Programme, while also overseeing ongoing projects and funding commitments from the previous 2008–2011 National Affordable Housing Programme. Homes funded under these schemes had to comply with the HQIs of 2007, current Building for Life standards, and the Design and Quality Standards (2007). In 2018, the HCA was then replaced by two separate bodies: Homes England and the Regulator of Social Housing, sponsored by the Ministry of Housing, Communities and Local Government, which is responsible for housing delivery and the regulation of private registered providers of social housing. The Shared Ownership and Affordable Homes Programme (2016–2021) was among the funding schemes that originated with the HCA.

The Commission for Architecture and the Built Environment (CABE) developed the Building for Life criteria in 2001, which were updated in 2015 and adopted in all existing council and housing association homes. This design tool guides housing stakeholders, including home builders, local authorities, and communities, in the delivery of "well-designed homes and neighbourhoods" (Birkbeck et al, 2014). Until 2010, eligibility for social housing grants depended on meeting three core performance measures and standards: HQIs (version 4) for internal environment standards, achieving a minimum sustainability rating of 3 on the Code for Sustainable Homes, and a minimum Building for Life score of 12 out of 20.

In 2010, the Housing Associations' Charitable Trust (HACT) study *Room to Swing a Cat? The Amount and Use of Space in New Dwellings in London & the South East* reviewed 89 homes marketed for sale by 17 housebuilders (Drury & Somers, 2010), concluding that homes were, on average, smaller than the draft London Plan (2010). This provided strong evidence supporting the reintroduction of space standards. Following a public consultation, the Greater London Authority published the *London Housing Design Guide* (2010), which included new and more ambitious space standards applied across all housing sectors (Figure 3.20). Homes built on land owned by the London Development Agency or funded by the HCA were expected to meet minimum gross internal floor area, storage provision, and open space requirements. However, the guide's "Priority 2" standards, specifying minimum floor areas and habitable room dimensions, were strongly recommended but not mandatory.

The Nationally Described Space Standard (NDSS), published in 2015 by the Department for Communities and Local Government, is England's first national space standard, and applies to both public and private housing. The NDSS room and dwelling dimensions replace all minimum standards used by local authorities, notably drawing from the *London Housing Design Guide* (2010) and HQIs. It applies to all new homes built to Categories 1 and 2 of Part M (Accessibility) of the Building Regulations. The NDSS requires minimum internal gross floor areas and bedrooms of at least 7.5 m^2 for singles (minimum 2.15 m width) and minimum 11.5 m^2 for doubles (minimum width of 2.75 m for the first double and at least 2.55 m for others).

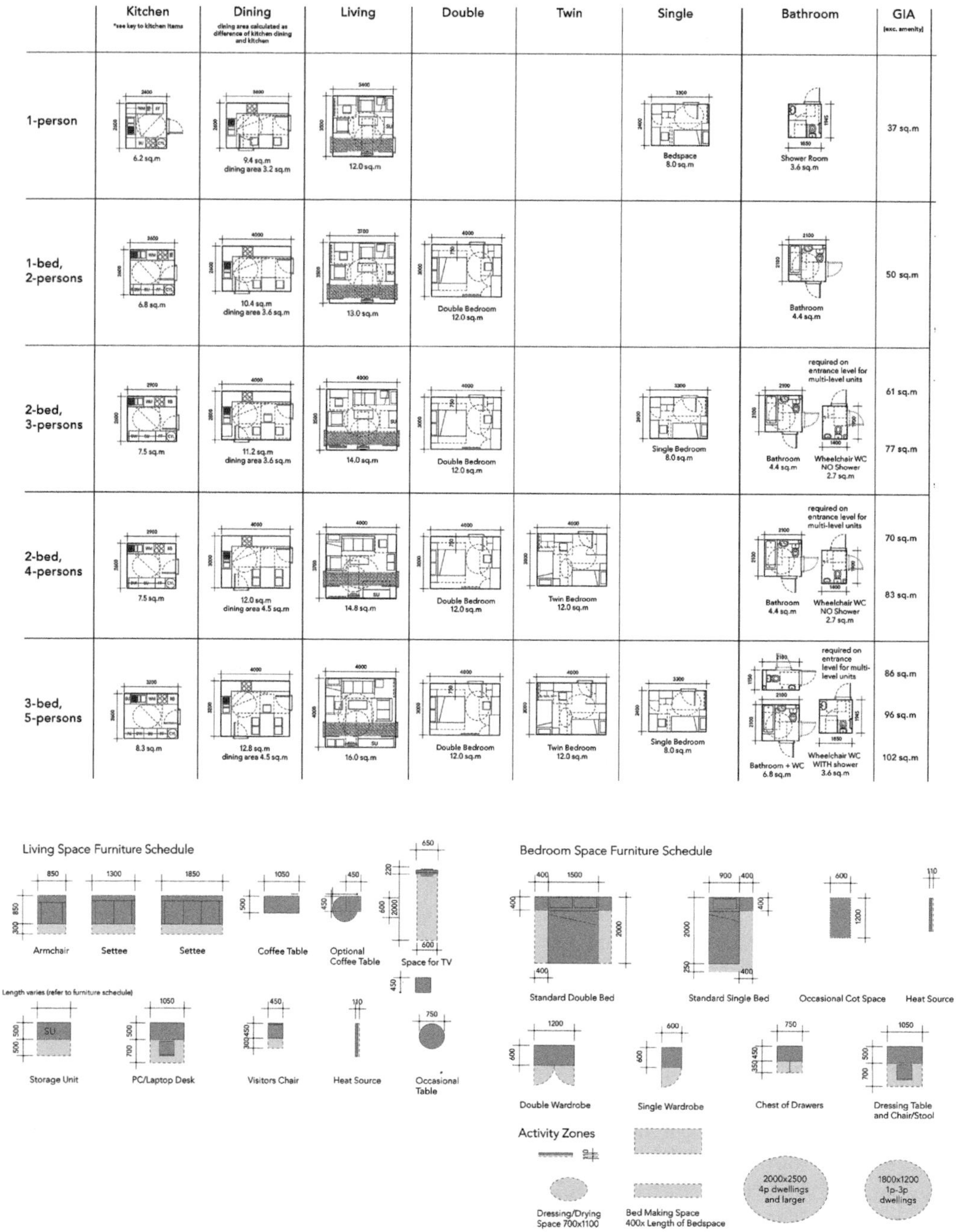

FIGURE 3.20 Graphic representation of space standards, furniture schedules, and circulation zones.

Source: Greater London Authority, *London Housing Design Guide* (2010).

However, the NDSS is not a building regulation but a technical planning standard, and thus part of the planning system. Each local authority must therefore individually adopt the NDSS after justifying its economic viability and need. To date, only 37% of local planning authorities have done so, and a study of recently built affordable housing in England found that 57% of new homes were below the overall dwelling sizes recommended by the NDSS (Özer & Jacoby, 2023). The only mandatory space standards are those incorporated in the Approved Document Part M of the Building Regulations (2015), which requires all new housing to meet minimum accessibility or so-called "visitability" standards and dimensions. While space standards became partially enforced via planning, permitted developments remained exempt from complying with the NDSS and its minimum floor area requirements of 37 m^2 until 2020.

Despite these substantial weaknesses in the implementation of space standards, the NDSS today is around 10% larger than the Parker Morris standards from the 1960s (Kearns, 2022; Park, 2017). The UK also had the fourth-highest usable floor area per person in Europe in 2010 (Ministry of the Interior and Kingdom Relations, 2010). This highlights not only significant increases in dwelling sizes over time, but also how measurement and comparison methods affect interpretations and perceptions – UK homes tend to be smaller than those in other European countries when compared by the number of bedrooms, but there is also greater underoccupancy in the private sector, explaining the high average usable floor area per person.

Following the Grenfell Tower Fire in 2017 and the COVID-19 pandemic, interest in housing quality, health, safety, and wellbeing increased significantly across the sector and among the public. Reports such as *The Cost of Poor Housing to the NHS* (BRE Group, 2021), *Improving Health and Wellbeing Through Housing* (Local Government Association, 2022), and *Health Equity in England* (Marmot, 2020) emphasise the importance of health and wellbeing in the home. In response to growing concerns, the Town and Country Planning Association launched the Healthy Homes Bill in 2020, with the aim to establish minimum standards for the size of homes, the provision of internal and external storage spaces, access to natural light in bedrooms, and thermal comfort.

In addition, the *Living with Beauty* report (Building Better, Building Beautiful Commission, 2020), the latest government-commissioned housing report chaired by Roger Scruton, promotes housing quality through aesthetic and place-based standards in housing development. Building on this, the Levelling-up and Regeneration Act 2023 responds to ongoing pressure from local authorities and the Local Government Association for greater planning powers and devolution. Key provisions include planning reforms, the introduction of a new infrastructure levy replacing most Section 106 agreements (which traditionally required developers to contribute to affordable housing and infrastructure provision), and updates to compulsory purchase order powers, designed to simplify and expedite land assembly for regeneration and public benefit.

Currently, the Decent Homes Standard – setting minimum requirements for repair, facilities, thermal comfort, and safety – is under review, with proposals to extend it to the private rental sector. Meanwhile, the Future Homes Standard, requiring all new homes to be low-carbon and energy-efficient, is set to take effect in late 2026. The government has also reinstated a national housing target of 1.5 million homes over five years (2024–2029), and introduced new planning reforms, including mandatory local housing targets, the introduction of grey-belts, and streamlined approval processes, alongside new funding for affordable and social housing. Housing aims, policy, and regulation therefore remain in constant flux. While design governance changes accordingly, as this historical review demonstrates, there are significant path dependencies specific to the changing housing contexts in England.

Conclusion

This study of design governance through key historical housing acts, regulations, and standards in England, particularly in relation to standardised housing design, highlights its deeply contextual and contingent nature. Housing design outcomes are determined by shifting political agendas, economic conditions, social values, and design and construction practices. They reflect significant historical events and changing priorities in housing, from public health concerns and post-war reconstruction efforts to an affordability crisis and the current drive for environmental sustainability. Design governance, therefore, is neither neutral nor static, but continuously influenced by and responsive to socio-political, institutional, and ideological transformations.

The historical analysis reveals some of the key path dependencies in design governance that continue to shape housing outcomes, regulations, and standards today. Past decisions about who defines standards, and how they are implemented and enforced, have lasting structural and practical effects on long-term housing provision, quality, and affordability. These path dependencies underscore how governance, regulatory cultures, and housing practices are embedded within broader housing systems, making it impossible to separate design standards and standardisation from the wider political, social, and economic contexts in which they are produced and applied. They also reflect the evolving roles of local authorities and private sector actors, whose capacity and priorities shape the adoption and enforcement of standards across regions.

Design governance processes and decisions rely on diverse forms of evidence, including statistical surveys, ethnographic studies, user feedback, condition surveys, practice reviews, case study analysis, and technical experiments with materials and construction methods. The evidence base has hereby evolved over time: from nineteenth-century public health concerns and statistics to early-twentieth-century technical research and material performance studies, to mid-twentieth-century sociological surveys and post-occupancy evaluations, and more recently to performance-based environmental regulation and quantifiable metrics. These shifts register changes in the questions asked, the actors involved, and prevailing political agendas around housing.

Government-commissioned housing reports such as the *Tudor Walters Report* (1918), the *Dudley Report* (1944), the *Parker Morris Report* (1961), and to a lesser extent the recent *Scruton Report* (2020) mark key historical moments when housing policy and design standards were extensively reviewed, recast, and redefined, shaping new housing agendas, promoting new lifestyles, and advancing construction and design practices. These reports exemplify advances in evidence-based policy and design, demonstrating how social science, health studies, design research, and technical testing inform the material, spatial, and social reasoning of new homes, as well as the standards that underpin their design (Figure 3.21). The adoption, abolition, or partial reinstatement of standards – for instance, the removal of the Parker Morris standards in 1980 – reflect both political priorities and the technical, social, and environmental challenges of their times, and can result in major changes in how the state defines housing aims and quality, as well as responsibilities for the supply of subsidised housing.

Central to these housing transformations has been the balance between material safety, physical health, and mental wellbeing. The focus has shifted from construction quality and public health to family and individual wellbeing, emphasising human-centred design that reflects lived experiences. Capturing this in housing policy and design controls – through post-occupancy evaluations, sociological studies, or surveys and interviews with residents – remains critical. While past approaches integrating design research and social studies offer important lessons, they often relied on normative or normalised assumptions of the home. Today, a more inclusive framework is required to account for diverse demographics, household compositions, housing typologies and densities, and marginalised voices. Without this, standards and design governance risk perpetuating outdated assumptions and failing to address emerging housing needs, including those of ageing populations. Housing outcomes must therefore not only be determined by economic, technical, procedural, or technocratic considerations but also by shared social and environmental values, expectations, and responsibilities.

These considerations must be understood within the broader historical and systemic context of housing in England. The long history of laissez-faire approaches, decentralised regulation, extensive council housing provision, and a rich social welfare history demonstrates both the complexity and adaptability of housing systems and design governance. While England is often associated with neoliberal housing policies prioritising private-market supply, homeownership, and deregulation, welfare state principles continue to influence political and societal housing decisions and investment. The systemic failure of the market to deliver sufficient affordable and adequate housing, despite deregulation and subsidiarity, has necessitated extensive state interventions at national and local levels, exposing fundamental structural problems in neoliberal housing models (Jacoby et al., 2022). Greater market dependency tends to marginalise and exclude not only low-income households but also increasingly middle-income households. At the same time, the coexistence of market-driven and social welfare approaches continues to shape current policy, regulatory practices, and housing design outcomes as well as expectations around housing quality, accessibility, equity, and environmental performance.

Given worsening housing affordability and limited progress in improving housing quality and living standards for those in greatest need, a fundamental reassessment of the role housing should play in society and the level of responsibility and investment required to support it is needed. This reconsideration must translate into housing standards and regulations that go beyond safeguarding minimal housing conditions, aspiring instead to socially and environmentally ambitious outcomes that integrate inclusive design, sustainable practices, and socio-spatial evidence collected across different household types, communities, and regions. To make design governance equitable and responsive to the lived realities of homes today, it is essential to rethink how supporting evidence is collected and whose experiences are considered.

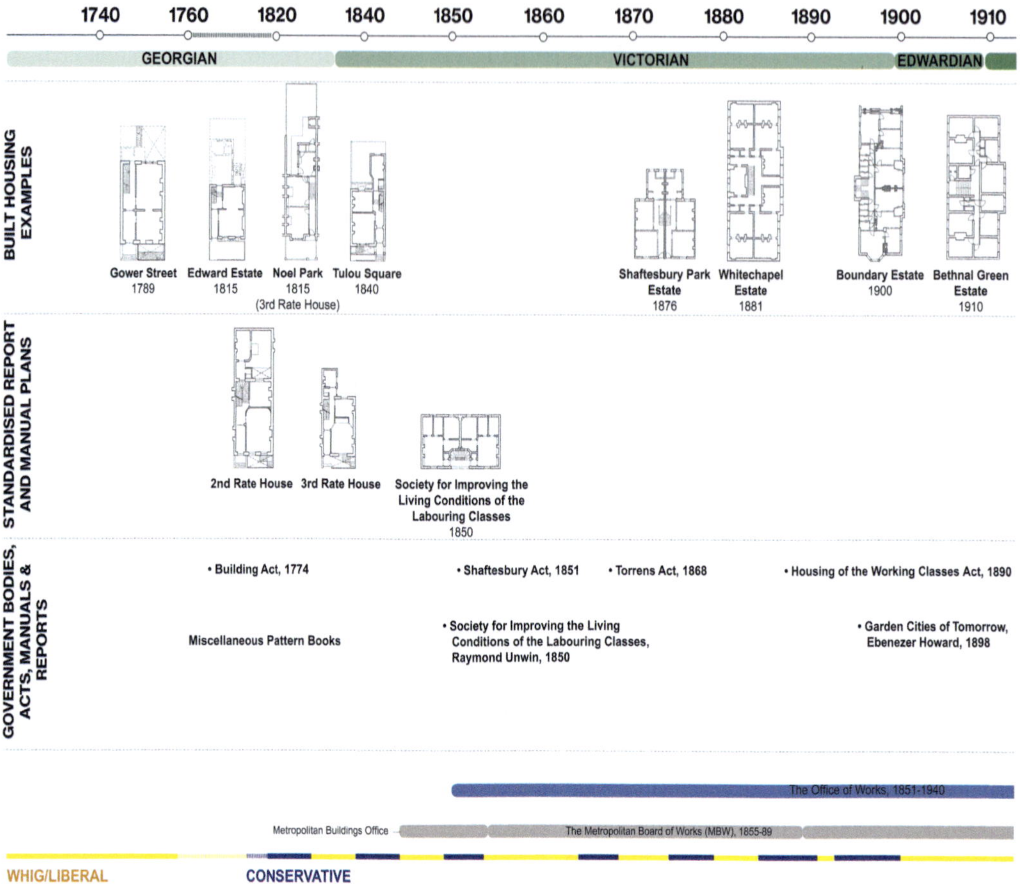

FIGURE 3.21 Timeline of key housing standards and regulations in England, including related standardised house plans.

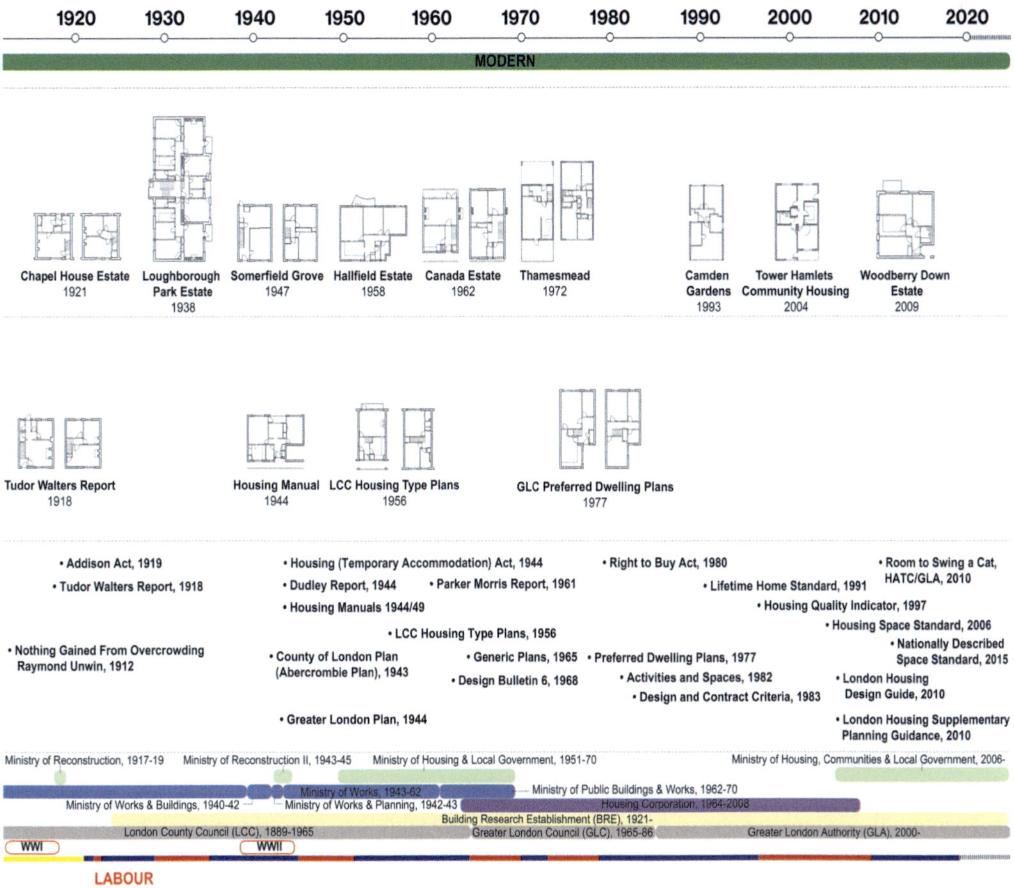
1920
1930
1940
1950
1960
1970
1980
1990
2000
2010
2020
MODERN
Chapel House Estate 1921
Loughborough Park Estate 1938
Somerfield Grove 1947
Hallfield Estate 1958
Canada Estate 1962
Thamesmead 1972
Camden Gardens 1993
Tower Hamlets Community Housing 2004
Woodberry Down Estate 2009
Tudor Walters Report 1918
Housing Manual 1944
LCC Housing Type Plans 1956
GLC Preferred Dwelling Plans 1977
• Addison Act, 1919
• Tudor Walters Report, 1918
• Nothing Gained From Overcrowding Raymond Unwin, 1912
• Housing (Temporary Accommodation) Act, 1944
• Dudley Report, 1944
• Parker Morris Report, 1961
• Housing Manuals 1944/49
• LCC Housing Type Plans, 1956
• County of London Plan (Abercrombie Plan), 1943
• Generic Plans, 1965
• Design Bulletin 6, 1968
• Greater London Plan, 1944
• Right to Buy Act, 1980
• Preferred Dwelling Plans, 1977
• Activities and Spaces, 1982
• Design and Contract Criteria, 1983
• Lifetime Home Standard, 1991
• Housing Quality Indicator, 1997
• Housing Space Standard, 2006
• Room to Swing a Cat, HATC/GLA, 2010
• Nationally Described Space Standard, 2015
• London Housing Design Guide, 2010
• London Housing Supplementary Planning Guidance, 2010
Ministry of Reconstruction, 1917-19
Ministry of Reconstruction II, 1943-45
Ministry of Housing & Local Government, 1951-70
Ministry of Housing, Communities & Local Government, 2006-
Ministry of Works, 1943-62
Ministry of Public Buildings & Works, 1962-70
Ministry of Works & Buildings, 1940-42
Ministry of Works & Planning, 1942-43
Housing Corporation, 1964-2008
Building Research Establishment (BRE), 1921-
London County Council (LCC), 1889-1965
Greater London Council (GLC), 1965-86
Greater London Authority (GLA), 2000-
WWI
WWII
LABOUR

4

THE EVOLUTION OF HOUSING DESIGN STANDARDS IN CHILE

Alvaro Arancibia

The evolution of housing design standards in Chile offers a unique lens through which to understand the limitations of the neoliberal housing supply and policy model. Chile's neoliberal approach presents a central paradox: while, in theory, it promotes self-regulation by the free market as the guiding mechanism, in practice it relies on sustained state intervention to ensure sufficient access to housing, particularly for the most vulnerable in society. This ongoing tension between market and state has made Chile a paradigmatic case, in which housing policy reflects both the possibilities and the constraints of the neoliberal model.

Through the extensive use of housing subsidies, the state has played a pivotal role in a housing system that would otherwise have failed to meet the housing needs of a significant portion of the population. The analysis in this chapter focuses on how the implementation of a neoliberal model in the 1980s marked an important turning point in the design and delivery of housing in Chile (Jacoby et al., 2022). It established housing subsidies as a key policy tool, initially targeting low-income groups but later extending its focus to middle-income households. While this improved overall housing access, these housing programmes were also criticised for failing to respond to the actual needs of families (Fuster-Farfán, 2019).

Around 14.5% of all newly built housing in Chile is wholly financed through state subsidies, while an additional 42% of homeowners receive partial subsidies for the acquisition of their homes (Rebolledo, 2023). Subsidised homes are exclusively developed for homeownership, which means that ownership is the only route to affordable housing and there is no official social rent provision. Due to this high level of subsidies – indicating basic market failures in affordable housing supply – housing design quality and space standards have historically been very low. Therefore, technical and social norms have been essential to safeguarding housing provisions, which, determined by the available amount of subsidy, have often remained substandard, pushing the idea of a minimum dwelling to its very limit. Subsidised housing standards have seen three important reviews over the last 40 years, in 1984, 2005, and 2011, with minimum dwelling sizes increasing from 24 m^2 in 1984 to 55 m^2 today – the current minimum area for a five-person home.

Beyond their technical dimension, design standards embody the political, economic, and social priorities of an era. For example, the Ley de Habitaciones Obreras (Workers' Housing Law)

DOI: 10.4324/9781032679204-7

marked the beginning of the regulation of housing for low-income groups by establishing basic health and safety requirements. The development of standards intensified with the introduction of new housing typologies, beginning with incremental housing models in the 1980s and later high-rise buildings in the 2010s. This chapter traces the importance of design governance and standards in Chile's housing history, from the first effort to mandate housing design controls in 1906 through the Ley de Habitaciones Obreras, which sought to improve the living conditions of the working class, to current housing policies that promote both greater social integration and increased housing density.

Through a historical examination divided into seven periods, the chapter explores how housing standards have evolved in response to the need to balance market demands and a high housing deficit with aspirations for improved housing quality and accessibility (Jacoby et al., 2022). It analyses key conceptual and practical limitations and their consequences, such as urban segregation and the standardisation of housing, which fail to reflect cultural diversity or individual needs. The chapter therefore addresses not only the technical aspects of design standards, but also their wider impact on social, economic, and urban dynamics. By analysing the interaction between public policies, the market, and residents' needs, this chapter offers a comprehensive understanding of how these forces have shaped Chile's housing landscape and the lives of its inhabitants, highlighting both achievements and ongoing challenges in the pursuit of dignified, inclusive, and accessible housing for all.

1906–1935: The First Housing Regulations

The origins of state-led housing policy in Chile were shaped not only by rapid urbanisation and public health concerns but also by Catholic social doctrine, particularly the influence of Pope Leo XIII's encyclical *Rerum Novarum* (Of New Matters, 1891), also known as *Rights and Duties of Capital and Labour*. This document inspired charitable housing initiatives by religious institutions in the late nineteenth century, conceived as moral and social interventions aimed at improving living conditions for the urban poor (Hidalgo Dattwyler et al., 2005). These early projects, although few, framed the dwelling as part of a broader system of care, linking the notion of shelter to that of hygiene, education, and social discipline.

Despite these charitable efforts, their reach was insufficient to address the scale of the housing crisis. For most of the urban working class, the dominant form of accommodation was the *conventillo*, consisting of subdivided rooms in old colonial houses, formerly occupied by upper-class families, arranged around a shared patio (Figure 4.1). Sanitary facilities such as latrines and water access were communal, and ventilation was poor, fostering the spread of infectious diseases. This overcrowded and unsanitary environment, together with the earlier philanthropic initiatives, created the conditions for the first state-led housing legislation.

The 1906 Ley de Habitaciones Obreras, inspired by European policies, most notably the French Loi Siegfried of 1894, translated these principles into the first binding technical framework for working-class housing (Hidalgo Dattwyler et al., 2005). It established Consejos de Habitaciones Obreras (Workers' Housing Councils) to supervise compliance with standards for cross-ventilation, minimum ceiling heights, daylight access, and the use of durable materials like fired brick and treated wood. These regulations conceptualised housing as a designed environment optimised for health, productivity, and moral order, rather than merely as shelter.

FIGURE 4.1 *Conventillo* courtyard in 1900.

Source: Photograph by Harry Grant Olds (1900), Collección: Museo Histórico Nacional Código BN: MC0007091.

One of the most emblematic projects of this period was Población Huemul I in Santiago (1911–1918), which was developed under the auspices of the Consejo Superior de Habitaciones Obreras. Conceived as a model neighbourhood, it included low-rise brick housing arranged along well-ventilated streets, integrated with public facilities such as a school, market, medical centre, and theatre (Hidalgo, 2019). Its layout reflected both the hygienist principles of the 1906 law and the moral aspirations inherited from earlier Church-led initiatives. While celebrated as a pioneering experiment in social housing, its relatively high construction standards, generous dwelling sizes, and the large-scale provision of community services made it difficult to replicate widely under prevailing budgetary and political constraints (Figure 4.2).

In architectural terms, the technical requirements of the 1906 law encouraged compact, standardised layouts that could be efficiently reproduced within the urban block. The cité typology – rows of compact patio house units organised along a narrow passageway – became the preferred replacement for the overcrowded *conventillo* (Hidalgo, 2019) (Figure 4.3). While cités improved ventilation, light penetration, and circulation in accordance with the new law, some continued to use shared sanitary facilities and only offered minimal private space, reflecting the persistent tension between sanitary ideals, affordability, and density (Rojas, 2012) (Figure 4.4).

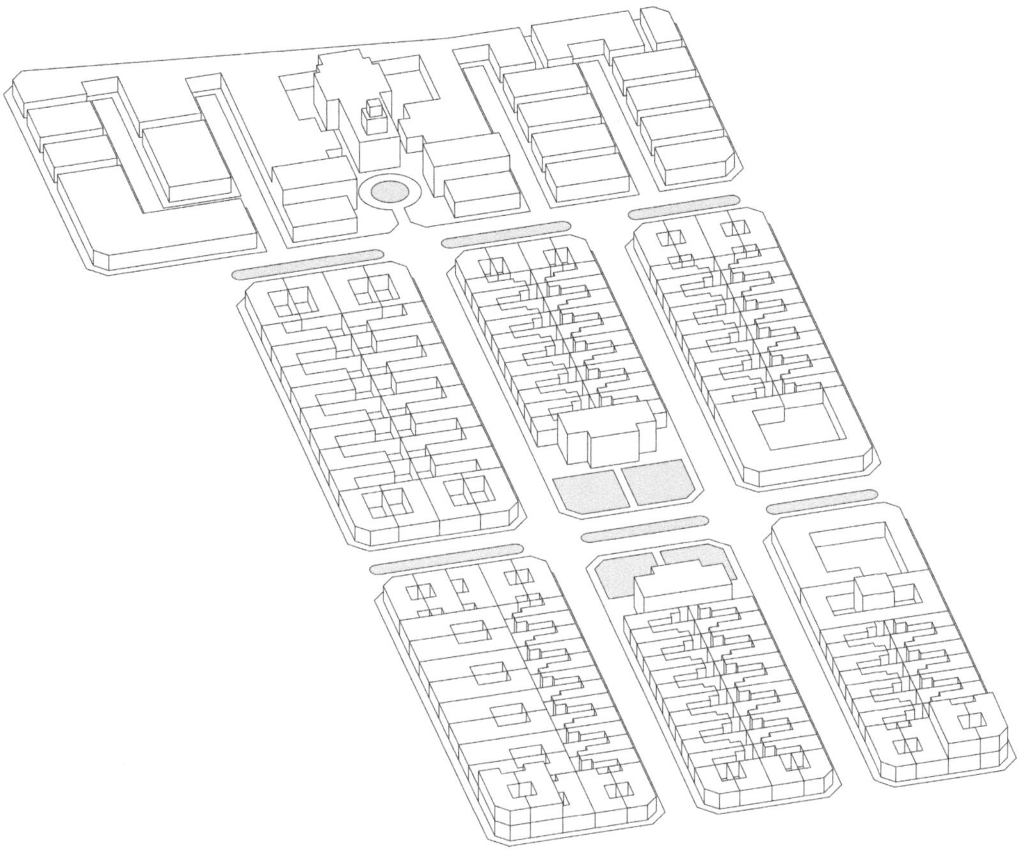

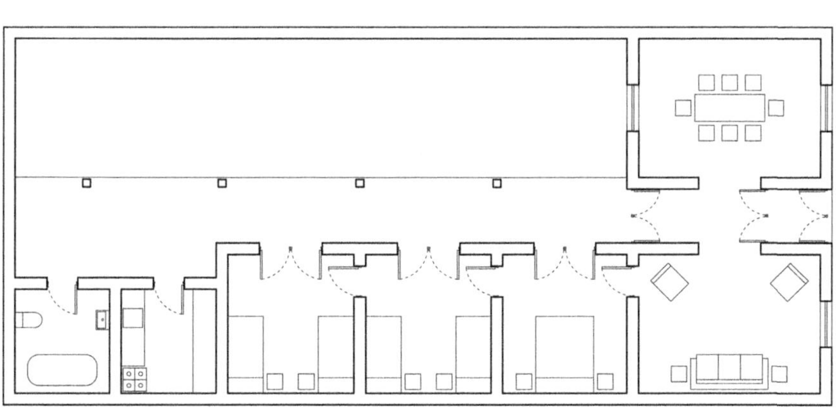

FIGURE 4.2 Población Huemul I (1911–1918) was conceived as a neighbourhood with a range of social services. The typical floor plan is influenced by colonial architecture and has a dual organisation around enfilade rooms and an exterior corridor.

Source: Adapted from Arancibia Tagle (2017).

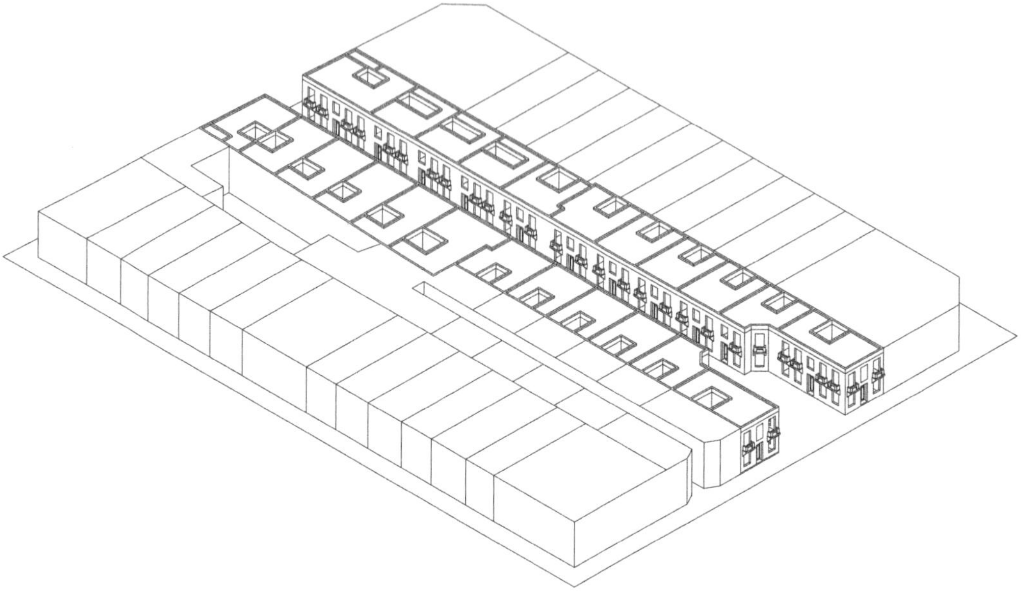

FIGURE 4.3 Cité Adriana Cousiño (1920). The cité, typically inserted within block interiors, had a pedestrian circulation connecting to one or more streets.

Source: Adapted from Arancibia Tagle (2013).

The 1925 Ley de Habitaciones Baratas (Low-Cost Housing Law) refined these standards, introducing minimum room dimensions, formalising requirements for potable water and sewerage connections, and mandating electric lighting where available (Hidalgo, 2019). It also included provisions for urban integration, requiring alignment with existing street grids, and offered tax incentives for developers who complied with it. These adjustments reinforced the push towards modular, rationalised designs that integrated functional efficiency with infrastructural connectivity. Alongside cités, modest single- and two-storey row houses with private kitchens – and occasionally private toilets – began to appear, though still within strict dimensional limits that reflected both economic constraints and prevailing conceptions of what could be defined as a minimum dwelling. An example of this is Conjunto Picarte of 1925, which combines the pedestrian street of the cité with a configuration of houses featuring a backyard, an arrangement that not only ensured cross-ventilation and natural lighting throughout the dwelling but also provided a utility zone for cooking and laundry, functionally separated from the main living areas (Figure 4.5).

By the early 1930s, these laws had established a core vocabulary of sanitary and functional housing standards such as ventilation, light, sanitation, durability, and urban integration, which would inform Chile's low-income housing architecture for decades (García, 2018). Yet their limitations were equally clear: even technically compliant projects often failed to eliminate overcrowding, and production volumes remained far below the needs of a rapidly growing urban population.

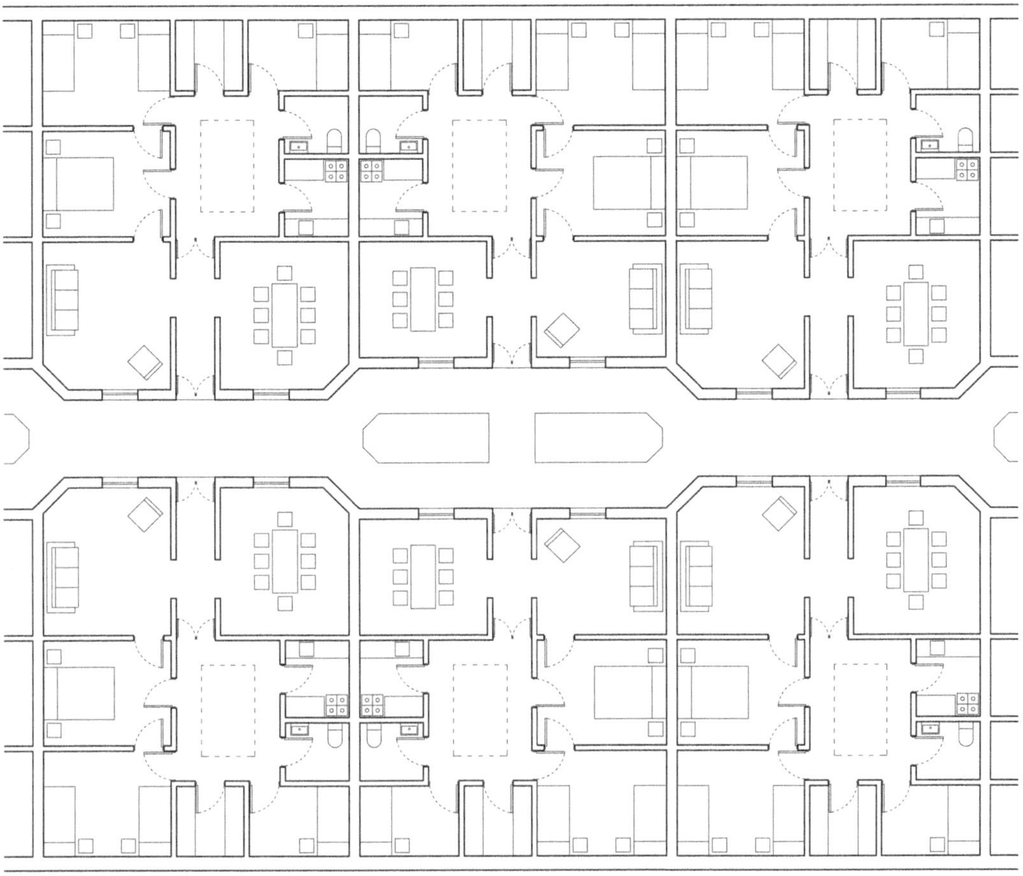

FIGURE 4.4 Cité Recreo (1906), illustrating the interior courtyard's dual role in organising housing and providing natural ventilation and light.

Source: Drawn by the author (2025).

1936–1964: Consolidation of the State in Housing Policy

The period from 1936 to 1964 was crucial in consolidating housing policies in Chile, marking a significant shift in how the state addressed the housing deficit. By the mid-1930s, the shortage of adequate housing had become a pressing national concern, affecting a large segment of the population. In this context, the establishment of the Caja de Habitación Popular (Popular Housing Fund) in 1936, a state agency created to finance and oversee the construction of low-cost housing for working-class families, marked a turning point. The institution played a key role in coordinating public housing efforts and establishing more detailed technical standards for residential construction (Hidalgo, 2000).

By the late 1936, the Caja de Habitación Popular had begun implementing its vision through model housing projects such as the Colectivo San Eugenio (1936) and Pasaje San Ignacio (1942) (Figures 4.6 and 4.7). In the former, these were blocks of flats housing multiple families, and

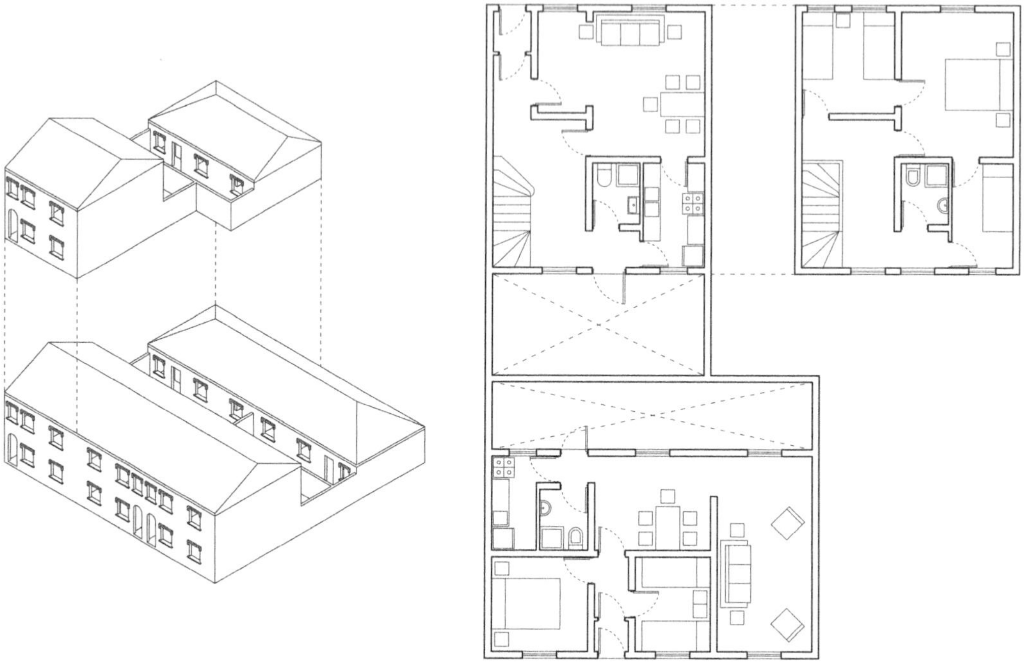

FIGURE 4.5 Conjunto Picarte (1925), exemplifying experimentation with one- and two-storey row housing, incorporating hygienist principles through patios functioning as service zones and for cross-ventilation.

Source: Adapted from Arancibia Tagle (2013).

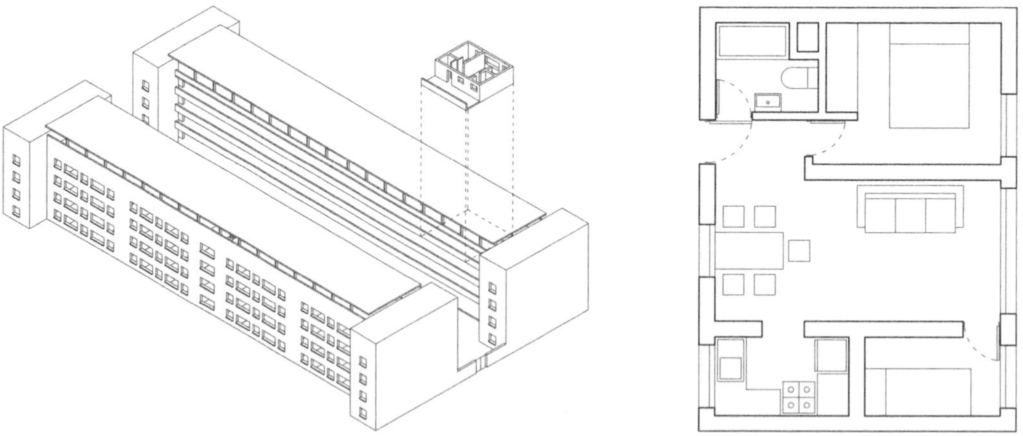

FIGURE 4.6 Colectivo San Eugenio (1936) is one of the first attempts to build mid-rise housing using the slab block typology, designed to maximise space and functionality within what the Caja de Habitacion Popular considered a minimum dwelling.

Source: Adapted from Arancibia Tagle (2017).

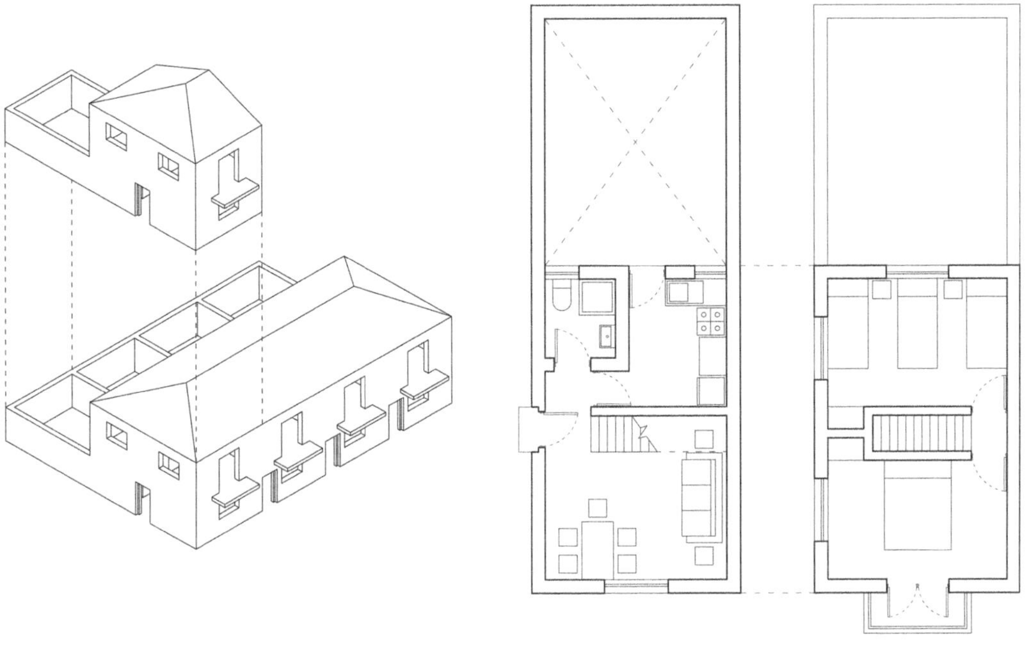

FIGURE 4.7 Pasaje San Ignacio (1942), an example of row housing designed to Caja de Habitación Popular standards. The project illustrates the pursuit of efficiency through minimal dimensions, guided by hygienist principles such as cross-ventilation and patios serving as a service zone.

Source: Adapted from Arancibia Tagle (2013).

in the latter, terraced houses, featuring units with individual bedrooms, integrated living–dining rooms, separate kitchens, cross-ventilation, and durable materials like fired brick – reflecting the functional and sanitary standards promoted by the Caja de Habitación Popular. Nonetheless, they largely catered to middle-income families and thus did not improve housing access for the most precarious parts of the population.

In 1948, the Ley Pereira (General Housing Law) expanded the provisions of the Caja de Habitación Popular by establishing more stringent regulations for housing construction. It introduced standards for minimum room and shared-area dimensions, and promoted the integration of communal spaces, such as green spaces and recreational amenities. These elements were incorporated more systematically into planned housing complexes that combined multi-family blocks with shared spaces to improve residents' quality of life. A notable example of this approach is Población Quebrada Márquez in Valparaíso (1949), which adopted block typologies that ensured cross-ventilation, used durable materials, and provided communal areas (Figure 4.8). Although the Ley Pereira represented an important advancement, its impact was limited by budgetary constraints that hindered the wider implementation of its provisions (Hidalgo, 2005).

The creation of the Corporación de la Vivienda (CORVI; Housing Corporation) in 1953 marked a shift towards the industrialisation of housing construction. The agency adopted modern, standardised construction methods to address the growing urban housing deficit. CORVI built approximately 25,000 low-cost housing units between 1953 and 1958, averaging around 4,100 units per year (Raposo, 1999). These homes featured significant improvements in construction materials,

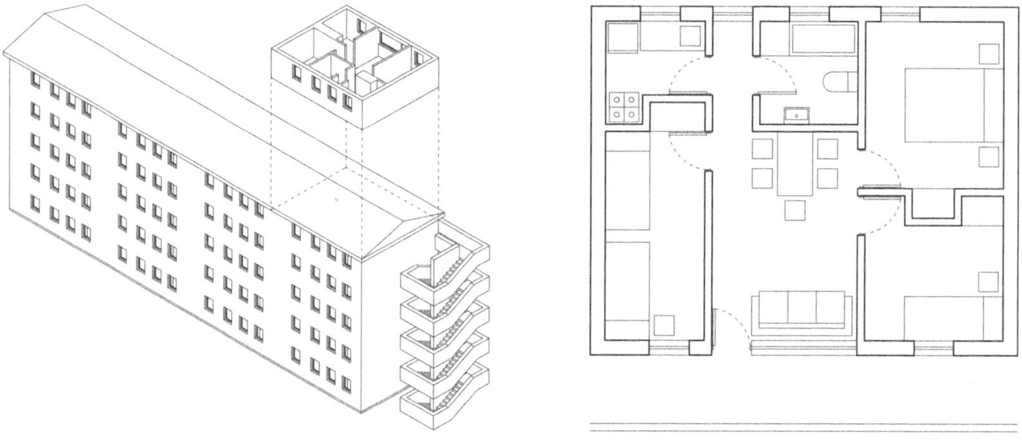

FIGURE 4.8 Población Quebrada Márquez (1949), exemplifying the period's pursuit of a functional floor plan with minimal dimensions, organised around a three-bedroom programme.

Source: Drawn by the author (2025).

such as reinforced concrete, which offered greater durability. Internal layouts also evolved, incorporating private kitchens and bathrooms, representing a major improvement over the shared facilities common in earlier decades. Such projects sought to optimise urban land use and improve access to basic services, contributing to more efficient housing design. A well-known example of this is Villa Portales, a large-scale housing complex built in Santiago during the 1950s, which exemplified CORVI's housing ambitions through the use of modern materials, rationalised mid-rise slab block layouts, and integrated public infrastructure (Figure 4.9).

In 1959, the Ley Sobre Habitaciones Económicas (Law on Low-Cost Housing Units) rationalised housing production for middle- and lower-middle income groups, offering tax and credit incentives for projects that met specific standards of cost, surface area, and habitability. For the first time, these standards codified a minimum housing programme that required at least two bedrooms per unit, along with a living–dining area, kitchen, and sanitary facilities (Ministerio de Obras Públicas, 1959). While the law allowed for single-family row houses and semi-detached units, it also promoted higher-density solutions, including multi-storey apartment blocks, to optimise land use and reduce per-unit construction costs. Typical dwellings ranged from 40 to 65 m^2, with two or three bedrooms, integrated living–dining areas, kitchens with cross-ventilation, and, in the case of houses, small backyards extending the living space outdoors. An example of this policy is Villa Frei in Santiago, which, unlike its predecessor, Villa Portales, combined mid-rise slab blocks with residential towers instead of row houses, marking a shift towards vertical density within an integrated neighbourhood plan (Figure 4.10).

However, despite progress in housing design regulation and construction during this period, the housing deficit remained a structural challenge. According to official estimates, Chile faced a shortage of approximately 140,000 housing units in the early 1950s – a figure that rose steadily throughout the decade (Instituto Nacional de Estadísticas [INE], 1952). By the early 1960s, the deficit was widely reported to exceed 400,000 units, reflecting not only the inadequacy of housing output but also the poor quality of much of the existing housing stock, as measured by overcrowding, precarious materials, and lack of basic services

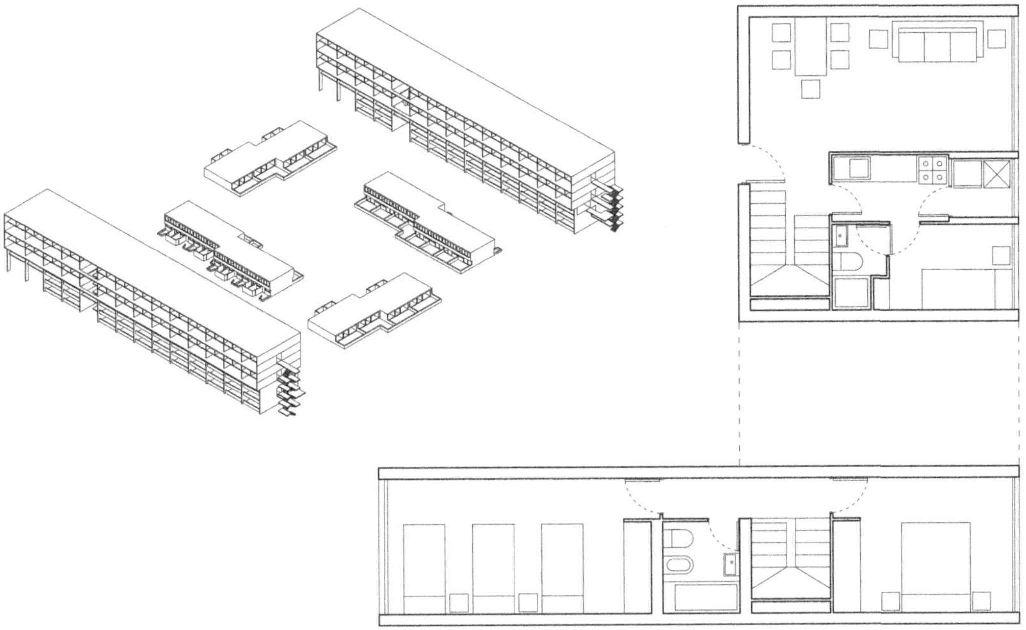

FIGURE 4.9 Villa Portales (1956–1966), one of CORVI's most emblematic projects, featuring large-scale slab blocks with duplex dwellings that included two formal bedrooms and a third bedroom next to the kitchen–laundry area.

Source: Adapted from Arancibia Tagle (2013).

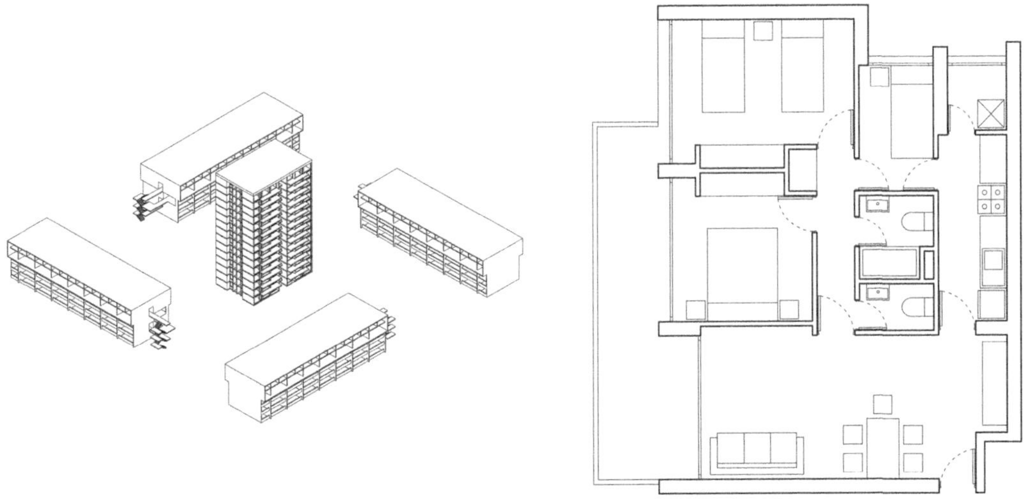

FIGURE 4.10 Villa Frei (1965–1968), an example of high-rise housing innovation. The standard tower floor plan includes three bedrooms, two bathrooms, and a kitchen integrated with a laundry area.

Source: Adapted from Arancibia Tagle (2013).

(Hidalgo, 2005). While middle-income groups benefited from the new housing standards and typologies, vulnerable social groups continued to face economic barriers, reinforcing housing inequalities (Arellano, 1985).

1965–1973: Self-help and Urban Renewal

From 1965 to 1973, Chile experienced rapid urban growth, exacerbating the existing housing shortage. According to estimates from the Corporación de la Vivienda, the housing shortfall exceeded 400,000 units by the early 1960s and was projected to surpass 500,000 by the end of the decade – equating approximately 30% of the national housing stock at the time (Hidalgo, 2005). While the 1960 census recorded a population of 7.4 million, this had increased to nearly 8.9 million by 1970, further intensifying pressure on urban infrastructure and housing supply (INE, 1970). During this period, housing programmes diversified in their approaches to address the shortfall. Operación Sitio (Plot Operation) introduced a more participatory model, enabling low-income families to secure serviced plots and progressively self-build their homes. By contrast, initiatives such as the Plan de Ahorro Popular (Popular Savings Plan) and projects by the Corporación de Mejoramiento Urbano (CORMU; Urban Improvement Corporation) relied on financial savings schemes and large-scale state-led developments. Despite their different logic, these policies shared an emphasis on design standardisation and the improvement of urban living conditions (Bruey, 2014).

Operación Sitio, launched in 1965 under the Eduardo Frei Montalva administration, was one of the most emblematic housing initiatives of the time. The programme provided urbanised plots of land to low-income families and promoted self-help housing through assisted self-construction, with the land sold at a very low cost through long-term subsidised loans. During its implementation, approximately 100,000 plots were allocated for urbanisation and construction, with a large proportion designated for self-built homes (Ministerio de Vivienda y Urbanismo [MINVU], 2005). The plots, averaging 162 m^2, included basic urban infrastructure such as streets, green areas, and community spaces. Although access to services like potable water and electricity was often limited, the model enabled families to build their homes according to their own means and needs.

Operación Sitio also established minimum urban development standards, including land levelling and plot demarcation. However, the quality of the homes built varied considerably, depending on a household's finances and access to technical advice. Architecturally, the programme led to a diversity of housing solutions, ranging from basic wooden structures to more elaborate brick constructions. Notable large-scale examples include Villa Francia (1969), built on extensive tracts of land provided by the state. In parallel, other initiatives pursued similar approaches, such as Villa La Reina (1966), a municipal programme that allocated serviced plots with the expectation of progressive self-construction (Figure 4.11). Although not formally part of Operación Sitio, Villa La Reina exemplified the same logic of rapid urban expansion, with minimal initial infrastructure, delegating much of the responsibility for the built environment to residents. While these strategies enabled many families to own land and their own home, inadequate infrastructure contributed to precarious living conditions for a substantial portion of the population. In Santiago alone, Operación Sitio allocated nearly 71,000 plots to more than 380,000 people between 1965 and 1970, yet many of these settlements lacked proper sanitation, paved roads, and access to public services, highlighting the limitations of a strategy focused primarily on land provision (Quintana, 2014).

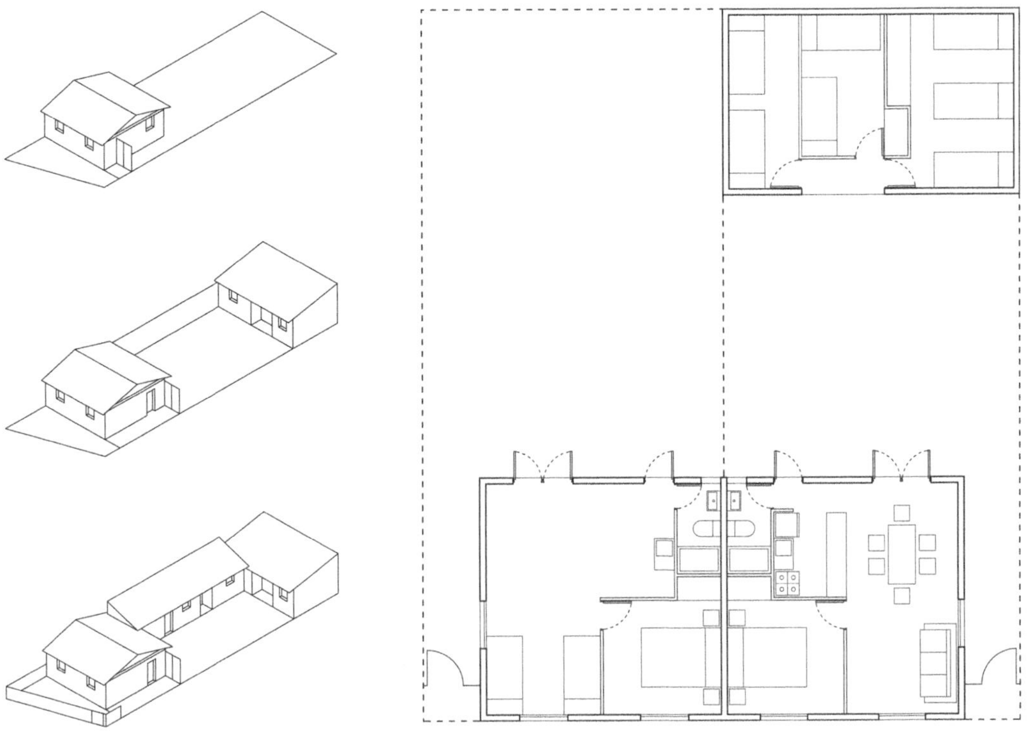

FIGURE 4.11 Standard housing solution in Villa La Reina (1967). The design strategy was based on an initial one-bedroom unit, with the remainder of the dwelling programme intended for incremental extensions by the inhabitants.

Sources: Axonometric projection from Francisco Quintana, "Urbanizando con tiza: Operación Sitio y Villa La Reina (1965–1970)" (2014). Floor plan drawn by the author, 2025.

The Plan de Ahorro Popular, implemented in the same decade, introduced a financing model that combined state subsidies with family savings to support homeownership. The programme subsidised the construction of approximately 60,000 homes during the 1960s, primarily targeting emerging middle-income groups (MINVU, 2004). Eligibility was based on enrolment in one of five savings plans, which required families to make a minimum of 20 monthly deposits – amounting to up to 20% of household income – at a time when many earned less than 100 USD per month (Biblioteca del Congreso Nacional de Chile, 2014). Applicants also had to demonstrate stable salaried employment and could not already own any property, reflecting a policy focus on disciplined saving as a pathway to homeownership. Beyond the financial mechanism, the programme sought to promote efficient, modestly sized dwellings that could accommodate a nuclear family while incorporating basic services and shared communal spaces. In doing so, it represented a shift towards more compact and standardised housing design compared to earlier decades. However, these stringent savings and employment requirements effectively excluded the most vulnerable households, which historically had been left out of previous homeownership schemes as well, thereby limiting the programme's redistributive impact (Castañeda & Quiroz, 1986).

Building on this, the concept of Vivienda Serializada (Serialized Housing) materialised through the testing of a catalogue of nearly 20 rationalised prototypes, ranging from one-storey

FIGURE 4.12 Examples of CORVI's serialised housing models (1966–1971): semi-detached houses (Model 136), slab block (Model 1010), and tower (Model 1050).

Source: Drawn by the author (2025).

semi-detached houses to four-storey slab blocks and even 15-storey towers (Montealegre et al., 2023) (Figure 4.12). Typically, between 50 and 70 m^2, these dwellings were conceived as compact yet efficient units for nuclear families, combining two or three bedrooms with a living–dining area, separate kitchen, and access to basic services and communal facilities.

Conceived as templates or type-solutions for large-scale replication, these models embodied the rationalisation of construction and the pursuit of economies of scale. The programme was not intended to produce a wide variety of housing types but rather to establish a limited catalogue of standardised options that could be reproduced across multiple sites, with only minor adjustments in layout or materials. This approach enabled CORVI and the Plan de Ahorro

Popular to reduce design costs, streamline construction processes, and accelerate delivery, establishing serialisation as a key tool for addressing the housing deficit. However, although presented as typologies that could be flexibly interpreted and adapted to different contexts, their structural, formal, and programmatic parameters were already tightly defined, which ultimately constrained the capacity of these dwellings to accommodate more diverse household structures or modes of inhabitation (Vergara et al., 2021). In this sense, the housing designs conceived under the influence of *Vivienda Serializada* illustrate both the promise and the limitation of typological replication: while it allowed housing production to scale up rapidly, it also reinforced a homogenisation of the built environment that left little room for variation in domestic life.

Meanwhile, CORMU, a government body established in 1965, led urban renewal and collective housing projects, achieving unprecedented housing output. During Salvador Allende's administration (1970–1973), CORMU intensified its efforts, building around 52,000 homes annually, with a peak of 89,000 units in 1971 (INE, 1971; Lawner, 2023; MINVU, 2023). Inspired by the principles of the Modern Movement, CORMU promoted industrialised construction and integrated urban planning. Its developments included apartment blocks and high-rise towers ranging from four to 20 storeys, with dwellings typically between 40 and 65 m^2. These homes had efficient internal layouts prioritising natural ventilation and lighting.

Such housing programmes predominantly supported homeownership rather than rental housing, reflecting a long-standing policy preference in Chile. Despite the absence of a formal or mandatory design standard, CORMU established precedents through pilot projects, developing its own design guidelines for dwellings, residential complexes, and urban spaces (Demiddel et al., 2023). These projects presented exemplar typologies that could be replicated or adapted across multiple locations. These guidelines aimed to promote socially cohesive urban development, with a focus on maximising urban density and access to essential services. Projects included green areas, recreational spaces, and community facilities such as schools and health centres – representing significant progress in integrating housing with the urban environment. An emblematic example of this vision was Remodelación San Borja in Santiago (1968–1975), composed of high-rise residential towers of around 20 storeys above continuous commercial and service podiums (Figure 4.13). The project integrated elevated pedestrian walkways, extensive communal areas, and public facilities, illustrating CORMU's modernist approach to combining high-density housing with a network of open spaces and urban amenities. However, as in previous periods, these housing initiatives continued to serve middle-income groups, leaving the needs of the most vulnerable unmet (Anguita & Becerra Ibañez, 2024).

As was also the case in previous eras, the housing deficit remained a structural problem, despite these advances. By the late 1960s, the shortall had risen to approximately 600,000 homes – around 40% of the national housing stock – driven by rapid urban migration and insufficient housing supply (Pugh et al., 1970). While the housing programmes during this period improved housing supply and design standards, budgetary constraints and unequal resource distribution continued to perpetuate housing inequalities across socio-economic groups.

1973–1989: Implementation of the Neoliberal Housing Model

In Chile, the neoliberal model fundamentally transformed housing policy, radically altering both the provision and role of housing itself. Introduced during Augusto Pinochet's military dictatorship, the model shifted responsibility from the state to individual households and the market, embracing privatisation, subsidiarity, and free-market competition as guiding principles of

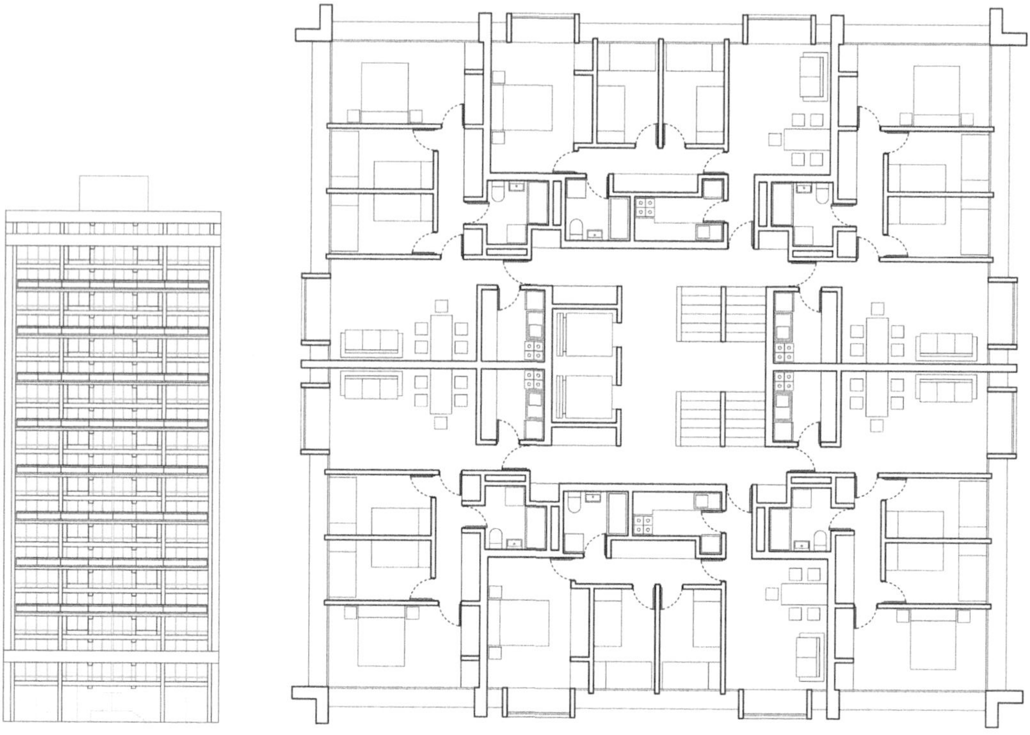

FIGURE 4.13 Remodelación San Borja (1968–1975) was originally planned as a complex of 28 20–22-storey residential towers, with six units of approximately 70 m^2 per floor, comprising three bedrooms and one bathroom.

Source: Drawn by the author (2025).

public policy, including housing. While this represented a radical break with the state-led construction programmes of the 1960s, it also built on earlier experiments such as Operación Sitio, which had already delegated part of the responsibility for housing provision to families through progressive self-construction. The pivotal moment in this transformation was the introduction of the first demand-side housing subsidy programme in 1977, which replaced state-led supply with subsidy provisions, laying the foundation for a market-oriented housing system (Ross & Pelletiere, 2014).

The implementation of the neoliberal housing model emerged in response to an intensifying housing crisis (Kusnetzoff, 1974). By 1974, authorities estimated a national housing deficit of nearly 1 million units – almost double the late-1960s estimate of around 500,000 – prompting the adoption of subsidy-based, market-driven housing policies (Koppelman, 2018). This dramatic increase reflected not only rapid urban growth but also the failure of previous state-led housing policies to meet the needs of the most vulnerable. Against this backdrop, the neoliberal model sought to restructure Chile's housing system, redefining the roles of the state and the market.

The neoliberal approach to housing in Chile first introduced at this time is based on the idea that supply and demand should be primarily regulated by the market. The state assumes a subsidiary role, intervening only in cases of market failure and limiting its role to providing demand-side subsidies for the most vulnerable. This strategy aims to reduce the housing deficit while minimising the government's responsibility for direct housing provision or long-term management. Housing at this point in time was reconceptualised as a consumer good and a tool for individual wealth accumulation, rather than as a social right or a component of collective well-being (Gil, 2015; Inter-American Development Bank, 2004).

The neoliberal housing model in Chile was structured around four core principles (Atria, 2013). First, housing supply was to be met by the private sector through free-market competition, eliminating the state's role as a direct provider. Second, homeownership was prioritised over rental housing, promoting property as a form of personal economic security. Third, the principle of subsidiarity guided state policy, with government intervention restricted to housing subsidies for vulnerable populations. Finally, the deregulation of planning and design standards aimed to accommodate subsidy constraints, ensure developer profitability, and facilitate mass housing construction.

Although these principles were consolidated during the Pinochet dictatorship, the preference for homeownership had deeper roots. Since the 1950s, public programmes had favoured individual ownership as a tool for social stability and a way to reduce long-term state obligations, thereby laying the groundwork for the later market-based housing policies. Initiatives such as the creation of CORVI in 1953 and Operación Sitio in the late 1960s explicitly promoted homeownership over rental models, reflecting a bipartisan consensus on the social value of owner-occupied housing. Under the neoliberal framework, subsidies supported access to mortgages, not rental alternatives, enabling thousands of families to purchase homes while excluding lower-income groups.

This neoliberal shift was reinforced by the 1979 Política Nacional de Desarrollo Urbano (Urban Development Policy), which declared urban land a non-scarce resource, encouraging expansive real estate development. The new regulatory framework enabled a proliferation of housing projects on the urban periphery, where land was cheaper but often lacked infrastructure and services (Barton & Ramírez, 2019). These large-scale developments prioritised low-cost housing supply over quality, further exacerbating urban segregation (Figure 4.14).

A representative example of this was the Programa de Vivienda Básica (Basic Housing Programme), launched in 1976. It provided homes with a minimum floor area of 24 m^2, designed to be extended by residents themselves through self-construction over time (Figure 4.15). Built on 9 × 18 m plots, this model minimised cost and allowed for future additions. However, the approach shifted responsibility for development onto individual households, exacerbating inequalities both in construction quality and in liveability, due to disparities in technical expertise, access to materials, and finances. The initial dwellings were often too small and lacked thermal comfort and adequate services.

While comparable to Operación Sitio of 1965 in its provision of urbanised land for self-construction, the Programa de Vivienda Básica introduced a critical innovation in 1984: the Cuadro Normativo de Espacios Mínimos para el Mobiliario (Minimum Space Standards for Furniture Framework) (Figure 4.16). These standards established minimum interior dimensions for bedrooms, bathrooms, and common areas, based on standard furniture sizes and room functions. Beyond its technical aspects, the Cuadro Normativo defined a conventional home and standard functional dwelling programme, including one bedroom, a bathroom, and a combined living–dining–kitchen area, with the possibility of adding two further bedrooms over time. However, as with Operación Sitio, the incremental nature of this programme meant that the eventual quality of housing varied greatly, depending on household income and resources. As a result, inequalities among new homeowners translated into significant differences in housing quality.

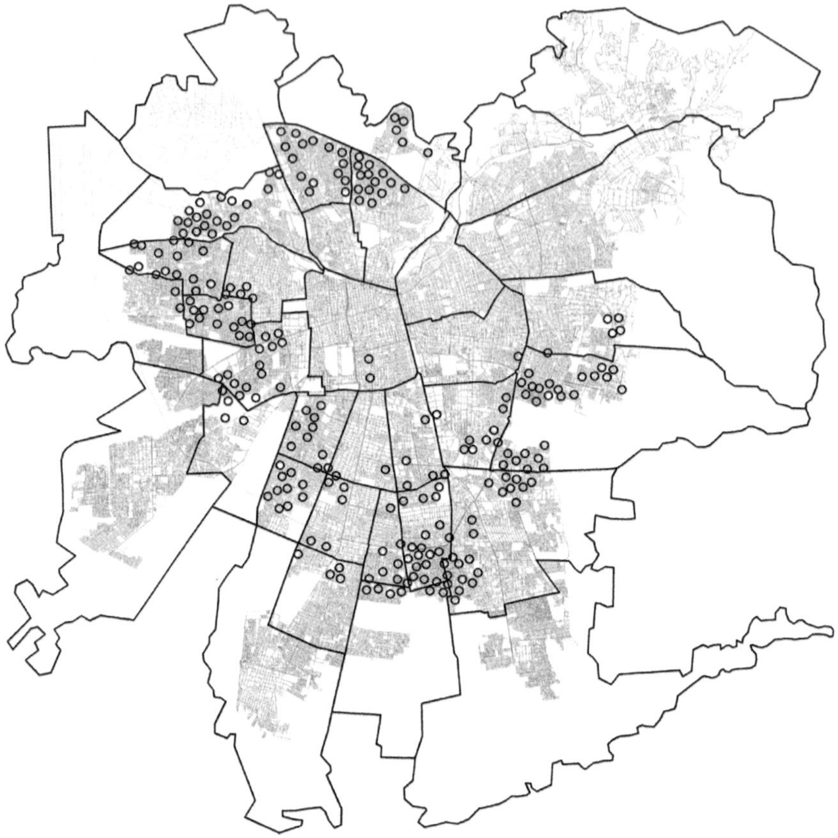

FIGURE 4.14 Location of subsidised low-income housing built between 1979 and 1989.
Source: Arancibia Tagle (2017).

The Cuadro Normativo became the blueprint for calculating minimum dwelling sizes and developing design guidelines for subsidised housing (Jacoby et al., 2022). Although reviewed and adapted over time, it remains influential today. As a regulatory tool, it served as a prototype for subsequent housing standards, aiming to address habitability challenges more systematically. However, while reflecting an effort to optimise and rationalise domestic space, it also highlighted the tensions inherent in a cost-constrained system. The objective was not to improve housing quality comprehensively, but rather to meet quantitative targets within tight budgets. This placed the burden of completion and improvement on homeowners, reinforcing a progressive housing model that expanded access while maintaining inequalities tied to household incomes.

This basic neoliberal housing model epitomised a minimalist approach that could be read in two ways. One interpretation is the provision of the bare minimum for physical survival and basic habitability, addressing only fundamental functional and biological needs. The other envisions housing as encompassing the necessary conditions for a normal social life, including sociability, flexibility of use, privacy, and individual expression. In practice, Chile's neoliberal model conformed almost exclusively to the first interpretation. This corresponded to what Karel Teige termed the "utilitarian minimum": housing reduced to its most elementary functional

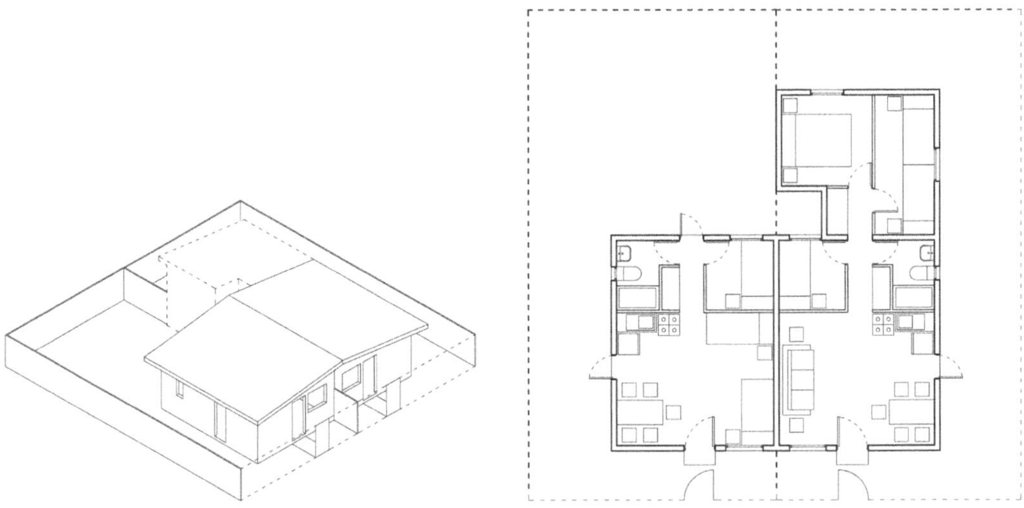

FIGURE 4.15 Example of a semi-detached house on a 9 × 18 m lot, the standard provision by the Programa de Vivienda Básica. The initial design included a single bedroom, with the rest of the dwelling intended for future extensions by residents.

Source: Adapted from Arancibia Tagle (2017).

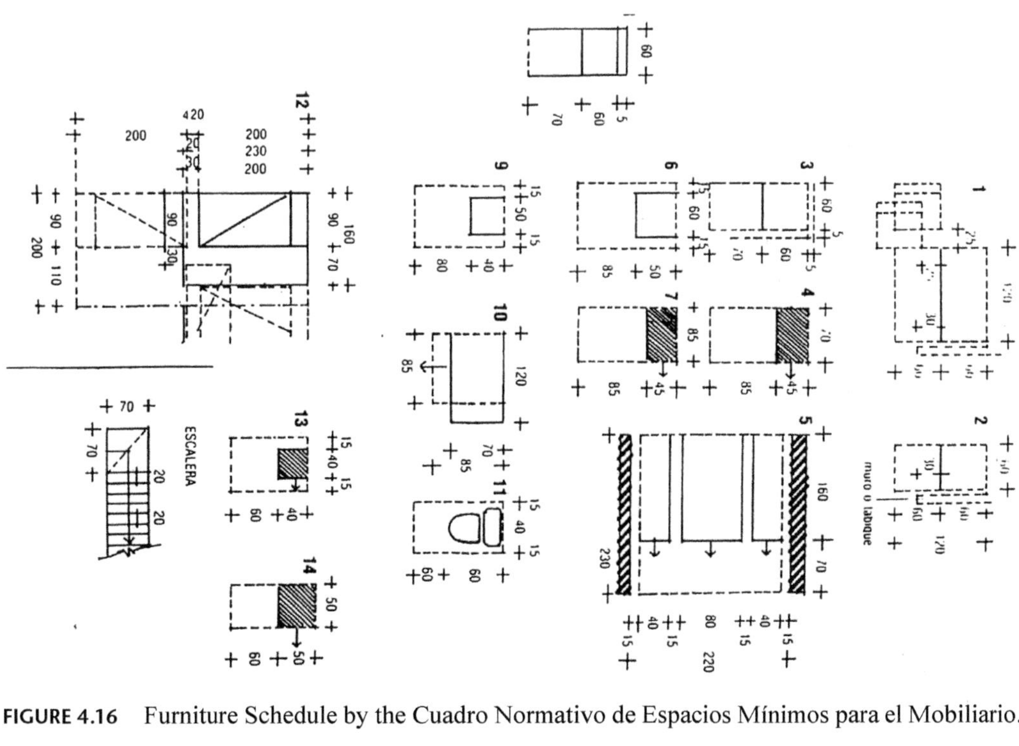

FIGURE 4.16 Furniture Schedule by the Cuadro Normativo de Espacios Mínimos para el Mobiliario.

Source: MINVU (1984).

requirements for human survival, while neglecting the broader social, psychological, and cultural dimensions of domestic life (Teige, 2002).

Another key component of the neoliberal housing model was the Saneamiento de Lotes (Lot Regularisation Strategy), which complemented formal housing programmes by allocating *casetas sanitarias* (sanitary cabins). This policy provided families with a serviced plot and a minimal masonry core containing a bathroom and kitchen, requiring the residents to self-construct the remaining living areas (Figure 4.17). These plots were part of rudimentary urban layouts, typically including dirt roads, basic electricity connections, and limited access to potable water. Designed for households in situations of extreme vulnerability, these units were conceived as the initial infrastructure upon which a future dwelling could be progressively built. As an emergency-oriented solution, they were exempt from meeting the space standards defined in the Cuadro Normativo. However, making them permanent depended on the financial means and time of households, once again reinforcing socio-economic inequalities.

The neoliberal model dramatically increased housing supply. In the 1980s, Chile built an average of 80,000 new homes annually (Rodríguez & Sugranyes, 2005). However, these gains came at a significant social and urban cost. Mass housing construction in urban peripheries reinforced patterns of urban segregation that persist to this day. These new developments often lacked public services, including transportation, schools, and healthcare facilities. The absence of mixed-use infrastructure further limited economic and social opportunities in these communities.

While housing supply increased, many homes failed to meet adequate housing standards, negatively affecting quality of life for thousands of families (Cortés-Urra et al., 2023). From a regulatory perspective, housing policy mirrored the constraints of the neoliberal model. Large-scale construction focused on reducing the housing deficit, but at the expense of long-term liveability and housing quality (Gil, 2019).

The promotion of homeownership as the dominant tenure model has had a lasting impact on Chile's social and urban fabric. The use of housing subsidies reinforced the belief that individual

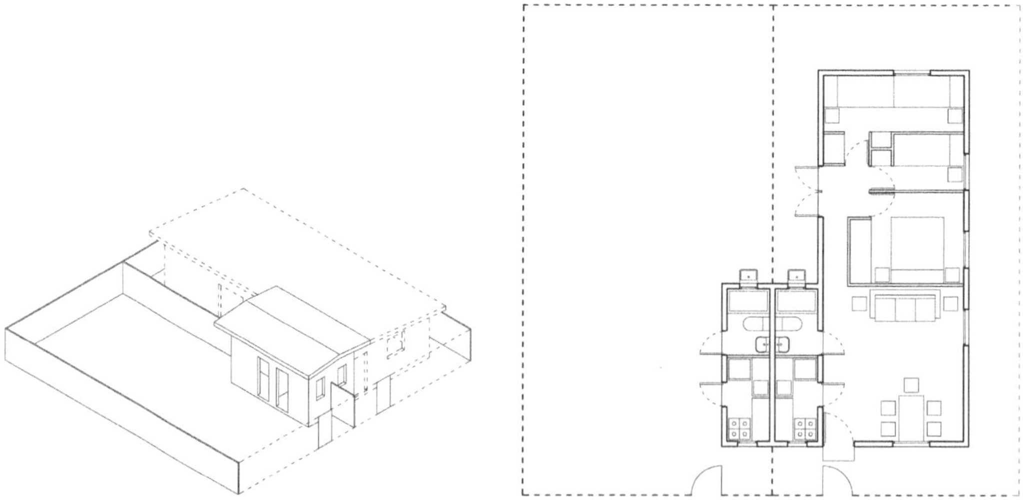

FIGURE 4.17 Example of a *cabina sanitara,* providing only a bathroom and kitchen, with the rest of the dwelling to be completed through future extensions by residents.

Source: Adapted from Arancibia Tagle (2017).

ownership is the most legitimate form of housing, stigmatising rental or collective housing alternatives (Beswick et al., 2019). This created a housing system favouring economic efficiency over equity and quality of life, leaving the most vulnerable populations underserved and widening socio-economic divisions. This legacy of segregation, precarity, and inequality has continued into subsequent decades.

1990–2002: Neoliberal Continuity and Incremental Housing

Building on the neoliberal principles established during the Pinochet dictatorship, Chile made significant progress in reducing its housing shortage between 1990 and 2002. Though official statistics suggested that the deficit had fallen to around 600,000 units by the late 1980s, alternative estimates placed it at over 900,000 in the early 1990s, reflecting broader definitions that included qualitative deficits such as overcrowding and inadequate services (Rodríguez & Sugranyes, 2005; Rojas, 1999; United Nations, 2018). Addressing these challenges required a partial rethinking of the inherited neoliberal framework.

The housing policy of this period maintained several key neoliberal principles, particularly the emphasis on privatisation and subsidiarity (Greene, 2004; Navarro, 2005). First, housing provision remained almost entirely in the hands of the private sector, with the state assuming only a regulatory and facilitatory role, mainly through the allocation of subsidies to low-income families. Second, homeownership continued to be prioritised over alternative forms of tenure, reinforcing the notion that securing housing was an individual responsibility, albeit one supported by public housing programmes. Third, design standards remained minimal to contain construction costs and maximise housing production, a factor which perpetuated disparities in quality and liveability.

The most prominent policy instrument of this era was the Programa de Vivienda Progresiva (Progressive Housing Programme), which offered an initial, minimal housing solution for families classified as vulnerable based on criteria such as income, housing conditions, and eligibility for social benefits. The programme provided an initial dwelling of 36 m^2, with the expectation that families would progressively expand and improve their homes over time. As an evolution of the earlier Programa de Vivienda Básica, it offered beneficiaries an urbanised plot equipped with basic services – including potable water, sewerage, and electricity – and a core housing unit typically comprising one bedroom, a bathroom, a kitchen, and a multifunctional space.

While earlier programmes had also delivered urbanised plots, the Programa de Vivienda Progresiva stood out for its effort to eradicate *campamentos* (informal settlements), where residents often lacked basic sanitation infrastructure. Thus, in addition to reducing the housing deficit, the programme aimed to improve public health and living conditions by relocating families to urbanised environments and encouraging their active participation in the incremental development of their homes.

The dominant housing typology of the Programa de Vivienda Progresiva was a two-storey row house, which typically featured a small front garden and backyard, providing space for future extensions (Figure 4.18).

These developments resembled terraced housing, laid out in a linear configuration. In parallel, particularly between 1995 and 2000, new housing typologies emerged, most notably *bloques tijera* (scissor blocks), used in larger-scale, higher-density housing projects. These three- to four-storey housing blocks offered compact flats that maximised land use for low-income families – typically not exceeding 40 m^2 (Figure 4.19). However, their rigid design

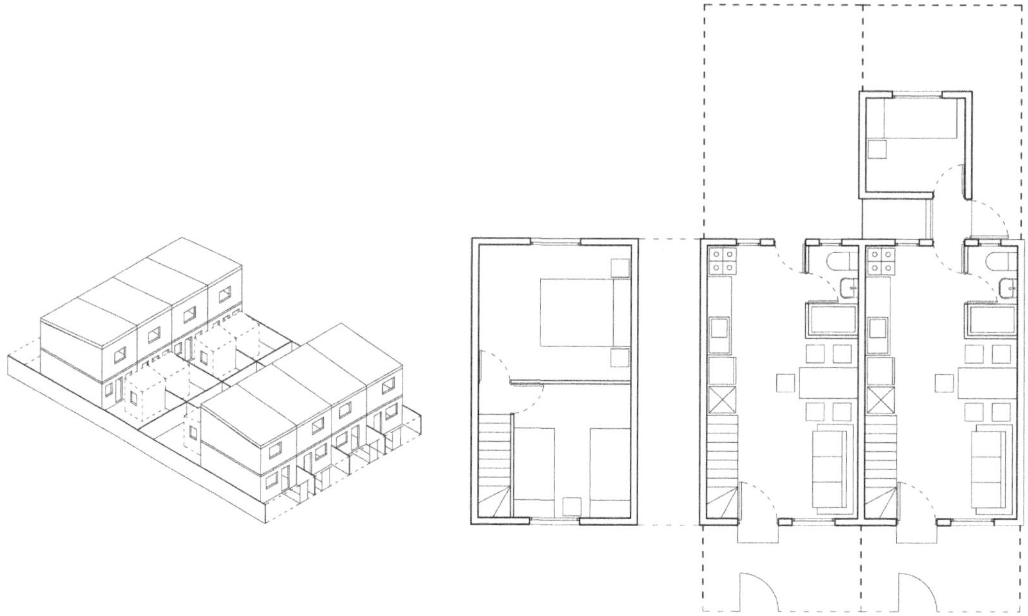

FIGURE 4.18 Example of a row housing typology developed between 1990 and 1995, originally conceived as a two-bedroom unit with provision for a rear-yard extension to add a third bedroom.

Source: Adapted from Arancibia Tagle (2013).

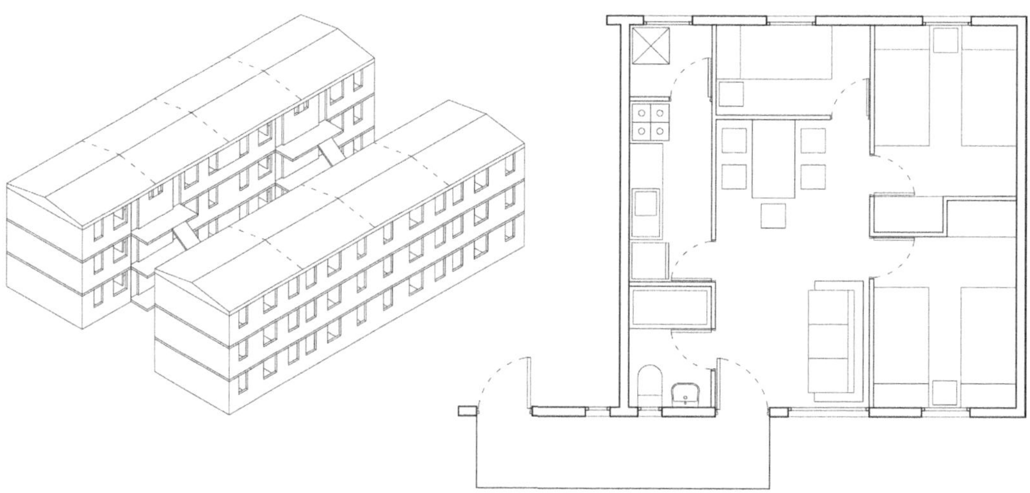

FIGURE 4.19 Example of a *bloque tijera* and a typical three-bedroom unit plan.

Source: Adapted from Arancibia Tagle (2013).

limited adaptability to evolving household needs, leading residents to extend their homes informally to the detriment of the building's appearance, safety, and functionality (Aravena & Iacobelli, 2012).

Although formal housing access increased significantly during this period, the subsidy- and self-construction-based model reinforced a new understanding of poverty (Rodríguez & Sugranyes, 2005). Many families, though no longer homeless, continued to experience housing precarity due to the peripheral location of many projects, which hindered access to essential services, employment, and public transport. Moreover, the initial housing units were often too small and constructed with low-quality, inexpensive materials that compromised durability and comfort.

The urban impact of these policies was also significant. The urban sprawl, driven by the extensive development of large-scale urbanised plots, entrenched patterns of spatial segregation that prevented the socio-economic integration of new neighbourhoods (Vargas, 2006). These areas were characterised by the uniformity of housing and a lack of commercial, social, and communal infrastructures, further isolating residents and reinforcing social exclusion.

Between 1990 and 2002, over 800,000 small housing units were built, outpacing the rate of new household formation and reducing the housing deficit to fewer than 500,000 units by the end of the decade (Gilbert, 2004). This was achieved through highly standardised construction processes, the use of low-cost materials, and the mobilisation of substantial state subsidies. However, this did not translate into a commensurate improvement in quality of life. Many households continued to face issues related to their homes' poor construction quality and suburban location (Figure 4.20). The rapid delivery of homeownership, while politically and statistically effective, masked the precarious conditions under which many families continued to live – highlighting the contradiction between owning a house and enjoying a dignified standard of living (Rodríguez & Sugranyes, 2005; Vargas, 2006).

2003–2010: Debate on Housing Quality, Size, and Density

Between 2003 and 2010, Chile experienced an important shift in housing policy, characterised by a reassessment of prior strategies and an intense debate surrounding the quality, density, and location of subsidised housing. This transformation was driven by a growing recognition of the limitations of the previous housing model, which had created extensive urban segregation and poor-quality homes (Caldera Sánchez, 2012). As a result, much of the debate focused on dwelling size, while equally important concerns, such as design standards, urban density, and spatial integration, were often overlooked (Hidalgo, 2019).

By 2002, the housing shortage still affected over 400,000 families, and past advances in housing supply had failed to address deeper structural issues (Hofmann & Ospina, 2010). For instance, the *bloques tijera* were increasingly criticised for their rigid design, which often led to low-quality informal flat extensions, physical deterioration, and social stigmatisation (Muñoz, 2011).

In response, Alejandro Aravena and his architecture studio Elemental emerged in 2003 as influential voices in the housing debate. They argued that the challenge was not merely addressing the insufficient minimum dwelling size, but also of density and how future expansions were planned (Aravena & Iacobelli, 2012). Their incremental housing model proposed that homes be designed to anticipate expansions, ensuring that future modifications could be seamlessly integrated into the original building structure, thereby avoiding the informality observed in the

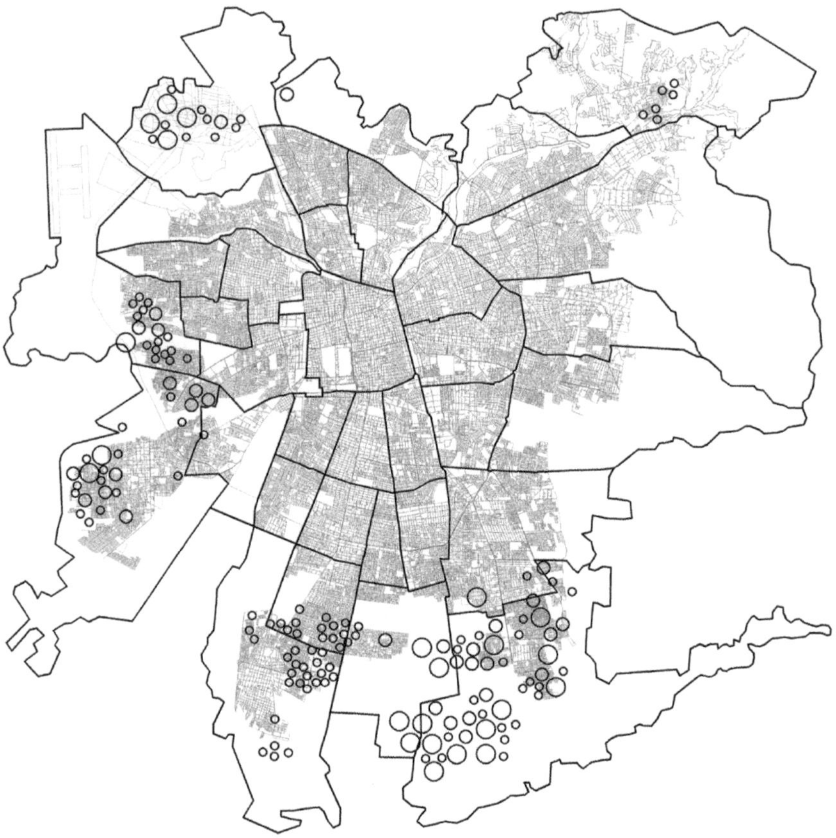

FIGURE 4.20 Location of subsidised low-income housing built between 1990 and 2000.

Source: Arancibia Tagle (2017).

Vivienda Progresiva's row houses and *bloques tijera* (Figure 4.21). This approach redefined the logic of subsidised housing, offering a design model that balanced design flexibility and quality without substantially increasing cost.

Elemental's incremental housing model proposed constructing only 50% of the final home, including essential elements such as a kitchen, bathroom, and structural framework, while leaving space for families to complete the rest in their own time. Although framed as an innovation, this principle of incremental expansion was not new: earlier programmes such as Operación Sitio and the Vivienda Básica had already relied on progressive self-construction to achieve a complete dwelling. What Elemental put forward was instead a new architectural wager: to create a more robust framework for incremental growth and to test whether such a model could be combined with higher densities. In practice, this took the form of three-storey designs with shared courtyards and modular façades that included completed sections for the initial half-house and open sections for future expansions (Figure 4.22). The underlying proposition was that density and design flexibility could coexist, reducing land costs and enabling the eventual provision of larger homes within the subsidy framework (Aravena & Iacobelli, 2012). However, this hypothesis remained largely theoretical, since the idea that incremental housing could be

FIGURE 4.21 A typical informal dwelling extension to a *bloque tijera*.

Source: Photograph by the author (2021).

viable and scalable at higher densities was never empirically demonstrated, and the model ultimately lacked replicability.

The reconfiguration of incremental housing sparked a wider critical debate about the minimum dwelling size and what should constitute an acceptable standard for subsidised housing (Carrasco & O'Brien, 2022). On the one hand, there was broad consensus on the need to increase space standards to ensure dignified living conditions. On the other, the architectural indeterminacy of incremental housing was questioned, with some arguing that larger, more complete, and conventional housing units could better meet common family needs, offering a formal final configuration and acceptable-quality materials, given that users often extend their houses in a chaotic and precarious manner (Figure 4.23).

This debate culminated in 2005 with the DS174 Programme and its Cuadro Normativo para el Programa Arquitectónico Mínimo y Mobiliario (Normative Framework for the Minimum Architectural Programme and Furniture), which established a new standard for subsidised housing (MINVU, 2005). It increased the minimum initial floor area from 24 to 45 m^2, with provisions for an additional 10 m^2 for future expansion, significantly surpassing the 1984 standards. It also defined a basic functional dwelling programme consisting of at least two bedrooms, one bathroom, a kitchen, and a living–dining area, with a possible third bedroom to be added later. These improvements responded to calls for more adequate spatial provisions, though they also reinforced the social norm of the nuclear family (Figure 4.24).

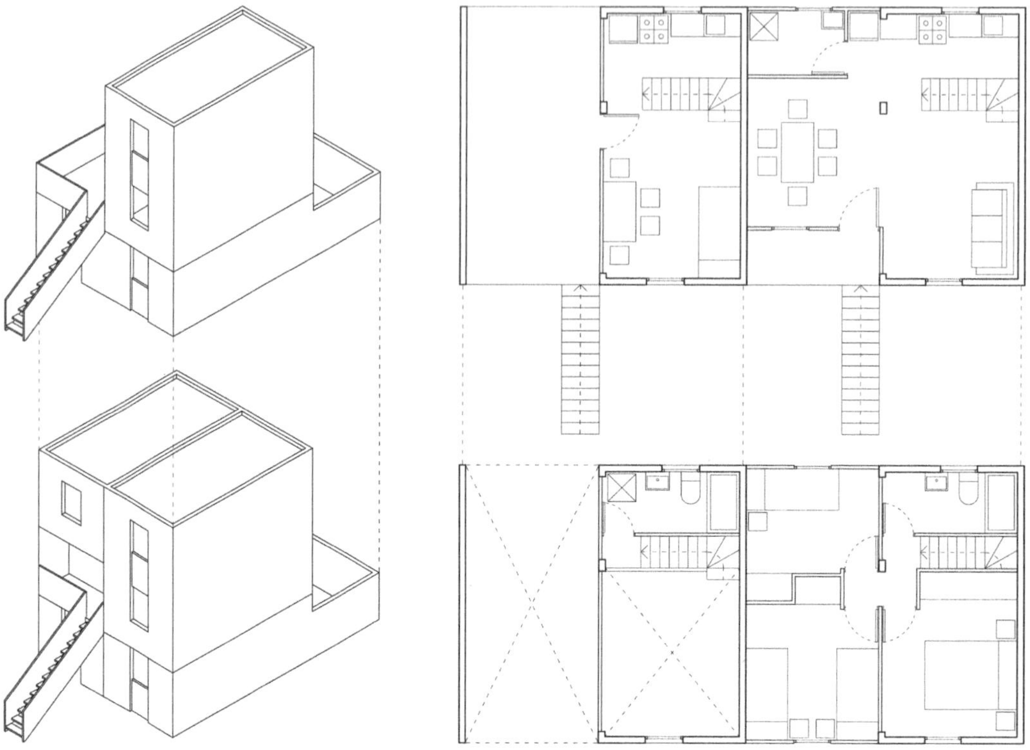

FIGURE 4.22 Quinta Monroy by Elemental Architects (2003), a half-house scheme, designed as an expandable framework for extension into a conventional three-bedroom house.

Source: Adapted from Arancibia Tagle (2013).

The new regulations introduced standards not only for space and layout but also for material quality and design, with the aim of improving daily living conditions. It thus tried to address both the technical–spatial aspects of housing and the social and familial dynamics that shape home life (López & Correa, 2007).

Despite these advances, a key issue remained unresolved: the delivery of subsidised housing at higher densities in central urban areas with high land prices. The lack of subsidised housing in central areas continued to perpetuate spatial and socio-economic segregation. This peripheralisation was due to limited subsidies, which made acquiring well-located urban land for development in a competitive market unviable.

The approval of the Cuadro Normativo by the DS174 programme brought an improvement in housing standards, both in terms of minimum surface areas and in a more demanding dwelling programme. However, the fundamental challenge of financing more centrally located land persisted. This limitation undermined the programme's effectiveness, as it continued to rely on the incremental house, a typology intrinsically tied to low-rise, ground-based solutions. Such a model proved inadequate for accommodating higher-density schemes capable of offsetting the costs of central urban sites. As a result, the most common architectural response to DS174 took the form of three-storey houses, typically located in peripheral urban areas due to land cost constraints. Even Elemental adapted their "half-house" scheme to this, reinterpreting it within

FIGURE 4.23 Images of the Quinta Monroy Housing Project by Elemental Architects (2003), showing how residents extend their homes beyond the original design vision.

Source: Courtesy of Cristóbal Palma (2021).

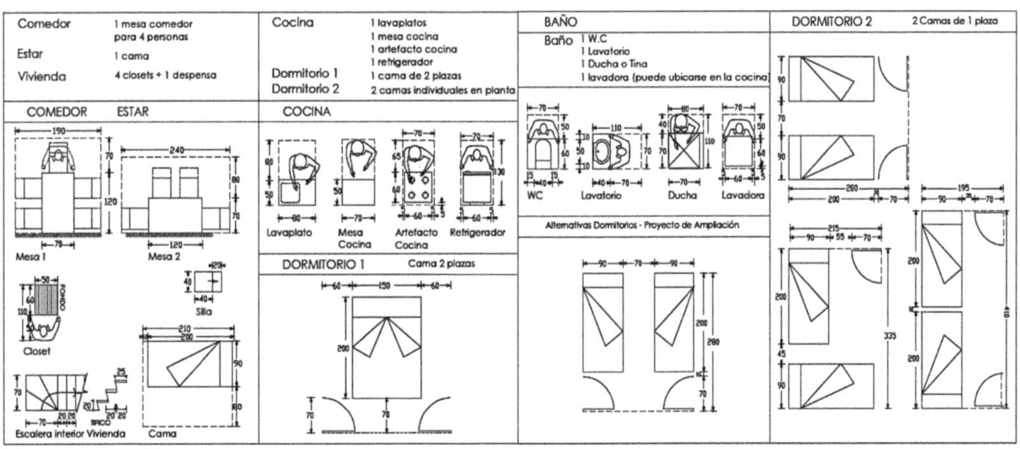

FIGURE 4.24 Furniture Schedule by the Reglamento Fondo Solidario de Vivienda: Cuadro Normativo D.S. 174.

Source: MINVU (2005).

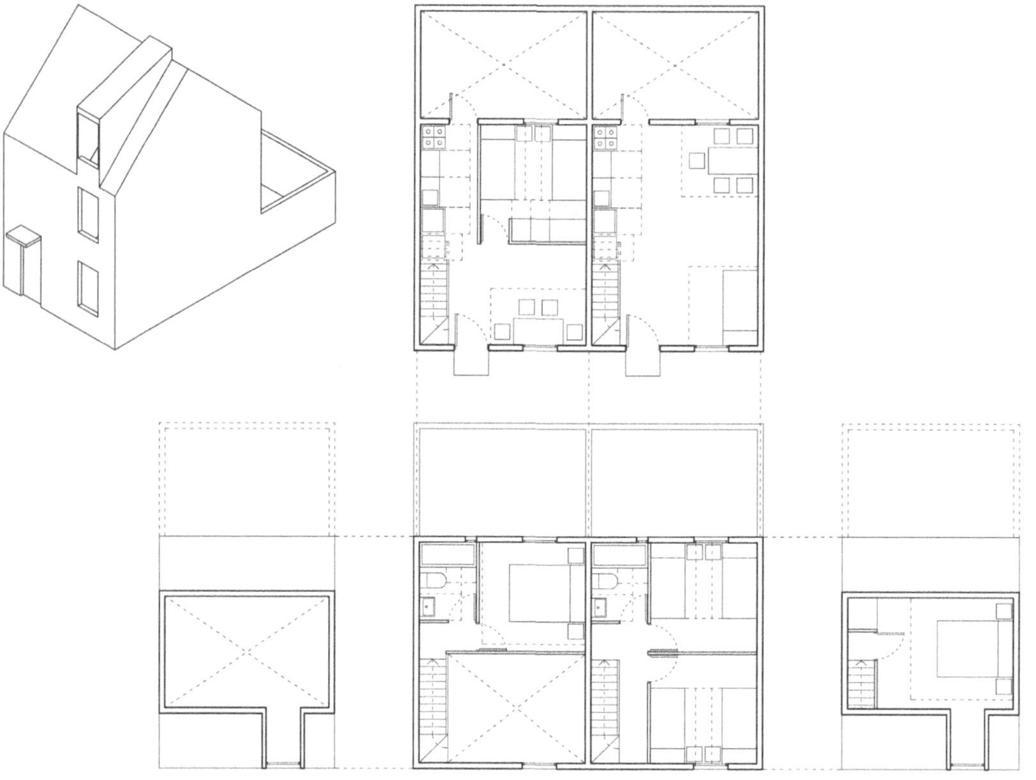

FIGURE 4.25 Lo Barnechea by Elemental Architects (2008), a three-storey row house allowing interior extensions.

Source: Adapted from Arancibia Tagle (2013).

a three-storey row house in which the upper levels were left as unfinished voids, allowing for the later construction of two additional bedrooms on the second and third floors, thus illustrating the persistence of the incremental approach despite the updated regulatory framework (Figure 4.25).

The only way to secure central sites was through its donation by municipalities or foundations, or by obtaining financing beyond the housing subsidy. Within this framework of external funding, Elemental's projects were no exception, as they too relied on a combination of public land contributions and supplementary resources (Carrasco & O'Brien, 2022). While the cost-saving argument centred on reducing construction costs, the overall viability of such projects ultimately depended on these additional sources of land and funding.

Despite the challenges in implementing the DS174 programme, by the early 2010s the government considered the housing shortage in Santiago nearly resolved, though housing policy based on incremental construction had proven inefficient (MINVU, 2013). The housing deficit had again reached approximately 500,000 units by 2010, and despite innovations in design and standards, Chilean policy continued to fall short in addressing urban segregation (Montgomery, 2022). Structural inequalities and persistent problems with housing quality remained major barriers to achieving more equitable and sustainable housing outcomes.

2011–2025: Consolidation of Housing Standards and Social Integration Policies

By 2011, the rising housing deficit in Chile underscored the need to re-evaluate national housing strategies. Growing housing demand – fuelled by population growth, changing household structures, and increased migration – outpaced housing supply and was exacerbated by decades of poorly planned urban expansion (Silva & Vergara-Perucich, 2021). The crisis also exposed the limitations of a housing approach that failed to meet the needs of both low- and middle-income households. Vulnerable populations faced financial barriers and limited access to subsidies, while middle-income families were often excluded from support, despite lacking the resources to secure adequate housing on their own.

This situation therefore called for a more inclusive and diversified policy framework aimed not only at housing supply but also at building more desirable and centrally located housing, with a balanced focus on densification, social integration, and improved quality of life (OECD, 2023). This re-evaluation required an updated regulatory framework and stronger incentives, particularly through differentiated subsidies that acknowledged the varied economic realities of Chilean families (Salvi del Pero, 2016). It was also essential to adopting an understanding of housing not only in physical terms but also as a key component of social cohesion and sustainable urban development – one capable of responding to aspirations for inclusion and well-being in an increasingly diverse society.

The persistent shortcomings of the incremental housing model further underscored the need for a different approach to subsidised housing production, particularly the need to build at higher densities of four storeys or more, where incremental self-construction was no longer viable (Jacoby et al., 2022). Therefore, the minimum housing provision shifted to fully completed homes, moving away from past incremental housing models.

This shift toward higher-density housing aligned with a broader reassessment of housing policy, which had evolved over nearly three decades of mass housing production under a demand-side subsidy model (Cortés-Urra et al., 2023). Since its first implementation in 1977, the state had invested nearly 4 billion USD in low-cost housing subsidies, amounting to approximately 0.5% of Chile's GDP annually – placing the country among the highest per capita investors in housing subsidies in Latin America (OECD, 2023; Gilbert, 2004). However, a government evaluation in the 2010s found that nearly 40% of the housing delivered to low-income families between the 1980s and early 2000s required demolition or major renovation, at an estimated cost of up to seven times the original subsidy (Secretaría Técnica Presidencial, 2005). These homes were described as deteriorated, obsolete, too small, and in need of large-scale urban regeneration or replacement (MINVU, 2014). This was particularly problematic, as most were privately owned, limiting direct state intervention. In response, the government implemented targeted programmes combining renovation subsidies, low-interest loans, and technical assistance in an attempt to address past failures without mass expropriation (Iglesias et al., 2014). These issues exposed the long-term social and fiscal consequences of poor-quality housing, reinforcing the urgency of an integrated and quality-oriented housing policy framework.

To support densification and expand housing subsidies beyond incremental strategies, in 2011 the Ministry of Housing and Urban Development introduced a new subsidy aimed at middle-income households, accompanied by new standards established through the Cuadro Normativo DS1 (DS1 Normative Framework) (Figure 4.26). Concurrently, the design standards for subsidised homes built for vulnerable groups were updated through the Cuadro Normativo DS49 (DS49 Normative Framework), replacing those from the 2005 Programa de Vivienda Básica (Figure 4.27).

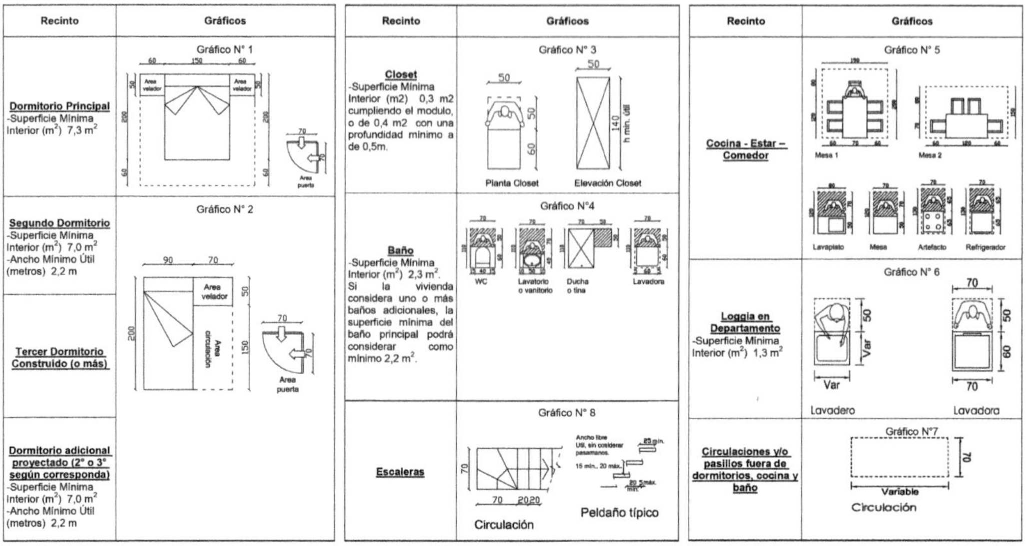

FIGURE 4.26 Furniture Schedule by the Tabla de Espacios y Usos Mínimos para el Mobiliario del DS N°1 e Itemizado Técnico para Proyectos del Título I del DS N°1.

Source: MINVU (2012).

Each subsidy scheme was associated with its own specific dwelling programme and space standards, embedded within a normative framework tailored to the needs of each target group. Under DS1, the Tabla de Espacios y Usos Mínimos para el Mobiliario (Table of Minimum Spaces and Uses for Furniture) was introduced, standardising the minimum dimensions for bedrooms, closets, bathrooms, kitchens, laundry areas, and circulation

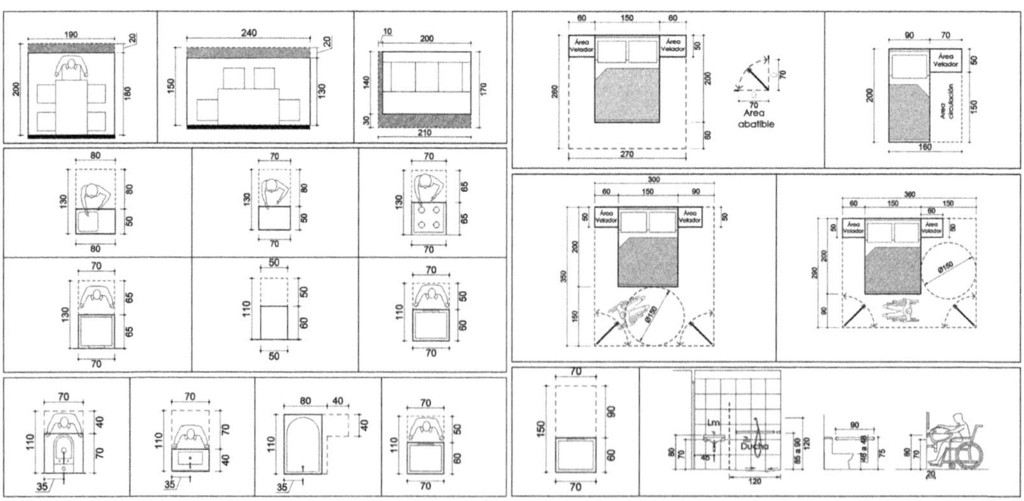

FIGURE 4.27 Furniture Schedule by the Cuadro Normativo y Tabla de Espacios y Usos Mínimos para el Mobiliario: Para Proyectos del Fondo Solidario de Elección de Vivienda Regulado por el D.S. N° 49.

Source: MINVU (2017).

spaces – issues not previously considered by design standards. However, no minimum was mandated for living areas, leaving these decisions at the discretion of developers. As a result, they often provide extremely small spaces, sometimes too small to accommodate a sofa without encroaching on the dining area. This also leads in poorly defined common spaces, forcing residents either to live with impractical spatial arrangements or without a functional living room.

Applied predominantly to high-density solutions, the DS1 programme has been implemented mostly in mid-rise blocks and high-rise residential towers. The DS1 framework established variable minimum sizes based on the number of bedrooms. For one-bedroom and one-bathroom flats, a minimum dwelling size of 37 m^2 was mandated. While no formal minimum existed for units with two or more bedrooms, application of the room-level standards meant that a two-bedroom unit typically ranged from 45 to 47 m^2, and three-bedroom units from 52 to 55 m^2. However, as in previous Cuadros Normativos, the dimensions of the kitchen, dining area, and bathroom remained fixed irrespective of occupancy levels, failing to recognise that larger households require more shared and services spaces (Figure 4.28). Despite increased regulatory control and detail, inconsistencies in housing quality persisted, as living areas and overall dwelling size remained effectively unregulated.

On the other hand, DS49 required a minimum area of 55 m^2 for a three-bedroom flat, which is rooted in the assumption of a nuclear family as the normative household model (Figure 4.29). This made the programme particularly rigid, especially when applied to high-density, multi-storey housing solutions where spatial and cost constraints are more pronounced. In contrast, detached houses were generally designed with two initial bedrooms within a minimum 42 m^2. These were expected to be expanded to 55 m^2 through the addition of a third bedroom, reflecting the continued influence of the incremental housing model inherited from earlier policies (Figure 4.30). While this 42-m^2 expandable approach could

FIGURE 4.28 Examples from Conjunto Urbano Gabriel Palma by Francisco Izquierdo (2017), showing the kitchen and living–dining area remained unchanged regardless of the number of bedrooms.

Source: Jacoby et al. (2022).

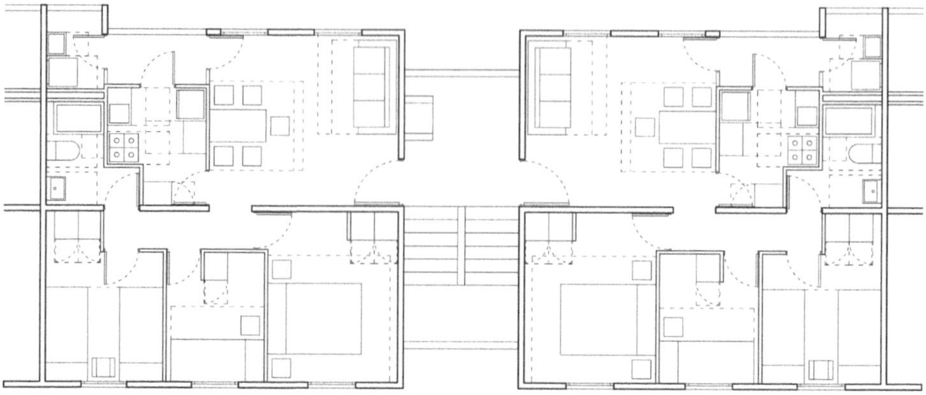

FIGURE 4.29 El Mariscal by Francisco Vergara (2021), an example of a 55-m² standard unit with three bedrooms built to the DS49 programme requirements in a five-storey building.

Source: Drawn by the author (2025).

theoretically better meet each household's specific needs, relying on low-density houses as the primary urban development model is counterproductive in today's context of densification and rising land values.

Recognising some of these limitations, the 2017 update to DS49 introduced new requirements for accessibility, parking, vehicular access, and circulation within housing developments.

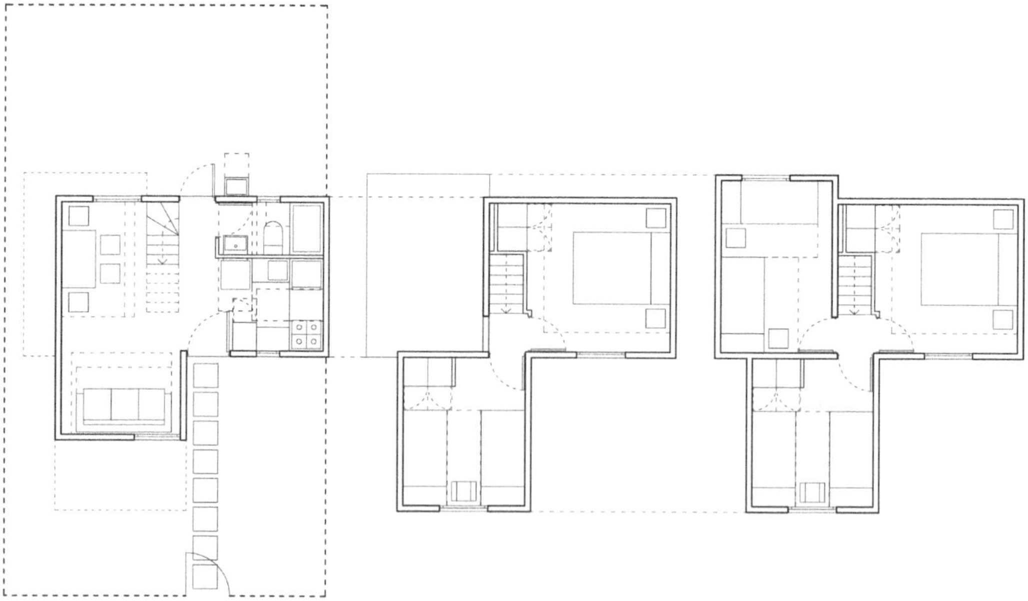

FIGURE 4.30 El Mariscal by Francisco Vergara (2021), an example of a two-storey 42-m² house designed to the DS49 programme requirements for future extension, increasing the number of bedrooms from two to three.

Source: Drawn by the author (2025).

These additions, particularly the need for lifts and other accessibility features, have significantly increased project costs and made implementation more difficult. Ultimately, one of the intrinsic challenges of the DS49's debt-free housing provision is that it must function as a universal solution, designed to fit any scenario. This inevitably produces a generic dwelling solution, reflecting a homeownership model that offers no real alternatives sensitive to the specific needs of each family or how those needs change over time.

The DS19 programme, introduced in 2017 under the Programa de Integración Social y Territorial (Social and Territorial Integration Programme), sought to tackle urban segregation and the disconnect between housing supply and urban dynamics. It promoted mixed-income developments by supporting the co-location of vulnerable and middle-income households, thereby fostering social and spatial inclusion.

Under the DS19 programme, housing projects were prioritised in central, well-connected urban areas, breaking with the historical peripheralisation of subsidised housing. Developers received financial incentives to build at least 20% of a project's homes for vulnerable households, as defined by the Registro Social de Hogares (Social Registry of Households), which classifies families based on income, household composition, and social dependency indicators, and 10% for "emergent" groups with limited debt capacity. While early developments tended to allocate different subsidy groups to separate building types, this practice was revised to promote mixed-tenure developments within the same building (Figure 4.31).

Architecturally, DS19 developments are increasingly high-density, with buildings typically being mid-rise solutions, starting at four storeys and now often exceeding 15 storeys, to optimise land use (Figure 4.32). Projects are required to be located within a defined proximity

FIGURE 4.31 Conjunto Urbano Gabriel Palma by Francisco Izquierdo (2017). One of the first projects featuring spatial and typological differentiation in accordance with the DS19 subsidy scheme.

Source: Photograph by the author (2025).

FIGURE 4.32 Mirador Laguna by Mobil Arquitectos and Alvaro Arancibia (2024), built for the DS19 programme, combining mid-rise and high-rise building typologies.

Source: Courtesy of Cristóbal Palma (2025).

to essential public infrastructures, such as schools, healthcare centres, transport, green spaces, childcare facilities, and commercial areas, ensuring equitable urban access for low-income residents (MINVU, 2016). However, this has introduced new challenges related to the quality of shared spaces, building materials, and fostering a sense of community among residents from different socio-economic backgrounds (Centro de Políticas Públicas UC, 2021; Centro de Políticas Públicas UC, 2023; Morales et al., 2024).

While the DS19 programme has been instrumental in building subsidised housing in central urban areas and promoting social integration, its regulatory framework has also reinforced a homogenisation of dwelling layouts. The coexistence of two regulatory standards – designed for two different socioeconomic groups – has not produced greater spatial diversity but rather led to the widespread replication of dense building schemes with standardised, elongated units, commonly known as *pastillas* (Figure 4.33). This configuration – with a single orientation, a kitchen–laundry at one end, a central living–dining room, and bedrooms connected by a corridor leading to one or two windowless bathrooms – has become the dominant template for large developers (Figure 4.34). Its appeal lies in its efficiency and ease of adaptation to different programme requirements, yet this very flexibility has produced a generic layout applied to diverse lifestyles, irrespective of household structure or everyday domestic practices.

The rigidity of DS19 standards has further reinforced this trend of standardisation, as key domestic spaces are designed with little variation: kitchens are consistently reduced to bare-minimum provision of space and equipment, dining areas are often relegated to circulation

FIGURE 4.33 Las Araucarias by Inmobiliaria Maestra (2023), a *pastilla* design characteristic of the DS19 programme.

Source: Photograph by Lucía Alonso (2023).

FIGURE 4.34 Las Araucarias by Inmobiliaria Maestra (2023), a DS19 project with different versions of *pastillas* that can be combined to achieve the required unit mix by the developer.

Source: Drawn by the author (2025).

zones with limited natural light, and living rooms are conceived merely to accommodate a sofa, rather than as integrated and versatile spaces connected to the cooking and dining areas. These design choices highlight the central challenge of the DS19 programme: reconciling efficiency and land optimisation with the creation of dwellings capable of supporting diverse modes of inhabitation while providing improved spatial and functional quality.

The DS19 delivery has become the Ministry of Housing's main focus, accounting for approximately 35% of total subsidies. By integrating elements of the DS49 and DS1 programmes, DS19 projects aim to provide more inclusive, better-integrated urban housing. Nonetheless, the programme continues to face critical challenges, particularly regarding high land prices and financial viability, which can limit its ability to reverse historical patterns of urban segregation. According to Casen 2022 data published by MINVU, the quantitative housing deficit is currently estimated at 552,046 units (7.9% of all households). The qualitative deficit, referring to dwellings that require improvements or expansions, meanwhile, is 1,263,576 units (MINVU, 2023). These figures offer a vital comparison to earlier eras and highlight how current legislation still has substantial ground to cover in addressing both the quantitative and qualitative dimensions of the housing deficit.

In sum, the DS19 programme embodies both the advances and contradictions of Chile's housing policy trajectory. It has expanded access to centrally located, high-density housing while aiming for social integration. Yet the standardisation of design, while increasingly instrumental for mass housing production, has also caused prevalent homogeneity, limiting not only the diversity of dwelling types, household compositions, and lifestyles, but also the way in which the dwelling programme is conceptualised and organised. At the same time, the persistence and recent growth of the housing deficit underscore that efficiency in production alone cannot resolve the broader challenge of ensuring adequate, inclusive, and adaptable housing for all.

Conclusion

The evolution of housing standards in Chile reveals how normative definitions of what constitutes adequate housing have continually shifted in response to changing institutional, political, and economic contexts. In the early twentieth century, public housing initiatives were primarily driven by health and social concerns, giving rise to standards focused on hygiene, ventilation, lighting, and the functional organisation of domestic life. These design and development priorities, often linked to disciplinary architectural paradigms, sought to improve both housing supply and living conditions.

In the second half of the twentieth century, housing policies expanded significantly. Institutions such as CORVI and later CORMU were established to lead subsidised housing provision and define homes fit for a "modern way of life" for working-class families. Although not always formalised through regulations, these efforts promoted integrated housing models that incorporated public space, shared facilities, and typological innovation. Housing design was closely tied to an urban project, with a strong emphasis on architectural and spatial quality, albeit not without contradictions or inconsistencies in the attempt to produce housing at a large scale. However, many of these initiatives functioned as pilot projects based on soft architectural criteria rather than clear, replicable standards. As a result, despite their contributions to housing quality, they proved difficult to scale or implement consistently across the country, limiting their capacity to respond to housing needs at a national level.

The neoliberal turn imposed during the military dictatorship in the 1980s marked a radical transformation. The state withdrew from its role as a direct provider of housing and instead adopted a subsidiary model based on individual subsidies. This paradigm shift redefined housing standards around cost-efficiency and the logic of minimal-dwelling provisions. Rather than aspiring to quality or long-term habitability, the system prioritised delivering the greatest number of units at the lowest possible cost. Minimum standards were defined narrowly, reducing housing to its most elementary form in order to meet housing targets. Programmes like the Programa de Vivienda Básica institutionalised the notion of the "utilitarian minimum", offering initial incremental dwellings of very limited size, with the expectation that families would complete their homes over time using their own resources. Housing provision ceased to be a finished solution and became merely a starting point.

Since the 1990s, the post-dictatorship period has introduced new programmes and instruments – most notably through Decrees DS49, DS1, and DS19 – that have diversified the housing provision and refined both design governance and subsidised housing. These policies have improved housing access and encouraged private-sector involvement, while enhancing housing locations, density, and design. Nevertheless, the definition of housing standards has remained largely constrained by economic calculations and a highly rigid regulatory framework.

In particular, the current subsidy system, consolidated during the neoliberal period, defines housing standards primarily in relation to dwelling size and a schedule of typical furniture requirements. This technocratic and prescriptive model understands design as a logistical problem to be solved through a normative approach, rather than as responding to diverse modes of living. The resultant minimum dwelling is thus evaluated less in terms of spatial quality or adaptability to use over time than by its standardised layout and function, expressed through room sizes and circulation patterns that leave little room for design variation or socio-cultural specificity.

This rigid framework has significantly limited the ability of architects and planners to respond to the profound transformations that affect domestic life today. Household composition has evolved, as have the ways in which housing is inhabited. Standards based exclusively on the optimisation of construction costs and furniture arrangement fail to address broader questions such as long-term flexibility, gendered uses of space, intergenerational living, or the integration of care infrastructure into the domestic sphere. The persistence of a normative dwelling layout constrains both flexible spatial organisation and more ambitious conceptualisations of what a minimum home could be, which are important problems for affordable housing and homes built for large households. More flexible layouts are therefore essential for greater long-term housing adaptability and sustainability.

The spatial consequences of this standardisation are visible in the repetition of standard house types, the monotony of housing developments, and the challenges they pose to urban integration. Despite some improvements in location and density, the formal expression and spatial potential of social housing remain constrained by spatial norms. The risk is therefore that architectural design becomes a mere box-ticking exercise, rather than a tool for enabling better standards of living.

The challenge for the future is to reframe the notion of the housing standard. This means not abandoning it but reconceptualising it. Instead of understanding it as a mechanism for simplification and control, it should be seen as a platform from which to articulate social, architectural, and territorial ambitions. Standards should establish thresholds of dignity and equity while allowing for typological experimentation, local adaptation, and the incorporation of residents' agency in shaping their living environments. There is an urgent need to move beyond fixed, absolute standards.

Another key challenge is developing more diverse affordable housing tenures to complement individual ownership, offering a broader spectrum of options such as rental homes, co-operative housing, and shared ownership models. These alternatives are essential to providing more flexible and inclusive responses to the diverse realities of households, life stages, and socio-economic circumstances. They also acknowledge the structural limitations of a homeownership-based approach, which can be financially inaccessible or unsustainable for low-income households, and often fails to accommodate the needs of an ageing population or those with special needs.

As Chile continues to face a housing crisis, intensified by growing inequalities, demographic shifts, and environmental pressures, the role of standards must be subject to open and interdisciplinary debate. The question is not only how much space a dwelling must offer, but what kind of life it enables. A housing policy committed to social justice must confront the limitations of its regulatory instruments and embrace the transformative power of architecture as an important dimension of public action.

PART III

Systems and Standards

5

HOUSING SYSTEMS

Subsidised Housing Design and Regulatory Instruments

Seyithan Özer and Sam Jacoby

This chapter analyses housing systems and their design-related dimensions by comparing the different forms of subsidised housing and design governance in England (London and beyond), Chile (Santiago), China (Shenzhen), the Netherlands (Amsterdam), Spain (Barcelona), and Switzerland (Zurich). These six cities and countries represent distinct approaches to subsidised housing provision within different housing markets and regulatory frameworks. The analysis specifically focuses on how the governance of subsidised housing design is linked to local housing systems.

The functions and processes of housing systems determine how housing is supplied, managed, and accessed, as well as the quantity, type, affordability, and quality of available housing. Conventionally, housing systems are classified as "dualist" or "unitary" rental markets to indicate how they regulate and relate to the private and social housing sectors (Kemeny, 1995). In dualist systems, subsidised housing is narrowly targeted at low-income populations and operates separately from the private rental sector. This often results in socio-economic segregation and greater sectoral differences in housing quality. In contrast, unitary systems offer access to subsidised housing to a broader income range and integrate it with the private rental sector in a single market. They therefore promote greater tenure and design equality, as well as affordability across the housing market.

While these typologies are useful for highlighting general distinctions – whether subsidised housing functions as a targeted social safety net or a more universal welfare provision – this binary classification and its welfare-based explanations are increasingly criticised for their Western European bias (Harloe, 1995). Critics argue that it overlooks the dynamics of emerging or transitioning housing markets in many non-Western countries (Flynn & Montalbano, 2024) and even fails to account for significant changes in European housing systems since these classifications were first developed (Stephens, 2020).

This chapter analyses the housing system of each studied country and city in relation to the composition of housing providers, forms of tenure, target populations, financing models (including subsidies), and investment in new housing, aiming to characterise and clarify the sociopolitical roles that subsidised housing plays in each context. As these roles directly shape

DOI: 10.4324/9781032679204-9

the standards of housing quality that are expected or prioritised in a place, they provide a basis for examining the relationship between housing systems and design governance. For example, when subsidised housing is conceived primarily as a welfare provision, quality benchmarks might prioritise basic habitability, whereas in contexts where economic growth and rapid urban development drive housing policy, cost efficiency might be emphasised.

Moreover, the way design regulations are applied often reflects these broader roles and priorities: they can be "universal", setting consistent standards across all housing sectors, or "differentiated", only imposing specific requirements on the subsidised housing sector. This distinction is shaped not only by policy objectives, but also by the actors involved in housing delivery – particularly the types of providers and financiers – who influence both design aspirations and the mechanisms through which standards can be implemented or enforced. For example, in market-led systems where housing delivery relies on private developers, regulation tends to be more flexible, negotiated, or inconsistently applied, often reflecting the limits of public oversight and the varying capacities or willingness of providers to meet quality benchmarks.

This chapter is organised into three sections. First, it provides an overview of the main types of subsidised housing found across the six countries, highlighting the different roles that subsidised homes play within each housing system. Second, it outlines how new affordable housing is delivered, focusing on the key actors and financing mechanisms available. Third, the chapter offers an analysis of design governance in each context and draws connections between broader housing system characteristics and the regulatory instruments used to control housing design outcomes.

Subsidised Housing Types

This section focuses on how subsidised housing is defined and understood in relation to its provision and respective housing systems. It discusses the forms of tenure, the characteristics and composition of subsidised housing, and the target groups it serves, describing who subsidised housing is provided for and under what terms (Table 5.1).

Subsidised housing can play various roles in a housing system. In England and the Netherlands, it is mainly meant to address shortcomings in the housing market by providing secure and affordable homes to low-income and vulnerable households. By contrast, in Chile and Spain, subsidised housing is largely intended to support homeownership. State support is channelled through demand-side subsidies paid to households for purchasing homes rather than for developing long-term rental options.

In comparison, Switzerland and China offer two distinct approaches to subsidised housing that go beyond the conventional market-led versus state-led divide. Switzerland's non-profit co-operative housing sector represents an alternative form of housing provision operating outside both the market and public sector. Based on the core principles of self-management and non-profit operation, it delivers long-term housing stability through controlled, low rents. However, its limited scale and selective access mean that it cannot address broader affordable housing challenges without greater state support.

China exemplifies a state-directed but market-responsive housing system, which has recently seen a significant return to state-led housing supply in large cities with major urban growth and affordability problems. This new affordable housing is delivered through state-owned but semi-independently operating development companies, allowing for large-scale housing provision while maintaining a degree of market logic. Through the introduction of a mix of affordable

TABLE 5.1 Subsidised housing types

Country	*Form of tenure*	*Tenure model*	*Target group*
England	Social rent	Long-term rental	Socially and economically vulnerable
	Intermediate rent	Short-term rental	Low- to mid-income households
	Shared ownership	Generally starts with 25% ownership	Mid-income households
Chile	Subsidised homeownership	Full ownership	Low-income households
		Full ownership	Mid-income households
China	Public rental housing	5 years	Low- to mid-income households with urban household registration (*hukou*)
	Affordable rental housing	5 years	Qualified new citizens, young people, and high-skilled workers.
	Housing for talent workers	5 years	High-skilled professionals
	Shared homeownership	Generally starts with 50% ownership	Mid-income households
Netherlands	Social rent	Long-term rental	Low-income households
	Intermediate rent	Long-term rental	Low- to mid-income households
Spain	Protected housing	Short-term rental	Mid-income households
		Full ownership	
Switzerland	Cooperative housing	Cooperative ownership	All incomes

Note: Full project data are available online: https://doi.org/10.60624/b68t-ae27.

housing programmes, China has been able to diversify tenure options to address the needs of different local populations while also attracting skilled workers to cities with a labour shortage.

Country Comparison

England and the Netherlands, two Western European countries that established large social housing systems after the end of World War II, have seen significant transformations since the 1980s along with the global neoliberalisation of housing policies (Blessing, 2015; Cooper & Kurzer, 2023; Czischke & van Bortel, 2023). England has become a nation of owner-occupiers, with 62% of the population living in homes they own. This is followed by the private rented sector (21%) and social rented sector (17%; ONS, 2025b). In London, however, the number of owner-occupiers is lower (47%), while both the private rented (31%) and social rented housing sectors (22%) are higher (Table 5.2).

Subsidised housing in England includes affordable homes that are rented or sold under different tenures and levels of affordability, targeting a wide range of households. The definition of "affordability" in England is generally based on local market rents and property prices rather than household income. Subsidised housing encompasses social rent (typically rented at around 50% of market rents), affordable rent and intermediate rent (up to 80% of market rents), rent

TABLE 5.2 Tenure distribution

Country	*Owner-occupied*	*Private rent*	*Subsidised rent*[1]
England[2]	62%	21%	17% [SR]
London[2]	47%	31%	22% [SR]
Chile[3]	61%	26%	0.1% [SR]
Santiago[3]	56%	34%	–
China[4]	79%	12%	2% [PR]
Shenzhen[5]	23%	72%	5%
Netherlands[6]	57%	14%	29%
Amsterdam[6]	47%	23%	30%
Spain[7]	75%	16%	2% [SR]
Barcelona[7]	69%	24%	1.8% [SR]
Switzerland[8]	36%	58%	2.8% [C]
Zurich (City)[8]	8%	65%	27% [C]

Notes:

[1] As nomenclature varies, the following terms are used for comparison: social rent [SR], public rent [PR], and cooperative housing [C]. Most subsidised housing in Chile and Spain is built for ownership and therefore not included under subsidised rent.

[2] ONS (2025b).

[3] Ministerio de Desarrollo Social y Familia (2023).

[4] National Bureau of Statistics of China (2021).

[5] Huang (2022).

[6] Centraal Bureau voor de Statistiek (CBS) (2024).

[7] Instituto Nacional de Estadísticas (INE) (2023).

[8] Bundesamt für Statistik (2025).

to buy (with a period of intermediate rents), shared ownership (part buy, part rent), and first homes offering a 30–50% discount (Ministry of Housing, Communities and Local Government [MHCLG], 2024a). In addition, London has its own rental categories of London Affordable Rent (less than 50% of market rents) and London Living Rent (typically one-third of average local household incomes).

Social rent homes are let at the lowest rates, based on a formula made up of: "70% of the national average rent multiplied by relative county earnings... by the bedroom weight... plus 30% of the national average rent multiplied by relative property value" (MHCLG et al., 2022). They are reserved for the most vulnerable and disadvantaged populations and subject to meeting strict eligibility criteria, including local connections, low household income, experience of homelessness, unsafe or overcrowded living conditions, fleeing domestic violence, and serious health or disability-related needs requiring stable and affordable accommodation. However, increasingly households cannot afford social rents when housing benefits do not fully cover them. Local authorities both assess housing needs and allocate social housing, even when homes are managed by other providers such as housing associations.

Intermediate rent homes include "affordable rent" that, at up to 80% of market rent, can still exceed the local median income in less affordable areas like London. For this reason, newer affordable rental tenures such as London Affordable Rent and London Living Rent set rent levels below the 80% threshold. Affordable rent homes are allocated based on income criteria determined by each housing provider.

Intermediate sale homes include "shared ownership" and a range of affordable housing options, typically for first-time buyers or key workers sold at a discount. Shared ownership allows buyers to own part of a home and pay rent on the remaining shares as well as a service charge.

Access to shared ownership depends on income criteria, which are often well above local median incomes. While there are growing calls for "genuinely" affordable housing, this term is not formally defined in England, making it difficult at times to agree on its meaning and implementation. The widely accepted rule of thumb that affordable housing should cost no more than one-third of household income is widely accepted. However, this is often unattainable in contexts where the cost of supplying new housing is high and property prices are disconnected from incomes.

Due to market-driven housing supply and austerity policies in England, supply-side subsidies for social rent homes are limited. In 2020–2021, only 12% of new affordable housing were for social rent, while affordable rent made up 54% and shared ownership 33% (Department for Levelling Up, Housing and Communities [DLUHC], 2022b).

Similar to England, most households in the Netherlands live in homes they own. However, the social rent sector accounts for 29% of the housing stock (CBS, 2024), making it the largest social housing sector in Europe (Table 5.2; Eurostat, 2025c).

In the Netherlands, "social housing" includes both purpose-built social rent homes provided by housing corporations and rent-regulated private sector homes. These are often grouped together because social housing is determined by rent regulation rather than tenure type. In 2025, rent controls applied to all rental homes that are below the so-called liberalisation threshold (*liberalisatiegrens*) of currently €900.07 per month (Table 5.3) and

TABLE 5.3 Social housing and benefit allocation in the Netherlands

Thresholds[1]	*Purpose*	*Monthly Rent (2025)*	*Income limit for rent allowance*[3]
Basic rent (*basishuur*)	The minimum rent every tenant must pay before housing allowance is calculated.	–	–
Quality discount limit (*kwaliteitskortingsgrens*)	The maximum total rent up to which 100% of the difference between the basic and total rent is covered by the housing allowance.	€477.20	€43,835
Lower capping limit (*lage aftoppingsgrens*)[2]	The maximum total rent up to which 65% of the difference between the quality discount limit and total rent is covered by the housing allowance. The lower capping limit applies to 1–2 person households and the upper capping limit to larger households.	€682.96	
Upper capping limit (*hoge aftoppingsgrens*)[2]		€731.93	€53,057
Liberalisation threshold (*liberalisatiegrens*)	Rent limit separating regulated (social) from unregulated (private) rental housing (eligibility also depends on WWS points).	€900.07	€58,282

Notes:

[1] Thresholds are set annually by the government; only the rent at the start of the tenancy is tested against that year's thresholds.

[2] Any rent above the capping limit is paid in full by the tenant.

[3] For 2 or more person households.

Source: de Rijksoverheid (2025).

achieve a maximum score of 186 points in the Housing Valuation System (Woningwaarderingsstelsel [WWS]). WWS points are calculated based on property size, location, quality, amenities, energy label, and the market value assessed at municipal level (Waardering Onroerende Zaken [WOZ]). A cap limits the influence of this annually assessed WOZ value to a maximum of 33% of total WWS points in order to prevent high valuations from pushing homes into the unregulated private sector. However, it still means that in expensive areas like Amsterdam, available rent-controlled, social homes tend to be smaller or lower quality than elsewhere.

Like all rental housing in the Netherlands, social rent homes are offered for an indefinite period, with rent increases regulated throughout the tenancy (de Rijksoverheid, 2025). However, social housing provides stronger protection, greater affordability, and more tenant security. The basic rent is income-based and commonly only around 25% of a tenant's monthly net income. While eligibility for social housing is primarily based on national income thresholds, housing corporations and municipalities can apply additional criteria to prioritise groups such as those in need of emergency accommodation, young adults, students, large families, people with disabilities, and the elderly.

The national policy regulating social housing access includes several income limits. Reflecting the social welfare role of housing corporations, the main income limit is defined by the Diensten van Algemeen Economisch Belang (DAEB), which prioritises lower-income households most in need of affordable housing. While housing corporations can normally allocate up to 7.5% of homes to households with incomes above this threshold, this can increase to 15% in areas with a high housing shortage and, therefore, greater housing demand (AEDES, 2025).

The second threshold is the "appropriate allocation" income limit, which ensures that households with lower incomes are matched with homes at rents that they can afford. Housing corporations must usually allocate at least 95% of these households to homes with rents below the corresponding capping limit (*aftoppingsgrens*). This income limit is also used to determine eligibility for rent allowance.

Even though almost one-third of all Dutch housing is classified as social, there is still a significant shortage of affordable homes. An average of 483 people apply for each advertised social rent home, and in 2021, the average waiting time was over 13 years (Kraniotis & de Jong, 2021), compared to around 6.6 years in London (Eichler, 2025).

In comparison to England and the Netherlands, Chile and Spain do not have affordable rent sectors of similar scale or structure. Instead, subsidised housing in both countries largely consists of homes that are built for ownership. Thus, subsidised housing is, in terms of tenure, indistinct from private-sector homes.

In Chile, 61% of households own their homes and 26% rent privately (Ministerio de Desarrollo Social, 2025), while the social rent sector is negligible at under 1%, despite demand and some limited, small-scale pilot projects. All housing supply relies on the private market, with prospective homebuyers supported by extensive demand-side subsidies. The subsidies are given as vouchers to low- and middle-income households to buy properties that are specifically developed by the private sector for the subsidised housing market. This means that these homes are built to comply with the particular requirements of subsidy programmes, for example, policies that support families, urban densification, and social integration. The amount of subsidy that households can receive depends on their income level and living conditions. Households in the lowest 10% of income distribution are eligible for subsidies covering up to

95% of the total cost of purchasing a home, with the rest typically made up through savings (Kast, 2009).

In 2017, 34.7% of all households in Chile who bought a home since 2012 had received a subsidy from the Ministry of Housing and Urbanism (MINVU, Ministerio de Desarrollo Social, 2018), with 25.2% supported by the maximum 95% subsidy and 9.5% having to combine their subsidy with a mortgage. However, due to higher housing costs, half of all new homes purchased during this period in the Santiago metropolitan area received a subsidy, showing significant regional variations. As policy supports homeownership by lower-income households – without offering alternative rent support or options – private rent is predominantly targeted at higher-income groups, with 32.3% of the wealthiest households renting compared to just 13.3% of the poorest.

Similar to Chile, Spain has high levels of homeownership at 75%, a small private rental sector (16%), and 8% living in housing provided by employers, relatives, and others (INE, 2023). The main form of subsidised housing in Spain is called "protected" housing (*vivienda protegida*), which is typically offered for sale with a temporary protection period of five to 20 years, during which it is shielded from market speculation and has to be the primary residence (Generalitat de Catalunya, n.d.).

Protected homes are subject to income limits and price caps (Table 5.4), which are, for example, set at 50–70% of market rates in the Barcelona metropolitan area. Once the protection period ends, the homes can be freely sold on the private market. However, recent regional policies are aiming to increase the protection period and expand the social rental sector. Between 2005 and 2018, only 19% of protected housing was offered for rent (Ministerio de Transportes, Movilidad y Agenda Urbana, DG de Vivienda y Suelo, 2020), with affordable homeownership often inaccessible for low-income populations. Nevertheless, only around 2% of households in Spain live in social rent homes, and in some cases, tenancy can have fixed-term limits after which residents have to move out.

Switzerland, unlike many other European countries, has neither a social or public rental sector nor a formal national subsidy system. Nevertheless, it is predominantly a country of tenants, with 58% living in the private rent sector and only 36% owning their homes – the lowest homeownership rate in Europe (Bundesamt für Statistik, 2025).

A small amount of affordable housing is provided by the non-profit rent sector, mainly through housing cooperatives, with some offered by housing associations and arms-length government organisations. There are over 170,000 cooperative homes in Switzerland, housing around 2.8% of all households (Wohnbaugenossenschaften Schweiz, 2022).

TABLE 5.4 Subsidised housing price caps in Catalonia

Category of subsidised housing	*Household income limit*	*House price (€/m², Zone A)*[2]
Special regime	≤ 2.5 × Sufficiency Income Indicator of Catalonia[1]	€2,343.19
General regime	≤ 5 × Sufficiency Income Indicator of Catalonia[1]	€2,666.02

Notes:

[1] This indicator defines the level of income below which living with dignity is considered impossible and is used to determine benefits eligibility; it was €9,341.92 in 2024 (Generalitat de Catalunya, n.d.)

[2] Zone A refers to the Barcelona metropolitan area.

While not all cooperatives are non-profit, those receiving government-backed credits and land subsidies must operate under a cost-rent model without profits, where rents cover only the actual costs of finance, maintenance, and management, thus protecting housing and tenants from speculation. This results in rents 20–40% below those in the private rent sector. Buildings are collectively owned by all cooperative members, who are then given in return the right to occupy a dwelling unit. Although the federal government recognises the important role of housing cooperatives in providing affordable housing by offering help in financing and land acquisition (exclusively to non-profit cooperatives), cooperatives remain fully responsible for allocation and management, and support varies regionally.

Over the last three decades, China has witnessed extensive market-oriented reforms, completely transforming its state-dominated housing sector from the Communist period into a largely privatised one. In this process, urban public housing was sold off, and private developers entered an emerging housing market (Cui & Arundel, 2025). However, this created growing affordability and maintenance problems and the need for housing support for low-income households.

In response, over the past two decades, China has introduced various subsidy programmes to tackle housing unaffordability by developing subsidised housing at an unprecedented scale and speed. Between 2011 and 2015, it delivered 40.13 million new affordable homes (Fang et al., 2020). In large cities like Guangzhou, affordable housing provision is expected to surpass the market supply for the first time in 2025 (Wang & Jacoby, 2023). While homeownership rates are very high nationally (around 79%), they are significantly lower in major metropolitan areas: 50% in Shanghai, 39% in Beijing, and 24% in the Guangdong province, which includes Shenzhen and Guangzhou (Office of the Leading Group of the State Council for the Seventh National Population Census, 2021).

China's main affordable housing programmes are public rental housing (*gonggong zulin zhufang*); affordable rental housing (*baozhangxing zulin fang*), and shared ownership housing (*gongyou chanquan zhufang*). These vary in size, target population, eligibility criteria, financing, and the regions in which they are offered, although they primarily focus on large urban areas.

Launched in 2010, public rental housing (PRH) is the oldest housing programme, providing homes for low- and middle-income urban residents. Eligibility requires an urban household registration permit (*hukou*), which controls access to public services, and income thresholds depending on each subsidy programme. More recently, housing eligibility has expanded to include some skilled migrants without an urban *hukou* and newly employed, highly skilled workers. As part of its 14th Five-Year Plan, China committed to building 6.5 million public rental housing units in 40 major cities between 2021 and 2025 (The State Council, 2022).

Affordable rental housing (ARH), introduced in 2021, is a more recent tenure targeting young and new urban residents who cannot otherwise afford homeownership. It has no income criteria or *hukou* requirements, aiming to attract skilled migrant workers. In some regions, a related programme called housing for "talent" workers (*rencai gongyu*) targets highly skilled young professionals with a university degree.

Finally, the shared ownership housing programme (SOH) allows those unable to buy a home outright in the market to purchase a share (typically around 50%) of a property, paying subsidised rent on the remainder, with the option to buy further shares later.

As the comparison shows, the forms of tenure, target groups, and levels of affordability (Table 5.5) can differ significantly, demonstrating the diverse functions of subsidised housing

TABLE 5.5 Housing affordability indicators

	House price to average income[1]	*Household rent to income ratio in the private sector*	*Social rent to private rent ratio*
England[2]	8.3	26%	49%
London	12.7	40%	37%
Chile[3]	16.4	27%	52%
Santiago		28%	
China[4]	29.6	19%	–
Shenzhen[5]	48.1	33%	30%
Netherlands[6]	11.8	33%	48%
Amsterdam	16.8	29%	40%
Spain[7]	–	32%	–
Barcelona	–	35%	–
Switzerland[8]	11.0	26%	86%
Zurich (Canton)	16.7	20%	–

Notes:

[1] House price to income ratio, based on Numbeo (2024) data unless otherwise stated.
[2] House price to average income, based on ONS (2024a). Other data are based on ONS (2024b) and DLUHC (2024b).
[3] Ministerio de Desarrollo Social (2023).
[4] Numbeo (2024).
[5] Chen (2024).
[6] CBS (2024) – house price to average income, calculated from the average sale price and average household income.
[7] INE (2023).
[8] House price to average income, calculated from average sale price and average household income (BfS, 2025).

within a housing system. Subsidised housing can serve as a policy tool for reducing inequality, stabilising markets, promoting homeownership, or supporting urban economic development. These varied roles reflect differing national or regional priorities and the historical contexts of housing systems.

For instance, in England and the Netherlands, affordable rental housing is a central part of the housing safety net and social welfare traditions, providing secure accommodation for lower-income households and helping to address market failures. In contrast, Chile and Spain prioritise subsidised homeownership, using public subsidies to support private property purchases rather than expanding rental provision. In these contexts, affordable housing tends to have a more transitional or aspirational role, with housing stability closely linked to individual ownership and greater self-reliance.

Meanwhile, Switzerland's cooperative housing sector offers a non-profit, collectively managed alternative to both state and market provision that succeeds in creating long-term affordable homes, albeit at a modest scale. Similarly, China adopts a multifaceted, state-led approach that combines rental and shared ownership schemes to support urban workers, migrants, and skilled professionals, positioning affordable housing as a key instrument of urbanisation, labour mobility, and social integration.

Subsidised Housing Supply

In the studied six countries, both the provision and financing of subsidised housing are highly diverse, shaped by varying degrees of state involvement, market orientation, and civil society engagement. While the state is still responsible for the regulatory and financial frameworks of affordable housing in all case studies, the actual supply increasingly relies on non-governmental and semi-autonomous providers (Table 5.6).

In England and the Netherlands, responsibility for developing and managing subsidised housing has largely shifted to non-profit organisations. Due to decreasing public investment in social housing, social landlords in both countries increasingly have to balance their social mission with market activities. Generating income through private rent and sales has thus become essential to cross-subsidising social housing. Planning obligations and favourable loans complement these efforts, but rising land and development costs, coupled with growing financial pressures, raise concerns about the long-term affordability of homes and the ability of housing associations to effectively maintain their social mission.

In Chile, a balance of low-cost housing demand and private sector supply relies on demand-side subsidies. While this blurs tenure distinctions, subsidised homes remain distinct from open market ones, as developers must follow subsidised housing regulations and specifications, which are typically significantly lower than those in the private sector. In contrast, low-cost private homes in England tend to be smaller than those built to subsidised housing standards.

In comparison, Spain and China have stronger state-led and state-affiliated housing supply models, dominated by municipal or local government bodies. Spain often relies on arms-length municipal organisations to develop its "protected" housing and China on state-owned development companies. Both countries leverage public land and subsidies – with the Chinese government as the largest urban landowner in the country, allocating about 10% of development land for affordable housing (Yuan, 2015).

In comparison, Switzerland has a distinct non-profit cooperative housing model operating on a cost-rent principle. However, the cooperative housing sector is small and unevenly concentrated in some regions.

TABLE 5.6 Subsidised housing providers and financing

Country	*Provider*	*Financing*
England	• Local authorities • Housing associations	• Government subsidies • Cross-subsidies • Planning obligations
Chile	Private housebuilders	Government subsidies
China	• Regional authorities • Subsidiary companies	Government subsidies
Netherlands	Housing corporations	• Cross-subsidies • Land subsidies
Spain	Arm's length municipal organisations	• Cost-sale • Cross-subsidies
Switzerland	Cooperatives	• Cost-rent • Land subsidies • Government-backed credits

Country Comparison

In England and the Netherlands, affordable housing is mainly provided by non-profit providers known as housing associations in England and housing corporations in the Netherlands. In both countries, they act as developers, landlords, and long-term asset managers.

There are around 1,400 registered housing associations in England. However, 234 of these each manage over 1,000 homes, owning collectively 96% of all social housing stock and thus dominating the sector (Regulator of Social Housing, 2019). The largest housing associations are Places for People (219,616 homes), followed by Clarion (125,000), L&Q (118,181), and Sanctuary (105,218) (McCabe, 2020). At the same time, 82% of housing associations manage fewer than 1,000 social homes, with most owning under 250 units. This is partially due to past affordable funding programmes having favoured larger housing associations, as well as the need to cross-subsidise social homes, creating pressure for an economy of scale, which encourages the merging of housing associations into larger organisations. However, this can mean that larger housing associations are responsible for a very diverse housing stock that is often largely inherited through mergers and might not align with their development standards or wider mission.

New affordable housing in England is typically developed through one of three procurement routes: first, by housing associations in receipt of subsidies from the Affordable Homes Programmes; second, by housing associations using income generated through their private-sector activity (cross-subsidisation) and loans; and third, via planning obligations attached to new private developments.

The UK government's recent funding for new affordable housing has been primarily delivered by Homes England, which mainly supports housing associations through its Affordable Homes Programmes 2011–2016, 2016–2021, and 2021–2026. The Housing Act 1974 enabled housing associations to receive public subsidies for the construction of new social housing, marking an important shift in housing provision from local authorities to non-profit providers. Most housing associations are therefore non-profit organisations that can access both government funding and private financing for their development. Within the policy context of declining public spending on affordable housing since the Spending Review in 2010 (partially reversed by the current Labour government), many housing associations had to adopt a cross-subsidy approach to fund the construction of new social homes and maintenance of the existing stock. This has driven a focus on profit generation via shared-ownership homes and, more recently, private sales and rental housing.

Nonetheless almost half (49%) of all new affordable housing is delivered through planning obligations imposed by local authorities on private developments (Inside Housing, 2022). Under the previous National Planning Policy Framework (which was in force until the end of 2024), local planning authorities were expected to reserve at least 10% of homes on major developments (more than 10 dwellings) for affordable homeownership (MHCLG, 2024b). However, many local plans imposed more onerous requirements, targeting higher overall proportions of affordable housing and including affordable rent tenures. Currently, targets are set by local planning authorities based on local needs without national minimum requirements. The problem with homes created through planning obligations is that there can be insufficient incentives for private developers to deliver well-designed housing.

Housing corporations in the Netherlands encompass municipal corporations, housing associations, and housing foundations recognised by royal decree as private entities with a statutory obligation to act in the interest of public housing. The responsibilities and regulations for housing corporations are set out in the Housing Act of 2015 (Woningwet), with the primary aim of providing affordable housing for low-income households. Notably, although 50% of homes owned by housing corporations have market-based rental values that would exceed local affordability thresholds, they are let below the regulated rent limits (Schiilder & Scherpenisse, 2018).

There are around 300 housing corporations (van Gent & Hochstenbach, 2020), holding 70% of all rental housing and one-third of the total housing stock (Veenstra et al., 2017). In Amsterdam, the largest housing corporations are Ymere (40,366 dwellings), followed by Eigen Haard (35,060), Stadgenoot (30,821), Rochdale (28,537), Lieven de Key (26,816), Alliantie (19,909), Woonzorg (1,969), DRC (1,510), DUWO (1,281), and Habion (201) (van der Molen, 2025).

Despite the sizable social housing stock, the Netherlands has, since the 1990s, also widely adopted policies promoting homeownership and reducing subsidies. This means that the government no longer provides sufficient direct subsidies to housing corporations. Instead, the latter develop new housing with the help of state-backed loans at favourable terms and their own cross-subsidies. Local governments are also empowered to impose planning conditions for new housing developments. Since 2018, the municipal government in Amsterdam has thus introduced new tenure requirements for projects on publicly owned land, requiring a tenure mix of 40% social rent, 40% mid-market, and 20% high-end. However, this has not been consistently implemented and therefore has only had limited impact (Hochstenbach & Ronald, 2020).

In contrast to England, the Netherlands, and Chile, where housing supply is provided through the private and non-profit sectors, in Spain and China subsidised housing is largely provided by entities closely linked to local and regional governments. In Spain, protected housing is developed by a variety of actors, including autonomous communities such as Catalonia, local governments, private and non-profit organisations, and housing cooperatives. However, delivery is primarily through arm's-length municipal organisations, with subsidies generally offered as land grants, which does not support the construction costs and therefore often leads to less affordable or accessible homes.

In comparison, affordable housing in China is planned, developed, and provided by local housing bureaus and state-owned property development companies. Affordable housing, in particular public rental housing, is largely publicly financed and further benefits from public land allocation, permitting very low rents. In addition, the government has been promoting private-sector involvement in subsidised housing through policy incentives and development partnerships, reflecting a pragmatic approach to diversifying housing delivery while retaining government oversight.

In Switzerland, cooperatives are the main providers of affordable homes. Housing cooperatives own on average only 80 homes, making them typically very small (Thiesen, 2020), although some, like the Allgemeine Baugenossenschaft Zürich (ABZ), manage over 5,000 units. There are also significant regional differences in the cooperative housing landscape (Duyne Barenstein & Koch, 2022). The city of Zurich has the largest share of the non-profit housing sector, with 45% of all cooperative homes located in the canton of Zurich (Wohnbaugenossenschaften Schweiz, 2022), making up 7.1% of the total housing stock in Switzerland (Bundesamt für Statistik, 2025), or 18% of housing in the city. However, much of this is older housing, with only 4,938 new cooperative homes built since 2010 (Stadt Zurich, 2025).

While cooperatives do not receive direct subsidies, the Swiss Confederation provides some indirect support. It offers low-interest loans through a revolving fund (*fonds de roulement*) for cooperative and non-profit housing providers, which has supported around 3% of new homes, equating to over 1,500 units per year since its introduction in 2003 (Koch, 2021). The

Confederation also acts as a guarantor, enabling housing cooperatives to access private capital for new housing projects at favourable interest rates.

There are, however, regional differences in subsidy arrangements. The city of Zurich has committed to making one-third of its housing stock non-profit by 2050. To this end, it has implemented new policies, including public land leases for 60 to 100 years to non-profit organisations and housing cooperatives at below-market rates. These ground leases to non-profit providers often require them to offer 20–30% of the subsidised units as quasi-social housing to those in need. By 2018, the city of Zurich had issued 220 new lease contracts to non-profit housing organisations (Debrunner & Hartmann, 2020). In addition to land leases, the city supports cooperatives by providing direct financing (e.g., through state pension funds investing in subordinate second mortgages to housing cooperatives) and by buying shares in cooperatives (Barenstein et al., 2022; Thiesen, 2020).

While the actors involved in subsidised housing supply differ across countries, a shared trend is the growing importance of hybrid financing models, combining public funding, land-use planning tools, private capital, and cross-subsidy strategies. However, the balancing act between financial viability and social outcomes remains a shared and persistent challenge. Countries with more market-reliant housing systems tend to experience greater problems with housing affordability and long-term access, whereas those with strong public or cooperative involvement in housing provision are often better positioned to deliver stable and inclusive housing, although typically at smaller scales and with limited capacity for growth.

Design Governance Approaches

Governance approaches are diverse and specific to a context, shaped by regulatory histories and ambitions. This section analyses how regulations, laws, and standards, both explicit and implicit, shape the design outcomes of subsidised housing.

Chile, China, and Switzerland have a targeted and clearly defined approach to design governance. For example, Chile and China apply strict additional standards to subsidised housing through laws and design guides, respectively. In Switzerland, cooperative housing must meet specific design-quality standards to be eligible for government financing and land subsidies. Neither Chile nor Switzerland has a unified, traditional social housing sector, with subsidised housing primarily provided through private ownership in Chile and collective ownership in Switzerland.

The expected quality of subsidised housing is informed by the main housing objectives and dominant housing providers in each country. In China, where housing provision is driven by large-scale developmental goals and delivered mainly by state-owned developers, and in Chile, where a significant share of the population still lacks adequate housing and delivery is through large private developers, design standards prioritise housing supply over housing quality. In contrast, in Switzerland, where supply is motivated by long-term affordability and housing quality, and delivery is primarily by small non-profit cooperatives, subsidised homes focus on spatial innovation, design quality, and social value.

In England, the Netherlands, and Spain, regulations and standards are generally universal across tenures, with few provisions applying exclusively to subsidised housing. Nonetheless, sectoral differentiation emerges in practice due to market pressures and limit in subsidies. In the Netherlands, capped rental prices, and in Spain, capped sales prices, directly influence the design of subsidised housing. In England, reliance on cross-subsidisation and delivery through planning obligations creates comparable budgetary constraints, discouraging experimentation. These financial pressures favour larger providers, who benefit from standardised designs and delivery at scale. As a result, they often adopt their own quality and development standards, which can become important drivers of housing differentiation and improvements in the sector.

The quality of design is thus closely connected to how subsidised housing is financed and delivered. Where subsidies are limited or reliant on cross-subsidisation, cost pressures tend to override design ambitions. In contrast, where land access or public funding is a key enabler of new housing supply, there is more capacity for consistent and centralised regulation as well as a long-term view. In Spain and Switzerland, for example, public land subsidies and financing also often require architectural design competitions, embedding design quality into the procurement process and enabling greater innovation in subsidised housing delivery.

The following section discusses the processes through which the various design controls for subsidised housing are implemented. Across all cases studied, the role of the state, whether as funder, planner, regulator, or landowner, remains critical in shaping what is possible in terms of affordable housing delivery and design, including in countries with advanced neoliberal housing policy frameworks.

Country Comparison

England has historically taken a differentiated approach to design governance. While mandatory building regulations control essential design aspects such as materials, structure, fire safety, ventilation, sanitation, and accessibility across all housing sectors and tenures, additional design requirements, specifically space standards, have been applied to subsidised housing since the early twentieth century. These were traditionally enforced through the conditions attached to housing subsidies.

From the early 2000s until 2015, requirements specific to subsidised housing were formalised in the Housing Quality Indicators (HQIs), which assessed factors such as unit size and layout (Housing Corporation, 1999). The Housing Standards Review (2012–2015) replaced this approach with a single national minimum space standard for all tenures: the Nationally Described Space Standard (NDSS), introduced in 2015. This moved space standards out of the subsidy framework and into the planning system as a technical standard, but without making them mandatory. Although the NDSS applies across tenures, its inclusion in local plans is discretionary and must be justified by evidence of need and economic viability.

In 2023, our survey of 322 local authorities (with a response rate of 79%, n = 253) found that only 37% (n = 93) had adopted the NDSS in their local plans and policies, while 8% (n = 21) used it solely as design guidance in their supplementary planning documents (Özer & Jacoby, 2023). Among authorities that had not adopted the NDSS, 85% (n = 112) reported not formally referencing any space standards in their local plans or planning guidance (Figure 5.1)

The regulatory policy shift from a subsidy to a planning framework coincided with broader changes in affordable housing delivery. Today, most affordable housing in England is developed without direct subsidies, primarily by housing associations through cross-subsidies or planning obligations (Figure 5.2). Importantly, as they are only included in the planning framework, space standards remain negotiable. This is less of a problem for homes delivered by housing associations, which often have their own internal development and design quality standards aligned with best practice (e.g., Peabody, 2025) – as they own their housing in principle in perpetuity, they can take a long-term view on initial housing investment and returns. However, it

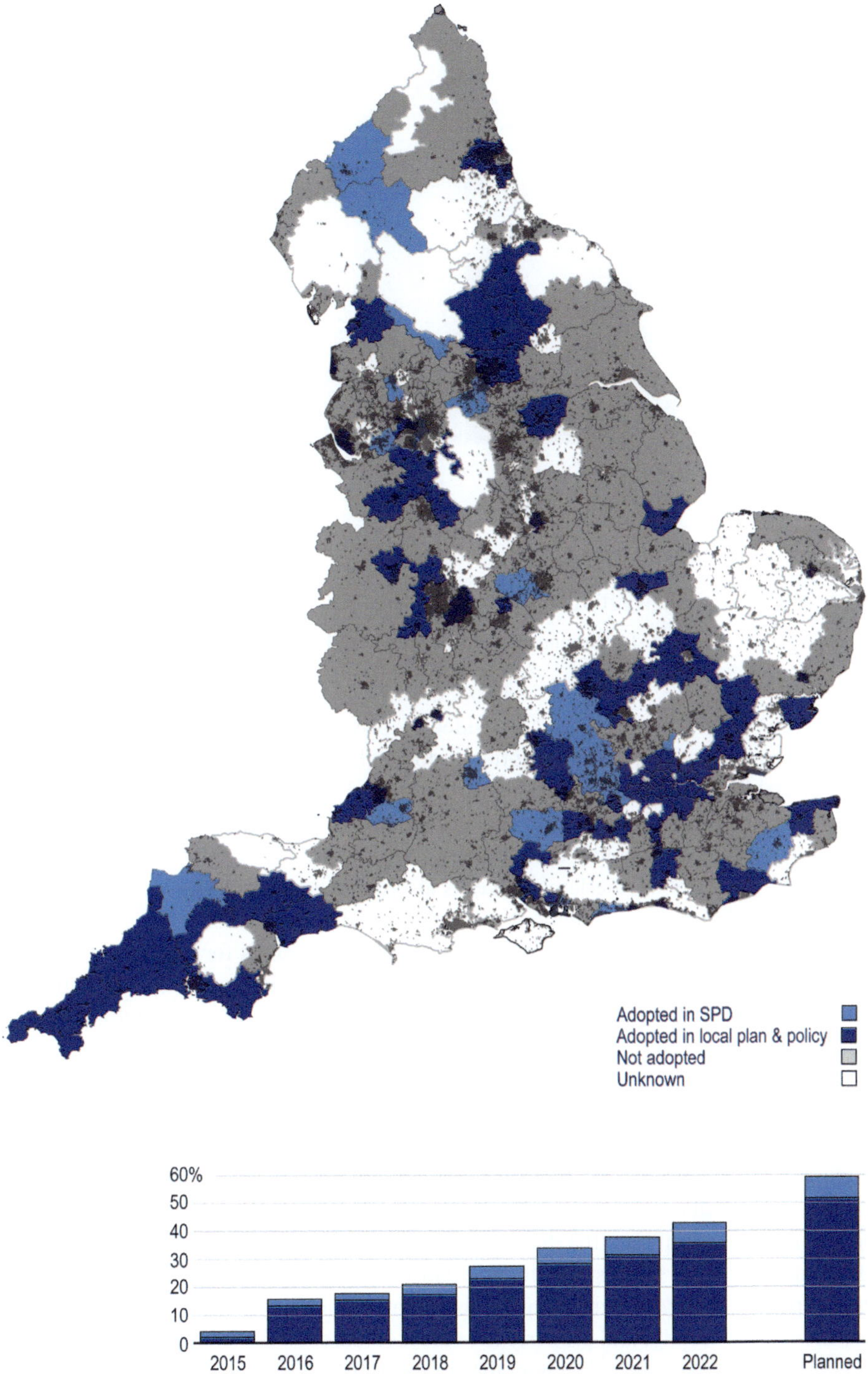

FIGURE 5.1 Local planning authorities who adopted the NDSS into their local plan or supplementary planning guidance.

Source: Özer & Jacoby (2023).

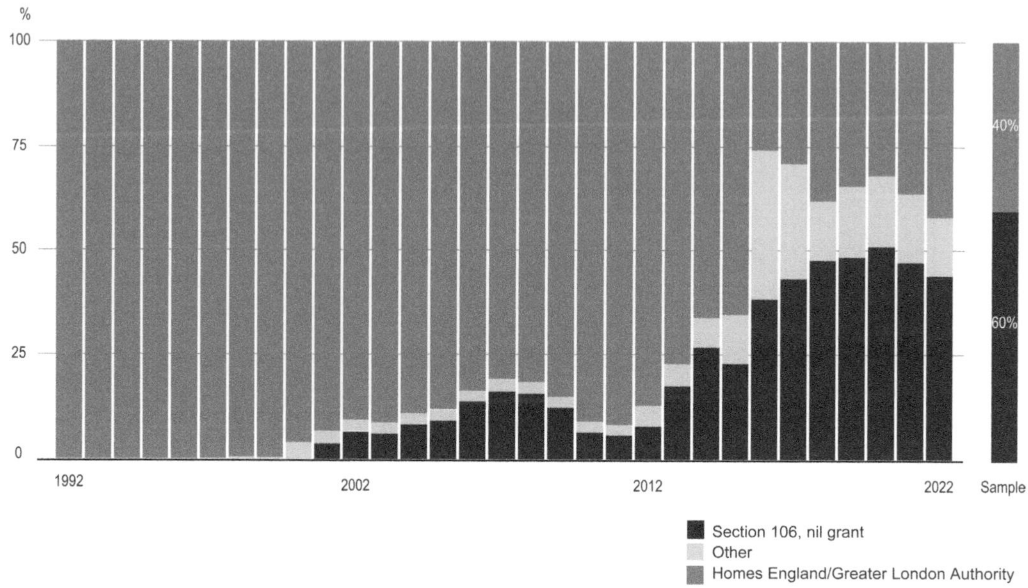

FIGURE 5.2 Financing of new affordable housing in England.

Source: Department for Levelling Up, Housing and Communities (2022b).

poses challenges in affordable housing provided by private developers as a planning condition, as design standards are frequently negotiated down. Developers often use site constraints or local market viability to justify deviations from national standards (Ferm & Raco, 2020; Sayce et al., 2017). As a result, enforcement of space standards is inconsistent, with subsidised housing often falling nationally well below the NDSS.

Similar to England, the Netherlands governs affordable housing design primarily through national and municipal plans and regulations that apply equally to all housing. This includes the 2012 Building Decree (Bouwbesluit), which provides technical standards for health and safety, usability, energy efficiency, and environmental performance. In addition, municipal planning requirements and regulations, as well as zoning plans (Bestemmingsplan, Wet Ruimtelijke Ordening) at municipal, regional, and national levels, regulate land use and impose developmental controls on building height, building footprint, building envelope, and roof shape, as well as the type and mix of housing units in developments. Municipalities also have design committees (*welstandscommissie*) that assess planning applications against local and architectural design standards.

Despite these regulatory layers, rent caps play an important role in shaping the design quality of social housing. As all rental homes below a certain rent threshold (*liberalisatiegrens*) are classified and protected as social rent, the definition of this threshold is critical. The rental value is calculated based on multiple factors, including location, unit and room sizes, kitchen and bathroom amenities, type and quality of built-in appliances, material finishes, outdoor spaces, communal or shared spaces, energy rating, and property tax values (Huurcommissie, n.d.). Some aspects of this assessment are highly detailed, especially those related to specifications such as the length of the countertop in the kitchen. In expensive areas such as Amsterdam, high land costs make it difficult for housing corporations to offer social rent homes, resulting in smaller units (often studios) and homes with basic amenities, unless they can afford to cross-subsidise the additional cost.

Similar to housing associations in England, housing corporations in the Netherlands often have their own functional and technical standards and employer requirements that define the quality of housing they provide (de Alliantie, 2017). These tend to align with the voluntary standards published by professional bodies. One example is the 2015 WoonKeur housing quality certificate (Handboek WoonKeur SKW Certificatie), which provides a "life-cycle proof" rating by measuring homes against set requirements for use, accessibility, flexibility, and adaptability. The Woonkeur manual contains six modules for both new constructions and existing buildings, covering aspects of design, installations, care provision, and mobility and accessibility. Another important reference is the *Housing Standard* (*Woonstandaard*) published in 2024 by the Stichting Netwerk Conceptueel Bouwen, a group of affordable housing providers in the Netherlands. It provides a breakdown of the minimum functional and technical requirements expected of affordable housing according to different rental classes, building types, and occupancy levels. However, these voluntary standards often prescribe floor areas, amenities, and technical requirements that exceed what current subsidy levels can support.

In Spain, the design of protected housing is governed by national and regional building codes. In Catalonia, mandatory design requirements are set out in the Decree on the Minimum Habitability Conditions of Dwellings (Decret 141/2012 Sobre Condicions Mínimes d'habitabilitat dels Habitatges i la Cèdula d'habitabilitat, DH). As in England and the Netherlands, these standards apply to all new housing regardless of tenure. However, one notable difference is the regulation of a maximum size for subsidised housing. According to the Catalan Decree 75/2014, Article 44, protected housing units must generally not exceed 90 m^2, except for accessible homes (maximum 100 m^2) and large family homes (maximum 120 m^2). Another country that regulates the maximum size of affordable homes is China, with rental housing typically ranging from 40 to 70 m^2 (Wang & Jacoby, 2023).

Similar to the Netherlands, design quality in Catalonia's subsidised sector is indirectly shaped by the cost of subsidised homes. Since there are no direct subsidies, providers must recover their development costs through sales, which, as protected housing prices are capped, creates pressure to reduce unit sizes and design quality. However, another factor influencing housing design quality is the use of architectural design competitions in the procurement process. Since in Catalonia protected housing developments in receipt of subsidies are considered public projects, they must be awarded through a competitive tendering process, meaning that every project is specifically designed for a site and programme.

Comparable to England and the Netherlands, Spanish social housing providers often have their own design guides and development standards. For instance, the Institut Català del Sòl (INCASOL) uses three standardised dwelling types and sizes for units: two-bedroom units for three people (50 m^2), two-bedroom units for four people (60 m^2), and three-bedroom units for five people (70 m^2) (INCASOL, 2019). Another key provider, the Institut Metropolità de Promoció de Sòl i Gestió Patrimonial (IMPSOL), has its own design standards and produces detailed good practice manuals for the architects they work with, covering diverse aspects of domestic life such as ventilation, housing flexibility, and gender equality.

Conclusion

Housing systems exert a direct and structural influence on housing design outcomes. How housing is regulated, financed, and delivered not only determines what affordable homes are built but also shapes their design and the standards that are applied to it. However, the approach to design governance, whether differentiated or integrated, does not directly correspond to broader system typologies, such as dualist or unitary models. China, for example, has a residualised public rental system with strictly differentiated design controls, whereas in England, where the subsidised sector is also strongly residualised, national building regulations and planning frameworks are universal across tenures.

Differences in delivery models have a substantial impact on design outcomes. In affordable housing built through policy interventions in the open market, particularly where the market is dominated by large-volume housebuilders, cost efficiency and scalability often result in extensive housing standardisation through the use of standard house or layout types and limited responsiveness to local or site contexts (Özer & Jacoby, 2023). This can be the case even where the housebuilders are non-profit organisations, such as housing associations. In comparison, smaller housing providers, such as many housing cooperatives, tend to be less focused on standardisation and more on project-specific design solutions.

Likewise, state-led delivery can result in very different housing design outcomes. While in China, state provision often relies on standardised layouts and highly rationalised planning processes to deliver housing at scale, in Spain, a more design-oriented supply model based on public tender competitions encourages site-specific and architecturally distinct affordable housing projects. However, the case studies show that design governance at the organisational level of the housing provider plays an important but often overlooked role in housing quality.

The increasing use of cross-subsidies to fund social homes is reshaping how social housing providers operate and think about design and housing standards. This can shift the priorities of social housing providers, encouraging them to adopt more market-oriented practices that can dilute their social mission or reduce support for design innovation and experimentation.

Another commonly overlooked influence on design outcomes is how affordability is calculated. For example, in the Netherlands, where affordability is more directly linked to household income and regulated rent ceilings, new social housing often consists of smaller dwellings. This allows providers to stay within rent caps but can limit access for larger households, which may struggle to find suitable homes. In comparison, England's affordable housing model pegs rent levels to a percentage of local market rates rather than household income. This can result in larger units being built, including family homes, but at rent levels unaffordable for many lower-income groups, producing more generous spatial standards which, however, do not always translate to greater accessibility for the intended target populations.

The structure of the housing system – who delivers it, how it is financed, and how affordability is defined – therefore directly and sometimes profoundly shapes housing design outcomes. Housing is thus a reflection of broader housing governance approaches that manifest in the way housing is designed, the regulations and standards it is built to, and how homes affect everyday life.

6

HOUSING STANDARDS

Socio-technical Design Controls

Seyithan Özer and Sam Jacoby

Many countries adopt a wide range of mandatory design controls to ensure that new homes meet essential technical and material standards related to health and safety, environmental performance, accessibility, and provision of infrastructures and amenities. These requirements are typically set out in building regulations or building codes and are legally enforceable (Table 6.1). In addition, many countries apply broader design requirements intended to safeguard and enhance quality of life and wellbeing, addressing design factors such as adequate space, access to amenities, prevention of overcrowding, environmental comfort, and usability. Unlike regulations, these standards are often voluntary and presented as best practice, but they frequently serve as eligibility requirements for housing subsidies. Together, mandatory regulations and voluntary standards

TABLE 6.1 Approved documents of the building regulations in England dealing with housing design standards

Safety	*Health and Comfort*	*Performance*
Part A – Structure	**Part E** – Resistance to the passage of sound	**Part L** – Conservation of fuel and power: Dwellings
Part B – Fire safety: Dwellings	**Part F** – Ventilation: Dwellings	**Part R** – Physical infrastructure and network connections for new dwellings
Part C – Site preparation and resistance to contaminants and moisture	**Part G** – Sanitation, hot water safety, and water efficiency	**Part S** – Infrastructure for charging electric vehicles
Part D – Toxic substances	**Part H** – Drainage and waste disposal	**Document 7** – Material and workmanship
Part J – Combustion appliances and fuel storage systems	**Part M** – Access to and use of buildings: Dwellings	
Part K – Protection from falling, collision, and impact	**Part O** – Overheating	
Part P – Electrical safety in dwellings		
Part Q – Security in dwellings		

DOI: 10.4324/9781032679204-10

play a critical role in ensuring that homes are fit for purpose and support the wellbeing and dignity of the people living in them.

All six countries studied in this book – England, Chile, China, the Netherlands, Spain, and Switzerland – have broadly comparable essential housing regulations, which set mandatory standards for all new homes. In addition, governments often introduce specific standards for subsidised housing to exert greater control over design outcomes. These include, for example, stricter requirements to improve accessibility and flexibility, measures to ensure natural ventilation in all rooms to reduce running costs, and, importantly, minimum dwelling sizes to guarantee the usability and adaptability of homes over time.

There are not only national but also regional differences in housing design standards and guidance. For example, the *Housing Design Standards LPG. London Plan Guidance* (Greater London Authority [GLA], 2023a) is a comprehensive local design guide in England, offering detailed supplementary advice on design policies and standards adopted by the London Plan, as well as recommending best design practice. Both of these standards and best practice recommendations constitute material considerations for local authorities when making planning decisions. The guidance addresses a wide range of design scales – from placemaking and the public realm (Part A), to shared and ancillary spaces (Part B), and homes and private outside space (Part C) – illustrating the breadth of common housing design and planning considerations (Table 6.2). The recommendations also include best practice space standards that are approximately 10% above the Nationally Described Space Standard (NDSS), reflecting changes in home use following the COVID-19 pandemic (Department for Communities and Local Government, 2015).

While dwelling size is only one aspect of housing design quality, it has become both the most regulated and widely recognised measure of housing standards and value. The protection of minimum dwelling sizes is particularly important in subsidised housing, where economic pressures are greater than in other sectors to reduce the size of homes, maximise density, and

TABLE 6.2 Scope of standards in the *Housing Design Standards LPG. London Planning Guidance*

Part A: Placemaking and the Public Realm	*Part B: Shared and Ancillary Spaces*	*Part C: Homes and Private Outside Spaces*
A1 – Response to context	B1 – Approach routes and entrances	C1 – Inclusion and accessibility
A2 – Land-use mix	B2 – Internal circulation and dwellings per core	C2 – Internal space standards
A3 – Streets and public realm	B3 – Storage of bicycles, mobility scooters, and wheelchairs	C3 – Choice and flexibility
A4 – Public open space, biodiversity, and urban greening	B4 – Car parking	C4 – Aspect, orientation, daylight, and sunlight
A5 – Inclusion and accessibility	B5 – Access for emergency and service vehicles and fire safety	C5 – Air quality, external noise, and soundproofing
	B6 – Dealing with waste and recycling	C6 – Thermal comfort
	B7 – Supplying energy efficiently (being clean)	C7 – Water usage
	B8 – On-site renewables (being green)	C8 – Digital connectivity
	B9 – Shared outside amenity space	C9 – Fire safety
	B10 – Management and maintenance	C10 – Private outside space

Source: GLA (2023a).

optimise land use due to the need to reconcile high construction costs with limited subsidies and funding. Space standards are therefore a key consideration in subsidised housing policy and design regulation, with financial feasibility having to be weighed up against the need for the long-term usability and adaptability of a home.

The amount of available space in a home affects the ability of households to prepare and share meals, socialise, store belongings, study and work from home, play, and rest. It also influences whether activities can take place simultaneously without conflict, whether household members have sufficient privacy, and whether homes can adapt to common changes in household circumstances, such as the number of occupants, ageing, or disability (HATC, 2006). Adequate space is therefore essential to physical and psychological wellbeing, enabling healthy social relationships while also providing for individual privacy and rest. Despite significant differences in average dwelling sizes across countries, the average space per person is broadly comparable, although this does not capture national variations in dwelling sizes between regions – for example, urban and rural areas – as well as housing sectors (Table 6.3).

Inadequate space is linked to overcrowding, mental health challenges, domestic accidents, lower educational attainment for children, and strained family relations (Kearns, 2022). Average

TABLE 6.3 Average dwelling sizes (all housing sectors)

	Average dwelling size	*Average household size*	*Average space per person*[1]
England[2]	96 m²	2.22	44 m²
London[2]	84 m²	2.51	–
Chile[3]	66 m²	2.80	18 m²
Santiago[3]	79 m²	2.90	–
China[4]	111 m²	2.92	42 m²
Shenzhen[4]	72 m²	2.25	–
Netherlands[5]	120 m²	2.10	53 m²
Amsterdam[5]	77 m²	1.84	–
Spain[6]	106.5 m²	2.50	43 m²
Barcelona[7]	78 m²	2.30	–
Switzerland[8]	99 m²	2.10	47 m²
Zurich (Canton)[8]	97 m²	2.00	–

Notes:

Full project data are available online: https://doi.org/10.60624/nnc8-1557.

[1] Calculations are based on average dwelling sizes and household sizes.

[2] Dwelling sizes: Ministry of Housing, Communities and Local Government [MHCLG] (2020a, 2025); household sizes: Office for National Statistics [ONS] (2025a). In 2024, the average usable floor space in social rented homes was 66m², in private rented homes 76m², and owner occupied homes 110m² in England.

[3] Dwelling size: Molina et al. (2020); household size: Ministerio de Desarollo Social (2023). Santiago: Instituto del Cemento y del Hormigón de Chile, 2019

[4] National Bureau of Statistics of China (2020); Shenzhen: Zheng (2023) and China-Census.org. (2025).

[5] Dwelling size: Centraal Bureau voor de Statistiek (2024); household size: Eurostat (2025a) and Amsterdam: Urbistat. (2023).

[6] Dwelling size: Eurostat (2025b); household size: Eurostat (2025a).

[7] Dwelling size: Blanchar (2020); household size: Barcelona Datastore (2025).

[8] Dwelling size: Bundesamt für Statistik (2024a); household size: Bundesamt für Statistik (2024b).

TABLE 6.4 Average dwelling sizes by tenure in England

	Owner occupied	*Private rent*	*Local authority*	*Housing association*
Average floor area	111 m²	76 m²	66 m²	67 m²
Space per person	50 m²	33 m²	28 m²	32 m²

Source: Based on data from DLUHC (2023).

dwelling sizes differ significantly between housing tenures (Table 6.4), with public or social rented as well as lower-cost private homes typically the smallest. However, averages can conceal important differences within tenures and disguise wider housing quality and maintenance issues. In England, for instance, around 23% of all private rented homes fail the Decent Home Standard, compared with 11% in the social rented sector (Department of Levelling Up, Housing and Communities [DLUHC], 2022a), highlighting that inadequate housing is not just a question of tenure or size.

The COVID-19 lockdowns further revealed how a lack of space and poor housing conditions can increase stress, strain household relationships, and limit the occupants' ability to carry out domestic activities in comfort and in parallel (Alonso Aranda & Jacoby, 2023; Brown et al., 2021; Jacoby & Alonso Aranda, 2022; Özer & Jones, 2022). Dwelling size and spatial design impact not only the usability of a home, but also its accessibility. For older people and those with mobility or access challenges, inadequately sized and poorly arranged spaces can be unsafe and create barriers to independence, limiting their quality of everyday domestic life.

Space standards vary considerably in their formulation and implementation. The way a standard is defined and formulated – whether at room level, dwelling level, or both – and the specific dimensions or performance benchmarks it prescribes can determine how it is translated into actual designs. Equally important is how a standard is implemented, including its regulatory status, which can range from binding legal requirements to voluntary guidelines issued by the government, professional bodies, or housing providers.

A key determinant of these variations is the role the state plays in controlling design outcomes and, consequently, what kind of regulatory function space standards serve. Depending on context, they can be a safeguard ensuring minimum acceptable conditions or a driver for improving housing quality. The implementation and impact of space standards is thus shaped by housing systems and design governance approaches. While many countries have introduced formal or informal benchmarks for minimum dwelling sizes, their influence on actual housing delivery depends on an interplay of regulations, market conditions, and development models. Taken together, these factors define different typologies of space-standard implementation.

In countries such as Chile and China, housing policy is largely target-driven, prioritising the reduction of housing deficits through large-scale developments rather than focusing on individual housing quality. Standards in these contexts tend to be narrowly defined within existing subsidy frameworks and fiscal constraints, promoting cost-efficient housing supply. The outcome is typically smaller homes with basic finishes and provisions, aiming to maximise housing access for both low- and mid-income populations under pressure from growing housing costs. Standards function primarily as regulatory tools to ensure that minimum design requirements are met, enabling the production of subsidised homes within limited budgets.

By contrast, many European countries, such as Switzerland, Spain, the Netherlands, and England, place greater emphasis on design quality, sometimes at the expense of overall housing supply. In some countries, such as England, standards operate as normative, formal constraints, closely guiding design outcomes. In others, like the Netherlands, they serve more as aspirational, voluntary guidelines, often compromised by cost ceilings and rent regulation. In Zurich, space standards are treated as a baseline, regularly exceeded within cooperative housing that prioritises spatial quality and flexibility of use.

Although the definition of affordable housing and its design standards varies, spatial adequacy is commonly framed in terms of human dignity, wellbeing, usability, and long-term values, reflecting traditions of housing as a core element of social welfare policy – despite the widespread erosion of welfare-based housing models through repeated policy changes and growing market pressures since the 1980s. Design standards are therefore understood not just as regulatory instruments but also as a social commitment to improving living standards. Housing design outcomes in these contexts thus tend to produce more generously sized homes with higher-quality finishes and better provision of services and amenities.

Housing Sample and Characteristics

The selection of developments and dwelling layouts for analysis focused on recent subsidised housing projects. Increasingly, subsidised housing is built for ownership and therefore less targeted at low-income and more at middle-income groups. As a result, subsidised housing developments are frequently delivered as mixed-tenure schemes for socio-economically diverse residents from both low- and mid-income populations. Given that land and construction costs are major constraints on delivering new subsidised housing, high-density building types, particularly blocks of flats, are the most typical design solutions. In the larger cities studied – London, Shenzhen, Amsterdam, Barcelona, and Zurich – flats dominate, although houses are still common in Santiago and less urban areas of England.

The sampling approach followed three main steps: (1) identifying the largest subsidised housing providers in each region or city, (2) selecting their most recently completed large-scale developments, and (3) collecting building and dwelling plans, together with information on housing types and tenure mix. This was obtained through online searches, planning application records, and information supplied directly by housing providers. Only developments for which sufficient data were available were included in the analysis (Table 6.5). This approach enabled, on the one hand, an examination of the standardisation practices of major housing providers, and on the other, a comparative overview of dwelling types and development standards across the samples from the six countries.

Many of the sampled developments are mixed-tenure due to shared policy ambitions for the spatial and social integration of subsidised housing, but also because insufficient state subsidies create a need for cross-subsidisation. The social mix of developments, however, can be very nuanced, although in most countries, subsidised housing is distinct from private developments and built on specifically allocated land. In England, private, public, and social housing are often combined in the same project; in China, subsidised housing is for both low-income groups and highly skilled workers; in Switzerland, subsidised housing is largely cooperatively owned; while in Chile, socio-economic groups are deliberately integrated. Likewise, the drivers of tenure integration differ; in Santiago, for example, this is due to an effort to address socio-spatial segregation of low-income groups traditionally excluded from urban infrastructure, with the 2016 DS19 policy offering subsidies to attract middle-income households and use this income to cross-subsidise the homes of low-income households in well-located and well-serviced mixed developments.

TABLE 6.5 Analysed subsidised housing projects in relation to providers and the representative number of dwelling units

Country	*Housing providers*	*Year built*	*No. of projects*	*No. of units*
England	10 largest regional and three national housing associations: L&Q and Peabody (Greater London), Vivid (Southeast), LiveWest (South West), Orbit (East of England), Bromford (West Midlands), EMH Group (East Midlands), Yorkshire Housing (Yorkshire), Karbon (North East), Torus (North West); and Clarion, Stonewater, and Home Group (national).	2020–2022	153	9,876
Santiago (Chile)	Recently completed subsidised housing.	2020–2022	11	2,754
Shenzhen (China)	Recently completed public rental and talent housing.	2020–2022	10	5,604
Amsterdam (Netherlands)	Two largest housing corporations: Ymere and de Alliantie.	2019–2022	11	855
Barcelona (Spain)	Main municipal arms-length housing organisations in Barcelona: Institut Metropolità de Promoció de Sòl i Gestió Patrimonial (IMPSOL).	2017–2023	8	516
Zurich (Switzerland)	Two largest housing cooperatives: Allgemeine Baugenossenschaft Zürich (ABZ) and Baugenossenschaft Zürich (BGZ).	2017–2022	8	1,012

Despite policy ambitions for "tenure-blind" housing development, spatial segregation between housing for rent and ownership and market homes persists in most schemes. Subsidised housing is still typically grouped in distinct blocks or areas away from other tenures, with separate access, and sometimes even separate provision of amenities. It is also common to use different finishes and materials in affordable housing than in private housing, visually distinguishing socio-economic differences and creating the perception of "cheaper" homes.

In addition, in contexts such as England and Chile, where the aspirational home is usually a house, the extensive use of flats in subsidised rent homes outside London or incremental building processes in Santiago reinforce typological stigma and negative associations between flats, informality linked to incrementally built homes, and social housing. Similarly, poor construction quality and limited maintenance can undermine long-term housing investment and value, as in Shenzhen, where flats older than 15 years are often described as "old" and viewed as undesirable to live in due to poor maintenance.

Nevertheless, the sampled housing includes a wide range of typologies, from terraced houses to blocks of flats to high-rises (Figure 6.1). They highlight the different degrees of housing standardisation – from the repetition of standardised units in two-storey houses to the repetitive vertical and horizontal layout of flats. The extent of the standardisation varies by context and housebuilder, being less common in Spain and Switzerland but producing highly rationalised plans in the case of England.

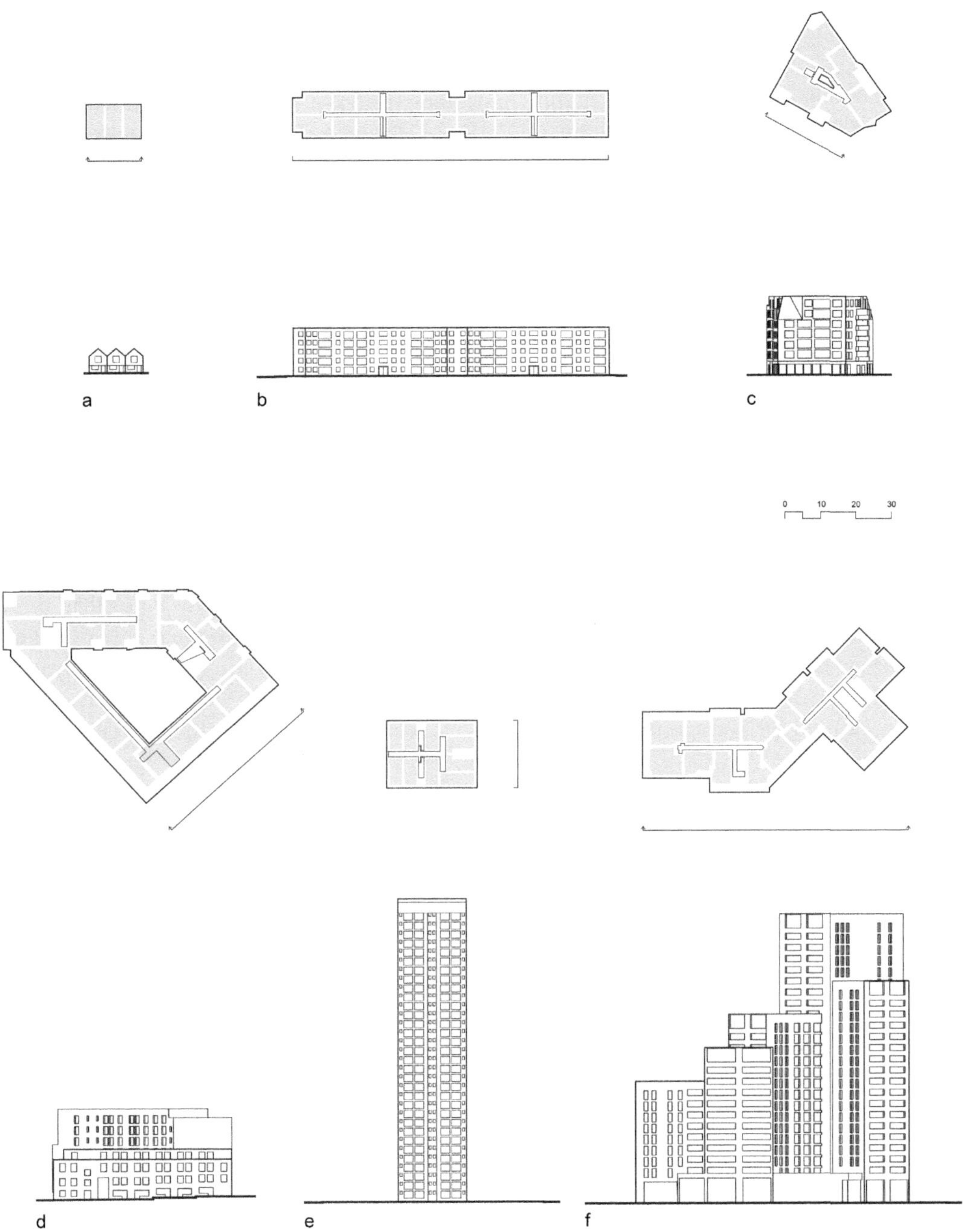

FIGURE 6.1 Common building typologies within the sample.

Source: Drawn by Claudia Andrea Chavarría.

Notes: a: terraced houses (Hampshire, England), b: slab block (Santiago, Chile), c: midrise block (Zurich, Switzerland), d: courtyard block (London, England), e: tower block (Shenzhen, China), f: tower cluster (London, England)

In England, the sample of 4,074 two- and three-bedroom houses was derived from only 244 standard type plans, which amounted to only 129 distinct type plans once repetition across developments and between different developers was considered (Özer & Jacoby, 2023). These homes were typically designed to comply either with the NDSS, introduced in 2015, or the earlier Housing Quality Indicators (HQI), a funding requirement for the National Affordable Housing Programme (2008–2011) and Affordable Housing Programme (2011–2015) by the Housing Corporation and the Homes and Communities Agency. Even dwellings that do not meet the current NDSS often comply with the former HQI standards, which required minimum dwelling sizes around 10% smaller that the NDSS. This indicates that most new-build homes are still based on some form of tangible space standard (Figures 6.2–6.3 and Table 6.6). The HQI assessed housing quality in its multiple dimensions, but the burden of complex assessment soon narrowed the focus to the basic dimensional criteria in the NDSS.

In England, 44% of new affordable housing is delivered through planning obligations that require private developers to include affordable units as part of their housing project under a so-called Section 106 agreement in order to gain planning consent (DLUHC, 2024a). While similar mechanisms exist in Amsterdam, where social housing is in contrast defined according to a rent cap and not its provider, in England even schemes led by registered providers usually mix affordable and market-rate homes, reflecting a financing model based on cross-subsidy and policy ambitions to integrate tenures.

However, affordable housing often employs different standardised house types than those used in the private market. A comparison of house types in England shows that only 6% of affordable and private housing by the same developer share the same house types. An analysis of 25 schemes by three major developers showed that private house types were more consistently reused – utilised on average in three developments, compared with two for affordable house

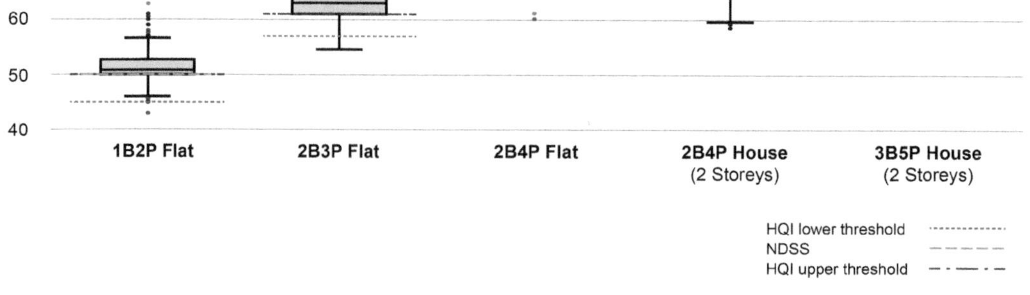

FIGURE 6.2 Dwelling size distribution per dwelling type in England.

Source: Özer & Jacoby (2023).

5.1 Unit type by area (75%) Please enter the number of units to which any of the following apply enter something on every line – use 'not applicable' for unit types not included in the scheme	Exceeds the upper figure by over 10%	Exceeds the upper figure by 1%-10%	Meets / falls within the range	Falls short of the lower figure by 1%-10%	Falls short of the lower figure by over 10%
5.1.1 1 bedspace 30 to 35 sq m					
5.1.2 2 bedspace 45 to 50 sq m					
5.1.3 3 bedspace 57 to 67 sq m					
5.1.4 4 bedspace 67 to 75 sq m					
5.1.5 5 bedspace 1 storey 75 to 85 sq m					
5.1.6 5 bedspace 2 storey 82 to 85 sq m					
5.1.7 5 bedspace 3 storey 85 to 95 sq m					
5.1.8 6 bedspace 1 storey 85 to 95 sq m					
5.1.9 6 bedspace 2 storey 95 to 100 sq m					
5.1.10 6 bedspace 3 storey 100 to 105 sq m					
5.1.11 7 bedspace 2+ storey 108 to 115 sq m					
5.1.12 7+ bedspace add 10 sq m per bedspace					
5.1.13 Other					

5.2 Units by living spaces (25%) *please enter the number of units to which any of the following apply. Enter something on every line*	**Number of units.**
5.2.1 At least the number of rooms required for the unit size are provided	
5.2.2 Additional bedroom above minimum required is provided	
5.2.3 Additional WC above minimum required is provided	
5.2.4 Additional bath/shower facility is provided in separate room from main bathroom	
5.2.5 Study/ separate work area is provided	
5.2.6 Separate utility room or separable utility space is possible	
5.2.7 Conservatory/enclosed sun porch/balcony (min. 3 sqm) is provided	
COMMENTS: Have any comments been entered on the comment page at the end?	

FIGURE 6.3 Housing Quality Indicator (HQI): internal environment core standard: unit type by area and units by living spaces.

Source: Housing Corporation (2008).

types. Notably, private sale homes were often smaller than their comparable affordable standardised house types (Figure 6.4).

The dataset compiled from housing developments across the six countries enabled both a comparison of average dwelling sizes by unit type and an analysis of the distribution of sizes within and across national contexts (Table 6.7). This highlights not only cross-country differences – such as the smaller homes typical of Santiago and the larger homes in Zurich – but also the degree of variation within a housing market. The data provide a comparative perspective on how space standards are applied or sometimes circumvented in the design and construction of affordable housing.

In London, newly built homes closely align with the NDSS. Median sizes for one-, two-, and three-bedroom flats almost exactly match the minimum requirements, for example, 50.8 m^2 for

TABLE 6.6 Technical housing standards – Nationally Described Space Standard (NDSS): Minimum gross internal floor areas and storage (m^2)

Number of bedrooms (b)	*Number of bed spaces (persons)*	*1 storey dwellings*	*2 storey dwellings*	*3 storey dwellings*	*Built-in storage*
1b	1p	39 (37)*	–	–	1.0
	2p	50	58	–	1.5
2b	3p	61	70	–	2.0
	4p	70	79	–	2.0
3b	4p	74	84	90	2.5
	5p	86	93	99	2.5
	6p	95	102	108	2.5
4b	5p	90	97	103	3.0
	6p	99	106	112	3.0
	7p	108	115	121	3.0
	8p	117	124	130	.03
5b	6p	103	110	116	3.5
	7p	112	119	125	3.5
	8p	121	128	134	3.5
6b	7p	116	123	129	4.0
	8p	125	132	138	4.0

Note: Redrawn, based on the Department for Communities and Local Government (2015).

a one-bedroom flat (a 50-m^2 standard dictated for two-person occupancy) and 70 m^2 for a two-bedroom flat (equalling a 70-m^2 standard for four-person occupancy). Limited variation in dwelling sizes suggests strong standardisation and little flexibility, with developers tending to build at the lower end of the permissible range, effectively treating the standards as a de facto maximum.

However, compliance with space standards varies across regions and dwelling types (Fig. 6.2). In England, 71% of flats meet the NDSS standards, compared with only 18% of houses, with compliance higher in London. This reflects both the predominance of flats in London (95% of affordable homes) versus 30% elsewhere, where houses are still common, and morphological differences. Space standards can be applied more efficiently in flats, whereas multi-storey houses face greater planning challenges due to building envelope and geometry constraints, the need to coordinate functions across floors, and additional circulation requirements. Although the standards allow for generous circulation areas, designers and developers often create more compact layouts, resulting in houses that fall below the NDSS despite having similar overall room provision to flats.

In addition, regional differences reflect uneven adoption of space standards. In London, space standards have existed since the introduction of the *London Housing Design Guide* in 2011. However, only 37% of local authorities in England, including all those in London, have formally adopted the NDSS since 2015 (Özer & Jacoby, 2023), creating significant regulatory divergence and regional disparities in housing standards.

In comparison to England, dwelling sizes in Amsterdam fall significantly short of the Woonstandaard. Median one-bedroom flats measure only 46.6 m^2, well below the recommended 60 m^2 minimum, while studios fail to meet the 42 m^2 benchmark. Even two-bedroom units, at 62 m^2 median, remain 10 m^2 below the recommended Woonstandaard dwelling size. This

FIGURE 6.4 Standardised house types in affordable and private housing (Bloor Homes).

Source: Özer & Jacoby (2023).

demonstrates that voluntary, aspirational standards such as the Woonstandaard have limited impact, particularly in social housing without sufficient subsidy support.

In Zurich, by contrast, cooperative housing considerably exceeds the standards of the Wohnungs-Bewertungs-System (WBS; Housing Evaluation System), a comprehensive design quality evaluation tool developed in 2015 by the Bundesamt für Wohnungswesen (BWO; Federal Office for Housing) to evaluate new developments, support architects in their planning, and determine the eligibility of homes for subsidies. Median one-bedroom flats measure 63.1 m^2, above the WBS-recommended 45 m^2, and two-bedroom units reach 84 m^2, again exceeding the 60-m^2 minimum. However, this has prompted calls for smaller homes to reduce climate impact

TABLE 6.7 Unit sizes and their distribution

	n	*mean*	*Min*	*M*	*max*
London* (n = 2,301)					
One-bedroom flat	747	51.5	40.2	50.8	77.0
Two-bedroom flat	1,104	71.8	61.0	70.0	110.2
Three-bedroom flat	450	91.6	74.3	87.0	109.0
England (excluding London)* (n = 1,829)					
One-bedroom flat	735	50.6	37.2	50.7	70.2
Two-bedroom flat	1,031	66.1	54.6	65.1	90.9
Three-bedroom flat	63	88.1	74.5	84.3	104.7
Santiago (n = 4,022)					
One-bedroom flat	318	33.8	29.3	33.9	37.5
Two-bedroom flat	2,276	50.7	45.6	51.2	62.6
Three-bedroom flat	1,428	58.8	45.6	59.7	62.4
Shenzhen					
One-bedroom flat	2,424	47.7	44.5	48.6	50.0
Two-bedroom flat	3,388	58.9	54.2	59.2	67.8
Amsterdam (n = 855)**					
Studio	238	40.6	22.6	40.9	48.5
One-bedroom flat	291	45.2	37.2	46.6	48.9
Two-bedroom flat	326	60.1	45.8	62.0	72.6
Barcelona (n = 516)**					
One-bedroom flat	22	44.2	43.6	44.1	44.4
Two-bedroom flat	267	60.0	47.0	60.3	67.2
Three-bedroom flat	227	70.9	33.1	75.0	86.1
Zurich (n = 1,012)**					
One-bedroom flat	227	63.7	51.1	63.1	68.2
Two-bedroom flat	452	87.4	74.6	84.0	126.2
Three-bedroom flat	333	100.3	95.6	100.6	111.5

Note: * Gross floor area. ** Usable floor area.

and operational costs. Although smaller than Swiss private-sector homes, cooperative housing still provides some of the largest subsidised dwellings in Europe. Benefitting from subsidised public land and loans, it prioritises long-term shared assets and adaptability over short-term cost efficiency. WBS standards are the most generous studied: a three-room unit (equivalent to a two-bedroom unit elsewhere) scores points for a 60–90-m^2 net internal floor area, with top marks given for 70–78 m^2. In comparison, in England the minimum gross internal floor area in the NDSS for a two-bedroom flat is 61 m^2 for three occupants and 70 m^2 for four.

Dwelling size standards in Switzerland are, however, just one element of the WBS, which encourages long-term adaptability and design innovation by basing its definition of housing quality on a comprehensive yet flexible multi-scalar scoring system that evaluates 25 key criteria from the urban environment to the building and unit scale, resulting in generously designed homes and supporting greater social and typological diversity (Table 6.8). Developments such as Mehr Als Wohnen in Zurich exemplify this approach and include cluster housing that combines private living spaces with shared kitchens and communal areas to support new forms of co-living. Similar experimentation is evident in Barcelona, where providers such as the Institut Municipal del Paisatge i la Sostenibilitat de l'Habitatge de Barcelona (IMPSOL) are setting new standards

TABLE 6.8 Twenty-five criteria of the WBS Housing Evaluation System

Urban Design	*Building Design*	*Unit Design*
K1 – Unit and type mix	K7 – Pedestrians and cyclists	K15 – Net floor area
K2 – Additional/supporting uses	K8 – Communal outdoor space	K16 – Room sizes
K3 – Mobility and transport	K9 – Private vehicles	K17 – Flexibility
K4 – Connection	K10 – Access	K18 – Furniture and use
K5 – Open space	K11 – Storage	K19 – Kitchen and dining
K6 – Participation	K12 – Spaces for communal use	K20 – Sanitary provision
	K13 – Washing and drying rooms	K21 – Storage
	K14 – Multipurpose communal spaces	K22 – Adaptability
		K23 – Private outdoor space
		K24 – Privacy and access
		K25 – Private storage outside the unit

for social housing design and integration. Design innovation is also driven by policies requiring larger projects in Switzerland and Spain to be tendered through design competitions. Not-for-profit housing cooperatives are particularly well-positioned to deliver these homes, as they enable more collective decision-making and can take a long-term view on development and costs.

Unit size and the number of bedrooms play an important role in balancing competing priorities within affordable housing provision. It directly influences construction costs, density, and the total number of units deliverable at a site. At the same time, it determines the capacity of the housing stock to accommodate households of varying sizes and compositions. Thus, the tension between maximising unit numbers and meeting the spatial needs of diverse households manifests differently across housing systems and economies.

In Chile, the national subsidy framework requires a minimum of two bedrooms per unit, with the typical aspirational home having three bedrooms. In houses, this is often achieved incrementally over time, as most initially only provide two bedrooms, unlike flats, which usually have three bedrooms. By contrast, in countries such as England and the Netherlands, where subsidies are constrained and delivery increasingly relies on planning obligations, rent-regulated frameworks, and cross-subsidies, there is greater pressure to maximise housing output, often resulting in homes with fewer bedrooms – although overall dwelling sizes might be comparable with the standard for a three-bedroom, five-person home in Chile (55 m^2) and a one-bedroom, three-person home in England (61 m^2).

In England, this pressure is particularly evident in areas with buoyant property markets. In London and the South East, one-bedroom units constitute a significant share of new developments (29% and 27%, respectively), whereas larger units like three-bedroom homes are more common in less expensive areas such as the north of England. Similarly, in the Netherlands, where social housing is defined by a rent cap based on a points system that factors in dwelling size, amenities, and location, housing corporations can only afford to deliver small homes in expensive cities like Amsterdam. Consequently, affordable housing provisions in Amsterdam increasingly consist of studios and one-bedroom flats under 50 m^2 in size.

The wide range of one-, two-, and three-bedroom floorplans in the sample from six countries therefore visually and dimensionally illustrates how dwelling layouts respond to local housing systems, space standards, household requirements, and socio-technical norms. These plans embody different design governance approaches and strategies used to balance efficiency, flexibility, and liveability, while also reflecting diverse regulatory and economic contexts (Figs. 6.5–6.7).

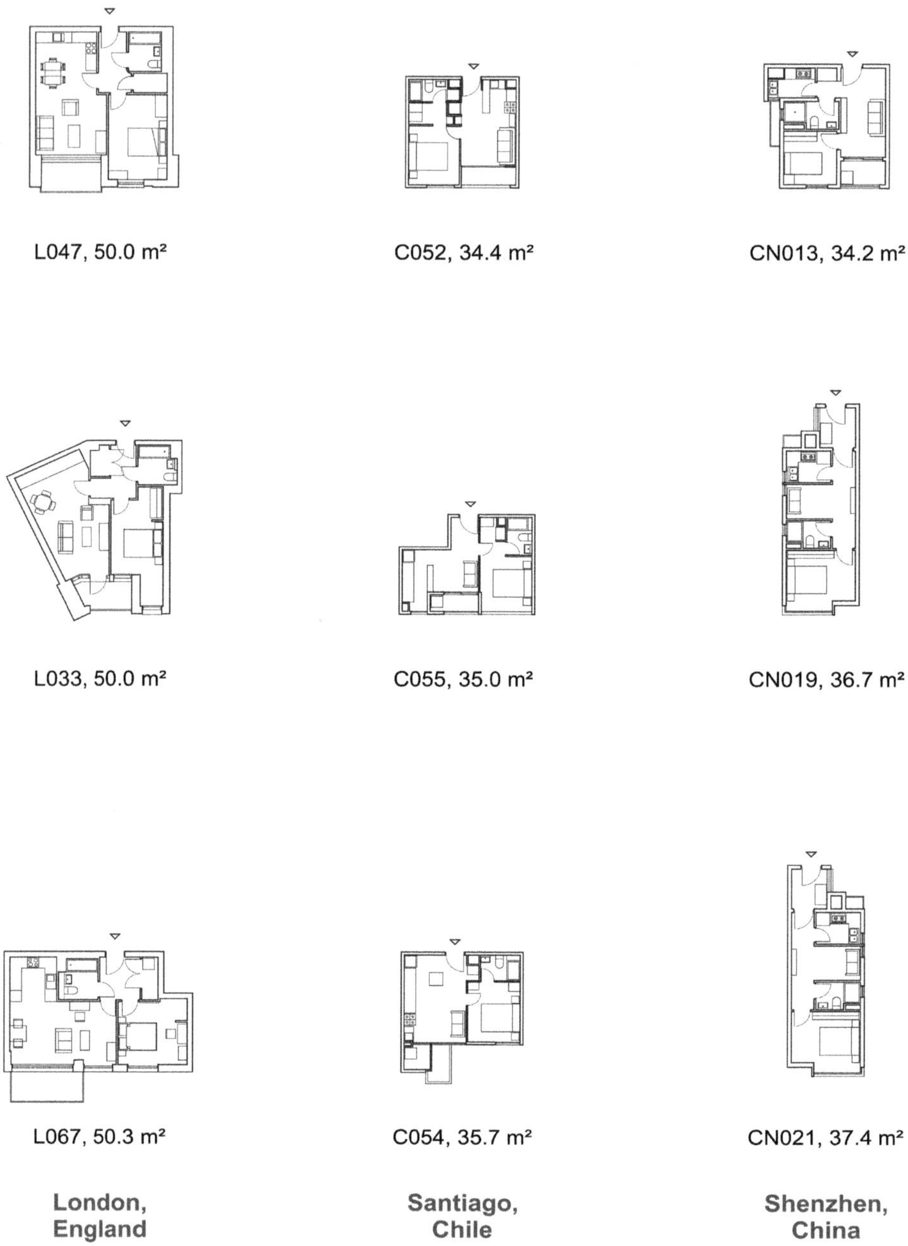

FIGURE 6.5 Sample of one-bedroom homes from London, Santiago, Shenzhen, Amsterdam, Barcelona, and Zurich.

Source: Drawn by Claudia Andrea Chavarría.

Note: For further plan data see: https://doi.org/10.60624/nnc8-1557.

FIGURE 6.6 Sample of two-bedroom homes from London, Santiago, Shenzhen, Amsterdam, Barcelona, and Zurich.

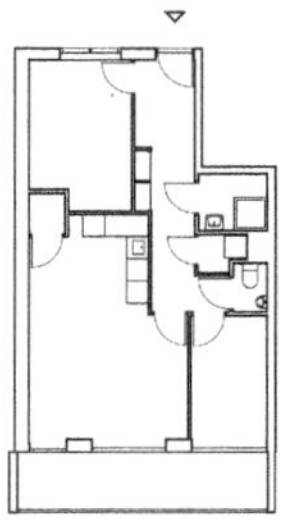

A044, 60.3 m²

B016, 59.9 m²

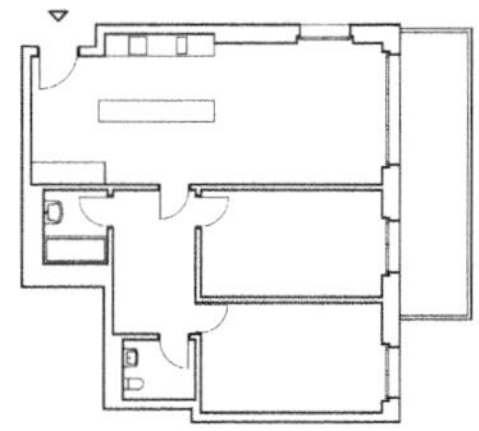

Z009, 82.4 m²

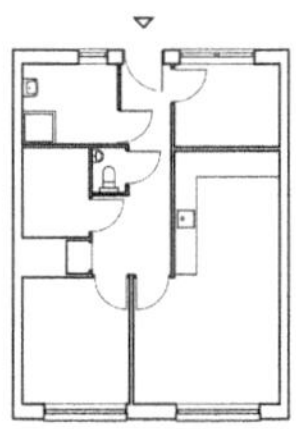

A063, 60.5 m²

B045, 60.8 m²

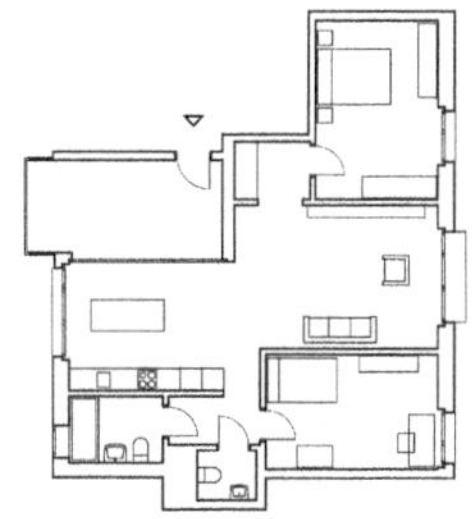

Z030, 83.1 m²

A065, 63.0 m²

B022, 62.4 m²

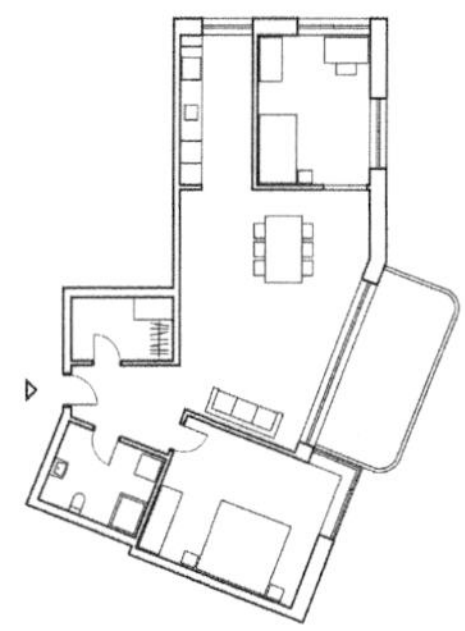

Z020, 84.6 m²

Amsterdam, Netherlands

Barcelona, Spain

Zurich, Switzerland

Source: Drawn by Claudia Andrea Chavarría.

Note: For further plan data see: https://doi.org/10.60624/nnc8-1557.

FIGURE 6.7 Sample of three-bedroom homes from London, Santiago, Shenzhen, Amsterdam, Barcelona, and Zurich.

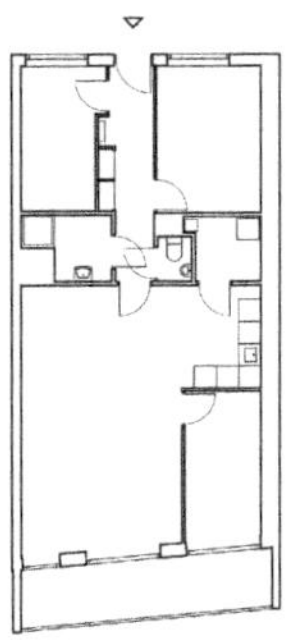

A050, 82.6 m²

B025, 71.3 m²

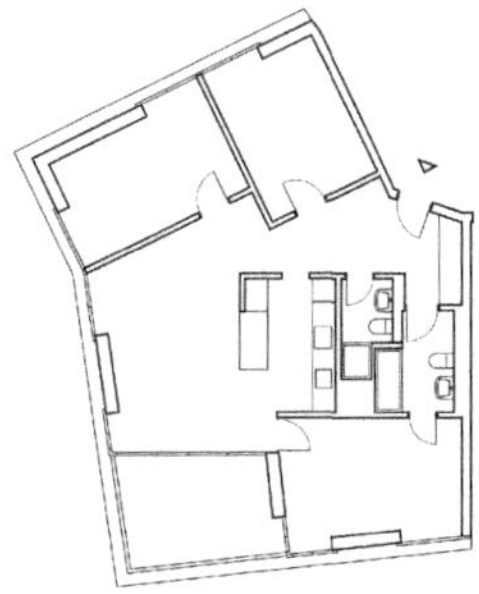

Z035, 98.6 m²

A060, 86.4 m²

B001, 71.4 m²

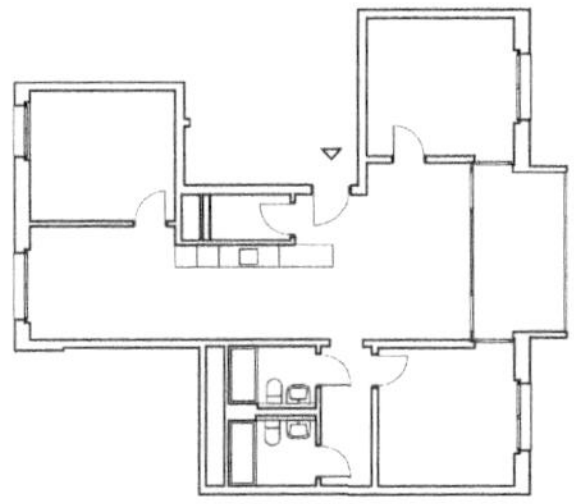

Z028, 100.6 m²

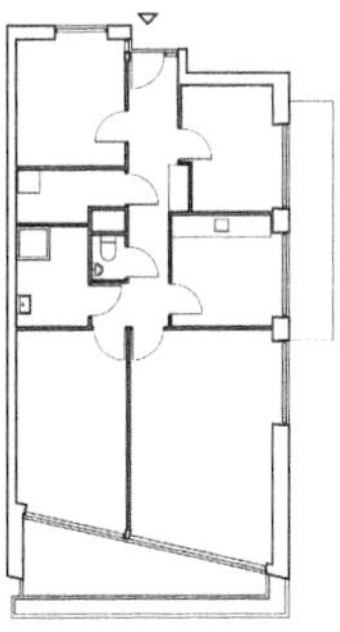

A071, 87.9 m²

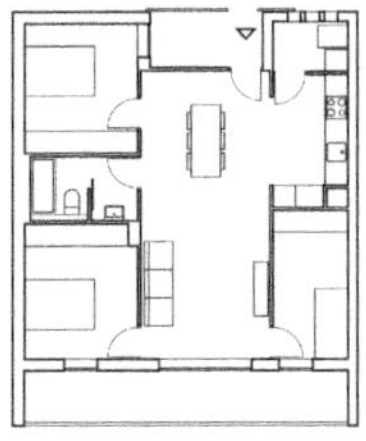

B006, 71.9 m²

Z005, 105.8 m²

Amsterdam, Netherlands

Barcelona, Spain

Zurich, Switzerland

Source: Drawn by Claudia Andrea Chavarría.

Note: For further plan data see: https://doi.org/10.60624/nnc8-1557.

Implementation of Space Standards

The implementation of space standards depends partly on the housing system and whether design controls are differentiated or universal in their application across housing sectors – broadly comparable to Kemeny's (1995) distinction between dualist and unitary rental markets. Although England, Spain, and Switzerland theoretically apply standards equally across all sectors, in practice this is more nuanced, and all six countries that were studied enforce or incentivise a separate and sometimes stricter application of standards for subsidised housing.

Voluntary standards are often developed by government agencies, professional bodies, or subsidised housing providers, either to supplement existing requirements or in place of mandatory standards, in order to promote best practice or support particular needs in the subsidised housing sector. These standards are frequently reinforced through government incentives and planning agreements, but also by insurance requirements, home warranties, or certification, which can blur the line between voluntary and regulatory measures. The countries studied illustrate the diversity of regulatory and voluntary approaches to space standards and how they apply to subsidised housing (Table 6.9).

TABLE 6.9 Space standards in England, Chile, China, the Netherlands, Spain, and Switzerland

Context	*Space standards*	*Details*
England	Nationally Described Space Standard (2015)	Specifies the internal space requirements for new dwellings but applies only when specifically adopted by a local planning authority.
Chile	Supreme Decree 19 (Social and Territorial Integration Programme, 2016) Supreme Decree 49 (Solidarity Housing Choice Fund, 2012)	Specify the design and space standards required by the two main subsidy programmes for low-income and mid-income households.
Shenzhen, China	Shenzhen Public Housing Design Standards (2021)	Specifies required public housing design standards, with distinct requirements for each affordable tenure.
Netherlands	Building Decree (Bouwbesluit, 2012)	Specifies statutory minimum dwelling floor areas.
	Housing Standard (Woonstandaard, 2024)	Voluntary design standard, categorised by housing type and cost according to rental class, published by a network of affordable housing providers.
Barcelona, Spain	Decree 13/2010	Law governing protected housing, defined as homes below a certain size, without specifying design standards.
	Decree 141/2012 (Minimum conditions for habitability)	Specifies the minimum and maximum floor area as well as internal space requirements of social housing.
	INCASOL Social Housing Standards (2019)	Organisation-specific social housing design standards for the Institut Català del Sòl, distinguishing between three unit types by size and number of bedrooms.
Switzerland	WBS Housing Evaluation System (2015)	The WBS is a scoring system used to assess eligibility for housing subsidies, evaluating 25 housing-quality criteria, from the location to the design of the development, building, and individual dwelling unit.

The legal status and consistency of space-standard adoption greatly depend on the regulatory tools used to implement them, as well as existing regulatory cultures and preferences. In England, for example, the NDSS, introduced in 2015 as a first cross-sector technical standard, is part of the national planning framework rather than a statutory regulation. It therefore only applies if adopted by local planning authorities within their local plans, leading to inconsistent implementation and enforcement.

In Chile and China, space standards only apply to subsidised housing and are strictly enforced through subsidy conditions. For instance, Chile's subsidy decrees – DS No. 49 Fondo Solidario De Elección De Vivienda (2012) for low-income housing and DS No. 1 Subsidio Para Sectores Medios (2016) for mid-income housing – specify design and dimensional requirements for dwellings. Similarly, Chinese regional and municipal governments publish their own detailed design standards for subsidised housing that both public and private developers must follow. However, in Switzerland, while dwelling sizes are not directly controlled by law, to qualify for land subsidies and access to special loans, housing cooperatives must achieve sufficient scores on the WBS, which assesses dwelling sizes and flexibility.

In contrast to these sector-specific and subsidy-linked requirements, in the Netherlands and Spain, basic dwelling sizes are legally regulated and thus apply to all new homes. In the Netherlands, minimum dwelling and room sizes are defined in a building decree (Bouwbesluit). In Catalonia (Spain), minimum space requirements are set out in the Habitability Decree (Decret 141/2012). In addition, Catalonia also generally limits the maximum size of subsidised homes to 90 m^2.

Beyond formal regulation, voluntary and provider-level design standards play a major role in subsidised housing design and supply, often linked to standardised dwelling layouts. English housing associations typically have their organisation-specific design and development standards, commonly aligned with the NDSS and best practice guides. This is exemplified by the *Peabody Design Guide* (Peabody, 2025), which in parts exceeds legal design requirements and sets sector-wide best practice. In the Netherlands, the social housing sector widely recognises the Woonstandaard (Housing Standard), which, although not legally binding, serves as a de facto design benchmark. Similarly, in Catalonia, the public housing agency Institut Català del Sòl (INCASOL) has developed its own design guide, including standardised dwelling and room sizes, while IMPSOL, Barcelona's public housing agency, issues aspirational design guidance for architects participating in its housing competitions.

Formulation of Space Standards

Space standards vary in their formulation and detail, with some specifying dimensions at the room or activity level, defining minimum room widths, floor areas, and floor-to-ceiling heights for bedrooms, kitchens, living rooms, or bathrooms, while others only set minimum floor areas for the entire dwelling. Most countries, however, adopt a hybrid approach. With the exception of Chile, the studied contexts provide both overall dwelling sizes and internal minimum dimensions for key functions and rooms such as kitchens, bedrooms, and living areas. This takes into consideration questions of spatial efficiency and economic feasibility, comfort and housing quality, as well as usability and regulatory enforceability.

The calculation of minimum dwelling, room, and activity-specific floor areas is based on the typical functional requirements of a home and its expected occupants. This includes accommodating standard furniture – such as beds, wardrobes, tables, chairs, sofas, desks, and storage units – together with the space required for their use, with requirements often defined in the form of a furniture schedule (Figure 6.8). It further accounts for the fixed elements and fittings in service spaces, including kitchen units (worktops, sinks, cookers, refrigerators, base units, and cupboards) and bathroom fixtures (toilets, washbasins, showers, or bathtubs), as well as the necessary clearances for safe and efficient use. In addition, activity zones associated with dressing, eating, studying, social interaction, or household tasks such as cleaning and laundry

			Number bedspaces / number furniture items required						
Space	**Furniture to be shown**	**Furniture size (mm)**	2	3	4	5	6	7	8
Living space	Arm chair (or number sofa seats in addition to minimum sofa provision)	850x850	2	3	1	2	3	4	1
	2 seat settee (optional)	850x1300							
	3 seat settee	850x1850			1	1	1	1	
	TV	220x650	1	1	1	1	1	1	1
	coffee table	500x1050 or 750 diameter							
	occasional table	450x450							
	storage units	500 x length shown (1 only required)	1000	1000	1500	2000	2000	2000	
Dining space	dining chair		2	3	4	5	6	7	+
	dining table	800 x length shown (1 only required)	800	1000	1200	1350	1500	1650	
Bedrooms									
Double Bedroom	Principal bedroom double bed; or	2000x1500	1	1	1	1	1	1	1
	Other double bedroom double bed; or	1900x1350	1	1	1	1	1	1	1
	single bed (2 number in twin)	1900x900	2	2	2	2	2	2	2
	bedside table	400x400	2	2	2	2	2	2	2
	desk and chair	500x1050	1	1	1	1	1	1	1
	chest of drawers	450x750	1	1	1	1	1	1	1
	double Wardrobe	600x1200	1	1	1	1	1	1	1
Twin bedroom	single bed (2 number in twin)	1900x900			2	2	2	2	2
	bedside table	400x400			2	2	2	2	2
	chest of drawers	450x750			1	1	1	1	1
	table and chair	500x1050			1	1	1	1	1
	double wardrobe	600x1200			1	1	1	1	1
Single Bedroom	single bed	1900x900		1	1	1	1	1	1
	bedside table	400x400		1	1	1	1	1	1
	chest of drawers	450x750		1	1	1	1	1	1
	table and chair	500x1050		1	1	1	1	1	1
	double wardrobe	600x1200		1	1	1	1	1	1
Bathrooms	WC + cistern	500x700							
	Bath	700x1700							
	Wash hand basin	600x450							
	Hand rinse basin	350x200							
Manoeuvring zone									
Bedrooms	Manoeuvring square as per requirements	1200x1200							
Living rooms	Turning circle; or	1500x1500							
	Turning ellipse	1400x1700							

FIGURE 6.8 DLUHC, *Approved Document M* (2016): Furniture schedule.

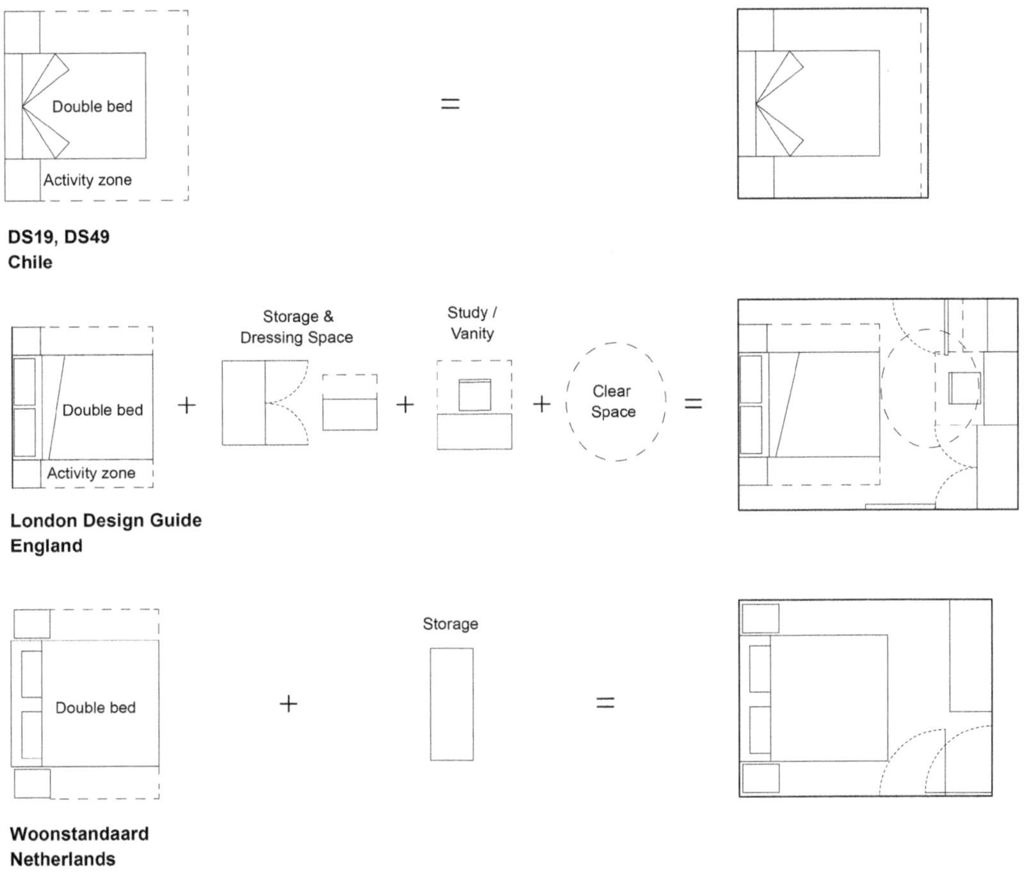

FIGURE 6.9 Bedroom sizes and their calculation in Chile, England, and the Netherlands.

are considered. Finally, the circulation spaces within and between rooms are included to ensure accessibility and functional efficiency throughout the home.

At the room level, minimum dimensions and floor areas differ depending on which furniture items are deemed essential and which activities or use zones are provided for (Figure 6.9). These area calculations therefore reflect not only the socio-cultural norms of domestic life and use, but also broader ambitions to improve housing standards, together with the market expectations that shape housing provision and design. In some contexts, the standard refers only to a room's core function, whereas in others it considers the entire room.

Overall minimum dwelling floor areas are, in principle, the sum of adding all room-level requirements or provisions plus the circulation spaces needed to connect them (Figure 6.10). Thus, space standards are both rational and technical in their calculation, often based on established design conventions as well as ergonomic and home-use studies (Neufert, 1926; Ministry of Housing and Local Government, 1968a). However, they are also contextual and a techno-bureaucratic translation of socio-political concerns and ambitions. These differences express not only regulatory priorities but also normative understandings of spatial adequacy. What is

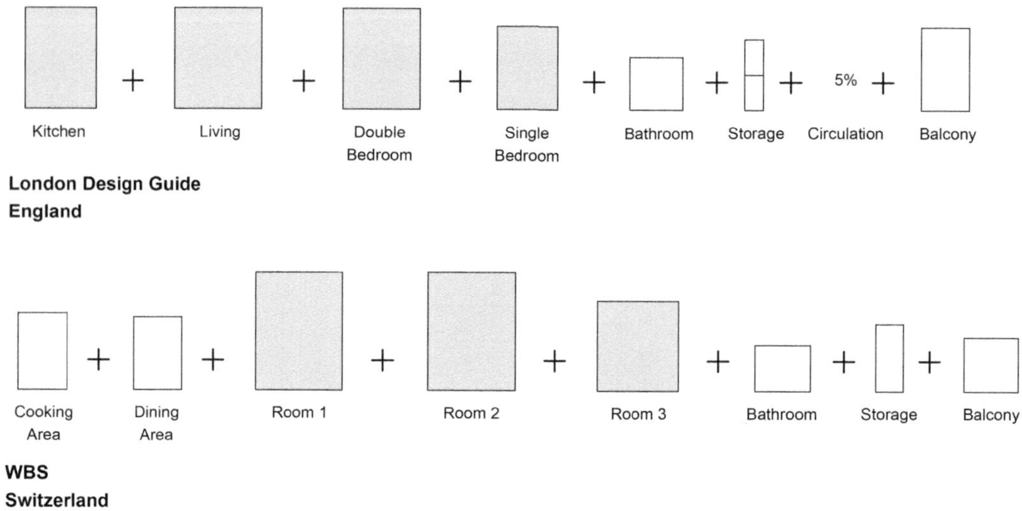

FIGURE 6.10 Dwelling size calculation in England and Switzerland.

considered "adequate" is thus shaped by empirical studies as well as socio-cultural norms, political agendas, and economic pressures. As a result, there are no universal space standards, and differences persist in prescribed dimensions and floor areas. For example, the minimum size for a two-bedroom dwelling ranges from around 50 m^2 in Spain and the Netherlands to 70 m^2 in England. Similarly, while a single bedroom of 5 m^2 is considered sufficient in China, the minimum size for a single bedroom in Switzerland is 10 m^2.

Space standards are defined in relation to the number of occupants, bedrooms, and habitable rooms, or prescribed for a dwelling without any reference to internal layout or occupancy. These varying levels of granularity in formulation reflect broader socio-political perspectives on housing, the extent of regulatory intervention in line with housing and economic policy, and assumptions about typical household use.

Some approaches, such as England's NDSS, directly link minimum dwelling sizes to household structure, specifying them by number of bedrooms and occupancy (e.g., two-person, three-person, four-person). This functionalist understanding of family life views the design of dwelling space as a rational response to familial patterns of cohabitation but can overlook wider demographic change in household compositions.

By comparison, Switzerland's WBS and China's space standards relate minimum sizes to room counts (e.g., two habitable rooms, three habitable rooms) rather than the potential maximum number of occupants. These systems adopt a more typological or spatial understanding of housing, defining adequacy in terms of the distribution of discrete functions such as sleeping, cooking, and living. This model allows greater cultural and household diversity, accommodating multi-generational households, non-nuclear families, or flexible uses of space without prescribing how rooms are used or by whom.

These differences in the approach to formulating space standards also determine how room-level standards are defined. They further inform the conversion of general housing requirements into specific spatial design dimensions for individual rooms, which are typically linked to particular domestic functions.

Room-level Standards

Room-based space standards translate the layout, functionality, and usability of a home into minimum room dimensions and floor areas. Many space standards are graphical to assist this translation, providing typical design and layout solutions that, with the dimensional information, can be visually assessed. The study included in the *London Housing Design Guide* (2010) is a very comprehensive example of such an approach (Figure 6.11) and was used to establish the basic floor area requirements of the NDSS (2015). This ensures that each room or functional zone can be properly used by preventing undersized or awkwardly shaped rooms. This graphical and dimension-based approach is easy to evaluate, particularly important in subsidised housing built to minimum standards. However, it can restrict design flexibility and long-term adaptability by assigning fixed uses to rooms at the design stage, limiting future change, and encouraging basic compliance rather than design ambition. The functionality and use of a home are therefore directly constrained by the domestic activities, furniture, and fittings explicitly included in the formulation and regulation of space standards.

In Chile, space standards are primarily defined at the room level, with dimensional requirements specified for different domestic functions alongside furniture schedules. While subsidy programmes only mandate some minimum dwelling sizes – 55 m^2 for a three-bedroom house for DS No. 49 and 47 m^2 for a house and 52 m^2 for a flat under DS No. 19 – the room-level functional requirements effectively establish minimum sizes for other unit types as well that can slightly differ. Under the DS No. 49 programme, for instance, design requirements result in a two-bedroom house of around 42 m^2, whereas under DS No. 1, a two-bedroom flat is around 47 m^2, highlighting how standards vary across target groups and subsidy schemes.

In Switzerland, dwellings are classified by the number of rooms rather than by the number of occupants. To score points under the "room size" criterion in the WBS, at least one room (typically the living room) must measure 14 m^2 or more, while all other rooms must be at least 10 m^2 (Fig. 6.12). The highest WBS scores are awarded to dwellings where all rooms are a minimum 14 m^2. According to the "furniture and use" criterion, rooms measuring 10–12 m^2 are considered suitable as single bedrooms and those over 12 m^2 as doubles; however, the WBS considers rooms in principle neutral in their function.

The WBS, based on a modular approach to rooms and functions, encourages flexibility by creating uniformly sized rooms that can be used interchangeably as a living room, bedroom, or working space (Figure 6.13). For example, points for "flexibility" are awarded when a 14-m^2 room includes at least a 3-m wall free of doors or windows, enabling the placement of larger furniture such as double beds or sofas. Rather than serving as restrictive minima, the dimensional requirements are applied to promote generously proportioned spaces that support diverse room functions and furniture arrangements.

The following sections compare room-level standards for habitable rooms. This includes bedrooms as well as kitchens and their integration with living and dining areas, comparing how functional requirements across different countries translate into specific spatial provisions and dimensions.

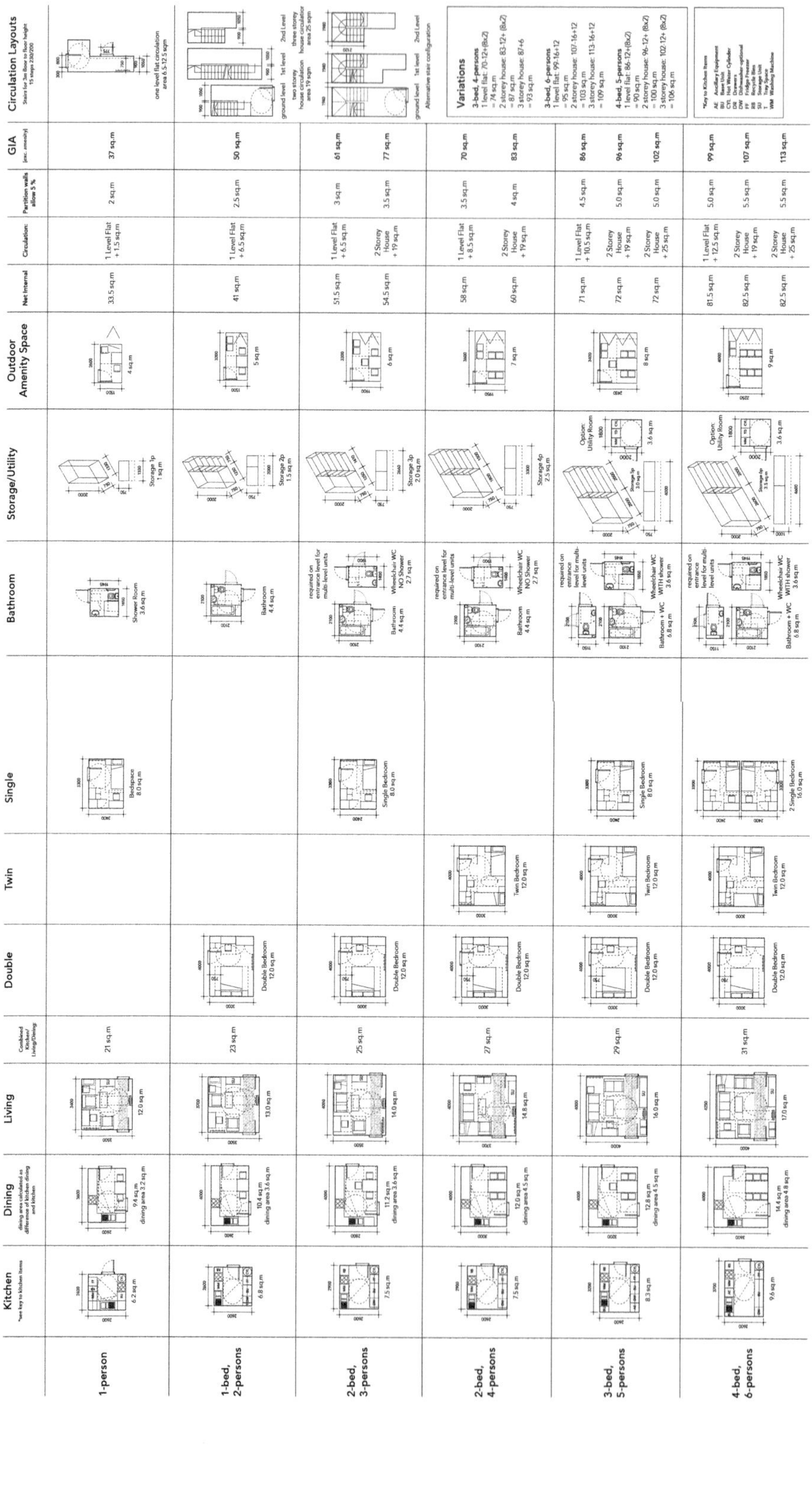

FIGURE 6.11 Space standards study.

Source: Greater London Authority, *London Housing Design Guide* (2010).

Grundausstattung

	Grösse der Wohnung 1-Zimmer	2-Zimmer	3-Zimmer	4-Zimmer	5-Zimmer	6-Zimmer	7-Zimmer
Zimmer (Anzahl Zimmer definiert die Grösse der Wohnung)							
Fläche (m^2)	≥14	≥14	≥14	≥14	≥14	≥14	≥14
		≥10	≥10	≥10	≥10	≥10	≥10
Nettowohnfläche (m^2)	30	45	60	80	100	120	140
Erschliessungszone	Breite 90 cm Kehrplatz 120 × 120 cm vor Zimmertür						
Kochbereich							
Anzahl Module	4.5	4.5	5.5	5.5	6.5	6.5	7.5
Fläche (m^2)	5	5	6	6	7	7	8
Essbereich							
Anzahl Sitzplätze	2	3	4	6	8	10	12
Dimension (cm)	160 × 160	160 × 270	180 × 270	240 × 270	300 × 270	360 × 270	420 × 270
Fläche (m^2)	2.5	4.5	5	6.5	8	10	11.5
Sanitärbereich							
Anzahl Räume	1	1	1	2	2	2	3
Fläche (m^2)	3.8	3.8	3.8	3.8	3.8	3.8	3.8
				2	2	2	2
Abstellbereich							
Anzahl Module	2	2	3	4	5	6	7
Fläche (m^2)	2	2	2.5	3.5	4.5	5.5	6.5
Aussenbereich (m^2)	3	3	4	4	5	5	6

FIGURE 6.12 Swiss WBS: Net living areas, rooms, functional zones, and corresponding fittings.

Source: Bundesamt für Wohnungswesen, *Wohnbauten planen, beurteilen und vergleichen: Wohnungs-Bewertungs-System WBS* (2015).

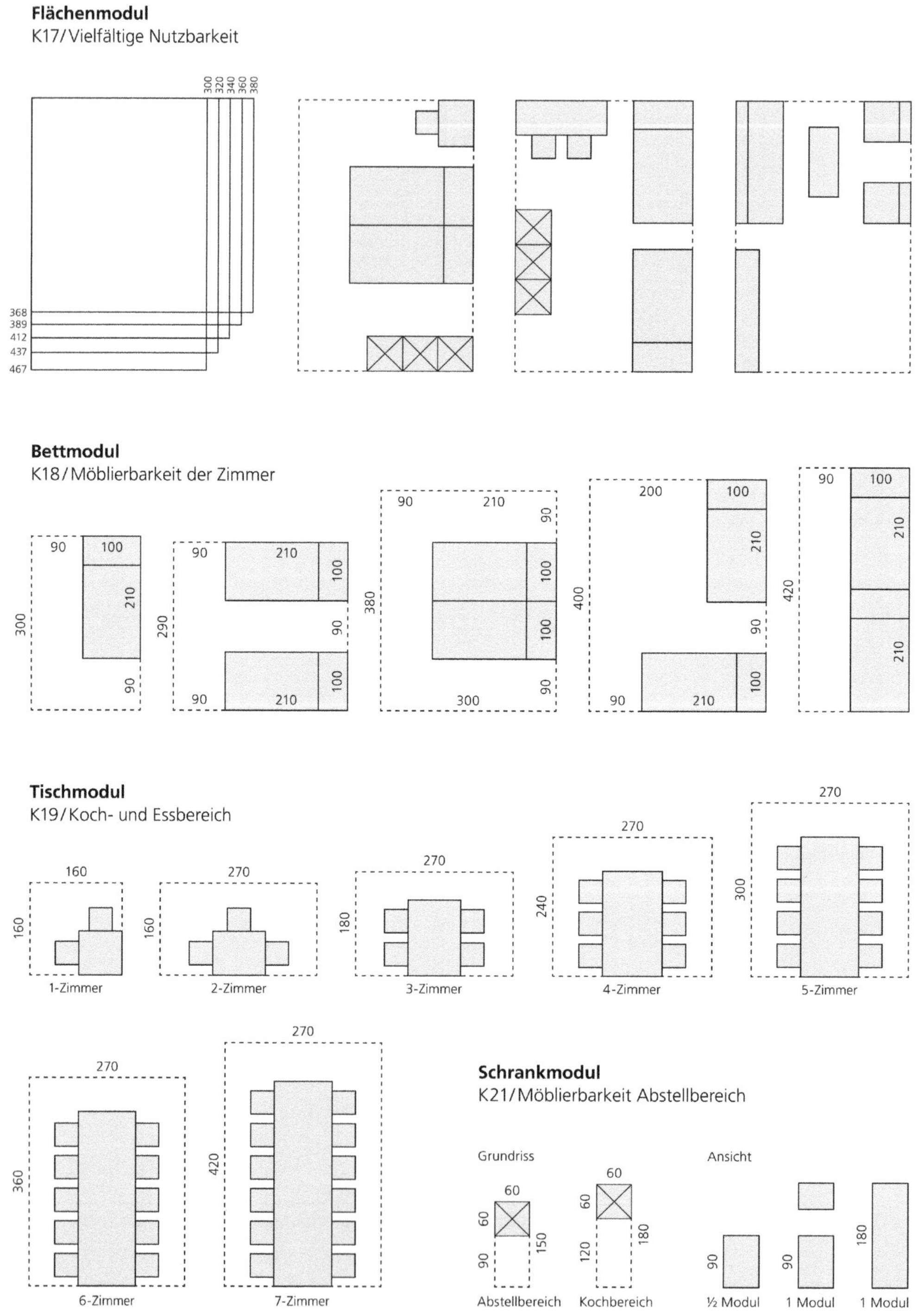

FIGURE 6.13 Swiss WBS: Templates for area, bed, table, and cupboard modules.

Source: Bundesamt für Wohnungswesen, *Wohnbauten planen, beurteilen und vergleichen: Wohnungs-Bewertungs-System WBS* (2015).

Bedroom Standards

Bedrooms are commonly the most used spaces in a home. Although generally considered a private habitable space predominantly associated with sleeping, both their history and actual use are more diverse (Perrot, 2018). For example, children's bedrooms are also typically used for playing and studying, and since the COVID-19 pandemic, many bedrooms have become a work-from-home space, at least some of the time.

Bedroom standards usually allow space for a bed, side table, wardrobe, and sometimes a desk or dresser. They prescribe a minimum floor area and, in some cases, a minimum room width. Since bedroom functions are well defined and have changed relatively little in modern homes, these standards – despite differences in furniture sizes, such as that of a standard double bed – remain broadly consistent across countries in their basic dimensions, despite variations in activity spaces and additional furniture (Figures 6.14–6.16).

The first (main) bedroom is generally expected to be occupied by a couple and is therefore designed as a double bedroom (Figure 6.17). Minimum requirements are typically represented graphically, showing furniture layouts, activity zones, circulation areas, and key dimensions, although they can also be presented in tabular form. A cross-country comparison shows that some standards are clearly prescriptive, specifying normative layouts for the entire bedroom, while others, such as Chile's, focus only on the main activity zone and essential bedroom elements. In some cases, the main bedroom is required to be larger than other double or twin bedrooms, reflecting its status within the dwelling and assumed familial social hierarchy.

Approaches to distinguishing between main and secondary bedrooms vary noticeably (Table 6.10). In England, all double bedrooms are treated equally, whether they are doubles

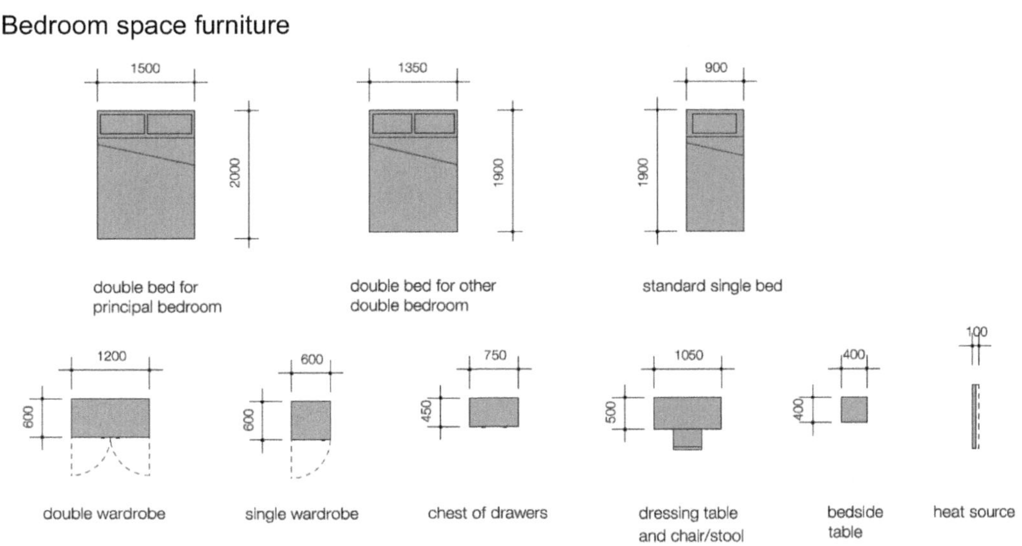

FIGURE 6.14 Furniture schedule for bedrooms.

Source: Greater London Authority, *Housing Design Standards LPG* (2023a).

1.1. DORMITORIOS

REQUISITOS			
TIPO DE DORMITORIO	**MOBILIARIO MINIMO**	**Superficie Mínima**	**Ancho Mínimo**
1- PRINCIPAL	**1 Módulo A + 1 Puerta + 2 Closet Simple o 1 fusionado**	**14,3 m²**	**260**
2- SEGUNDO	**2 Módulos B + 1 Puerta + 2 Closet Simple o 1 fusionado**		**220**
3- CONSTRUIDO ADICIONAL	**1 Módulo B + 1 Puerta + 1 closet Simple**	**4,5 m²**	**160**
4- PROYECTADO	**2 Módulos B + 1 Puerta+ 1 closet Simple**	**8 m²**	**220**

Modulo A (cama de 2 plazas y 2 veladores)

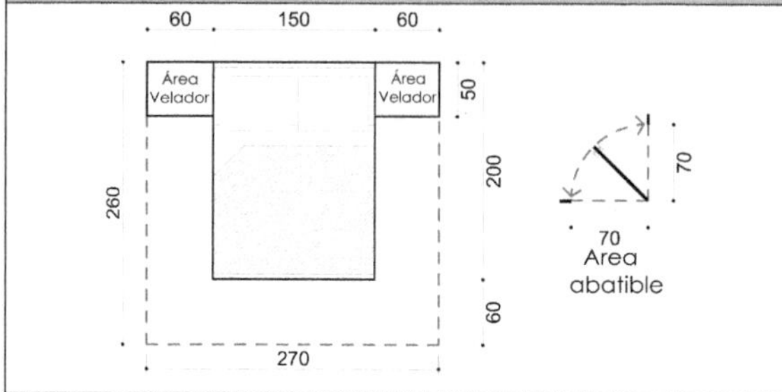

Módulo B (1 cama de 1 plaza y 1 velador)

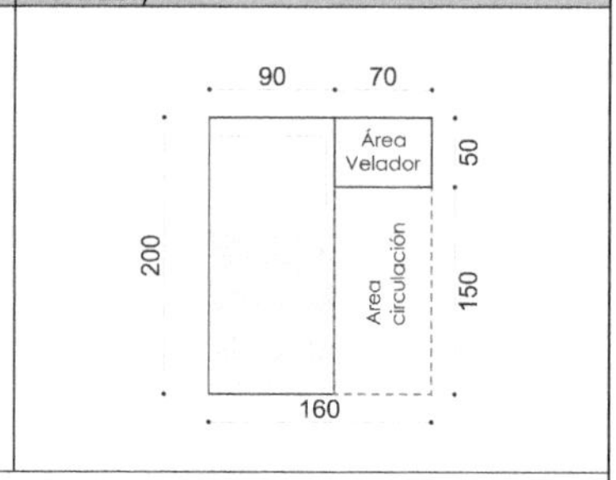

Notas:

- A las circulaciones de los módulos A y B, sólo podrán superponerse las áreas de puerta y de uso de closet.
- Cuando en un recinto se disponga las 2 camas en forma paralela se pueden fusionar las áreas de circulación y velador, respetando ancho mínimo y la superficie y ancho del recinto.
- El área del velador no podrá superponerse con áreas de circulación, uso de closet y puerta.
- La superficie mínima del dormitorio Principal más el Segundo será de 14,3 m².
- El área para closet, definida en el punto 1.6 del presente documento, es adicional a las superficies útiles señaladas para los dormitorios.
- En viviendas que aplique en subsidio de densificación en altura señalado en la letra d) del artículo 35 del citado reglamento, y que se encuentren destinadas a núcleos de hasta 2 integrantes, donde al menos uno de ellos sea adulto mayor o persona en situación de discapacidad con movilidad reducida, no deberán constituir el tercer dormitorio construido adicional, sin perjuicio de contar con la superficie mínima exigida para la aplicación de dicho subsidio complementario.

1.2. CLOSETS

REQUISITOS

La cantidad de módulo de closet dependerá de los dormitorios de la vivienda, salvo en viviendas con 1 sólo dormitorio conformado en su etapa inicial, donde se deberán considerar 4 módulos de closet como mínimo.

DIMENSIONES Y ÁREAS DE USO MÍNIMAS

Modulo simple

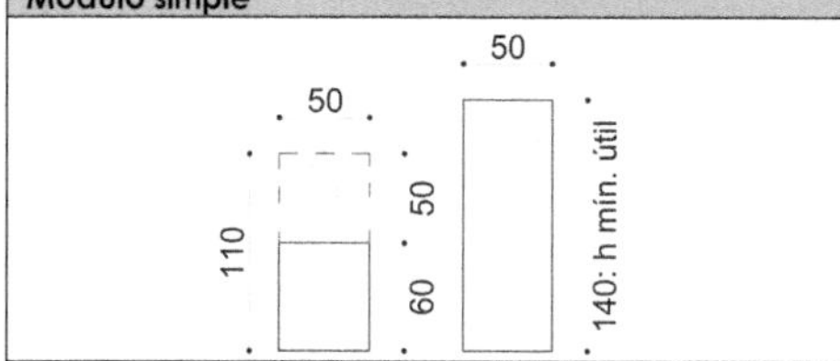

Modulo doble o fusionado

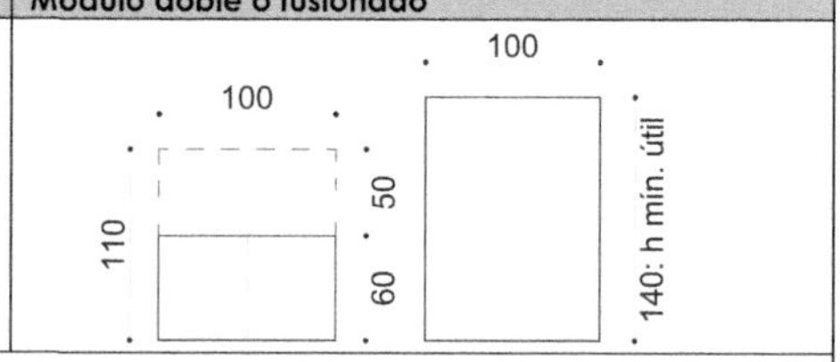

Notas:

- El área de uso del closet sólo puede superponerse al área de circulación de dormitorios o pasillos, respetándose siempre el ancho de la circulación y no puede superponerse con los veladores.
- Todos los closets deberán quedar conformados en fondo, altura y paramentos laterales. Se podrán fusionar hasta 2 módulos de closet de ancho mínimo 100 cm., sin necesidad de ejecutar la división entre ambos módulos.
- En viviendas con 1 sólo dormitorio conformado en etapa inicial, se puede fusionar hasta 4 módulos de ancho mínimo total de 200 cm. sin necesidad de ejecutar la división entre ambos módulos.
- Si existe un frente mayor al mínimo, la dimensión sobrante no se resta de los otros módulos.
- En caso de ubicar el módulo de closet sobre la escalera se deberá respetar lo indicado en Art. 4.2.6 de la OGUC.

FIGURE 6.15 Standards for bedrooms in Fondo Solidario de Elección de Vivienda, DS No. 49.

Source: Ministerio de Vivienda y Urbanismo de Chile, *Cuadro normativo y tabla de espacios y usos mínimos para el mobiliario* (2017).

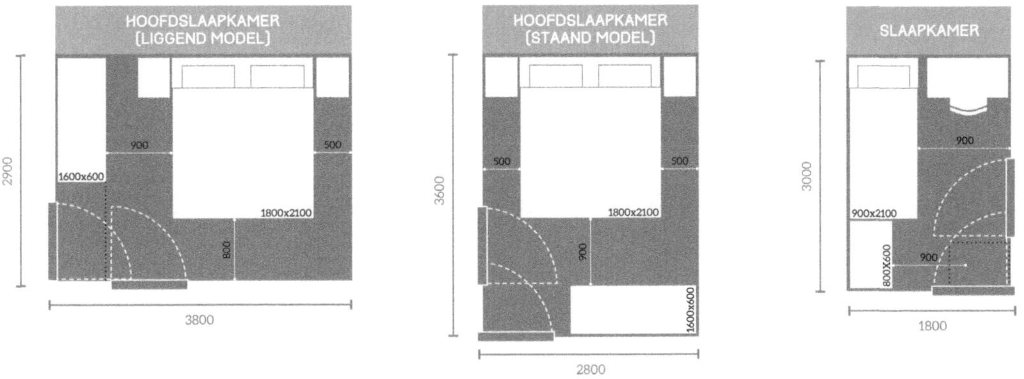

FIGURE 6.16 Bedroom standards.

Source: Netwerk Conceptueel Bouwen & Aedas, *De Woonstandaard* (2024).

or twins, while in Spain a hierarchy exists, with the main bedroom expected to be larger and, in larger homes, also wider. Chilean subsidy rules are the most restrictive, prohibiting a second double bedroom based on the assumption that all households are traditional families and therefore mandating a standard two-bedroom, three-person house (with a future additional bedroom) or three-bedroom, five-person flat. Some standards are very modest, clearly designed for bedrooms that are just used for sleeping, whereas the standards in Switzerland and England are more generous, acknowledging that bedrooms might be used for a range of activities.

Kitchen, Dining, and Living Room Standards

Kitchen, dining, and living areas are the principal shared spaces within a home. Although each has a distinct functional role – cooking, eating, and everyday living – their arrangement and layout have changed considerably over time. In traditional homes, these rooms and functions were separate, with the kitchen often considered a service space and the dining and living rooms used for more formal household and social interaction. Until the mid-twentieth century and the *Design of Dwellings* housing report by the Dudley Committee (Ministry of Housing and Local Government, 1944), even in public housing, the provision of a parlour, a formal reception room mainly used to entertain guests and at special family occasions, was common. More recently, open-plan layouts frequently combine cooking, dining, and living functions, reflecting more informal lifestyles.

Of these spaces, kitchens are the most functionally specific, with their layout often dictated by the efficient arrangement of appliances, worktops, and storage areas, and the relationships between them. Despite this high degree of standardisation, provision differs, with designs ranging from the most common, compact galley kitchens in smaller homes, to generous L-shaped or island layouts and their integration with dining or living areas (Figure 6.18).

Standards for kitchens, dining areas, and living rooms usually account for key furniture and fittings such as kitchen units, dining tables, and sofas or armchairs, as well as the required

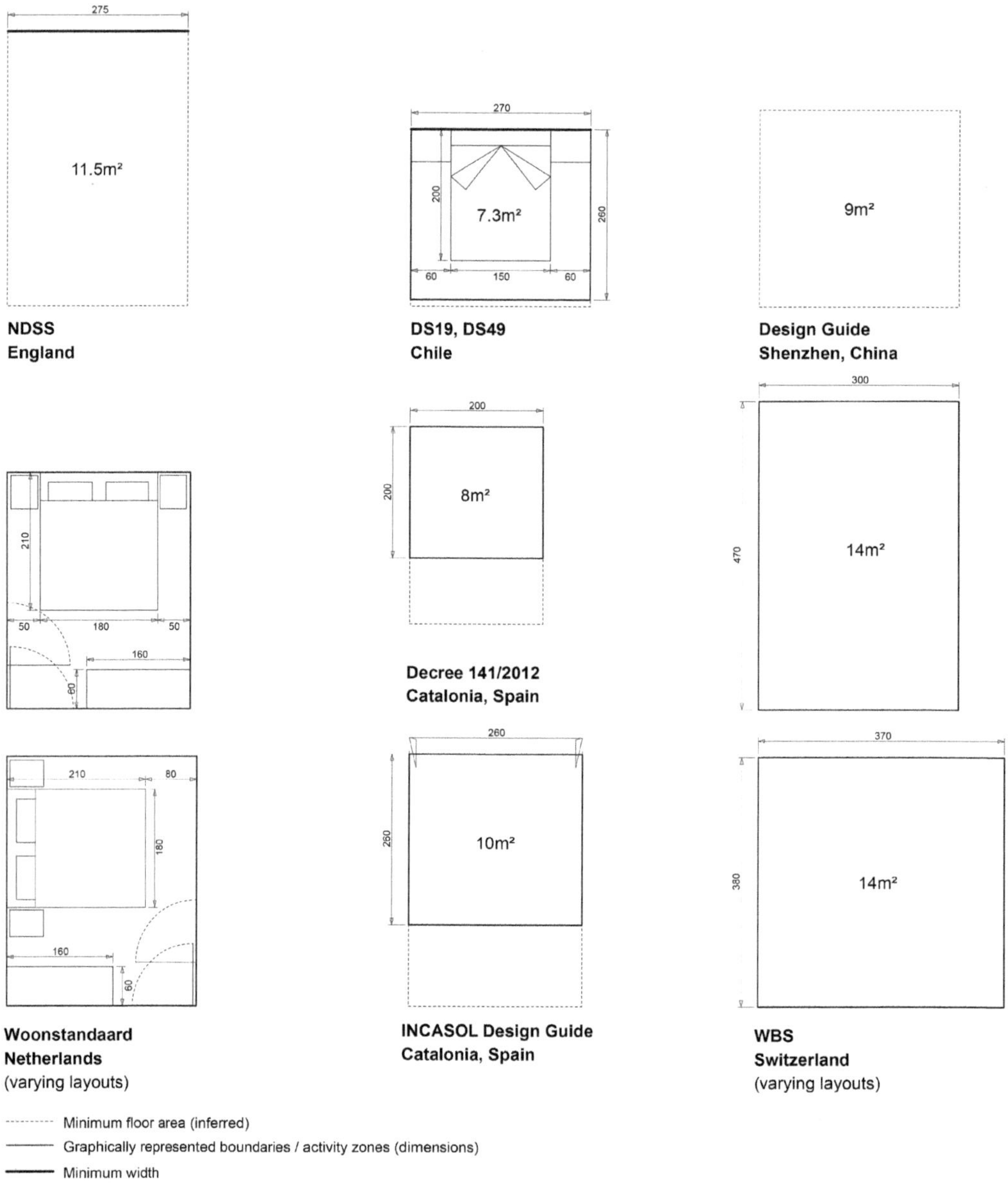

FIGURE 6.17 Minimum standards for the first bedroom in England, Chile, China, the Netherlands, Spain, and Switzerland.

Note:

[1] England: NDSS (2010).

[2] Chile: Minimum first bedroom from DS No. 1 (2012) and DS No. 49 (2017).

[3] Shenzhen: Minimum double bedroom size from Shenzhen Public Housing Design Standards (2021).

[4–5] The Netherlands: Minimum double-bedroom size from Woonstandaard (2024).

[6–7] Barcelona: Minimum double-bedroom sizes from Decree 141/2012 and INCASOL Social Housing Standards (2017).

[6] Switzerland: Minimum second-room size (first room is counted as a living room) from WBS (2015).

TABLE 6.10 Minimum bedroom standards

Context	*Space standards*	*Definition*	*First bedroom*	*Second bedroom*[1]	
			Double	*Double/Twin*	*Single*
England	Nationally Described Space Standard (2015)	Minimum floor area	>11.5 m²	>11.5 m²	>7.5 m²
		Minimum width	>2.75 m	>2.55 m	>2.15 m
Chile[2]	Supreme Decree 19 (Social and Territorial Integration Programme, 2016)	Minimum floor area	>7.3 m²	N/A	>7 m²
		Minimum width	-	N/A	>2.2 m
		Graphic standards[3]	2.7 m × 2.6 m	N/A	2.0 m × 1.6 m
	Supreme Decree 49 (Solidarity Housing Choice Fund, 2012)	Minimum floor area for the total of two rooms in a two-bedroom flat	>14.3 m²		
		Width	>2.60 m	–	>2.20 m
		Graphic standards[3]	2.7 m × 2.6 m	–	2.0 m × 1.6 m
Shenzhen, China	Shenzhen Public Housing Design Standards (2021)	Floor area	9 m²	9 m²	5 m²
Netherlands	Housing Standard (Woonstandaard, 2024)[3]	Graphic standards[4]	3.8 m × 2.9 m 3.6 m × 2.8 m	N/A	3.0 m × 1.8 m
Barcelona, Spain	Decree 141/2012 (Minimum conditions for habitability	Minimum floor area	6 m²	6 m²	6 m²
		Minimum width	>2.0 m >2.6 m (in 3B+)	>2.0 m	>2.0 m
	INCASOL Social Housing Standards (2019)[4]	Minimum floor area	10 m²	8 m²	6 m²
		Width	>2.6 m	>2.4 m	>2.0 m
Switzerland	WBS Housing Evaluation System (2015)	Floor area	>14 m²	>10 m²	>10 m²
		Graphic standards[3]	3.8 m × 3.7 m 4.7 m × 3.0 m	4.2 m × 1.9 m 3.0 m × 2.9 m	3.0 m × 1.9 m

Notes:

[1] As nomenclature varies, for comparison, "first" and "second" bedrooms are used. Typically, the largest bedroom has separate requirements. Except in Chile, the second bedroom can be a double, twin, or single.

[2] In Chile, the minimum subsidised dwelling is a two-bedroom, three-person family unit; a second double bedroom is not permitted.

[3] Dimensions refer to furniture size (bed, bedside table, circulation space, and sometimes wardrobe).

[4] Dimensions refer to exemplary bedroom sizes.

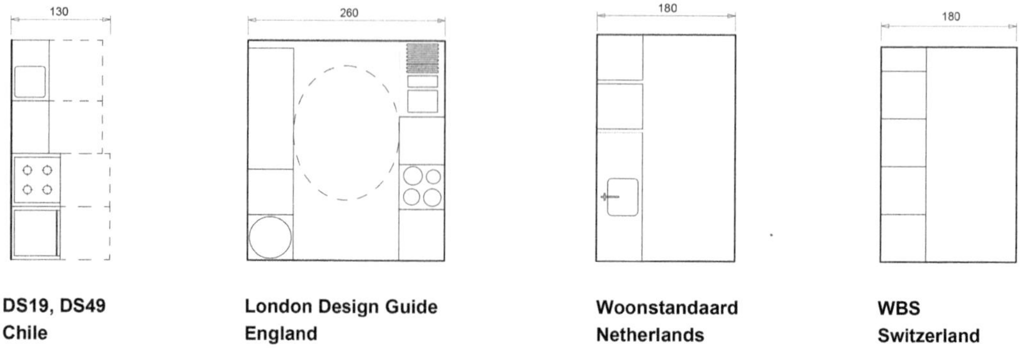

FIGURE 6.18 Kitchen sizes and their calculation in Catalonia (Spain), England, the Netherlands, and Switzerland.

activity and circulation zones (Figures 6.19–6.22). Dining areas are relatively fixed in their function, while living areas allow more flexibility and can adapt to changing domestic habits and lifestyles. Some countries prescribe minimum room areas (e.g., England), while others specify only activity zones and essential elements (e.g., Chile). With the exception of Chile, standards depend on the number of occupants, with provisions increasing with household size.

The variations of minimum internal standards for kitchens, dining areas, and living rooms reflect differences in cultural preferences for layout and use, housing policy, and regulatory approaches that favour either prescriptive or flexible standards, but also economic considerations, particularly in the subsidised housing sector (Table 6.11). For example, in London and Chile, open-plan layouts that integrate kitchen, dining, and living areas are common in subsidised homes, particularly flats. Combining these functions allows developers to maximise usable space and create the perception of larger, more flexible living areas, but in Chile, due to insufficient space standards, it is a necessity. However, even in London, where open-plan living is a more popular lifestyle choice, guidance from some boroughs warns that it is not suitable for all households, particularly those from cultural backgrounds that prefer a separation between cooking and social or sleeping spaces (GLA, 2023b). There are further noticeable differences in standards between tenures or target groups, for example, between different subsidy programmes in Chile.

Dwelling-level Standards

In contrast to detailed room standards, dwelling-level space standards only specify the total floor area of a home (Table 6.12). The method used to calculate minimum dwelling sizes is typically based either on the number of bedrooms or on the number of occupants and bedspaces (Figures 6.23–6.25). The control solely of the overall dwelling size can offer housebuilders greater flexibility in the distribution of internal space and better adaptation to site constraints and local property markets, potentially encouraging design innovation. However, this approach often prioritises economic planning considerations over design, focusing on the balance between construction costs, available subsidies, and housing quality. This can therefore undermine

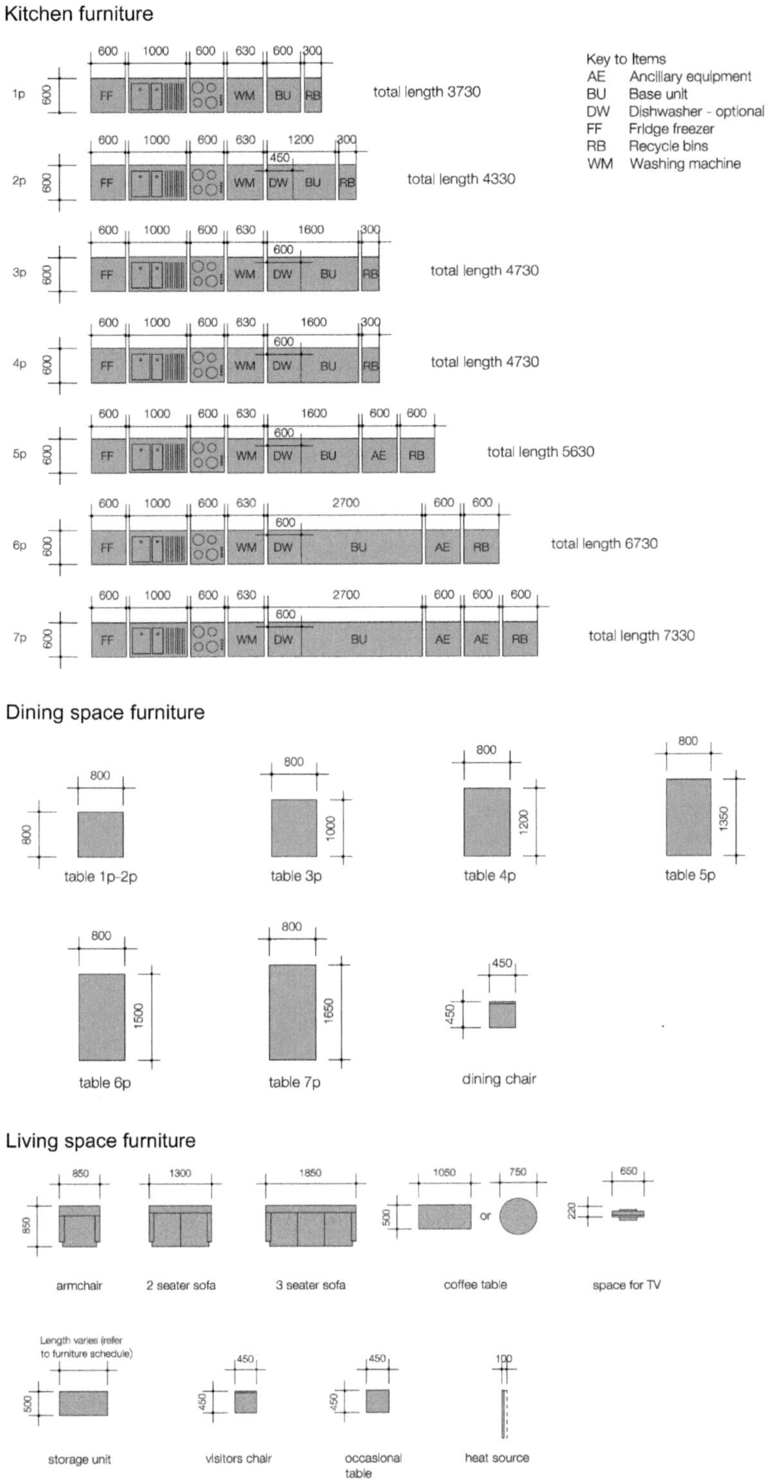

FIGURE 6.19 Furniture schedule for kitchens, dining spaces, and living spaces.

Source: Greater London Authority, *Housing Design Standards LPG* (2023a).

1.3. ESTAR – COMEDOR

REQUISITOS

Se debe considerar la cabida de módulo de comedor, más el módulo de estar

MOBILIARIO BÁSICO Y ÁREAS DE USO MÍNIMAS

COMEDOR

Alternativa 1

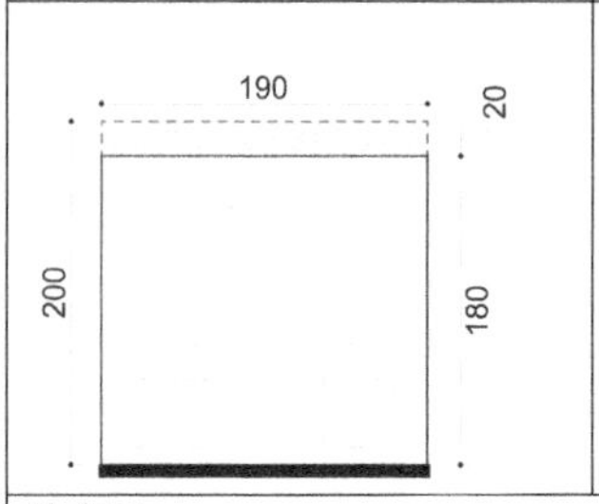

Alternativa 2

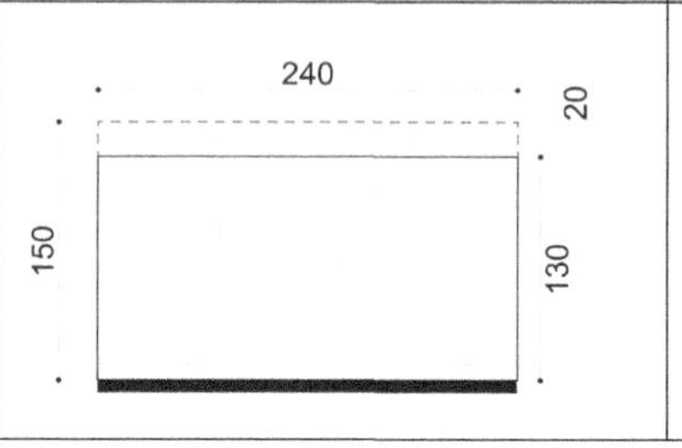

ESTAR

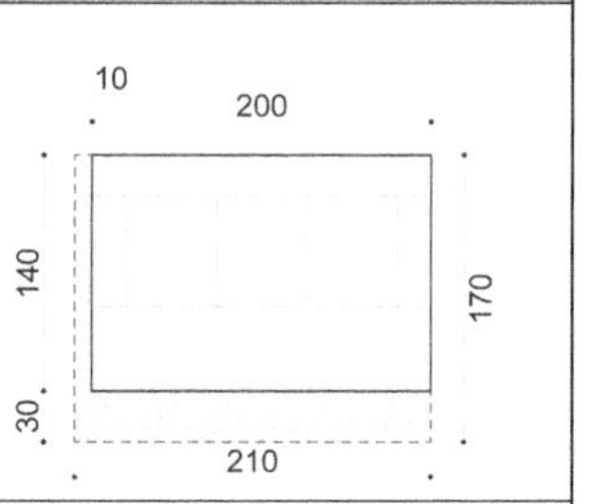

Notas:

- Aun cuando el recinto de estar y comedor se puede integrar al recinto cocina, cada uno de estos recintos debe cumplir en sí mismo con el requerimiento de mobiliario y áreas de uso definidos para cada caso graficado para cada recinto.

1.4. COCINA

REQUISITOS

- En la cocina, integradas o no, los artefactos y mobiliario deberán disponerse como una agrupación, que permita reconocer el espacio cocina como una unidad, el que se entenderá como el polígono donde se inscribe el mobiliario requerido y sus respectivas áreas de uso.
- Se debe incluir área para los siguientes mobiliarios/artefactos y sus respectivas áreas de uso:

MOBILIARIO BÁSICO Y ÁREAS DE USO MÍNIMAS

Lavaplatos

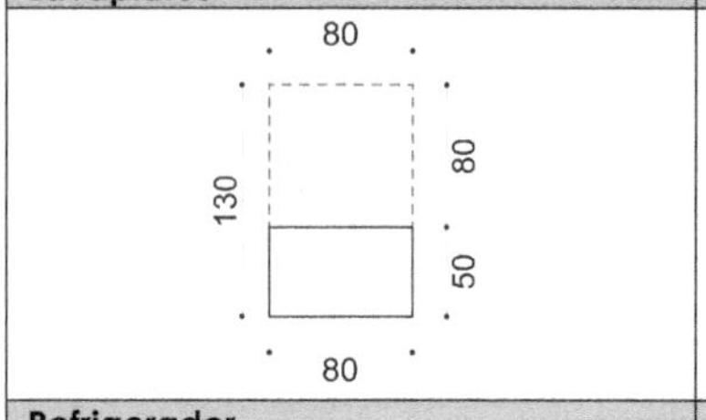

Mesa de Cocina

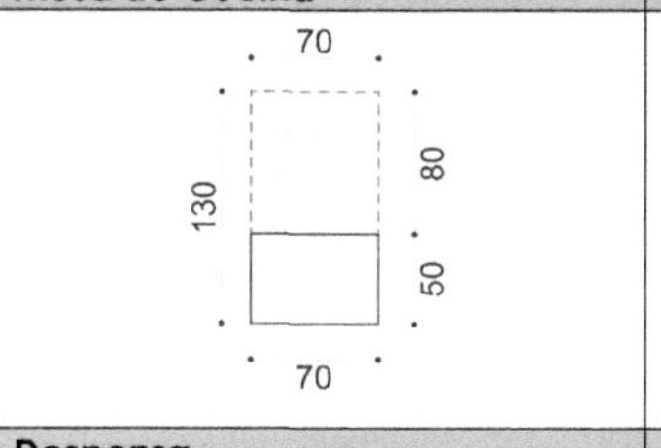

Artefacto cocina

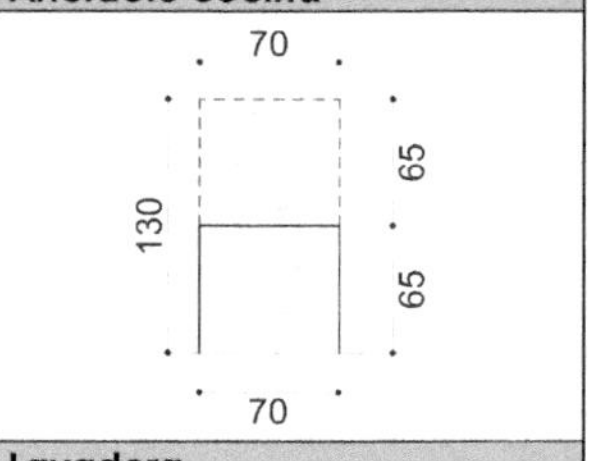

Refrigerador

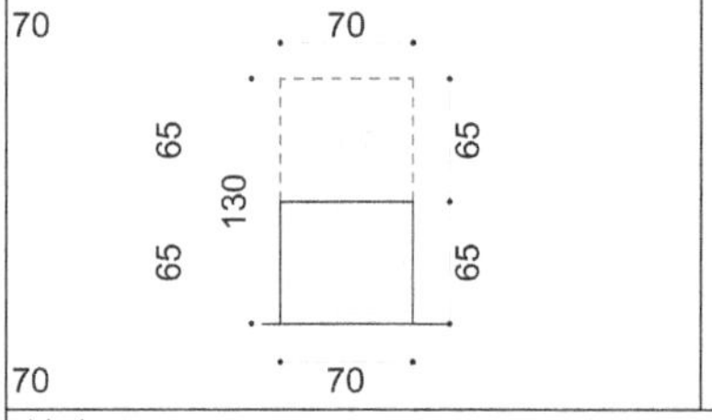

Despensa

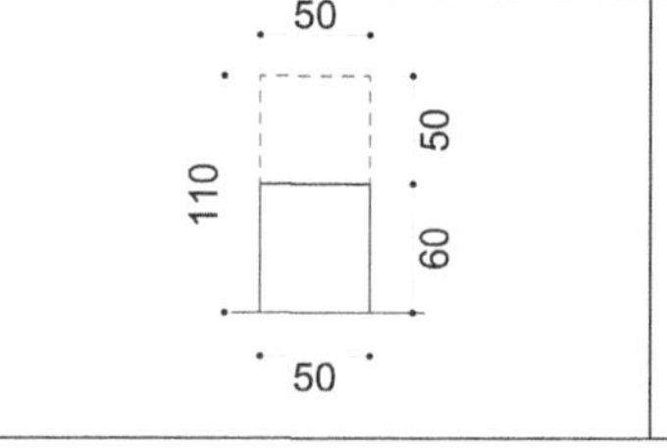

Lavadora

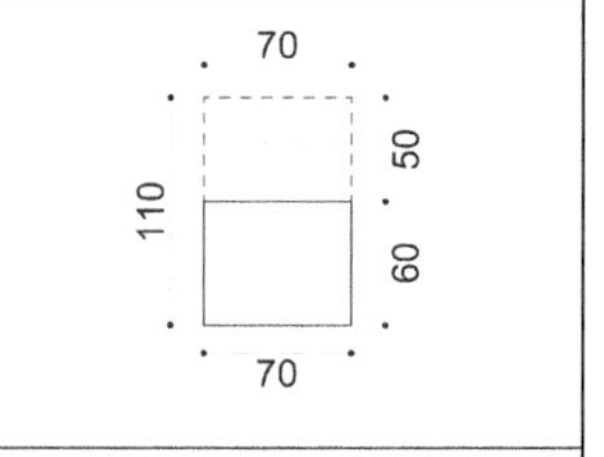

Notas:

- La lavadora podrá estar en el Baño, en la Cocina o en la logia.
- El área para la despensa puede ubicarse fuera de la Cocina en el Estar-Comedor o Pasillo y no requiere quedar conformada.
- El artefacto cocina no podrá ubicarse contiguo al artefacto refrigerador.
- La cocina deberá contemplar una puerta de salida al exterior o logia, distinta de la puerta de acceso principal de la vivienda. Cuando esta puerta converja al mismo espacio exterior que la puerta principal, podrá ubicarse en estar, comedor o pasillo.

FIGURE 6.20 Standards for the dining room, living room, and kitchen in Fondo Solidario de Elección de Vivienda, DS No. 49.

Source: Ministerio de Vivienda y Urbanismo de Chile, *Cuadro normativo y tabla de espacios y usos mínimos para el mobiliario* (2017).

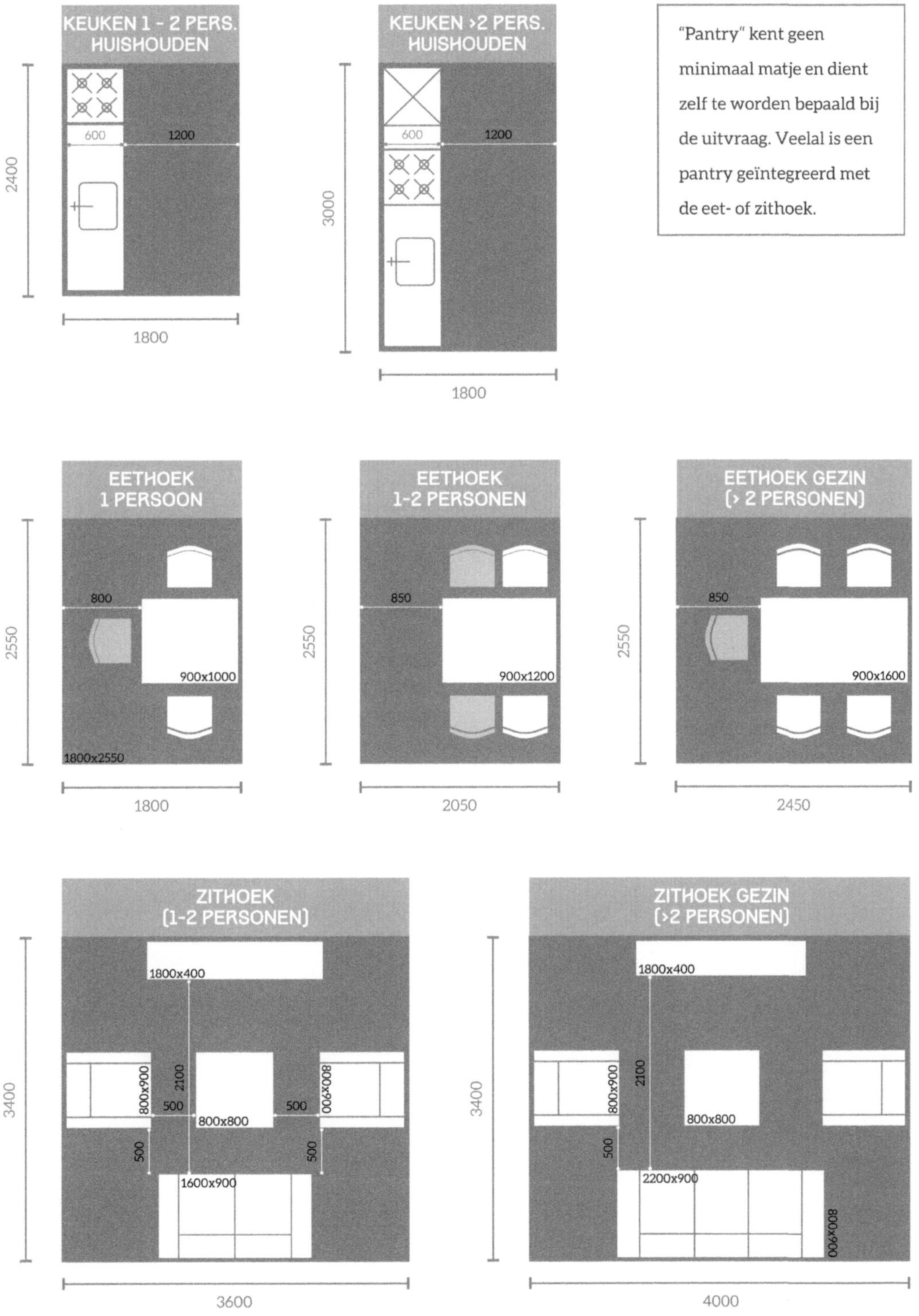

FIGURE 6.21 Space standards for kitchens, dining areas, and seating.

Source: Netwerk Conceptueel Bouwen & Aedas, *De Woonstandaard* (2024).

FIGURE 6.22 Comparison of minimum kitchen, dining, and living area dimensions in England, Chile, Shenzhen, the Netherlands, Catalonia, and Switzerland.

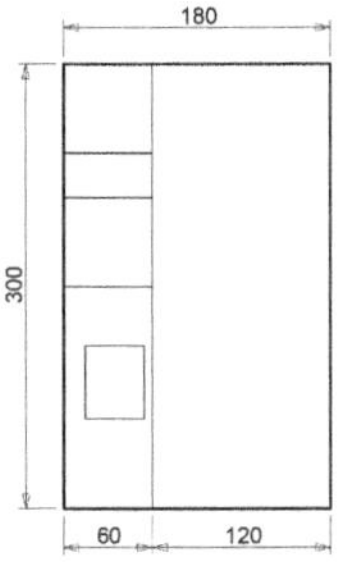

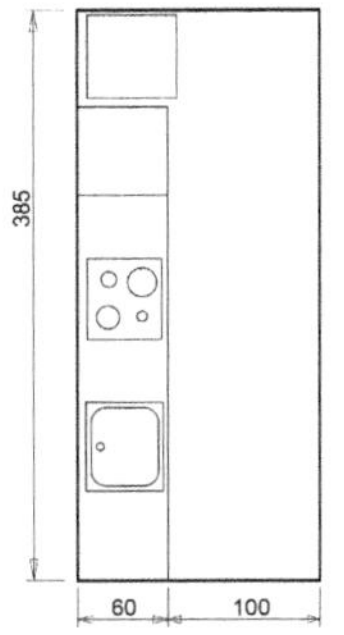

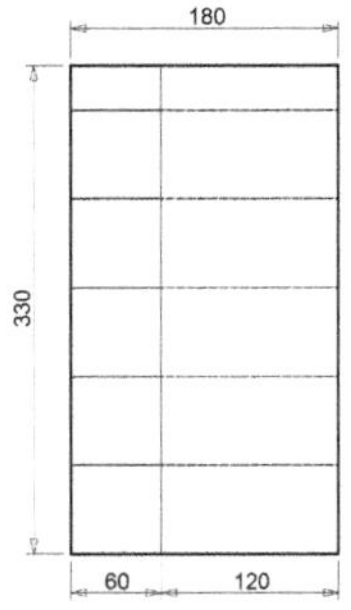

IINCASOL Design Guide
Catalonia, Spain

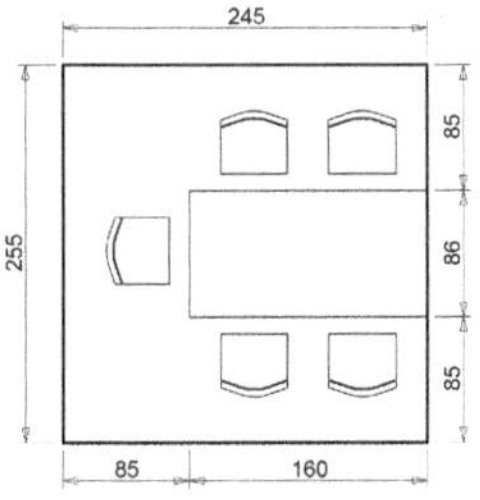

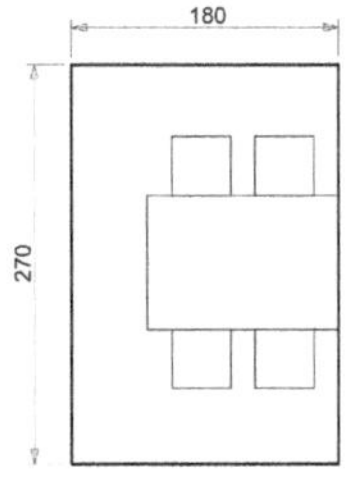

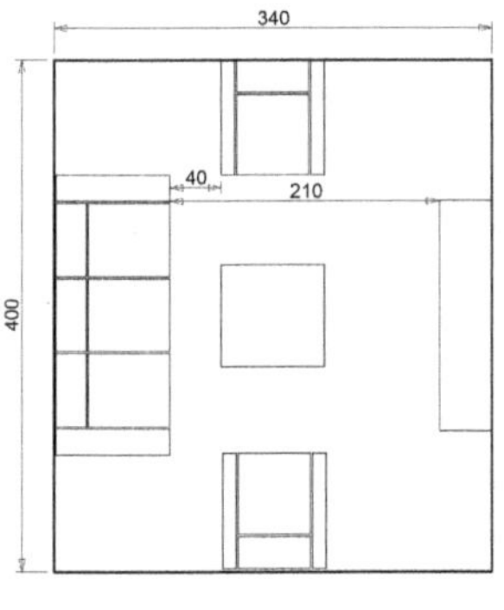

Woonstandaard
Netherlands

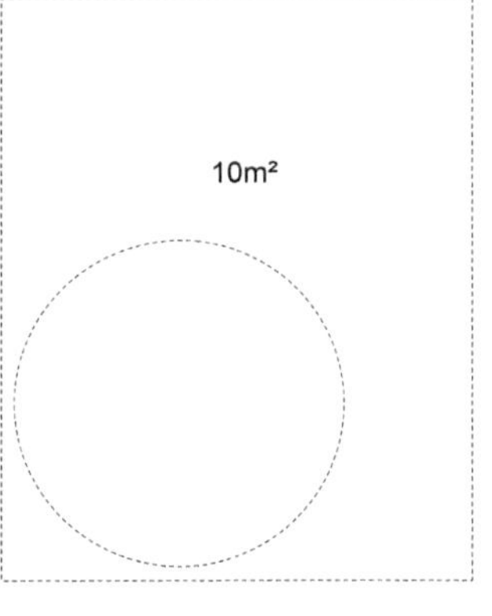

Decree 141/2012
Catalonia, Spain

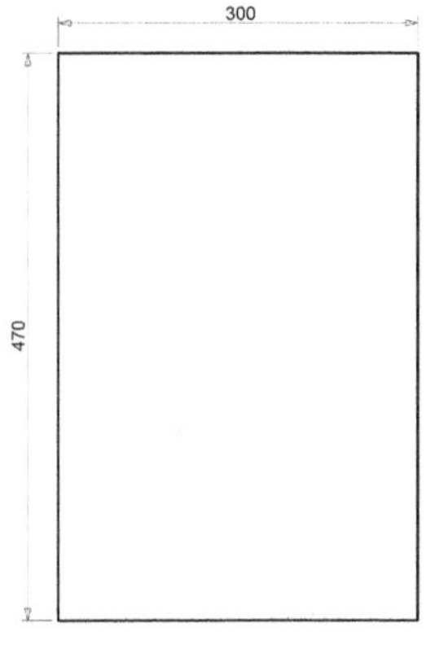

WBS
Switzerland

------------ Minimum floor area (inferred)
——— Graphically represented boundaries / activity zones
━━━ Minimum width

TABLE 6.11 Minimum internal standards for kitchen, dining and living areas

Context	*Space standards*	*Definition*	*Kitchen*[1]	*Dining*[1]	*Sitting area/ Living room*[1]
England	London Design Guide (2010)[2]	Minimum floor area Graphic standards[3]	7.5 m² 2.9 m × 2.6 m	4.5 m²	14.8 m² 4.0 m × 3.7 m
Chile	Supreme Decree 19 (Social and Territorial Integration Programme, 2016)	Graphic standards[3]	2.9 m × 1.3 m	2.0 m × 1.9 m 2.4 m × 1.5 m	–
	Supreme Decree 49 (Solidarity Housing Choice Fund, 2012)	Graphic standards[3]	3.7 m × 1.3 m	2.0 m × 1.9 m 2.4 m × 1.5 m	2.1 m × 1.7 m
Shenzhen, China	Shenzhen Public Housing Design Standards (2021)	Minimum floor area	3.5 m²	–	10 m²
Netherlands	Housing Standard (Woonstandaard, 2024)[3]	Graphic standards[3]	3.0 m × 1.8 m	2.55 m × 2.45 m	4.0 m × 3.4 m
Barcelona, Spain	Decree 141/2012 (Minimum conditions for habitability)	Minimum total floor area Minimum width		20 m² >2.80 m	
	INCASOL Social Housing Standards (2019)	Minimum width Graphic standards[3]	– 3.85 m × 1.6 m	– –	>3 m –
Switzerland	WBS Housing Evaluation System (2015)	Minimum floor area Minimum dimensions	6 m²	5 m² 1.80 m × 2.7 m	14 m² –

Notes:

[1] Kitchen, living, and dining space sizes change with occupancy; standards provided relate to two-bedroom (three habitable room, four-person) flats for comparison.

[2] NDSS (2015) provides no minimum sizes for kitchen, dining, and living areas; overall floor areas are based on the room-by-room descriptions of the interim *London Design Guide*.

[3] Sizes refer to example layouts accommodating minimum furniture requirements.

basic home usability, unless complementary internal spatial design guidelines are provided. For this reason, room-level specifications are often issued alongside overall dwelling standards, establishing clear links between the activities considered essential, the furniture required to support them, and often also the typical layouts that meet the requirements.

In some contexts, both minimum and maximum subsidised dwelling sizes are regulated. For instance, China mandates maximum dwelling sizes, while Switzerland's WBS penalises units that are either too small or excessively large, awarding maximum scores when floor area per

TABLE 6.12 Comparison of dwelling size standards in England, Chile, China, the Netherlands, Spain, and Switzerland

Context	*Space standards*	*Definition*	*Minimum*	*Nos. of bedrooms*[1]	*Maximum*
England	Nationally Described Space Standard (2015)	Gross internal floor area for: • Number of floors / building type • Number of bed-rooms (B) • Designed occupancy	37 m²	1B flat: > 37 m² (1P), > 50 m² (2P) 2B flat: > 61 m² (3P), > 70 m² (4P) 3B flat: > 86 m² (5P), > 95 m² (6P)	–
Chile	Supreme Decree 19 (Social and Territorial Integration Programme, 2016)	Net usable floor areas	–	Min. 47 m² (house) Min. 52 m² (flat)	–
	Supreme Decree 49 (Solidarity Housing Choice Fund, 2012)	–	–	–	–
Shenzhen, China[2]	Shenzhen Public Housing Construction Standards (2021)	Gross internal floor area described for: • Type of affordable housing • Number of habit-able rooms (HR)	35 m² (PRH/ TH), 65 m² (ARH)	1B flat: 35–40 m² (PRH), 35–40 m² (TH) 2B flat: 60–65 m² (PRH), 65–70 m² (TH), 65–70 m² (ARH) 3B flat: 80–85 m² (PRH), 85–90 m² (TH), 85–90 m² (ARH)	Max. 80 m² (PRH), 90 m² (ARH), 150 m² (TH)
Netherlands	Building Regulations (Bouwbesluit, 2012)	–	18 m²	–	–
	Housing Standard (Woonstandard, 2024)	Gross internal floor area described for: • Building type • Number of bed-rooms (B)	–	1B flat: 24–50 m² 2B flat: 50–65 m² 3B flat: 65–80 m²	–

(*Continued*)

TABLE 6.12 (Continued)

Context	*Space standards*	*Definition*	*Minimum*	*Nos. of bedrooms*[1]	*Maximum*
Barcelona, Spain	Decree 13/2010	The maximum size can increase to < 100 for accessible and < 120 for large family homes	–	–	< 90 m² (General needs)
	Decree 141/2012 (Minimum conditions for habitability)	–	36 m²	–	–
	INCASOL Social Housing Standards (2019)	Net internal floor area described for: • Number of bedrooms (B) • Designed occupancy (P)	–	2B flat: 50 m² (3P), 60 m² (4P) 3B flat: 70 (5P) m²	–
Switzerland	WBS Housing Evaluation System (2015)	Net internal floor area described for: • Number of rooms (HR)	–	1B flat: > 45 m² 2B flat: > 60 m² 3B flat: > 80 m²	–

Notes:

[1] Space standards are described according to the number of bedrooms (B), number of habitable rooms (HR), or maximum number of people (P) living in a home. For comparison, a 1-bedroom (1B) dwelling is considered equal to a dwelling with 2 habitable rooms (2HR) or a dwelling designed for the occupancy of 2 people (2P). Similarly, 2B = 3HR = 3–4P and 3B = 4HR = 5–6P.

[2] PRH: Public Rental Housing, TH: Talent Housing, ARH: Affordable Commercial Housing.

capita is optimised in relation to both space provision and operational cost. Similarly, Catalonia's protected housing sector sets maximum thresholds, generally of 90 m² but increased to 120 m² for large families or those with accessibility needs. This highlights that the role of subsidised housing standards is not only to ensure adequate space provision, but also to control the equitable use of public resources.

What is considered an adequate dwelling is culturally defined and depends on local expectations and domestic practices or preferences. An example of this is the kitchen in China, which even in small studio flats is always in a separate, enclosed room. Another example is the space for drying or washing clothes. In China, many residential buildings provide communal outdoor drying areas with washing machines commonly installed on the balcony, and in Switzerland, where the homes tend to be the largest analysed, housing developments often include shared laundry facilities. This reduces the need for provisions within individual homes. In contrast, despite having some of the smallest homes, Chilean subsidised flats always have a loggia for washing and drying. Similarly, in Barcelona, even relatively compact flats are expected to provide a dedicated area for drying clothes, often integrated into the balcony or kitchen and screened from external view. In contexts like the Netherlands, external ground- or basement-level storage for each dwelling unit is also commonly provided. However, many of the more voluntary standards depend on the development practices and standards of individual housing providers.

PMC	**PMC 6** *studio concept*	**PMC 7** *2 kamer concept*	**PMC 8** *3 kamer concept*
Huurniveau	Kwaliteitskortingsgrens	Eerste aftoppingsgrens	Tweede aftoppingsgrens
Gebouwtype	Gestapeld	Gestapeld	Gestapeld
Productkwaliteiten *Gebruikskwaliteit*			
Functionaliteit woning (matjes, verkeersruimte kunnen worden gecombineerd)	• Zithoek voor één- of tweepersoonshuishouden • Pantry • Eethoek voor éénpersoonshuishouden • Slaapkamer • Badkamer • Toilet (in combinatie met de badkamer) • Wasmachine aansluiting	• Zithoek voor één- of tweepersoonshuishouden • Keuken / Pantry • Eethoek voor één- of tweepersoonshuishouden • Hoofdslaapkamer • Slaapkamer • Badkamer • Toilet (kan in combinatie met de badkamer) • Wasmachine aansluiting	• Zithoek gezin • Keuken • Eethoek gezin • Hoofdslaapkamer • Slaapkamer (2x) • Badkamer • Toilet (2x) (2e i.c.m. badkamer) • Wasmachine aansluiting
Geadviseerde bandbreedte GO in m² (i.v.m. huurniveaus)	24 -50 (m²)	50 – 65 (m²)	65 – 80 (m²)
Geadviseerde beuk /of bouwsysteem maat	3,2 – 5,0	4,0 - 6	6,8 – 7,6
Milieu			
Energie	BENG	BENG	BENG
Gezondheid en comfort			
Comfort	De woningen voldoen aan de kwaliteitseisen volgens het geldende Bouwbesluit.	De woningen voldoen aan de kwaliteitseisen volgens het geldende Bouwbesluit.	De woningen voldoen aan de kwaliteitseisen volgens het geldende Bouwbesluit.
Technische en esthetische kwaliteit			
Basis	Vigerend Bouwbesluit	Vigerend Bouwbesluit	Vigerend Bouwbesluit
Uitstraling	Variatie in gevelbeeld en stedenbouwkundige opzet	Variatie in gevelbeeld en stedenbouwkundige opzet	Variatie in gevelbeeld en stedenbouwkundige opzet
Uitrusting	• Overal vlakke vloeren, geschikt voor afwerking met vloerbedekking • Wanden behangklaar • Plafond afgewerkt • Elektrische installatie conform NEN 1010 klaar voor gebruik • Mogelijkheid voor plaatsing wasmachine en aansluitingen hiervoor • Ventilatiesysteem • Verwarmingssysteem • Waterinstallatie • Volledig ingericht sanitair, natte cellen, met vloer en wand afwerking • Keukenblok aangesloten en afgestemd op pantry opstelling volgens leverancier. • De woningen voldoen aan de kwaliteitseisen volgens het geldende Bouwbesluit • Bergingsruimte (evt geclusterd in aparte bergingsruimte / bergings verdieping volgens bouwbesluit) • 10m heipalen • Terreininrichting (geen parkeren op eigen grond) • Centrale entree met het bellentableau met videofoon en brievenbusfronten	• Overal vlakke vloeren, geschikt voor afwerking met vloerbedekking • Wanden behangklaar • Plafond afgewerkt • Elektrische installatie conform NEN 1010 klaar voor gebruik • Mogelijkheid voor plaatsing wasmachine en aansluitingen hiervoor • Ventilatiesysteem • Verwarmingssysteem • Waterinstallatie • Volledig ingericht sanitair, natte cellen, met vloer en wand afwerking • Keukenblok aangesloten en afgestemd op pantry opstelling volgens leverancier. • Werkende aansluitingen nuts (warmtenet indien van toepassing, water, elektra, riool) • Bergingsruimte (evt geclusterd in aparte bergingsruimte / bergings verdieping volgens bouwbesluit) • 10m heipalen • Terreininrichting (geen parkeren op eigen grond) • Centrale entree met het bellentableau met videofoon en brievenbusfronten	• Overal vlakke vloeren, geschikt voor afwerking met vloerbedekking • Wanden behangklaar • Plafond afgewerkt • Elektrische installatie conform NEN 1010 klaar voor gebruik • Mogelijkheid voor plaatsing wasmachine en aansluitingen hiervoor • Ventilatiesysteem • Verwarmingssysteem • Waterinstallatie • Volledig ingericht sanitair, natte cellen, met vloer en wand afwerking • Woning voorzien van een standaard keukenblok, opstelplaats fornuis en koelkast (minimaal 3 boven- en 3 onderkastjes) • Werkende aansluitingen nuts (warmtenet indien van toepassing, water, elektra, riool) • Bergingsruimte (evt geclusterd in aparte bergingsruimte / bergings verdieping volgens bouwbesluit) • 10m heipalen • Terreininrichting (geen parkeren op eigen grond) • Centrale entree met het bellentableau met videofoon en brievenbusfronten
Onderhoud in eerste 15 jaar	Inzicht in onderhoudsbehoefte en -kosten	Inzicht in onderhoudsbehoefte en -kosten	Inzicht in onderhoudsbehoefte en -kosten
Proceskwaliteiten			
Ontzorgen (zie taakverdelingslijst hieronder)	Conceptaanbieders verantwoordelijk voor ontwerp, engineering, realisatie en vergunningen	Conceptaanbieders verantwoordelijk voor ontwerp, engineering, realisatie en vergunningen	Conceptaanbieders verantwoordelijk voor ontwerp, engineering, realisatie en vergunningen
Bewonerscommunicatie	Door opdrachtgever	Door opdrachtgever	Door opdrachtgever

FIGURE 6.23 Requirements for self-contained regulated social housing in multi-storey buildings.

Source: Netwerk Conceptueel Bouwen & Aedas, *De Woonstandaard* (2024).

Dwelling size is largely a quantitative measure of dwelling design, while the internal arrangement of rooms, access points, and circulation routes determines the quality of the space and how it functions in daily life. The relationship between access, circulation, and room grouping are therefore key to understanding the effectiveness of space standards and can reveal important differences in both spatial priorities and regulatory traditions (Fig. 6.26).

In English flats, access is typically via an entrance corridor. Bedrooms, bathrooms, and service spaces are grouped together in functional zones, creating clear separations between private and shared areas. This arrangement supports privacy but dedicates a relatively large amount of space for circulation. In Santiago and Shenzhen, access is generally directly into the main living area. Movement between rooms relies on internal corridors, and bedrooms are functionally grouped. This retains a conventional separation of day and night zones and enables compact

	Dormitoris	Sup. útil maxima	Cuina: Tipus	Cuina: Equipament		Bany: Principal	Bany: Petit	Zona de rentat
LLOGUER PER A COL·LECTIUS ESPECÍFICS 50 m²	1 doble sup.> 10m² (practicable) + 1 simple sup. > 6 m²	50 m²	Oberta	Armaris Placa focs Forn Campana Lluminària Rentavaixella Nevera	Alts i baixos Elèctrica Si Si Si Previsió Espai	Rentamans Inodor Dutxa (Practicable)	No	Estenedor Caldera Instal·lació per a rentadora
LLOGUER DE 60 m²	1 doble sup.> 10m² (practicable) + 1 doble sup. > 8 m²	60 m²	Tancada o semi incorporada	Armaris Placa focs Forn Campana Lluminària Rentavaixella Nevera	Alts i baixos Elèctrica Si Si Si Previsió Espai	Rentamans Inodor Dutxa (Practicable)	No	Estenedor Caldera Instal·lació per a rentadora
LLOGUER DE 70 m²	1 doble sup.> 10m² (practicable) + 1 doble sup. > 8 m² + 1 senzill sup.> 6 m²	70 m²	Tancada o semi incorporada	Armaris Placa focs Forn Campana Lluminària Rentavaixella Nevera	Alts i baixos Elèctrica Si Si Si Previsió Espai	Rentamans Inodor Dutxa (Practicable)	Rentamans Inodor	Estenedor Caldera Instal·lació per a rentadora

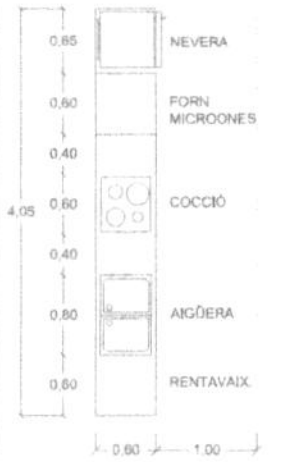

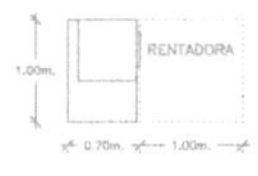

Sala
- Amplada mínima 3 m.
- Pre-instal·lació d'aire condicionat.

Cuina tancada o semi incorporada
- Mobles alts i baixos.
- Espai de 0,60 x 0,65 m. a tota l'alçada per la nevera.
- Moble de 0,60 x 0,60 m. a tota l'alçada pel forn i l'espai del microones.
- Equipada amb aparell de cocció elèctric de 4 focs, campana extractora, forn elèctric i aigüera de 2 sinus.
- Els electrodomèstics no es situaran darrere de zona de llits.
- Moble baix de 0,60 m. d'amplada al costat de l'aigüera, amb portes fàcilment desmuntables, perquè l'usuari instal·li un rentavaixelles.
- Per la instal·lació del rentavaixelles, preveure endoll, desguàs i presa d'aigua freda i calenta sota l'aigüera.
- Punt de llum general amb lluminària LED càlida instal·lada.
- Punt de llum sota el moble alt amb lluminària LED càlida instal·lada.

Dormitori doble practicable
- Superfície mínima 10 m², i amplada mínima 2,60 m.
- Espai per armari d'1,50 x 0,60 m, que no serà encastat.

Dormitori doble
- Superfície mínima 8 m² i amplada mínima 2,40 m.
- Espai per armari d'1,50 x 0,60 m, que no serà encastat.

Bany practicable
- Rentamans, WC i plat de dutxa.
- Mirall, portarotlles, tovalloler i barra per la cortina de la dutxa.
- Punts de llum amb lluminària LED càlida instal·lada al sostre i al mirall.

Zona de rentat i/o estenedor

Zona de rentat:
- La rentadora estarà protegida de l'aigua de pluja.
- Endoll estanc, desguàs i presa d'aigua freda i calenta.
- Si està en un espai exterior, preveure punt de llum amb lluminària LED càlida instal·lada.

Zona d'estenedor:
- S'ha de preveure un espai permanentment ventilat i protegit de vistes, amb 4 m o més de tendall, en trams no inferiors a 1 m. Pot incorporar altres usos com la caldera, l'espai d'emmagatzematge d'escombraries...
- El pati mínim per estendre la roba ha de permetre la inscripció d'un cercle d'1,80 m. de diàmetre.

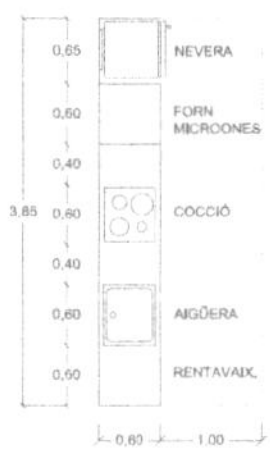

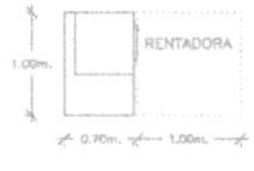

Sala
- Amplada mínima 3 m.
- Pre-instal·lació d'aire condicionat.

Cuina oberta
- Mobles alts i baixos.
- Espai de 0,60 x 0,65 m a tota l'alçada per la nevera.
- Moble de 0,60 x 0,60 cm a tota l'alçada pel forn i l'espai del microones.
- Equipada amb aparell de cocció elèctric de 4 focs, campana extractora, forn elèctric i aigüera de 2 sinus.
- Els electrodomèstics no es situaran darrere de zona de llits.
- Moble baix de 0,60m. d'amplada al costat de l'aigüera, amb portes fàcilment desmuntables, perquè l'usuari instal·li un rentavaixelles.
- Per la instal·lació del rentavaixelles, preveure endoll, desguàs i presa d'aigua freda i calenta sota l'aigüera.
- Punt de llum general amb lluminària LED càlida instal·lada.
- Punt de llum sota el moble alt amb lluminària LED càlida instal·lada.

Dormitori doble practicable
- Superficie mínima 10 m², i amplada mínima 2,60 m.
- Espai per armari d'1,50 x 0,60 m, que no serà encastat.

Dormitori senzill
- Superficie mínima 6 m2, i s'ha de poder inscriure un quadrat de 2 m.
- Espai per armari d'1,00 x 0,60 m, que no serà encastat.

Bany practicable
- Rentamans, WC i plat de dutxa.
- Mirall, portarotlles, tovalloler i barra per la cortina de la dutxa.
- Punt de llum amb lluminària LED càlida instal·lada al sostre i al mirall.

Zona de rentat i/o estenedor

Zona de rentat:
- La rentadora estarà protegida de l'aigua de pluja.
- Endoll estanc, desguàs i presa d'aigua freda i calenta.
- Si està en un espai exterior, preveure punt de llum amb lluminària LED càlida instal·lada.

Zona d'estenedor:
- S'ha de preveure un espai permanentment ventilat i protegit de vistes, amb 4 m o més de tendall, en trams no inferiors a 1 m. Pot incorporar altres usos com la caldera, l'espai d'emmagatzematge d'escombraries...
- El pati mínim per estendre la roba ha de permetre la inscripció d'un cercle d'1,80 m, de diàmetre.

FIGURE 6.24 Dwelling and room standards.

Source: Institut Català del Sòl, *Estàndards d'habitatge social* (2019).

表 5.2.1 人才住房各类套型基本指标

最小套内建筑面积（m²）	27	49	63	87	109
套型建筑面积区间（m²）	35-40	65-70	85-90	115-120	145-150
居住空间个数	1-2	3	3-4	4-5	≥5
可使用人数	1-2	3	≥4	≥4	≥4

表 5.2.2 人才住房各类套型功能空间最小使用面积

套型建筑面积区间（m²）	35-40	65-70	85-90	115-120	145-150
起居室（厅）（m²）	10	10	10	12	15
双人卧室（m²）	9	9	9	10	12
单人卧室（m²）	-	5	5	8	8
厨房（m²）	-	4	4	5	6
卫生间（三件洁具）（m²）	2.5	2.5	2.5	3	3.5
卫生间（两件洁具）（m²）	2.0	2.0	2.0	2.5	2.5

表 5.2.3 安居型商品房各类套型基本指标

最小套内建筑面积（m²）	49	63
套型建筑面积区间（m²）	65-70	85-90
居住空间个数	3	3-4
可使用人数	1-3 ≥4	

注：建设条件受限制的安居商品型房项目，在确保最小套内建筑面积的前提下，

表 5.2.4 安居型商品房各类套型功能空间最小使用面积

套型建筑面积区间（m²）	65-70	85-90
起居室（厅）（m²）	10	10

表 5.2.5 公共租赁住房各类套型基本指标

最小套内建筑面积（m²）	27	38.5	45.5	59.5
套型建筑面积区间（m²）	35-40	50-55	60-65	80-85
居住空间个数	1-2	2-3	3	3-4
可使用人数	1-2	2-3	4	≥5

注：建设条件受限

表 5.2.6 公共租赁住房各类套型功能空间最小使用面积

套型建筑面积区间（m²）	35-40	50-55	60-65	80-85
起居室（厅）（m²）	10	10	10	10
双人卧室（m²）	9	9	9	9
单人卧室（m²）	-	5	5	5
厨房（m²）	-	3.5	4	4
卫生间（三件洁具）（m²）	2.0	2.5	2.5	2.5
卫生间（两件洁具）（m²）	2.0	2.0	2.0	2.0

FIGURE 6.25 Subsidised housing characteristics and minimum usable floor areas.

Source: Shenzhen Housing and Construction Bureau, *Public Housing Construction Standards* (2021).

Notes:

Table 5.2.1: Basic characteristics of talent housing units.

Table 5.2.2: Minimum usable area of functional spaces in talent housing units.

Table 5.2.3: Basic characteristics of public rental housing units.

Table 5.2.4: Minimum usable area of functional spaces in affordable commercial housing units.

Table 5.2.5: Basic characteristics of affordable commercial housing units.

Table 5.2.6: Minimum usable area of functional spaces in public rental housing units.

FIGURE 6.26 Typical circulation and dwelling layout in the studied sample.

layouts, as the main living functions and circulation areas overlap. However, this can also create challenges for daily life and limit privacy.

In Barcelona, Amsterdam, and Zurich, too, the main access and circulation are commonly integrated with the living area; however, space standards are more generous to avoid overlapping functional and circulation zones. Bedrooms are less clustered, creating a more open, interconnected layout that enhances daylight penetration and perceived spaciousness, albeit at the cost of reduced privacy. However, in Zurich's large homes, as recommended by the WBS, often small, undefined spaces are inserted between rooms to compensate for this and can serve multiple functions as needed to improve long-term adaptability.

Access: living area
Circulation: living area
Bedrooms not grouped

B005, 50.9 m²

B043, 53.0 m²

B001, 71.4 m²

Amsterdam
Netherlands

Access: living area
Circulation: living area
Bedrooms not grouped

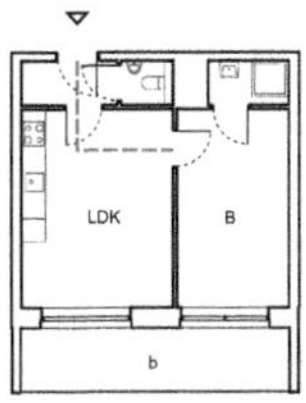

A004, 38.3 m²

A007, 45.8 m²

A038, 70.8 m²

Barcelona
Spain

Access: living area
Circulation: living area
Bedrooms not grouped

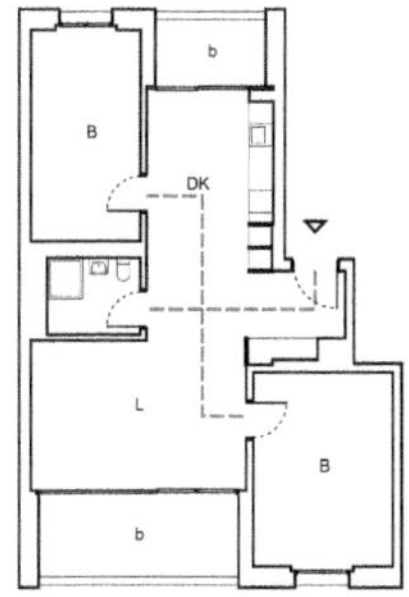

Z013, 79.5 m²

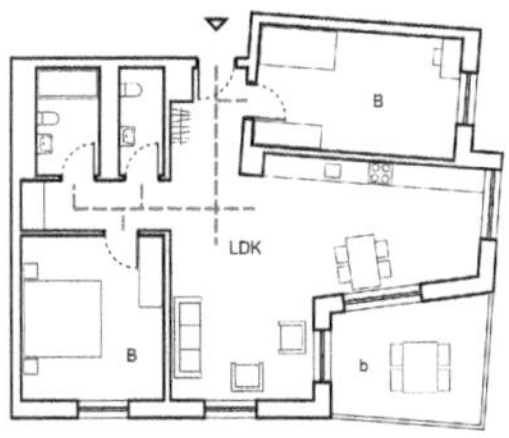

Z017, 81.0 m²

Z005, 105.8 m²

Zurich
Switzerland

These differences highlight a trade-off between functional zoning and spatial fluidity. Hall-and-corridor layouts prioritise privacy and clarity but use more floor area, while living-room-centred layouts maximise usable space and openness at the cost of privacy. Minimal or absent space standards allow very compact units, whereas generous standards enable more flexible layouts that can extend a home's functional lifespan. Unit layout is therefore not only technical or regulatory but also social and cultural: the same floor area can support very different uses depending on household routines, preferences, and interactions. However, dwelling size and use also need to be considered in relation to the quality of a space and how well it is maintained.

Conclusion

Overall, the formulation and implementation of standards demonstrate the tensions between prescription and flexibility in housing regulation. They reflect differing regulatory cultures and approaches about who should define adequacy and under what conditions. In highly codified systems such as Chile's subsidy decrees, minimum sizes leave little room for interpretation and design experimentation. By contrast, in England, the Netherlands, and particularly in Switzerland, more discretionary regimes allow housing providers to interpret adequacy in relation to economic feasibility but also their own institutional ambitions and practices.

The study of six contexts highlights that the regulation of housing space is as much a cultural and political question as it is a technical one, reflecting embedded ideas of domestic life, household formation, and what constitutes an "adequate" home from a regulatory as well as everyday lived perspective. These principles are shaped by national political economies, housing market pressures, and socio-technical conventions, embedding universal regulatory concepts in highly specific ways.

Standards embody a negotiation between efficiency, equity, and quality, whether the priority is to maximise the quantity of built units, safeguard minimum thresholds of liveability, or raise standards and the quality of life of occupants. Where they are binding through subsidy systems, as in Chile and China, standards tend to tightly define both scale and organisation, enabling compact but functional layouts within strict economic limits. In more flexible systems, such as the Netherlands or parts of England, aspirational or selectively applied standards leave greater scope for the influence of market forces, often resulting in smaller homes in expensive areas. Zurich's cooperative sector, however, demonstrates an alternative model: generous unit sizes and flexible layouts that exceed minimum requirements, supported by a regulatory and subsidy framework focused on creating long-term value rather than short-term supply.

Unit sizes, types, and layouts are greatly interconnected. While space standards set a baseline, market conditions, land values, and development models dictate how these parameters are realised and translated into design. In contexts with minimal or less onerous standards, layouts tend to be compact and efficiency-driven. Where standards are more generous – or where institutional practice exceeds them – there is scope for greater design innovation and the design of spaces that are non-prescribed in function. These impacts of less onerous or more generous standards can be exacerbated or compensated by differences in density and housing typologies.

Understanding subsidised housing through the lens of architectural design research enables a differentiated understanding of how socio-cultural norms, regulatory cultures, and design governance interact and shape housing design outcomes. Examining dwelling plans alongside system-level analysis reveals the spatial consequences of policy decisions and market pressures, making visible both housing inequities and regulatory successes or constraints. This underscores the need for interdisciplinary approaches that integrate social studies, policy analysis, and architectural design, producing richer, more nuanced insights with tangible impacts for both practice and research.

PART IV
Homes and Lived Experiences

7

IN-DEPTH CASE STUDY CARTOGRAPHIES

DOI: 10.4324/9781032679204-12

1 Residents

Jerry, England (London)

Nergiz, Ariyana & Noor, England (London)

Jake & Heather, England (London)

May & June, England (London)

Michael, England (London)

Maria, England (London)

Caroline, England (Eastleigh)

Emma, England (Eastleight)

Hannah, England (Liss)

Jennifer, England (Oxford)

Poppie, England (Oxford)

Soledad & Lautaro, Chile (Santiago)

Fernando & Veronica, Chile (Santiago)

Johana & Manuel, Chile (Santiago)

Carolinne & Filipe, Chile (Santiago)

Karin Alex & Benjamin, Chile (Santiago)

Christina & Alma, Chile (Santiago)

Erica & Matias, Chile (Santiago)

Weiping, China (Shenzhen)

Jiaxin, China (Shenzhen)

Mei, China (Shenzhen)

Chi, China (Shenzhen)

Babet, Netherlands (Amsterdam)

Anja, Netherlands (Amsterdam)

Marielle, Netherlands (Amsterdam)

Maartje, Netherlands (Amsterdam)

Bart, Netherlands (Amsterdam)

Kerala, Netherlands (Amsterdam)

Yeray & Pilarica, Spain (Barcelona)

David & Angeles, Spain (Barcelona)

Isabel, Claudia & Ximena, Spain (Barcelona)

Javier & Cristina, Spain (Barcelona)

Andre, Switzerland (Bülach)

Letitia, Switzerland (Bülach)

Candide, Switzerland (Zurich)

Sandra, Switzerland (Zurich)

2 Home-Use Studies

Jerry, England (London)

Nergiz, Ariyana & Noor, England (London)

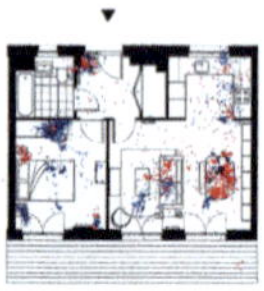

Jake & Heather, England (London)

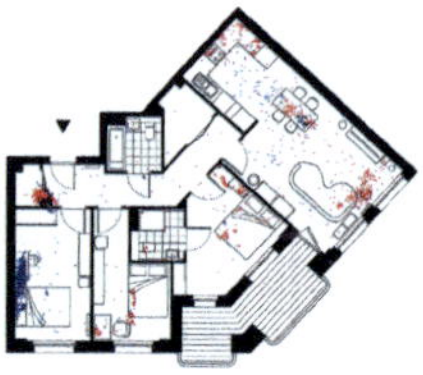

May & June, England (London)

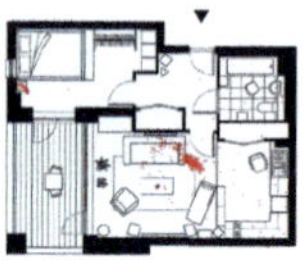

Michael, England (London)

Maria, England (London)

Caroline, England (Eastleigh)

Emma, England (Eastleight)

Hannah, England (Liss)

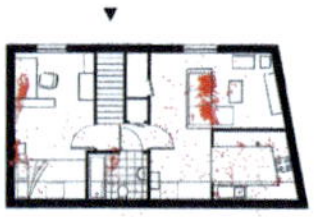

Jennifer, England (Oxford)

Poppie, England (Oxford)

Soledad & Lautaro, Chile (Santiago)

Fernando & Veronica, Chile (Santiago)

Johana & Manuel, Chile (Santiago)

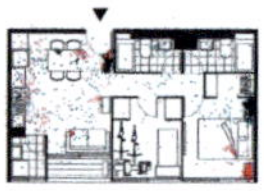

Carolinne & Filipe, Chile (Santiago)

Karin Alex & Benjamin, Chile (Santiago)

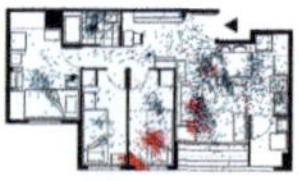

Christina & Alma, Chile (Santiago)

Erica & Matias, Chile (Santiago)

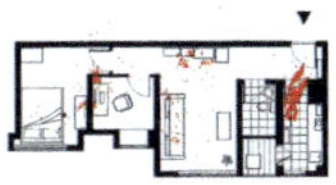

Weiping, China (Shenzhen)

Jiaxin, China (Shenzhen)

Mei, China (Shenzhen)

Chi, China (Shenzhen)

Babet, Netherlands (Amsterdam)

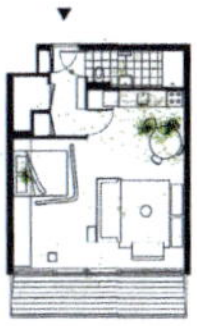

Anja, Netherlands (Amsterdam)

Marielle, Netherlands (Amsterdam)

Maartje, Netherlands (Amsterdam)

Bart, Netherlands (Amsterdam)

Kerala, Netherlands (Amsterdam)

Yeray & Pilarica, Spain (Barcelona)

David & Angeles, Spain (Barcelona)

Isabel, Claudia & Ximena, Spain (Barcelona)

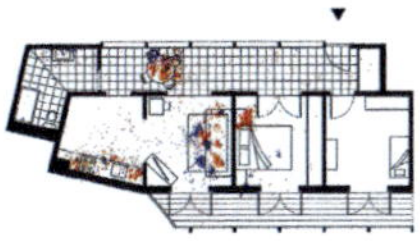

Javier & Cristina, Spain (Barcelona)

Andre, Switzerland (Bülach)

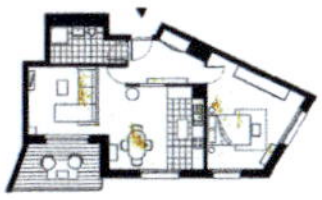

Letitia, Switzerland (Bülach)

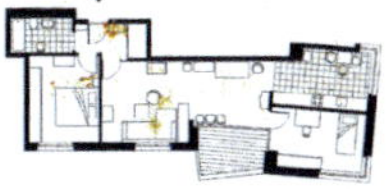

Candide, Switzerland (Zurich)

Sandra, Switzerland (Zurich)

3 Living Rooms

Jerry, England (London)

Nergiz, Ariyana & Noor, England (London)

Jake & Heather, England (London)

May & June, England (London)

Michael, England (London)

Maria, England (London)

Caroline, England (Eastleigh)

Emma, England (Eastleight)

Hannah, England (Liss)

Jennifer, England (Oxford)

Poppie, England (Oxford)

Soledad & Lautaro, Chile (Santiago)

Fernando & Veronica, Chile (Santiago)

Johana & Manuel, Chile (Santiago)

Carolinne & Filipe, Chile (Santiago)

Karin Alex & Benjamin, Chile (Santiago)

Christina & Alma, Chile (Santiago)

Erica & Matias, Chile (Santiago)

Weiping, China (Shenzhen)

Jiaxin, China (Shenzhen)

Mei, China (Shenzhen)

Chi, China (Shenzhen)

Babet, Netherlands (Amsterdam)

Anja, Netherlands (Amsterdam)

Marielle, Netherlands (Amsterdam)

Maartje, Netherlands (Amsterdam)

Bart, Netherlands (Amsterdam)

Kerala, Netherlands (Amsterdam)

Yeray & Pilarica, Spain (Barcelona)

David & Angeles, Spain (Barcelona)

Isabel, Claudia & Ximena, Spain (Barcelona)

Javier & Cristina, Spain (Barcelona)

Andre, Switzerland (Bülach)

Letitia, Switzerland (Bülach)

Candide, Switzerland (Zurich)

Sandra, Switzerland (Zurich)

4 Kitchens

Jerry, England (London)

Nergiz, Ariyana & Noor, England (London)

Jake & Heather, England (London)

May & June, England (London)

Michael, England (London)

Maria, England (London)

Caroline, England (Eastleigh)

Emma, England (Eastleight)

Hannah, England (Liss)

Jennifer, England (Oxford)

Poppie, England (Oxford)

Soledad & Lautaro, Chile (Santiago)

Fernando & Veronica, Chile (Santiago)

Johana & Manuel, Chile (Santiago)

Carolinne & Filipe, Chile (Santiago)

Karin Alex & Benjamin, Chile (Santiago)

Christina & Alma, Chile (Santiago)

Erica & Matias, Chile (Santiago)

Weiping, China (Shenzhen)

Jiaxin, China (Shenzhen)

Mei, China (Shenzhen)

Chi, China (Shenzhen)

Babet, Netherlands (Amsterdam)

Anja, Netherlands (Amsterdam)

Marielle, Netherlands (Amsterdam)

Maartje, Netherlands (Amsterdam)

Bart, Netherlands (Amsterdam)

Kerala, Netherlands (Amsterdam)

Yeray & Pilarica, Spain (Barcelona)

David & Angeles, Spain (Barcelona)

Isabel, Claudia & Ximena, Spain (Barcelona)

Javier & Cristina, Spain (Barcelona)

Andre, Switzerland (Bülach)

Letitia, Switzerland (Bülach)

Candide, Switzerland (Zurich)

Sandra, Switzerland (Zurich)

5 Bedrooms

Jerry, England (London)

Nergiz, Ariyana & Noor, England (London)

Jake & Heather, England (London)

May & June, England (London)

Michael, England (London)

Maria, England (London)

Caroline, England (Eastleigh)

Emma, England (Eastleight)

Hannah, England (Liss)

Jennifer, England (Oxford)

Poppie, England (Oxford)

Soledad & Lautaro, Chile (Santiago)

Fernando & Veronica, Chile (Santiago)

Johana & Manuel, Chile (Santiago)

Carolinne & Filipe, Chile (Santiago)

Karin Alex & Benjamin, Chile (Santiago)

Christina & Alma, Chile (Santiago)

Erica & Matias, Chile (Santiago)

Weiping, China (Shenzhen)

Jiaxin, China (Shenzhen)

Mei, China (Shenzhen)

Chi, China (Shenzhen)

Babet, Netherlands (Amsterdam)

Anja, Netherlands (Amsterdam)

Marielle, Netherlands (Amsterdam)

Maartje, Netherlands (Amsterdam)

Bart, Netherlands (Amsterdam)

Kerala, Netherlands (Amsterdam)

Yeray & Pilarica, Spain (Barcelona)

David & Angeles, Spain (Barcelona)

Isabel, Claudia & Ximena, Spain (Barcelona)

Javier & Cristina, Spain (Barcelona)

Andre, Switzerland (Bülach)

Letitia, Switzerland (Bülach)

Candide, Switzerland (Zurich)

Sandra, Switzerland (Zurich)

6 External, Work, and Communal Spaces

Jerry, England (London)

Nergiz, Ariyana & Noor, England (London)

Jake & Heather, England (London)

May & June, England (London)

Michael, England (London)

Maria, England (London)

Caroline, England (Eastleigh)

Emma, England (Eastleight)

Hannah, England (Liss)

Jennifer, England (Oxford)

Poppie, England (Oxford)

Soledad & Lautaro, Chile (Santiago)

Fernando & Veronica, Chile (Santiago)

Johana & Manuel, Chile (Santiago)

Carolinne & Filipe, Chile (Santiago)

Karin Alex & Benjamin, Chile (Santiago)

Christina & Alma, Chile (Santiago)

Erica & Matias, Chile (Santiago)

Weiping, China (Shenzhen)

Jiaxin, China (Shenzhen)

Mei, China (Shenzhen)

Chi, China (Shenzhen)

Babet, Netherlands (Amsterdam)

Anja, Netherlands (Amsterdam)

Marielle, Netherlands (Amsterdam)

Maartje, Netherlands (Amsterdam)

Bart, Netherlands (Amsterdam)

Kerala, Netherlands (Amsterdam)

Yeray & Pilarica, Spain (Barcelona)

David & Angeles, Spain (Barcelona)

Isabel, Claudia & Ximena, Spain (Barcelona)

Javier & Cristina, Spain (Barcelona)

Andre, Switzerland (Bülach)

Letitia, Switzerland (Bülach)

Candide, Switzerland (Zurich)

Sandra, Switzerland (Zurich)

7 Buildings

Jerry, England (London)

Nergiz, Ariyana & Noor, England (London)

Jake & Heather, England (London)

May & June, England (London)

Michael, England (London)

Maria, England (London)

Caroline, England (Eastleigh)

Emma, England (Eastleight)

Hannah, England (Liss)

Jennifer, England (Oxford)

Poppie, England (Oxford)

Soledad & Lautaro, Chile (Santiago)

Fernando & Veronica, Chile (Santiago)

Johana & Manuel, Chile (Santiago)

Carolinne & Filipe, Chile (Santiago)

Karin Alex & Benjamin, Chile (Santiago)

Christina & Alma, Chile (Santiago)

Erica & Matias, Chile (Santiago)

Weiping, China (Shenzhen)

Jiaxin, China (Shenzhen)

Mei, China (Shenzhen)

Chi, China (Shenzhen)

Babet, Netherlands (Amsterdam)

Anja, Netherlands (Amsterdam)

Marielle, Netherlands (Amsterdam)

Maartje, Netherlands (Amsterdam)

Bart, Netherlands (Amsterdam)

Kerala, Netherlands (Amsterdam)

Yeray & Pilarica, Spain (Barcelona)

David & Angeles, Spain (Barcelona)

Isabel, Claudia & Ximena, Spain (Barcelona)

Javier & Cristina, Spain (Barcelona)

Andre, Switzerland (Bülach)

Letitia, Switzerland (Bülach)

Candide, Switzerland (Zurich)

Sandra, Switzerland (Zurich)

8 Aerials

Jerry, England (London)

Nergiz, Ariyana & Noor, England (London)

Jake & Heather, England (London)

May & June, England (London)

Michael, England (London)

Maria, England (London)

Caroline, England (Eastleigh)

Emma, England (Eastleight)

Hannah, England (Liss)

Jennifer, England (Oxford)

Poppie, England (Oxford)

Soledad & Lautaro, Chile (Santiago)

Fernando & Veronica, Chile (Santiago)

Johana & Manuel, Chile (Santiago)

Carolinne & Filipe, Chile (Santiago)

Karin Alex & Benjamin, Chile (Santiago)

Christina & Alma, Chile (Santiago)

Erica & Matias, Chile (Santiago)

Weiping, China (Shenzhen)

Jiaxin, China (Shenzhen)

Mei, China (Shenzhen)

Chi, China (Shenzhen)

Babet, Netherlands (Amsterdam)

Anja, Netherlands (Amsterdam)

Marielle, Netherlands (Amsterdam)

Maartje, Netherlands (Amsterdam)

Bart, Netherlands (Amsterdam)

Kerala, Netherlands (Amsterdam)

Yeray & Pilarica, Spain (Barcelona)

David & Angeles, Spain (Barcelona)

Isabel, Claudia & Ximena, Spain (Barcelona)

Javier & Cristina, Spain (Barcelona)

Andre, Switzerland (Bülach)

Letitia, Switzerland (Bülach)

Candide, Switzerland (Zurich)

Sandra, Switzerland (Zurich)

9 Models

Jerry, England (London)

Nergiz, Ariyana & Noor, England (London)

Jake & Heather, England (London)

May & June, England (London)

Michael, England (London)

Maria, England (London)

Caroline, England (Eastleigh)

Emma, England (Eastleight)

Hannah, England (Liss)

Jennifer, England (Oxford)

Poppie, England (Oxford)

Soledad & Lautaro, Chile (Santiago)

Fernando & Veronica, Chile (Santiago)

Johana & Manuel, Chile (Santiago)

Carolinne & Filipe, Chile (Santiago)

Karin Alex & Benjamin, Chile (Santiago)

Christina & Alma, Chile (Santiago)

Erica & Matias, Chile (Santiago)

Weiping, China (Shenzhen)

Jiaxin, China (Shenzhen)

Mei, China (Shenzhen)

Chi, China (Shenzhen)

Babet, Netherlands (Amsterdam)

Anja, Netherlands (Amsterdam)

Marielle, Netherlands (Amsterdam)

Maartje, Netherlands (Amsterdam)

Bart, Netherlands (Amsterdam)

Kerala, Netherlands (Amsterdam)

Yeray & Pilarica, Spain (Barcelona)

David & Angeles, Spain (Barcelona)

Isabel, Claudia & Ximena, Spain (Barcelona)

Javier & Cristina, Spain (Barcelona)

Andre, Switzerland (Bülach)

Letitia, Switzerland (Bülach)

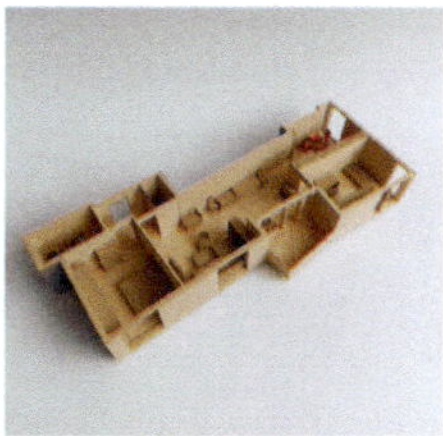
Candide, Switzerland (Zurich)

Sandra, Switzerland (Zurich)

10 Floorplans

Jerry, England (London)

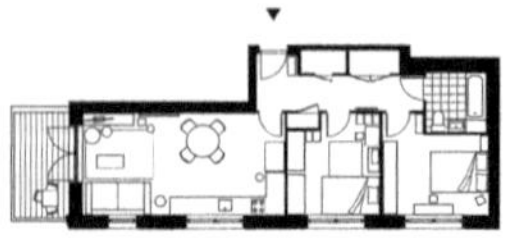

Nergiz, Ariyana & Noor, England (London)

Jake & Heather, England (London)

May & June, England (London)

Michael, England (London)

Maria, England (London)

Caroline, England (Eastleigh)

Emma, England (Eastleight)

Hannah, England (Liss)

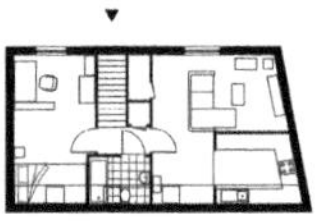

Jennifer, England (Oxford)

Poppie, England (Oxford)

Soledad & Lautaro, Chile (Santiago)

Fernando & Veronica, Chile (Santiago)

Johana & Manuel, Chile (Santiago)

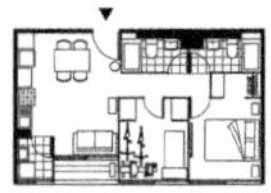

Carolinne & Filipe, Chile (Santiago)

Karin Alex & Benjamin, Chile (Santiago)

Christina & Alma, Chile (Santiago)

Erica & Matias, Chile (Santiago)

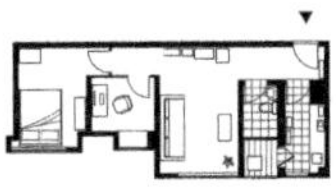

Weiping, China (Shenzhen)

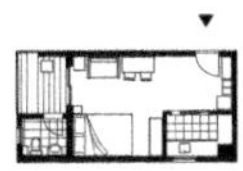

Jiaxin, China (Shenzhen)

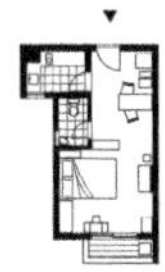

Mei, China (Shenzhen)

Chi, China (Shenzhen)

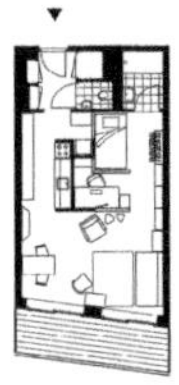

Babet, Netherlands (Amsterdam)

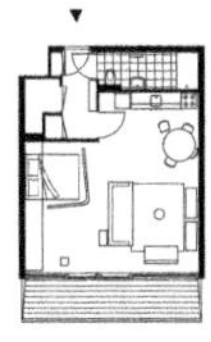

Anja, Netherlands (Amsterdam)

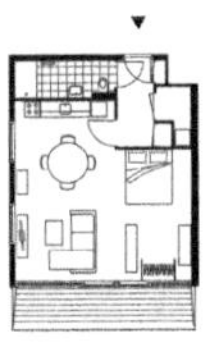

Marielle, Netherlands (Amsterdam)

Maartje, Netherlands (Amsterdam)

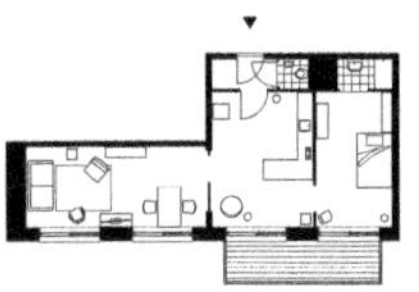

Bart, Netherlands (Amsterdam)

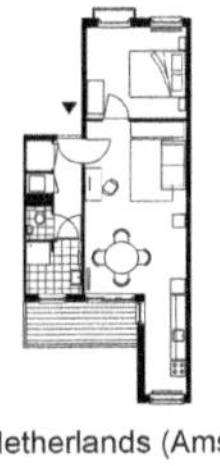

Kerala, Netherlands (Amsterdam)

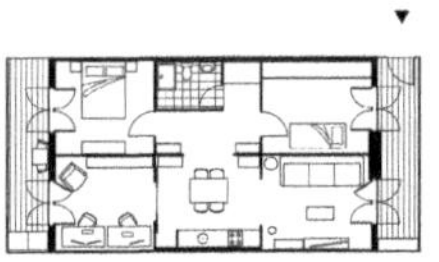

Yeray & Pilarica, Spain (Barcelona)

David & Angeles, Spain (Barcelona)

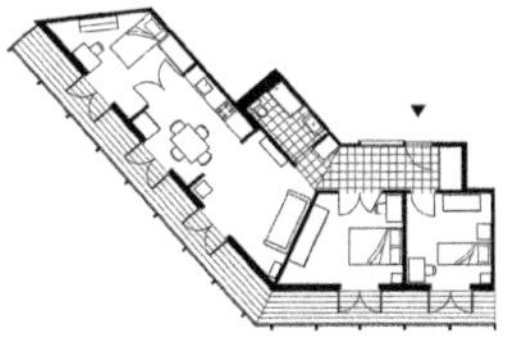

Isabel, Claudia & Ximena, Spain (Barcelona)

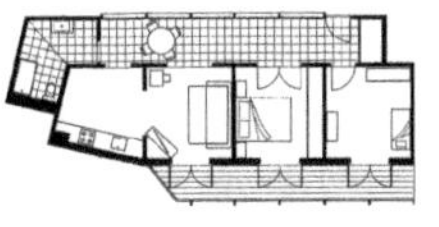

Javier & Cristina, Spain (Barcelona)

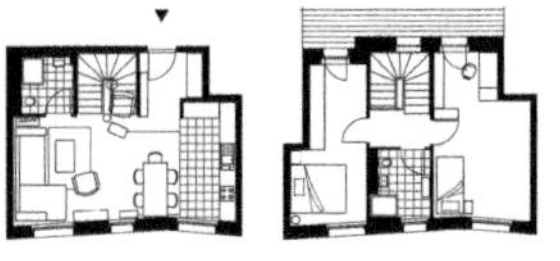

Andre, Switzerland (Bülach)

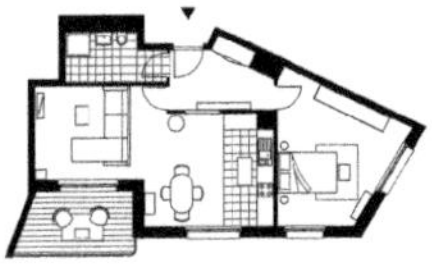

Letitia, Switzerland (Bülach)

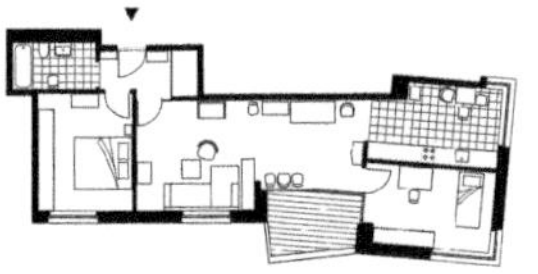

Candide, Switzerland (Zurich)

Sandra, Switzerland (Zurich)

Note: For further information see: https://doi.org/10.60624/nnc8-1557.

8

HOME-USE STUDIES

An Insight into Lived Experiences

Lucia Alonso Aranda, Consuelo Albornoz Marambio, and Sam Jacoby

Household dynamics, social norms, and cultural expectations shape not only how people live but also what they expect from their homes. Yet surprisingly little is known about how residents use domestic spaces and how design influences their daily routines, habits, and social interactions. Housing policies and design standards instead often rely on idealised assumptions about household life, resulting in a disconnect from how homes are actually lived in, particularly in affordable and subsidised housing, where spatial constraints and changing lifestyles can create unique pressures. To capture both the physical characteristics of homes and the lived experiences of their residents, we adopted a mixed-method approach, integrating architectural documentation, live-motion tracking, and interviews.[1] Understanding how people adapt their homes to evolving social, economic, and technological demands is essential to informing housing design that is both functional and resilient.

The study involved interviews and live tracking across 37 homes in ten cities: London, Liss, Eastleigh, and Oxford (England); Santiago (Chile); Shenzhen (China); Amsterdam (the Netherlands); Barcelona (Spain); and Bülach and Zurich (Switzerland). Over five days, the activities of residents living in subsidised homes were monitored using wearable tags and anchors placed in each room. The movement tracking data facilitated conversations with participants around specific design aspects such as the size, layout, and functionality of their home.

Housing studies have suggested the need for evidence-based changes in housing standards based on residents' lived experiences (Kearns, 2022; Royal Institute of British Architects (RIBA), 2011), yet little concrete research supports these claims. Previous research on everyday domestic life has often had a limited scope. Hillier and Hanson's *The Social Logic of Space* (1984) pioneered methods for analysing spatial configuration and its social implications, establishing a new theoretical foundation for understanding the relationship between space and social life. Their approach translated floorplans into spatial graphs and used algorithms to assess the degree of integration or segregation of different spaces. Ethnographic studies such as *Life at Home in the Twenty-First Century* (2012) by the UCLA Center on Everyday Lives of Families (CELF) explored how families navigate work, play, and domestic labour within their homes. Researchers installed cameras and tracked family members through their daily routines, representing the data as diagrams and descriptions rather than floorplans. More recently, smart-home research

DOI: 10.4324/9781032679204-13

projects, such as the Center for Advanced Studies in Adaptive Systems (CASAS) Smart Home Project and Aware Home Research Initiative (AHRI) at the Georgia Institute of Technology, have used sensor-based technology to monitor household behaviour and functions. Perhaps the simplest and most pragmatic example comes from the TV programme *Sarah Beeny's Renovate Don't Relocate*, which uses cameras to record how people use their homes and converts this information into heat maps to inform interior design decisions.

Each of these studies – whether grounded in ethnography, computational modelling, or spatial theory – offers a unique lens on how domestic routines are shaped by social norms, spatial design, and, increasingly, technology. Despite these contributions, a critical gap remains in developing a holistic approach: few studies integrate spatial analysis, behavioural patterns, and lived experience into a single framework capable of informing evidence-based housing design. Research tends to focus on either ethnography (CELF) or data-driven approaches (CASAS, AHRI) without integrating subjective experience through sensor data. For example, how residents perceive, reflect on, or adapt their routines in relation to the data being gathered is rarely studied. There is also a lack of comparative data across cultures, housing typologies, and non-nuclear family households. This study tries to address some of these gaps and responds to the urgent need for post–COVID-19 research to examine how new uses have reorganised daily spatial patterns and furniture configurations in the home.

In addition to ethnographic studies, post-occupancy evaluations (POEs) can help identify whether housing meets functional, spatial, and technical requirements. However, POEs are often quantifiable user satisfaction surveys rather than an attempt to qualitatively capture actual behaviour and use of spaces. As a result, housing policies tend to prioritise quantitative metrics – such as floor areas or the number of rooms – over qualitative aspects like spatial relationships and experiential qualities, which visual ethnography shows to be highly significant to those using the space. While surveys may record how much time people spend at home, they rarely reveal how time is distributed across rooms, activities, or different household members, leaving a critical gap in understanding the lived reality of housing. A significant research challenge is connecting data in a way that enables translation of behavioural insights into design regulations that better reflect how people inhabit their homes.

This study addresses this challenge by combining quantitative and qualitative approaches to provide a richer, holistic understanding of domestic life. Rather than relying on abstract standards or anecdotal evidence, we examine how people actually inhabit their homes – room by room, activity by activity – and how their homes support or constrain this. By integrating spatial metrics, behavioural patterns, and resident perspectives, this study moves beyond traditional architectural case studies and post-occupancy evaluations, which often rely on broad indicators like dwelling size or user surveys. Instead, it offers an evidence-based understanding of domestic life and homes as lived environments, accommodating work, leisure, care, and social interaction in nuanced and sometimes unexpected ways. The findings aim to inform more adaptive and responsive housing design, addressing emerging needs such as remote working, flexible family arrangements, and multi-use spaces, while challenging static assumptions embedded in current design standards and policies.

Methodology

Each home was recorded through a detailed photo survey, measured floor plans, and 3D interior scans, creating an accurate spatial record of its layout and furnishings. To understand how these spaces were used day to day, participants wore location-tracking devices for five to seven consecutive days. The real-time location system (RTLS), also known as an "indoor positioning system", is a technology solution commonly used for real-time tracking of inventory, staff, and equipment. Stationary anchors placed in each room captured movement patterns with room-level accuracy (around 30 cm), providing a continuous record of how occupants distributed their time and activities throughout the home. The anchors and location tracking device sent data to a controller unit, typically one per floor, although in very large homes or where connectivity was poor, two units were used. The RTLS operated offline to ensure data security, requiring minimal interaction from participants beyond wearing the device. To contextualise the tracking data, residents kept short daily activity logs, noting key tasks or events.

Participants gave informed consent before taking part, with all data stored securely and anonymised unless explicit identification was agreed. Data from location tracking, diaries, and interviews were analysed to examine patterns of home use and experiences of housing design quality. The study had ethics approval from both the Royal College of Art and the Pontificia Universidad Católica de Chile.

The data is visualised as dots on a floorplan, with each dot marking the participant's location at 30-second intervals. The colours used are to differentiate between countries as well as households in which two or more residents participated. Using a motion-tracking system rather than video recordings or similar visual methods ensures that the participants' privacy is preserved, as well as their anonymity where requested.

One challenge encountered was the lack of sufficient electrical sockets to connect the anchors. In some cases, thick concrete walls or dense building materials weakened the signal. Additional challenges included children or pets interfering with the hardware and participants forgetting to charge the wearable trackers. Since the person's location was recorded every 30 seconds, it was challenging to capture the exact repetition or sequence of smaller movements. Another challenge was the variation in the level of detail in the self-reported daily activity logs. While some described the activities carried out in each room and time slot, others only noted the times they were absent from the home. Awareness that their movements were being tracked also affected the behaviour of some residents, who reported changing the use of certain spaces during the study.

Home Use and Awareness of Space

The home-use studies and interviews revealed everyday spatial preferences, negotiations, and choices that residents make, as well as how different household members use domestic spaces and how activities can overlap. They showed that while some residents are highly aware of their movement and routines, others pay little attention to how they interact with their living spaces. By analysing daily habits, the negotiation of shared space, and underused spaces, home-use pattern studies provide a deeper understanding of how homes function beyond their intended design.

For some, home use is structured around clear, habitual patterns. In London, for example, Jake and Heather described their routine as "quite regimental", with clear preferences for where they work, relax, and sleep. Heather consistently sat near the window, stating, "That's my side close to the window. I just like sitting next to the light, and I like being next to the lamp". Jake was also very aware of his habits: "I have the double doors next to me wide open. So, you know, I might as well be outside if I'm sat here". His choice of seating, workspace, and

FIGURE 8.1 Comparison of the original layout planned by the architect Hawkins\Brown (a) and the actual furniture layout and use of the home by Jake and Heather (b), London (2023).

relaxation spots reflected a deliberate way of using and experiencing different parts of his home. He also recognised that certain areas serve multiple functions: "If I'm at the dining table, I'll be working from the dining table, I'll eat from the dining table, and then I'll read from the dining table". Jake and Heather furnished their flat much like the developer's original floorplan, changing only the dining table because of its importance to them and frequent use (Figure 8.1).

The routine and repetitive use of space was also evident in Jerry's flat in West London. Jerry's schedule was very similar during workdays, using a designated space for work at the dining table and his sofa for relaxing and eating. In the kitchen, he predominantly used one spot for meal preparation. In South London, May and June also had an established pattern at home. June worked a demanding job during the day, but when she was home, she mostly spent her time in her bedroom recording social media content and relaxing. Meanwhile, her cousin, May, who worked from home most days, used almost every available space. In comparison, Maartje's routine was less static (Figure 8.2). Nevertheless, she felt the size of her 37-m^2 studio flat in North Amsterdam dictated her movements, describing herself as "a tiger in a cage. . . pacing up and down a lot".

In comparison, other residents engaged with their homes in less intentional ways. Some spaces remained underused without any clear reason or even awareness of this. Isabel in Barcelona, for example, rarely used her living room but struggled to explain why, suggesting that her busy lifestyle left little time for relaxation. Interestingly, her daughters also avoided the living room, illustrating how collective behaviours can shape home use. Similarly, Anja in Amsterdam rarely used her sofa and seem to prefer eating, working, and socialising from the same spot at the dining table (Figure 8.3). By contrast, Babet in Amsterdam deliberately avoided using her dining table, choosing to eat her meals on the sofa instead.

For Hannah in Liss, the home-use tracking made her aware that she would like to "make more use of some of the areas of the home". This reflects the common notion that homes should be used efficiently and evenly. Spaces such as bathrooms, dining tables, or

FIGURE 8.2 Home-use studies: Jerry in London (a), May and June in London (b), and Maartje in Amsterdam (c), 2023.

balconies, while not used frequently or for extended periods, are still highly valued and sometimes essential. In Shenzhen, Jiaxin barely uses her kitchen at home because eating out or ordering food is common and affordable, yet she insists that "having a kitchen is still important" (Figure 8.4). However, another resident in Shenzhen expressed a preference for a larger balcony instead of a kitchen, showing how individual priorities shape home design preferences.

In some homes, it was challenging to capture these dynamics, as not all household members chose to take part in the home-use tracking. The negotiation of shared spaces becomes particularly relevant in smaller homes, where multiple activities often overlap. In Chile, for example, residents frequently adapt single rooms for different uses throughout the day, balancing work, dining, and social activities in the same space. This, for example, is evident in Cristina and Alma's tracking data, even though they were the only two out of five household members participating, as their busy floorplan demonstrates the many activities occurring in the same room at the same time. Cristina explained that the living room is where the family gathers the most; however, the tracking showed that her daughter, Alma, tended to spend most of her time in her bedroom. A similar pattern was evident in Karin's household, where three of four occupants participated:

FIGURE 8.3 Home-use studies: Isabel in Barcelona (a) and Anja in Amsterdam (b), 2023.

while the living room was collectively used, Benjamín, the eldest son, spent most of his time in his bedroom (Figure 8.5). These examples show the intensive use of shared areas of the home and the contrasting tendency of some household members to retreat to their private rooms.

Working

Having a separate room for working was common among smaller households, especially in single-person ones. For example, Sandra in Zurich and Hannah in Liss both used a separate room as an office space, as well for exercising and storage. In Shenzhen, while most studied flats were studios, one participant had two bedrooms, including a small spare one. As he had applied for a larger flat to allow his parents to live with him for at least six months a year, this extra bedroom needed to accommodate a bed. However, finding the room too small for this purpose, he chose to use it with a desk to work from home instead. Similarly, Yeray and Pilarica in Barcelona were very conscious about needing three bedrooms: one for working from home and another for when they had a baby. Other participants highlighted that having additional rooms gave them greater flexibility. For instance, Andre in Bülach, Switzerland, used his second bedroom, formerly his daughter's, as a hobby room for assembling train sets.

FIGURE 8.4 Home-use study: Jiaxin in Shenzhen (2024).

For others, however, having a separate room for work was not possible, leading to compromises and adaptations within their living areas or bedrooms. Isabel in Barcelona and Heather in London, for example, chose to set up desks in their bedrooms. Jennifer in Oxford also worked from her bedroom but divided the space to separate work from rest. Babet, living in a studio flat, similarly divided her space to create separate areas for sleeping, working, and living. Some residents were able to fit a designated desk for work within their open-plan living room, while others, particularly in Amsterdam and London, where open-plan spaces are more common, used dining tables for the dual purpose of eating and working. In two-person households where both worked from home, two working spaces were needed, often with one using the bedroom and the other the living room. Others, like Jennifer in Chile alternated between using the dining table and working from her bed. Although she was comfortable working from home, she noted that the lack of a proper workspace was a downside, in addition to her children interrupting her during meetings. These examples highlight how participants had to adapt their home use to meet remote working needs.

Participants in Shenzhen were often away from home for much of the day. Most left for work around 8:30 am and returned by evening, sometimes as late as 11:00 pm. In addition, food delivery in the city is very affordable, meaning many meals were eaten outside the home, which explains the limited use of kitchens. One participant who cooked on weekends for herself had more kitchen and dining table activities in her home-use tracking; however, her dining table sometimes doubled as a desk for work. This made it difficult to distinguish between uses of her dining table for eating, working, or socialising with friends, with limited space forcing an

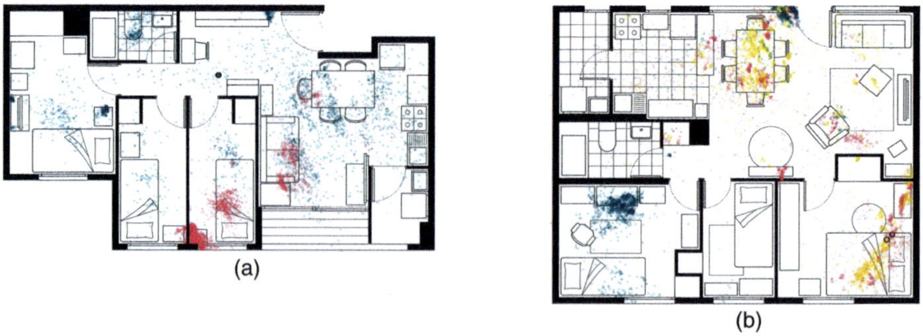

FIGURE 8.5 Home-use studies: Cristina and Alma (a) and Karin, Alex, and Benjamin (b) in Santiago (2023).

overlap of functions. Other participants had clearer divisions of use, with desks specifically set up for different purposes, such as working or gaming.

While most participants could sometimes work from home due to their desk-based employment, others, especially in Santiago, adapted their homes more radically to accommodate additional bedrooms, but also, for example, to work from home in a small shop or an improvised hair salon. To fully understand the differences in home workspaces, two types of domestic production and income generation should be distinguished: work-from-home and home-based work. "Work-from-home" refers to salaried work taking place at home (Islam, 2022), while the term "home-based work" encompasses various productive activities in which the house is the principal workplace (Wagemann et al., 2024). This distinction is important, especially in the Global South, where work-from-home alone does not capture the diverse work experiences (Islam, 2022; Wagemann et al., 2024).

Home-based work was more common in Santiago than in other cities. Examples of this are two self-employed homeworkers, both single parents and primary providers for their households. Erica worked as a pet groomer and hairdresser, using two spaces at her home for her occupations: a foldable grooming table in the living room when attending to pets, and a hairdressing station set up in the corridor near the bathroom to wash the hair of her clients. Soledad, meanwhile, left her job to care for her mother and set up a convenience store at home, selling food and soft drinks within the housing complex. She removed the partition wall between the third bedroom and the living room to make space for the shop, using the bedroom window overlooking the external hallway and a doorbell to sell her goods without having to open the main door (Figure 8.6).

This supports Verrest and Post's (2007) claim that tenure security enables home-based work, with individual homeownership being a key factor in developing home-based economic activities. In both Santiago cases, the participants made spatial modifications, installing furniture or rearranging the room layout, that would not have been possible without owning their home.

Kitchen and Dining Areas

The way kitchens are used varies considerably depending on household size, spatial configuration, and socio-cultural norms. Research on domestic space highlights how kitchens function both as sites of production and social interaction (Arnold et al., 2017), but their use is often contingent on household composition and lifestyle.

In single-person households, kitchen use is often limited to specific, efficient routines. For example, Jerry in London used just one designated area for meal preparation, while in Oxford, Poppie preferred to use only a small corner of her worktop for quick cooking. For some, kitchens were barely used at all. Hannah, living alone in Liss, explained: "I'm not really a cook, so I don't spend much time in the kitchen. I literally grab whatever's in the fridge, and usually I eat upstairs too. . . either on my bed or in the spare room on the computer". This highlights that convenience and individual routines often replace traditional meal practices in single-occupant households (Yates & Warde, 2017). This also suggests that for those living alone, kitchens can become purely utilitarian and sometimes underutilised spaces.

In multi-person households, however, kitchens often take on more dynamic and interactive roles, particularly when two or more people share cooking and cleaning responsibilities. Kitchens can become spaces of daily interaction and bonding, as seen in Jake and Heather's London

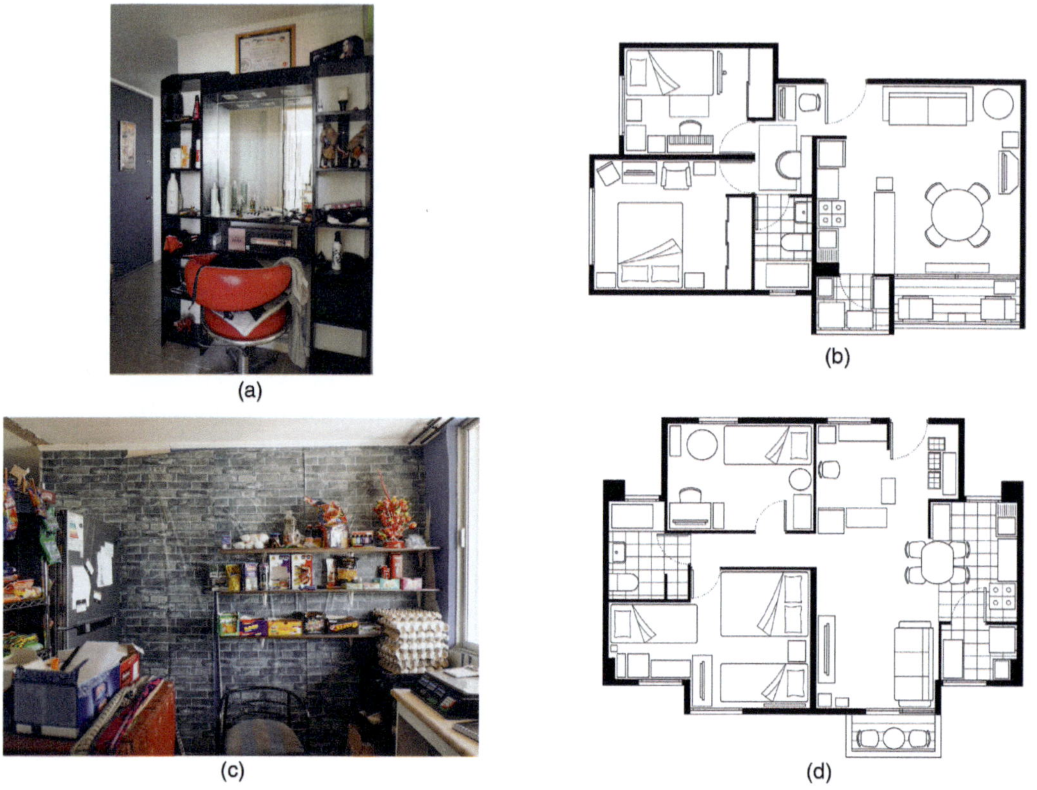

FIGURE 8.6 Working from home in Santiago: hairdressing in Erica and Matías' home (a, b) and Soledad's shop (c, d) (2023).

home, where they cooked together almost every evening and saw the kitchen as a "space of convergence" to talk and reconnect after work. They also preferred an open-plan kitchen, where they could comfortably cook and socialise at the same time. Similarly, Jennifer in Santiago noted the social importance of the open-plan kitchen: "when someone comes over, I don't miss anything when they're talking". These experiences support common arguments that open-plan designs foster sociability by removing physical barriers between cooking, dining, and living spaces (Sal Moslehian et al., 2023).

However, gender dynamics continue to shape kitchen use in many households. In Barcelona, all participants lived in two- to three-person households, but patterns of kitchen use varied. In two homes, cooking and cleaning tasks were shared equally, as with Yeray and Pilarica, yet in others the kitchen remained primarily the domain of women. For instance, in Javier and Cristina's home, Cristina was the primary kitchen user (Figure 8.7). In Isabel's household, although her daughters used the dining table, it is also evident that Isabel did most of the cooking and cleaning. Similarly, in Santiago, Veronica primarily used the kitchen and laundry room, with her partner Fernando admitting that he rarely used the latter. These findings echo feminist spatial analyses (Beck & Arnold, 2009), which argue that domestic spaces such as kitchens and laundry rooms are often socially and culturally coded as female domains.

(a)

(b)

FIGURE 8.7 Comparison of kitchen use: Cristina and Javier (a) and Yeray and Pilarica (b) in Barcelona (2023).

Kitchen layouts strongly influence how kitchens and the space around them can be used. Open-plan kitchens, like Jake and Heather's in London, facilitate social cooking and shared tasks, while closed kitchens often limit interaction, reinforcing more traditional, solitary cooking roles. Smaller kitchens in compact apartments may not accommodate a dining table, leading some participants, such as Michael (London), Jennifer (Oxford), or Caroline (Eastleigh) to prefer eating on their sofas. Others felt that their space was sufficiently flexible to give them both options, as seen in Sandra's Zurich flat, which could fit a small dining table in either the kitchen or living room, and Maria's London apartment, which could comfortably accommodate both a small breakfast bar and a four-person dining table. In Santiago, while Chilean space standards specify the required provision for key appliances like the oven, fridge, sink, and washing machine and activity zones, they do not provide detailed guidance on how these should be positioned in the small homes to optimise the floorplan and user efficiency. Thus, while Karin and Alex in Santiago like having an open kitchen, it requires sharing circulation space with the living room and keeping the area tidy, as the counters and dishwasher are visible from the flat's front door, which limits its use.

Some households made minimal use of their kitchens. This was evident not only in Shenzhen but also in homes where residents did not enjoy cooking or eating in the kitchen for various reasons. For example, Hannah in Liss rarely used her kitchen or dining table, instead preferring to eat upstairs on her bed or in the spare room. Likewise, Carolinne and Felipe in Santiago also ate in bed most of the time, illustrating how personal habits, space constraints, and lifestyle choices can make kitchens less essential, even in homes with full appliances and traditional cooking facilities. This contrasts with Michael's London home, where his kitchen lacked an oven, or homes in Shenzhen, which had only minimal appliances and where some residents would have liked better provisions.

Open-plan Living: Preference and Functionality

Subjective experiences, cultural backgrounds, and practical needs shape preferences between open-plan living and enclosed spaces with functions separated into different rooms. While many residents appreciate the spacious feel of open-plan layouts, others preferred the greater privacy, functionality, and storage that enclosed spaces can provide. Some residents, therefore, adapted their living spaces to their needs and tastes by strategically placing furniture, adding partitions, or trying out different arrangements to find the right balance between openness and practicality for themselves.

Open-plan living is often associated with a contemporary and flexible lifestyle. Some residents described it accordingly as "modern", "the way forward", and "handy", while acknowledging that it can mean "losing a few square meters". In Chile, in particular, limited space standards encourage the overlap of kitchen, dining, living, and circulation areas, resulting in very small living spaces. As a consequence, many participants removed the walls between the kitchen and living areas to create a more spacious open-plan arrangement. For example, Carolinne and Felipe in Santiago did this to create an "illusion" of space. But this perception was also highlighted by a resident in England who said open-plan living "gives people more of a sense of space without actually giving them the space".

Some also prefer open-plan living as it feels more culturally familiar. May in London, for example, found traditional flat layouts in England unfamiliar compared to the open-plan layouts she was used to in Asia. She disliked entering a home through a door that opened directly into a corridor with more separating doors. Emma in Eastleigh, too, preferred an open kitchen–living area, as her current layout forced her to close the kitchen door just to open the fridge. She found the kitchen isolating, especially when her son was in the next room and they could not easily communicate. She therefore felt that an open kitchen would improve both functionality and interactions, particularly when multiple people were sharing the space at the same time.

While preferences for open-plan living are subjective, they often depend on individual situations. Some residents value distinct spaces for different functions, especially for privacy. Caroline in Eastleigh, for example, appreciated having a separate kitchen that allowed her a retreat from her children for private conversations or work. However, she wished that a dining table could fit inside her kitchen to make it more functional (Figure 8.8).

Interestingly, some residents' attitudes toward open-plan living evolved over time. In London, Jerry, who grew up in a traditional terraced house where "everything is delineated" and "everything has a door", was initially hesitant about open-plan living. However, after experiencing it, he came to love the openness and its benefits when hosting guests. Nergiz, temporarily accommodated in her London flat while waiting to move into her new permanent home, expected to have a separate kitchen in the latter, since in three-bedroom houses, "kitchens are always separate because of the size of the property". This highlights that there is also a socio-cultural expectation regarding housing typologies and open-plan living.

FIGURE 8.8 Caroline's kitchen in Eastleigh (2023).

Although both Jerry and Nergiz had seen floorplans of their homes prepared before moving in, their actual use of the spaces differed once they began living there. Jerry, for example, divided his kitchen area with a bookshelf that doubled as a bar and paired it with a three-seater, L-shaped sofa. Nevertheless, he felt that, regardless of how he arranged the furniture, his kitchen still felt smaller because the storage was poorly designed and placed in the corner. In Nergiz's case, while her flat was originally planned with the living space closer to the kitchen, she chose to move the dining space closer to the kitchen to better suit her lifestyle. She also added storage to the hallway, as the developer's original provision had been insufficient (Figure 8.9).

In Shenzhen, studio flats usually have, in addition to a main space for living and sleeping, a separate kitchen, as this is the cultural norm. One resident also placed a storage unit between her bed and dining table to create a visual and functional divide, ensuring her bed was not

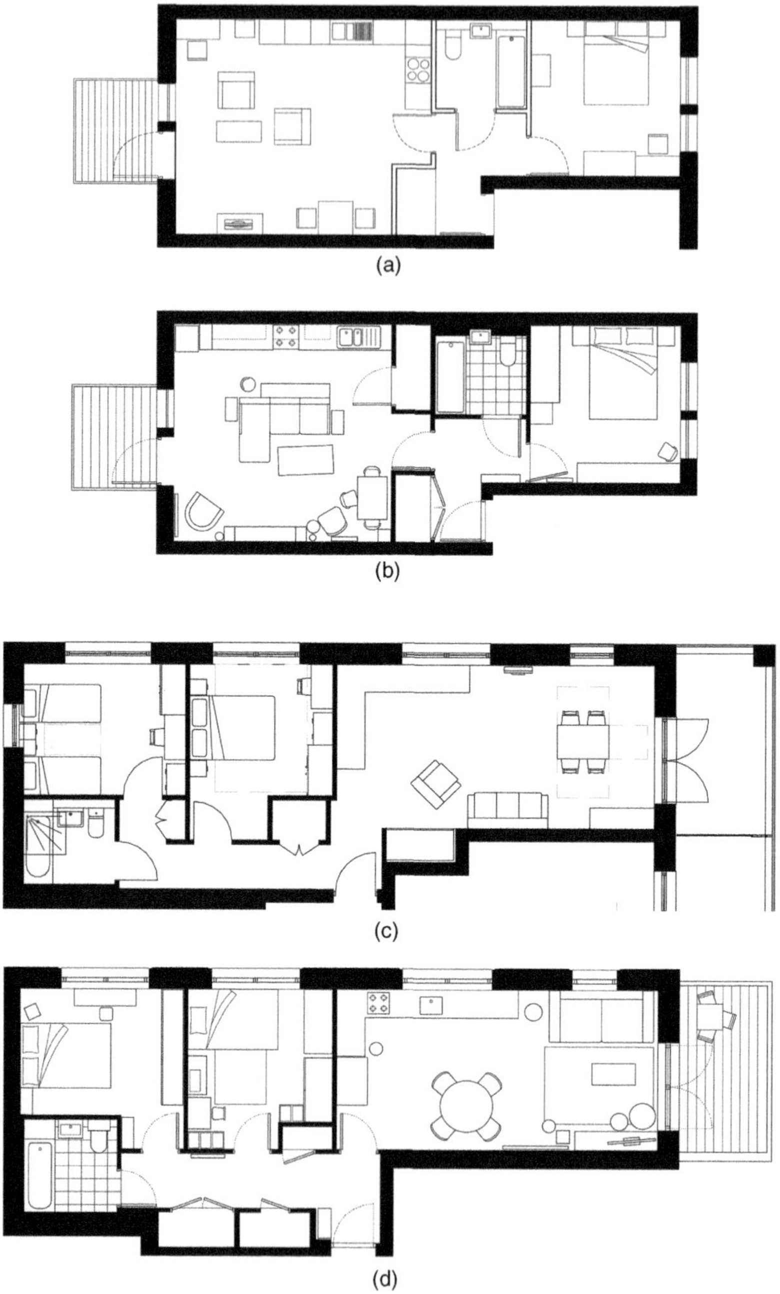

FIGURE 8.9 Comparison of home use in London (2023): Jerry's home as designed by the developer (a) and its actual furniture layout (b); and Nergiz, Ariyana, and Nooh's home as originally designed (c) and the actual layout (d).

(a) (b)

FIGURE 8.10 Studio flat in Shenzhen (a, 2024) and Marielle's home in Amsterdam (b, 2023).

immediately visible from the front door. This highlights a common challenge in very compact open-plan spaces: the lack of walls, which many residents found limiting not only for privacy but also for furnishing. As Marielle (Amsterdam) put it, "There is enough space, but there aren't enough walls, which makes it quite complicated". Without walls, residents have fewer options for storage, decoration, and even mounting televisions, making it challenging to organise their living spaces efficiently. In Marielle's case, the lack of walls and also the large windows offered little privacy. She therefore placed a large bookshelf to divide the living room from her sleeping area (Figure 8.10).

Accessibility Beyond Standards

Housing accessibility standards are prescribed by regulations, design guidelines, and standardised layouts, but real-life experiences can reveal significant gaps between these standards and actual use and usability. Meeting formal requirements does not always translate into functional, inclusive living spaces.

Many homes are, unsurprisingly, furnished differently from the layouts planned by designers and developers. For example, Michael's flat – a two-person, wheelchair-accessible dwelling – was designed with a living room fitting only a two-seater sofa. This did not accommodate his need for a three-seater sofa to lie down due to his chronic condition, leaving little room to manoeuvre in his wheelchair (Figure 8.11). But also, more generally, it is common for small single- or two-person households to have larger two- or three-seater sofas or L-shaped chaise sofas to accommodate more people than the actual occupants.

Although Michael lived in an officially designated "accessible flat" due to his limited mobility, many aspects of his home were impractical. For example, because he was a wheelchair user, his kitchen's traditional design forced him to transfer from his wheelchair to a higher office chair to reach the sink or upper cabinets (Figure 8.12). Even fire safety features, such as resistance springs on doors, made everyday tasks, like opening the doors, more difficult rather than safer. His frustration highlights a key flaw in accessible housing design: spaces are often created

FIGURE 8.11 Comparison of the layout by the developer (a) and the actual furniture layout in Michael's home (b), London (2023).

to comply with regulations rather than to respond to actual user experience. As he suggested, "If someone is designing a building and they're having a disabled flat, then put the disabled person in a chair in there, let them use the space, and then listen to them".

Some residents took matters into their own hands by modifying their homes to suit their needs better. In Amsterdam, for example, Bart removed interior doors to create an open space

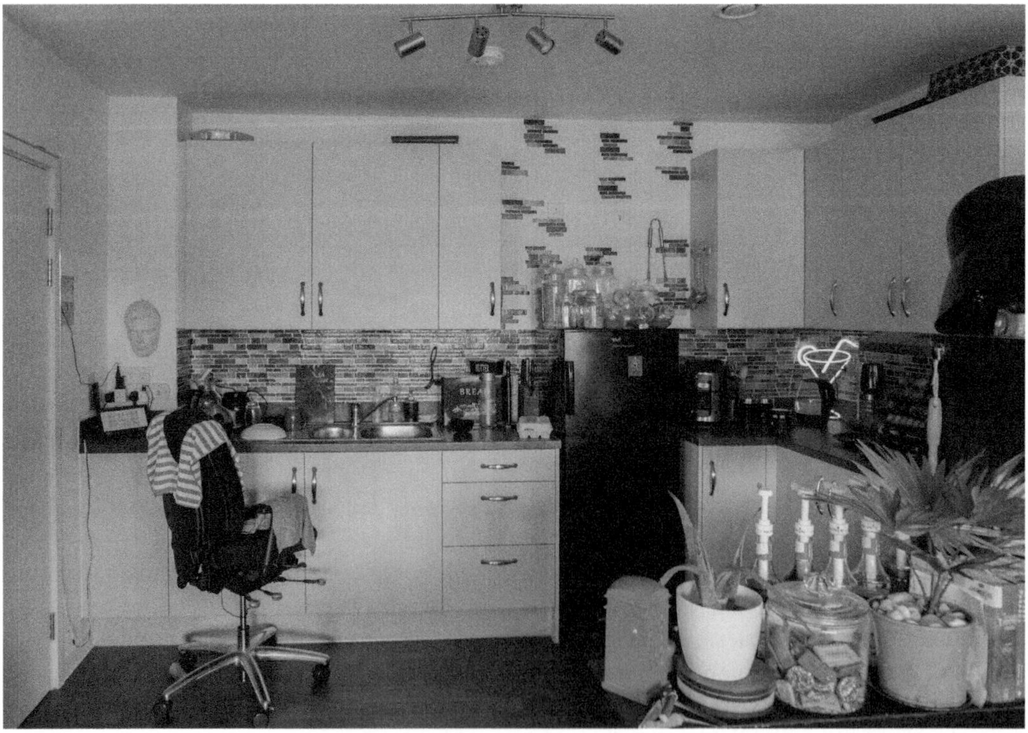

FIGURE 8.12 Michael's kitchen.

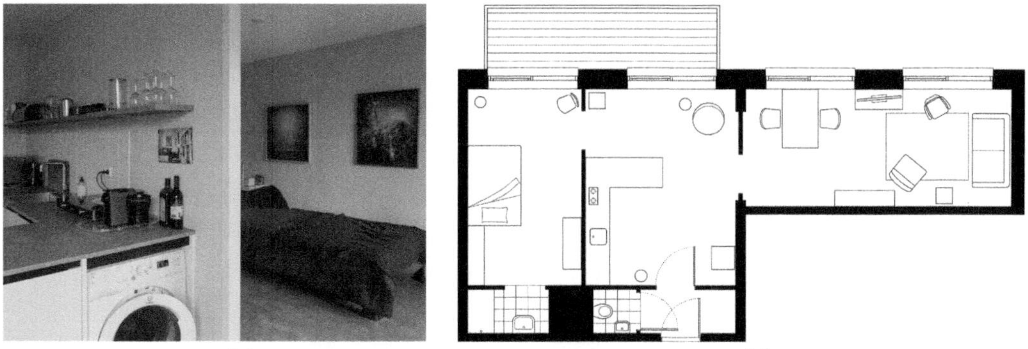

FIGURE 8.13 Bart's kitchen without cabinets but with private washing machine in Amsterdam (a, b, 2023).

that accommodated his reduced eyesight. He also replaced standard kitchen cabinets with pull-out units positioned for better visibility and installed a washing machine to avoid having to use shared facilities on the ground floor (Figure 8.13). While these adjustments have improved his daily life, they underscore how standardised accessible requirements can fail to meet specific individual needs. For Bart, good accessibility extended beyond the physical design of his home to include the communal resources available within his building. For example, three days a week, someone cooked for him in the shared kitchen: "I get my meals in the other block. They make meals and then they and I have to get. . . a plate, and I eat them here".

The experiences of individuals with disabilities demonstrate that accessibility is not a one-size-fits-all problem, but rather a dynamic and multifaceted issue that evolves with individual needs and changes in life circumstances.

Furnishing

Ultimately, the perception of space is not just about size and square metres but about how a home functions for its residents. Furniture plays an important role in shaping this perception and in determining whether a space meets expectations and can accommodate intended use. Some residents felt they had enough space but lacked the flexibility to rearrange furniture or use bedrooms differently from how architects and developers had planned them, sometimes due to simple design issues, such as the placement of services and circulation. Residents would regularly demonstrate to us how they adapted their home or its use to suit their personal needs and preferences. While some spaces could only be furnished as designed, residents – especially in Santiago – often had to adapt them for their specific needs, adding bedrooms, a small shop, or even an improvised hair salon.

Many residents felt that basic technical design decisions, such as the positioning of the TV port and electric sockets, significantly restricted how they could arrange their furniture and use their homes, as one resident noted: "whoever designed this had a very set idea of how you would live within these properties". Another resident felt the television ports were placed on the wrong

FIGURE 8.14 Poppie's home in Oxford (2023).

wall, since she could not fit her larger sofa opposite where she would have liked to place the television. This was also the case for Poppie in Oxford, who switched her sofa and television from the intended arrangement (Figure 8.14).

Thus, flexibility is determined by assumptions about how homes will be used by designers, the furniture owned by occupants, and accessibility to spaces. For example, Jake and Heather (London) chose a dining table with benches, so that the benches could go under the table while they worked out in their living room (Figure 8.15). Kerala in Amsterdam adjusted her furniture according to the season and light, as flexibility was crucial for her needs at any given moment. However, even external specifications can affect home use, for example, Maria in London found that her sofa choices were constrained by the small size of the elevator.

Furnished floorplans play an important role during the planning of a housing project, demonstrating to planners and developers that a home can accommodate the furniture and functions typically expected or legally required. They are also commonly used to illustrate to prospective tenants how a home might be arranged and lived in. Without an accurate plan, tenants cannot assess room sizes, anticipate where their furniture might fit, or determine whether the home meets accessibility or mobility needs. However, even when a floorplan is accurate, it still requires the ability to read them. Illustrated layouts can be prescriptive, with inaccurate furniture sizes or irrelevant furniture. Importantly, how people furnish and use their homes is highly individual and often diverges from the arrangements envisioned by architects or developers. Yet the way a home is furnished is one of the most significant determinants of its potential and actual use.

Homes in Amsterdam illustrate how residents in small studio flats often struggle not only practically but also psychologically with the lack of clear spatial and functional divisions, highlighting the importance of flexibility in arranging furniture. Anja, for example, felt that having "a bed in the living room is like being old, and it didn't feel very good. Before, when this thing [screen] wasn't here, it felt like sleeping in the kitchen". To address this, she created a movable screen to cover the bed, maximising the use of space and improving privacy. Babet, another studio-flat resident in Amsterdam, built a small, enclosed sleeping area and separate office space using partitions, cleverly repurposing her work monitor as a TV screen when it was turned toward her sofa (Figure 8.16). Likewise, Maartje also put up a dividing screen in her studio, since she did not "want to be looking at the kitchen all the time". These interior changes show

FIGURE 8.15 Jake and Heather's dining table (London).

how unfurnished and undefined spaces both encourage creativity and offer flexibility, allowing residents to customise their homes to meet their emotional and functional needs, but also highlight that they can require greater effort to make spaces liveable. Surprisingly, although less variation between idealised and actual home furnishing might be expected in smaller homes due to a lack of space and layout options, they in fact show some of the greatest divergences and innovations in use.

In comparison, some projects in Zurich and Barcelona with more generous or unique layouts tended to have much greater alignment between the original architectural plans and how residents ultimately furnished and used their homes. Yet even in these cases, subtle variations emerged, particularly in the Modulus Matrix housing in Barcelona. Yeray and Pilarica used one spare bedroom as an office and the other as a guest room, while David and Angeles turned one room into a storage space and others simply rotated or repositioned furniture

(a) (b)

FIGURE 8.16 Anja's movable screen to hide her bed (a) and Babet's office space (b) in Amsterdam.

relative to the suggested layouts (Figure 8.17). Interestingly, the award-winning Modulus Matrix project by the architects Marta Peris and José Toral (RIBA International Prize, 2024) was deliberately designed to eliminate corridors and instead uses an enfilade layout to connect rooms, creating more versatile living spaces. Although a recommended layout was provided, the uniform room sizes made each room interchangeable and suitable for multiple uses. This demonstrates how architectural design choices can give tenants greater flexibility in using their homes.

In Zurich, both Candide's and Letitia's flats were furnished very similarly to their original design, partly because each room had a prescribed function (Figure 8.18). However, the room sizes still allowed some flexibility. Letitia, for instance, chose to position her sofa facing the wall, with the television on a rack, rather than placing its back to the wall as suggested in the original plan. This arrangement prioritised comfortable TV viewing over the spatial efficiency and outward-facing orientation envisioned by the architects. The comparatively generous spaces in Barcelona and Zurich, in contrast to those in Amsterdam or Shenzhen, therefore, gave residents more options for arranging their furniture. This flexibility made it easier to accommodate personal preferences, daily habits, and practical needs.

In England, residents' use of their homes often differed significantly from the original planned layouts. While houses still followed typical functional distribution – separate bedrooms, kitchens, and living rooms – rooms tended to be smaller than those in Zurich or Barcelona. Consequently, residents had to adapt furniture arrangements and use in response to spatial constraints, leading to greater variation in how the spaces were used. In some cases, minor features affected functionality: for instance, the swing of the kitchen door limited access to appliances. In constrained spaces, furniture was often placed in a compromised manner that limited access. In other cases, larger rooms offered more flexibility: spacious bedrooms in homes like that of Hannah in Liss offered multiple options for bed placements, showing that even in prescriptive designs, residents can adapt layouts to suit their lives (Figure 8.19).

FIGURE 8.17 Yeray and Pilarica's office and guest room (a, b); original layout planned by the developer (c) and actual furniture layout in David and Angeles's home (d) in Barcelona (2023).

In Chile, the difference between the plans drawn by architects showing legally required standard furniture and actual furniture use was particularly apparent. These prescribed floorplans only show essential and small furniture such as beds, sofas, and dining tables, giving a false sense of spaciousness. Once the side tables, desks, chests of drawers, or TV stands widely used in Chilean homes but not included in the drawings are brought into a home, there is little space left to use or move around them, clearly showing that the space standards are insufficient to accommodate what most people expect to have and need in their home (Figure 8.20).

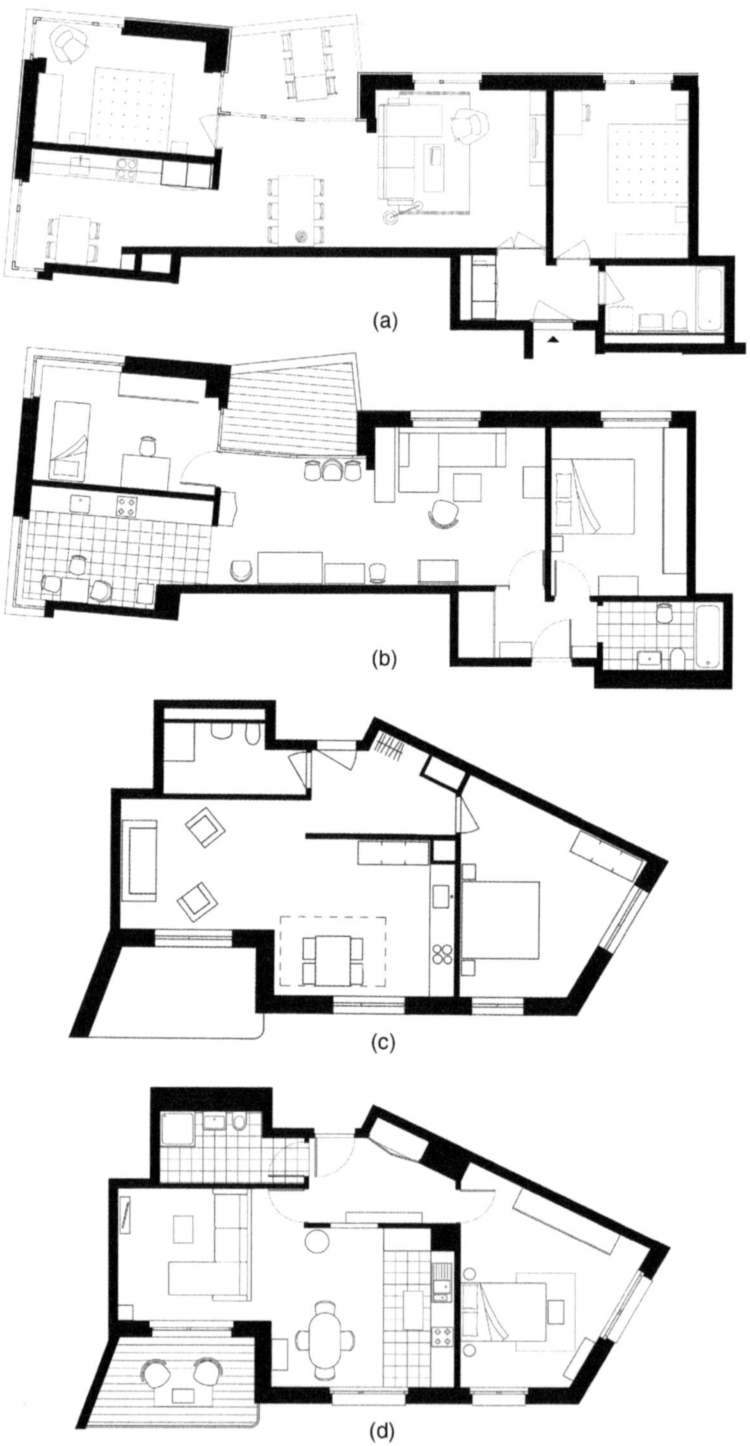

FIGURE 8.18 Comparison of home use in Zurich (2023). Candide's flat as planned by the developer (a) compared with its actual furniture layout (b); and Letitia's flat as planned (c) compared with its actual layout (d).

FIGURE 8.19 Comparison of home use in England (2024): Emma's home in Eastleigh as planned by the developer (a) and its existing furniture layout (b); and Hannah's home in LIss as planned (c) and its existing layout (d).

FIGURE 8.20 Comparison of the layout planned by the developer (a) and the existing furniture layout in Erica's home (b), Santiago (2023).

Conclusion

This home-use study offers a detailed analysis of everyday domestic life, revealing how residents negotiate, adapt, and often transform their living spaces to suit their individual needs and circumstances. The study shows how diverse factors can influence how people inhabit their homes: different household compositions, shifts in work patterns, ageing, and physical and mental health challenges. These findings point to a critical need for research methods that can capture lived realities. Approaches such as ethnographic research and home-use studies are particular valuable because they document how spaces are used everyday. Without this kind of evidence, design regulations and housing policies risk relying on outdated assumptions about household behavious and domestic life.

By combining live motion tracking, interviews, and spatial documentation, this study demonstrates the value of integrating objective movement and location data with subjective experience.[1] This approach moves beyond the conventional use of abstract standards or idealised and normative furnished floorplans, which often misrepresent actual use. Furniture layouts provided by housing associations, developers, architects, and designers are only a partial measure of usability. Although they can be useful for illustrating potential functions and suggested uses, they often mislead or fail to meet the expectations and preferences of residents, as they rarely reflect the way people live, work, and socialise. Similarly, furnished floorplans reflect a rigid understanding of space, overlooking the diverse ways in which a room may be used over the course of a day, as well as how its function may vary throughout the lifetime of a household or the lifespan of a home.

Residents bring unique cultural expectations, personal habits, and lifestyle preferences to their homes. Importantly, smaller homes do not necessarily produce more uniform behaviours; instead, spatial constraints often drive greater variety and creativity, as occupants have to find ways to make limited space serve multiple purposes. Yet, this does not mean that smaller spaces are necessarily used more efficiently – habits and social expectations continue to shape how homes are used or perceived. This challenges the common assumption that well-designed home layouts equate to efficient use, and that there is an entirely rational relationship between households and dwelling size. Rather, the findings show that flexibility and adaptability must be design priorities – an approach exemplified by Switzerland's Wohnungs-Bewertungs-System (Housing Evaluation System) – allowing residents to adjust spaces to their changing needs.

The findings also highlight that the value of a space is not necessarily proportional to how often it is used. Spare rooms, balconies, or kitchens may be used only intermittently yet hold high importance for residents, whether for their symbolic and social value, potential functionality, or ability to support changing life needs. Redundancy and inefficiency play different but important roles in a home. For example, underutilised space can be essential for adaptability, enabling homes to accommodate new patterns of work, care, and leisure without requiring major alterations. At the same time, questions of accessibility illustrate how regulatory compliance does not guarantee usability; only direct engagement with end users can reveal how spaces succeed or fail in practice.

This study demonstrates that greater consideration of end users, especially in relation to accessibility, is needed to improve the design of homes. Accessibility involves understanding how daily routines unfold within a home – and its neighbourhood – when household members have physical disabilities. Similarly, the active involvement of larger households, especially those with children, is essential in these studies. These households often face greater challenges related to the simultaneous use of spaces and storage needs, which prescriptive layouts can fail to register. By incorporating residents' perspectives, housing design and policy can better respond to diverse needs, leading to homes that are more adaptable, flexible, and inclusive.

Awareness of how people use their home and spaces can enhance everyday living, offering residents an opportunity to rethink their space through changes in behaviour or changes in furniture and layout. This study therefore argues for housing design and policy that is grounded in real lived experience, as these practices reveal important insights into how housing actually functions. Involving residents more directly in design processes, adopting tools that capture how homes are used, and moving beyond prescriptive furniture layouts can help produce housing that is both resilient and genuinely adaptive to the needs of its occupants.

Acknowledgements

The fieldwork for this research was undertaken with the invaluable support of Seyithan Özer and Alvaro Arancibia, who have assisted in the data collection. We are very grateful to Robin Roussel for developing the home-use software and assisting us remotely through the process. We are deeply grateful to Dr Raül Avilla-Royo (ETSAB Barcelona), Associate Professor Lu Wang (South China University of Technology), Gianna Bottema, and Salome Rohner (ETH Wohnforum) for their contributions in each country and helping us connect with residents and conduct the work. We also thank the housing providers ASIG, Baugenossenschaft Glattal Zürich, Clarion Housing Group, de Alliantie, AMB:IMPSOL, Peabody, and Ymere for their vital support of this study.

Most importantly, we extend our sincere thanks to all study participants in England, Chile, China, Switzerland, Spain, and the Netherlands for their generosity and the time they dedicated to sharing their home and experiences with us.

Note

1 Full project data is available online: https://10.60624/nnc8-1557.

9

WELLBEING AND HOUSING QUALITY

Comparative Case Studies in Six Countries

Lucia Alonso Aranda and Consuelo Albornoz Marambio

Housing is never simply a technical matter: it emerges through the interplay of political agendas, technical norms, and cultural expectations. Nowhere is this more evident than in the housing sector, where questions of design quality are inextricably linked to broader societal definitions of need, value, and progress. Housing space standards and design decisions are often presented as objective or technocratic in nature. However, they are underpinned by assumptions about what constitutes a good life, a good home, or a good society. As Porter (1996, p. 8) notes, "a decision made by numbers has at least the appearance of being fair and impersonal. . . quantification is a way of making decisions without seeming to decide". Metrics such as minimum space standards and definitions of overcrowding are not neutral indicators but often reflect social, political, and economic compromises. They provide structure and measurability yet frequently fail to capture subjective experience – such as when residents feel satisfied with housing that official frameworks might classify as inadequate.

This chapter examines how residents themselves interpret and negotiate questions of housing quality, affordability, safety, privacy, and community. Drawing on the documentation of 37 homes and semi-structured interviews with their residents and the tracking of how they use their homes, conducted across ten cities, this study explores the diverse ways people make sense of design and space, ranging from material aspects, such as finishes and room size, to psychosocial dimensions, including warmth, safety, and a sense of belonging. By foregrounding lived experience, the chapter highlights the need for metrics and standards to value housing as a site of identity, wellbeing, and aspiration.

The study of subjective wellbeing in housing, a relatively recent development, emerged from disciplines such as economics and psychology, and often uses life satisfaction as a measurable indicator. However, defining and measuring wellbeing remains complex, as housing satisfaction is not an intrinsic component but significantly impacts overall wellbeing (Clapham et al., 2017).

Housing quality can be assessed through various measures, including economic, subjective, and objective metrics, but each has its limitations. Economic indicators, such as prices, rent levels, affordability ratios, and subsidies, remain dominant in policy discourse; however, they oversimplify the complexity of housing markets and overlook individual needs and preferences. Subjective measures, such as life satisfaction and wellbeing indices, offer insights into personal

DOI: 10.4324/9781032679204-14

experiences of housing but are susceptible to interpretive ambiguity and may neglect physical conditions. Interpretations of subjective housing satisfaction vary – some focus solely on physical conditions, while others encompass psychological and social factors, such as security and a sense of belonging. Objective standards – including space per person, rates of overcrowding, or minimum quality benchmarks – facilitate comparability but risk imposing universal definitions of adequacy. Evaluating housing outcomes through economic, objective, and subjective lenses (Clapham & Foye, 2019) reveals the complexity of lived experience and the inadequacy of relying on a single metric. Yet subjective research also poses challenges, as people interpret concepts like "satisfaction" differently based on cultural norms, social expectations, and personal trajectories.

Capabilities-based approaches, drawing on the work of Amartya Sen (2009) and Martha Nussbaum (2011), shift the focus to what people are effectively able to do in their housing environments, such as preparing meals, studying, or sustaining social relationships. These perspectives recognise housing not merely as shelter but as a foundation for broader life opportunities.

This is where subjective, individual research, despite its aforementioned flaws, becomes essential. Although economic and objective indicators continue to dominate policy discussions, there is a growing recognition of the importance of subjective wellbeing, housing satisfaction, and power of choice (Clapham & Foye, 2019; Nussbaum, 2011). Indeed, studies consistently link poor housing conditions to adverse outcomes for health, wellbeing, and social stability (Evans et al., 2003; Marsh et al., 2000; Shaw, 2004).

These dynamics are even more complex when considered across international and cultural contexts. Notions of affordability, quality, and design vary widely across space and time. In some contexts, aspirations are driven by material growth and space acquisition (Park, 2017; Williams, 2009); in others, values such as modesty, multi-generational living, or climate adaptation shape spatial expectations. These differences reflect not only divergent housing markets and policy regimes but also underlying values and cultural scripts that inform what people expect from a home. Understanding how design governance functions thus requires attending to both systemic structures and everyday expectations – what housing is supposed to *do*, and *for whom*.

Questions about housing quality and design, framed in the language of architects and designers, can be understood in different ways. Some respondents focus on physical aspects, such as high-quality materials, while others emphasise psychosocial elements, like feeling warm or safe. This variability highlights the limitations of relying on a single evaluative framework. By combining multiple methodologies in studying people's homes, we thus aim to capture the multifaceted nature of residents' housing experience.

This chapter is structured into four sections. The first, "Space and Size", explores how space is measured and perceived across countries, demonstrating how it can be highly subjective due to factors such as household composition, ability to utilise space, aspirations, and the amount of storage space. The second section, "Affordability and the Allocation Process", details the process that residents undergo to rent or purchase a home, questioning what affordability means to them and whether their homes are truly affordable. The third section, "Design and Housing Quality", highlights what is meant by high housing quality and explores what residents expect from their homes, how they adapt their homes to suit their needs, and the main maintenance challenges they have faced. The last section, "Housing, Community, and Wellbeing", examines how housing design, space, and neighbourhood environments shape residents' relationships, wellbeing, and sense of safety, highlighting both the opportunities and constraints that homes and communities create for everyday social life.

Methods

Participants for the home-use study from 37 households were recruited through a survey on housing quality, affordability, and overcrowding (Table 9.1). The survey was distributed with the assistance of housing associations, cooperatives, and local authorities, as well as by post. It targeted residents living in newly built affordable or subsidised housing, and respondents

TABLE 9.1 Participant and household characteristics

Country	*Participant*	*City*	*Household size*	*Bedrooms*	*Size (m^2)*	*m^2 per person*
England (London and beyond)	Jerry	West London	1p (single household)	1 bedroom	53	53
	Nergiz, Ariyana, and Noor	West London	3p (mother, 2 children)	2 bedrooms	72	24
	Jake and Heather	South London	2p (couple)	1 bedroom	54	27
	May and June	South London	2p (cousins)	3 bedrooms	107	53.5
	Michael	North London	1p (single household)	1 bedroom	61	61
	Maria	North West London	1p (single household)	1 bedroom	51	51
	Hannah	Liss	1p (single household)	2 bedrooms	80	80
	Caroline	Eastleigh	5p (mother, 4 children)	4 bedrooms	96	19.2
	Emma	Eastleigh	2p (mother, child)	2 bedrooms	70	35
	Jennifer	Oxford	1p (single household)	1 bedroom	53	53
	Poppie	Oxford	1p (single household)	2 bedrooms	71	71
Chile (Santiago)	Soledad and Lautaro	La Florida	2p (mother, child)	2 bedrooms	63	31.5
	Fernando and Verónica	Peñalolén	3p (extended family)	3 bedrooms	62	20.6
	Johana and Manuel	San Bernardo	4p (parents, two children)	4 bedrooms	93	23.25
	Carolinne and Felipe	Independencia	2p (couple)	2 bedrooms	48	24
	Karin, Alex, and Benjamín	Estación Central	4p (parents, two children)	3 bedrooms	62	15.5
	Cristina and Alma	Cerrillos	5p (parents, 3 children)	3 bedrooms	52	10.4
	Jennifer and Cesar	Padre Hurtado	4p (parents, two children)	2 bedrooms	54	13.5
	Erica and Matias	Cerrillos	2p (mother, child)	2 bedrooms	54	27

(*Continued*)

TABLE 9.1 (Continued)

Country	*Participant*	*City*	*Household size*	*Bedrooms*	*Size (m^2)*	*m^2 per person*
China (Shenzhen)	Weipeing	Shenzhen	1p (single household)	2 bedrooms	43	43
	Jiaxin	Shenzhen	1p (single household)	Studio	23	23
	Mei	Shenzhen	1p (single household)	Studio	25	25
	Chi	Shenzhen	1p (single household)	Studio	25	25
The Netherlands (Amsterdam)	Babet	Amsterdam Noord	1p (single household)	Studio	48	48
	Anja	Amsterdam Noord	1p (single household)	Studio	48	48
	Marielle	Amsterdam Noord	1p (single household)	Studio	48	48
	Maartje	Amsterdam Noord	1p (single household)	Studio	37	37
	Bart	Amsterdam Oost	1p (single household)	1 bedroom	57	57
	Kerala	Amsterdam Oost	1p (single household)	1 bedroom	50	50
Spain (Barcelona)	Yeray and Pilarica	Cornellà de Llobregat	2p (couple)	3 bedrooms	78	39
	David and Angeles	Cornellà de Llobregat	2p (couple)	2 bedrooms	57	28.5
	Isabel, Claudia, and Ximena	Gavà	3p (mother, 2 children)	3 bedrooms	72	24
	Javier and Cristina	Gavà	3p (parents, child)	2 bedrooms	62	20.6
Switzerland (Zurich and Bülach)	Andre	Bülach	1p (single household)	2 bedrooms	92	92
	Letitia	Bülach	1p (single household)	1 bedroom	66	66
	Candide	Zurich	2p (mother, child)	2 bedrooms	83	41.5
	Sandra	Zurich	1p (single household)	2 bedrooms	62	62

Note: Full project data are available online, including interviews with participants: https://doi.org/10.60624/nnc8-1557.

were invited to take part in a follow-up study that included 3D scans of their homes, video and photographic documentation, location tracking, and an in-depth interview. Participants were compensated for their time.

The home-use study combined three primary forms of data collection: location tracking, a visual survey, and an interview. At least one participant per household was required to be 18 or older, with parental or guardian consent obtained for minors. Participation was voluntary, and residents could withdraw at any time before the public dissemination of data. Where requested, names and locations as well as images, films, or quotations that might identify participants or their homes were anonymised. All procedures complied with UK data protection laws and received approval from the Royal College of Art Ethics Committee and the Pontificia Universidad Católica de Chile.

Following informed consent, two researchers visited each participant's home. During the first visit, homes were documented photographically and through a LiDAR 3D scan. Although floorplans were sometimes provided, rooms were measured to record interior layouts, furniture, and fittings. Location-tracking equipment was then installed, including one to two anchors per room, a controller per floor, and a wearable tag for each participant. This system mapped residents' movements across five days to capture how different rooms were used. Participants also kept a daily activity diary during this period. On the last day, researchers returned to remove the equipment and conduct a semi-structured interview.

The interviews examined how residents utilised and perceived their homes in relation to design quality. Topics included household composition and daily routines; the influence of work or study on home use; processes of home allocation or selection; perceptions of housing design, space, safety, and privacy; flexibility, adaptability, and wellbeing; and experiences of affordability, overcrowding, repairs, and maintenance. Follow-up questions drew on home-use data, surveys, and visual documentation, allowing participants' accounts to be situated within both their everyday practices and broader understandings of housing quality.

In some contexts, such as Chile, where subsidies covered the majority of dwelling costs, participants were initially reluctant to discuss problems or deficiencies in their housing, fearing they would appear "ungrateful". Similar dynamics were observed among participants in England, Amsterdam, and Barcelona, reflecting the social sensitivities that shape how residents of subsidised homes articulate housing satisfaction and critique.

Space, Size, and Storage

Perception of space in the home is highly subjective, shaped by personal preferences, experiences, household composition, cultural norms, and the way different spaces are utilised. While official definitions may classify a home as overcrowded, some residents might still feel that their space meets their needs. For example, Nergiz (Figure 9.1), a mother living with her 18-year-old

(a) (b)

FIGURE 9.1 Nergiz, Ariyana, and Noor's home, London (a, b) (2023).

daughter and six-year-old son in London, found her home comfortable, despite it being legally overcrowded. She shared a bedroom with her daughter and intentionally purchased a large sofa for the living room to provide an alternative sleeping arrangement when needed. For her, the arrangement worked because she could accommodate her children's needs within the existing space, and there was a level of adaptability that made the situation comfortable.

By contrast, another mother in England struggled with the lack of space in the four-bedroom, 96-m^2 house which she shared with her four children. While it almost met England's Nationally Described Space Standard (NDSS) for a five-person household (97 m^2), frequent visits from her partner and her son's partner pushed the occupancy beyond what the space was designed for. The issue is therefore not just about square metres but about how overcrowding is perceived. She clarified that she did not think that "it's a tiny house, it's not; but a lack of privacy" created stress for her children and herself, impacting both her physical and mental health. For her, overcrowding was not simply a matter of adjusting sleeping arrangements but a fundamental issue of insufficient personal space. She often preferred to sleep in the living room because it offered her more space and privacy.

Privacy and noise are also crucial factors that shape how residents perceive their space. Larger households often expressed a need for a balance between shared and private areas, as shared spaces must accommodate multiple activities simultaneously. For Jennifer in Oxford, for example, preventing overcrowding meant considering not only the space provided per person but also shared facilities such as a washing machine and fridge. She grew up in an overcrowded home and then lived in multiple house shares in England, which made her understand the importance of individual and shared spaces. Based on her experiences, she suggested: "I think above a certain number of people, that's when you start to need, like, a second living room or a second shared space of some kind".

The perception of overcrowding is also often contextual, as evidenced by Carolinne and Felipe in Santiago, who felt that their privacy had been compromised by the transition from a house to a flat; they could now hear, and be heard from, other homes. Thus, overcrowding is not just about numbers – it is about how space is used, shared, and experienced. While some find ways to adapt, for others, it becomes a source of stress, affecting their wellbeing and quality of life.

Some participants did not want more space, but rather a different distribution of existing space with an additional small room that could serve multiple functions, such as storage, an office, or a guest bedroom. More space does not always equate to greater satisfaction: a family in Santiago believed their home was the right size, as a larger one would require more cleaning and could reduce the time they spent together. The way space is distributed can also impact perceptions of comfort. May in London, for example, questioned the large size of her balcony, arguing that more indoor space would have been more practical, while Weipeing in Shenzhen wished for a larger balcony to fit more than just his washing machine, installed, as is customary in the city, in this part of the flat (Figure 9.2).

The perception of space is also often directly influenced by comparisons to previous homes. In Chile, the space standards for homes supported by the Programa Fondo Solidario de Elección de Vivienda (DS49; Housing Choice Solidarity Fund Programme) and Programa de Integración Social y Territorial (DS19; Social and Territorial Integration Programme) subsidies require a minimum dwelling size of 55 m^2. As a result, residents who previously lived in private homes that did not have to meet this standard sometimes felt that their new homes were bigger. Likewise, residents who previously lived with their parents in larger homes tended to perceive their current flat as having less space. At the same time, those coming from informal housing, accustomed to sharing their home with non-family members, or those who were renting just a room viewed their current home as larger.

FIGURE 9.2 (a, b) May and June's home, London (2023). (c, d) Weipeing's home, Shenzhen (2023).

Cultural and regional differences in standards also influence how space is allocated and experienced. In Barcelona and Zurich, habitable rooms tend to be more equal in size, allowing for greater flexibility in their use, whereas in England and Santiago, there is a clear functional and spatial distinction between single and double or living rooms. This can limit how rooms are used and adapted over time, especially in the case of small single bedrooms as children grow (Figure 9.3).

For example, Andre in Zurich had two equally sized large bedrooms, allowing him to "move, here, stuff around quite easily, as the bedroom was foreseen as my hobby room now and vice versa, so it gives a fair amount of flexibility". In Barcelona, the large bedrooms that Isabel and her daughters had felt to them "as if each of us had a flat", but at the same time, they also had enough shared space to interact.

In comparison, space standards in Santiago are very low and do not account for the flexibility required by different household compositions or the life cycles families undergo. In a standard subsidised home, the secondary bedrooms are always designed for single beds and are assumed to be for children. The second bedroom is typically a twin, with a minimum floor area of 6.2 m^2, and the third bedroom is a single of 4.5 m^2. This space accommodates single beds, bedside tables, and small wardrobes, but is insufficient for a desk. For instance, in Jennifer's household

FIGURE 9.3 Floorplans of homes in Barcelona (a) and Zurich (b), where rooms tend to be more equal in size. In England (c) and Santiago (d), rooms have clear functional and spatial distinctions.

with two children aged two and 10, the youngest slept in a cot in the main bedroom. The older child slept in the twin bedroom, where a desk was also installed (Figure 9.4). When both children eventually have to share a room in the future, they will sleep in bunk beds to have more space, a problem not considered in the current standards.

Space and layout expectations were also a concern for some residents. In Eastleigh, Caroline found the room proportions in her social-rent home unusual, with a disproportionately large

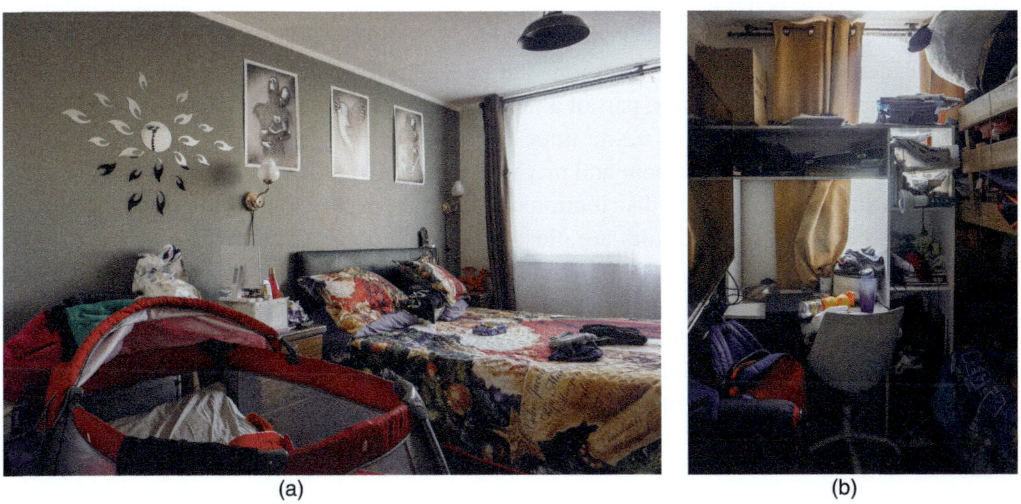

FIGURE 9.4 Jennifer and Cesar's main bedroom (a) and her older child's bedroom (b) in Santiago.

FIGURE 9.5 Caroline's home, Eastleigh (a), and Maartje's home, Amsterdam (b) (2023).

accessible bathroom on the ground floor, but very small bedrooms where beds had to be placed against the wall to allow enough space around them, without room for a desk for homework or working from home. Maartje, after walking into her flat in Amsterdam Noord for the first time, was so overwhelmed by how small it seemed that she cried (Figure 9.5). Maria in North West London, too, was frustrated by the limited layout options in her bedroom, where even placing a bedside table was difficult due to space constraints. In Zurich, Candide's narrow and long home, despite having enough space for her and her son, also caused problems when furnishing: "I try so many places. . . for my tables, for example, I don't know where I put my table, in the middle of the room?. . . It's not so easy to find a harmony".

The participants' perception of available space often reflected their household composition. In particular, those living alone had different opinions on the ideal amount of space per person. Although living in a studio flat, Jiaxin in Shenzhen believed 80 m^2 per person was necessary, Marielle in Amsterdam considered 50 m^2 sufficient. Chi in Shenzhen suggested that a living room should be around 15 m^2 and a bedroom 10 m^2, while Andre in Zurich insisted that he "would always go for better quality, less square metres", preferring a well-designed 70-m^2 home over a larger, lower-quality space. At the same time, Carolinne, living with her partner in Santiago, considered their 48-m^2 two-bedroom flat adequate for them but not for a family with children. In the same city, Jennifer, part of a family of four, found their 54-m^2 two-bedroom flat cramped, while Karin felt that her 62-m^2 three-bedroom flat was "just right" for four people, as it gave each child their own bedroom and privacy (Figure 9.6).

While the size, flexibility, and distribution of rooms are central to how residents experience adequacy in the home, these factors are closely intertwined with the availability of storage. Even when households consider their overall living space sufficient, a lack of appropriate storage can undermine comfort, limit adaptability, and intensify perceptions of overcrowding. Storage is expected and provided in many different sizes and shapes. In Zurich and Amsterdam, separate individual storage spaces outside the home are often offered on the ground floor or in a basement. In Shenzhen, there are communal storage areas for bicycles or motorbikes (Figure 9.7). England, meanwhile, has built-in storage requirements included in its space standards.

However, storage is a common problem in small, subsidised homes. A resident in London felt that her bedrooms were big enough for wardrobes, but storage in the kitchen was insufficient, as she could not store food in addition to pots and pans (Figure 9.8). While a resident in Amsterdam

FIGURE 9.6 Floorplans of homes: Marielle in Amsterdam (a), Carolinne and Felipe in Santiago (b), Jiaxin in Shenzhen (c), Andre in Zurich (d), and Chi in Shenzhen (e), 2023.

FIGURE 9.7 Storage space in Amsterdam (a) and communal storage for bicycles in Shenzhen (b).

FIGURE 9.8 Insufficient kitchen storage in London.

was thankful to have enough storage space in her basement, she worried about using it, as it had flooded twice already, and she lived in a flood-prone area. Residents in Santiago and Barcelona, in particular, felt that they lacked sufficient storage space. However, Isabel in Barcelona took a pragmatic stance on the issue: "We've discussed the idea of having an additional storage unit [*trastero*] for extra belongings, but having a storage unit also means accumulating things".

In Chile, DS49-subsidy developments do not include any storage units, either within the flat or in the building, unlike DS19 developments, where storage units can sometimes be purchased separately. The main storage provision in the homes is minimal, including wardrobes (standard size: 60 × 50 × 140 cm) and cupboards in the kitchen (Figure 9.9). No storage space is provided for household items such as suitcases or seasonal clothing, or large appliances like vacuum cleaners.

Residents in Santiago, therefore, expressed mixed views about the adequacy of storage space. Some felt that the available storage was insufficient, while others believed the problem lay in their choice of furniture (Figure 9.10). As Karin said: "You have to own only the necessary. If you don't use something, you should either sell it or get rid of it". But many residents had furniture from their previous homes that was often ill-suited to the size of the new space. Due to the lack of space, residents often stored items in unconventional places, such as the laundry area

FIGURE 9.9 Standard kitchen cupboard provision in Santiago.

FIGURE 9.10 Non-standard furniture in Santiago.

or, as in Jennifer's case, piling belongings in the second bathroom's bathtub. Although Erica in Santiago felt that she had enough space, she was using an external storage unit.

In addition to storage, outdoor space also emerged as a recurrent theme in residents' accounts, underscoring its importance for both practical and psychological wellbeing. Yeray in Barcelona described how stepping onto the balcony provided fresh air, sunlight, and a change of perspective while working or studying from home, helping "clear your mind" (Figure 9.11). Similar opinions were echoed by Jake and Jerry in London, who highlighted the value of their balconies. Jake mentioned that he enjoyed watching birds and insects visit his plants and had conversations with his next-door neighbours. Isabel in Barcelona also emphasised how the perimeter balcony allowed for multiple uses of each room.

The case studies demonstrate that perceptions of domestic space cannot be reduced to objective measurements alone, but are mediated by social, cultural, and experiential factors. Formal standards may establish minimum thresholds, yet they often overlook the significance of privacy, adaptability, and the distribution of space within the dwelling. However, for residents, the perception of space is influenced by the number of rooms available, their individual size, the flexibility of those spaces, and the level of privacy they provide. For some residents, creative adjustments mitigated spatial limitations, while for others, inadequate layouts, lack of flexibility, and insufficient storage exacerbated feelings of overcrowding. Thus, adequate housing should be understood not only in terms of size, but in relation to how spatial arrangements and storage capacity can sustain activities, privacy, and quality of life.

(a)

(b)

FIGURE 9.11 Outdoor space in Barcelona (a) and London (b).

Affordability and Allocation Process

Affordability is not a fixed measure but rather a matter of perception, influenced by factors such as income, household composition, lifestyle, and personal goals. For some residents, it meant keeping housing costs within a particular share of their income, while for others, it was about whether a home met their specific needs and aspirations. Governments often set benchmarks – for example, affordability is commonly defined as spending no more than one-third of a household's income on housing – but many households exceed the threshold. In the United Kingdom, for instance, a large proportion of households spend over 40% of their disposable income on rent or mortgage payments (Ministry of Housing, Communities, and Local Government, 2017). Policies such as social rent, affordable rent, or shared ownership aim to ease this burden, but even at 80% of market value, many low-income households continue to struggle.

Residents' own definitions of affordability often diverged from official standards (Table 9.2). Some compared their housing costs with prices on the private market. Yeray in Barcelona, for example, described his subsidised home as good value because it cost him only half of what a similar property in his area would have sold for – €350,000–370,000. Others measured affordability against household income. Jennifer and Cesar in Santiago felt secure because both earned wages, while Isabel, a single mother in Barcelona, found her home far less affordable without a partner's contribution. Another single mother, Caroline in Eastleigh, had to rely on Universal Credit to pay her rent and service charge, without which she would not have been able to pay for it. Similarly, Michael in London faced a shortfall because housing benefit caps did not cover his full rent, forcing him to use part of his pension to cover the difference.

Affordability also intersects with aspirations and financial stability. Kerala in Amsterdam defined it as the ability to save, which she could not achieve while living "paycheck to paycheck". For others, certain tenures created opportunities. Shared ownership offered Poppie in Oxford a route into homeownership that would have been otherwise impossible, and Jake and Heather in London chose it for long-term stability. However, they would have preferred regulated rental options similar to those found in other countries.

Beyond rent or mortgage, day-to-day costs also shaped how residents perceived affordability. Some struggled with furnishing or fitting out their homes, such as Maartje in Amsterdam, who could not afford to furnish her flat. Likewise, in Eastleigh, Caroline's inability to afford wardrobes or a bed frame shows how aspects beyond the space can significantly impact overall affordability. Utility bills and service charges were another pressure point. Marielle in Amsterdam found her housing broadly affordable thanks to a stable job, but high floor-heating costs left her with limited flexibility in her budget. Likewise, Nergiz in London reported monthly bills of £200–250, and in Santiago, condominium service charges proved unmanageable for some, leading to non-payment.

In Chile, where state policy strongly promotes homeownership, affordability was often understood differently. Fully subsidised housing was widely perceived as a gift, since households only had to contribute some of their savings without facing ongoing mortgage payments. Soledad described this arrangement as fair, and Fernando and his wife felt the same after receiving a subsidy to build their home as part of a small condominium. However, others emphasised that affordability was not just financial but also procedural: Cristina explained that saving was manageable, but waiting years to access subsidies was the hardest part. Timing could also be decisive. Carolinne felt fortunate to have bought her home just before the COVID-19 pandemic, as rising prices would otherwise have pushed ownership beyond her reach.

TABLE 9.2 Residents' definitions of affordability by country.

England	*London*	*Santiago*
70% of income goes to her shared ownership flat costs due to very high service charge. (Poppie, Oxford) 35% of income goes to her shared ownership flat. (Jennifer, Oxford) "I went from about £600 to £1300 a month so that's a big jump." (Caroline, Eastleigh, social rent)	55% of household income goes to their shared ownership flat: "How can developers or housing associations brand that as affordable?" (May and June) 25% of household income goes to social rent. (Jerry) "It's very affordable to pay. It's not much, £460, something like that." Nergiz (social rent) Rent is £670 per month: rent capped at £370 a month and has to provide other £300 from his pension. (Michael)	"It was alright; I don't think we paid a lot for the flat" (Soledad) "[Affordable] at least for us, since we both work." (Jennifer and Cesar) "Mortgages nowadays are so expensive that this house is practically a gift." (Johana) They had saved $750,000 and now only pay shared expenses. (Karin and Alex)
Amsterdam	*Barcelona*	*Zurich*
"Rent should not never be more than 20% of your paycheck … or 25 maybe but now I feel it's almost half" (Kerala) "Half of my income goes to my house, and it's not even mine" (Marielle) 700 Euro per month (Bart)	"This home cost me €176,500—there's no comparison [to the private market]" (David, ownership) "Considering the market prices, I find it reasonably priced. While it may not be cheap, it's certainly a good value compared to other options." (Isabel, ownership) "The monthly payment we make shouldn't exceed 30% of what we both earn." (Javier, rental)	"1,600 Swiss francs. Compared to the other flat in Zurich it's quite affordable." (Candide) 800 Swiss francs for city centre (Sandra) "Shouldn't be more than one third of your income." (Letitia)
Shenzhen		
2,000 Yuan for three months (Chi)	1,950 Yuan for three months (Jiaxin)	"20% of [my] whole costs." (Mei)

Therefore, affordability is experienced in highly diverse ways, shaped not only by income and tenure but also by household composition, hidden costs, and the timing of access to purchase or subsidies. Standard measures such as income ratios capture only part of the picture, while residents' accounts highlight how affordability is ultimately defined by whether housing supports stability, security, and everyday life.

Allocation Process

The process of securing housing varies widely across countries, reflecting different policy frameworks, market conditions, and levels of state involvement. Some systems rely on waiting lists, lotteries, or cooperative membership, while others require financial contributions or savings. Each approach brings specific benefits and challenges, shaping not only the accessibility of housing but also how residents experience their homes – whether with satisfaction, frustration, or a sense of uncertainty.

In Amsterdam, eligibility for social housing depends on household income. In 2025, the cap was €49,699 for single-person households and €54,847 for multi-person households. Social housing is allocated through a points system; if an individual's housing situation is urgent, they will be considered faster. Allocation occurs through the Woningnet system, in which applicants can register and apply for properties, although waiting times vary considerably. While Anja secured a home after 12 years on the list, Kerala waited over 20, and Marielle only three. The COVID-19 pandemic added further complications, forcing some, such as Anja and Maartje, to make housing choices based only on floorplans and photographs.

In Spain, protected housing schemes offer both rental and ownership pathways. Prospective tenants must be on the Register of Applicants for Subsidised Housing, which enters them into a lottery when a new housing project becomes available. For example, applicants must be registered in the municipality of Barcelona for one interrupted year prior to submitting their application and not be homeowners. A maximum income threshold needs to be met as well. Priority is given to groups such as single-parent families, people requiring accessible homes, and those under 35 years old. For homeownership, savings are required for a 5% deposit. If buyers back out, they face a €2,000 fine. However, the subsidised homes are sold significantly below the market rates and are thus seen as an affordable option. Residents such as David described the process as transparent and relatively straightforward, though lengthy. They mentioned that while savings are required, buildings in the area are priced between €350,000 and €400,000, compared to the €176,500 that they paid. In comparison, the social rental system offers an initial seven-year contract, which can be extended for a further three years.

In England, affordable housing includes social and affordable rent. Shared ownership provides another route, often seen as the only way onto the "property ladder", though it requires residents to manage both rent and mortgage alongside service charges. Hannah, living in Liss, Hampshire, explained that it was possible to increase her share of ownership, but only through 20% increments, creating financial barriers. To be eligible for shared-ownership housing, the applicant must be a first-time buyer with a household income below £80,000 a year outside London (or £90,000 in London).

Allocation processes in England depend on the tenure and circumstances of the applicant. For social rent, the applicant must have a housing need, such as overcrowding, homelessness, medical needs, very low income, or a dangerous living situation. Residents may receive priority due to estate regeneration, demolition, or through the general housing system. Experiences varied considerably: in London, Jerry described his active involvement in a regeneration project through assisting meetings, while Nergiz endured temporary overcrowding during relocation to a larger house. Both Caroline's and Michael's experiences were more negative due to time constraints. In London, Michael was given only four days to move into an accessible flat, with no support, and continued to wait months for disability adaptations. In Eastleigh, Caroline, though placed at the top of the waiting list, felt she had little choice when offered just one property, as her current situation was critical.

Zurich's cooperative housing model (*Genossenschaften*) offers a different pathway. Each cooperative has its own selection criteria, including length of membership, household size, fit with the existing community, financial situation, and urgency of housing need. As one resident explained, they had to write a letter justifying why they wanted to join the cooperative before they were accepted. Residents are sometimes allocated homes without physically visiting them due to demand, relying solely on floorplans. Recalling her experience, Letitia said, "I got declined at first, but two months later, they called me. After that, it moved really fast – I didn't even have a chance to say no".

In Shenzhen, social housing allocation can also be tied to professional status in the Talent Worker Scheme, targeting recent master's graduates who work for the government. Subsidised rentals are granted for three years, extendable by another three, with flat size depending on whether the applicant lives alone or with family. This system directly links housing access to labour market position, privileging certain groups.

In Chile, processes are shaped by subsidy schemes, particularly DS19 and DS49. The DS19 subsidy requires buyers to reserve units through developers, often with support in navigating bank mortgages. While some described this as straightforward, others, like Carolinne, faced barriers to child-free households, noting fewer options for single people or non-traditional families. The whole process of buying a subsidised home usually takes two years. However, for families accessing housing through the DS49 subsidy, it can take over a decade. To qualify, they must first join a Housing Committee, supported by a Sponsor Entity (SE) that will develop the housing project. The SE development and a Social Accompaniment Plan have to be approved by the committee and the SERVIU (Servicio de Vivienda y Urbanización; Housing and Urban Planning Service) overseeing the programme before construction begins. Long delays from the process of forming committees and securing land often prompt committees to negotiate improvements with SERVIU, sometimes escalating to protests or occupations, which can result in better housing conditions, such as larger flats and improved infrastructure. For instance, Karin's committee secured an additional 7 m^2 per flat, increasing the standard 55 m^2 mandated by DS49 to 62 m^2.

The DS49 programme also includes modalities such as the Programa Pequeño Condominio (Small Family Co-Housing Programme), which supports the densification of an existing residential plot of land by its owners by providing funding for the construction costs of a condominium with multiple homes for co-ownership by two to 12 households and offering temporary rent support for a six-month construction period. The process typically takes one to two years and is funded through family savings of 15 UF (£483), a base subsidy of 583 UF (£18,780), and, in some cases, additional contributions from municipalities, foundations, or companies. The eligibility criteria are the same as those for other DS49 programme modalities.

Fernando, for instance, used this scheme to replace his mother's self-built and overcrowded house with a new three-storey building containing three subsidised dwellings, preserving family land while accessing larger, debt-free housing. The plot initially contained a self-built home from the Operación Sitio (Operation Site) housing programme in the 1960s. This programme initially provided only a demarcated building lot, outlined in chalk, along with a small bathroom and kitchen connected to basic services, as well as basic infrastructure and urban layout (Quintana, 2014). With the help of the Consolida programme, he was able to replace this house with a standardised and industrialised three-storey reinforced-concrete building, containing three 60-m^2 three-bedroom dwellings (Figure 9.12).

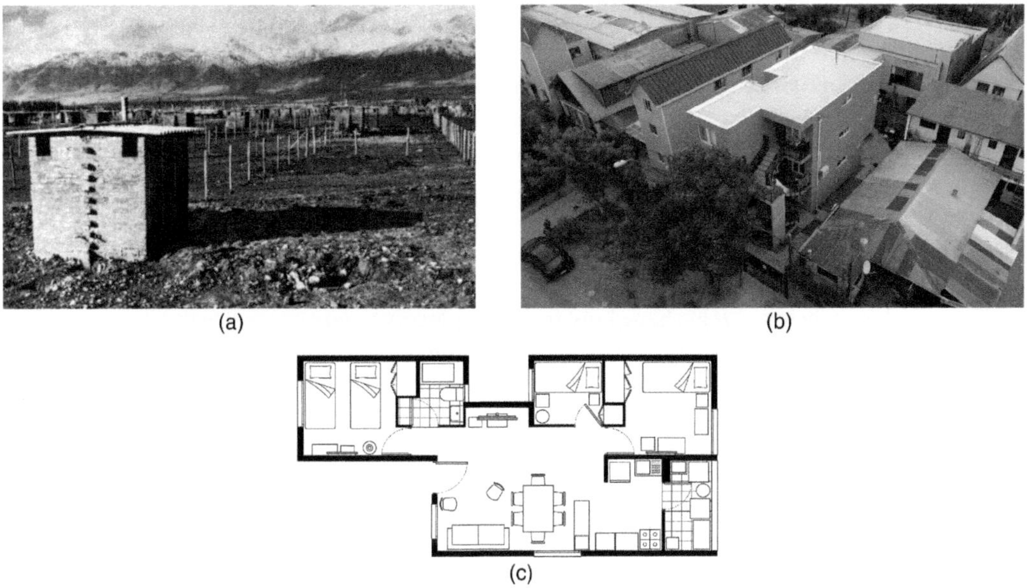

FIGURE 9.12 Developed land with sanitary facilities (kitchen and bathroom) under Operación Sitio (a). Photograph by Iván Csillag in Corporacion de la Vivienda, *Chile – 1960* (1960). Redevelopment of former Operación Sitio site through the Small Family Co-Housing Programme (b and c). The cream-coloured building with a grey roof on the left is one of the first models of this programme, built by the same developer.

Due to the allocation process, applicants often do not have the same rights or information when making a decision as those in the private market. Residents, therefore, highlighted various aspects they would have liked to have known about before moving into their homes. Expectations versus reality were a theme for many residents, both positively and negatively. One common concern was the unexpected noise levels and the surrounding environment. In Zurich, for instance, Letitia found the noise from the neighbour's children overwhelming at times, while Andre, despite being aware of the nearby motorway and railway, underestimated how much noise they would generate, which impacted his sleep. Michael, too, noted that his London home felt like a "car park with prefab walls", detailing how issues with sound insulation led him to experience anxiety and distress. At a different scale, in Amsterdam Noord Anja was disappointed by the design choices made after she moved in, such as the unattractive plants placed in the hallway, which she felt diminished the quality of the shared spaces.

Transparency in the home-buying process varied across participants' experiences. For instance, Jennifer in Oxford felt that the process was clear and straightforward, since she had purchased her shared-ownership home from her cousin. Fernando in Santiago emphasised the role of ongoing institutional support, as he recalled regular updates and meetings with the developer throughout the process. By contrast, Maria in London was frustrated with the lack of transparency, mainly because she had only viewed the show unit before committing to the purchase and encountered unforeseen problems after moving in, such as poor finishes in paint and tiles and high indoor temperatures. In the same city, May found the buying process particularly unclear, especially when it came to the timeline for completion, which was delayed by almost a year and still incomplete when she moved in. This caused administrative challenges, including setting up bills in their newly built homes because of missing land registry entries and incomplete documentation. Similarly, maintenance and infrastructure issues also caught some residents off guard: in Liss, Hannah discovered a hole in her back door on the day she moved in, which made it impossible to lock; Babet in Amsterdam expressed concerns about the dusty ventilation system and its detrimental impact on her health; and in London, Jake was unaware that the bike storage would not be available for the first four months of living in the building, and that parking would not be permitted, which was highly inconvenient.

Overall, these examples demonstrate that housing allocation systems are not merely bureaucratic procedures; they actively shape how residents perceive and experience their homes. Long waiting times, limited choice, and administrative inefficiencies can generate frustration and insecurity, while transparent processes, ongoing support, and affordability relative to market conditions foster satisfaction and stability. In this sense, allocation is not only a pathway to housing but also a determinant of whether residents experience their home in a positive or negative way.

Design and Housing Quality

Design and housing quality are multidimensional concepts shaped not only by regulations and technical standards but also by cultural practices, everyday routines, and the residents' own expectations and perceptions of adequacy. What constitutes a well-designed or high-quality home varies widely across contexts: for some, it is measured by materials, finishes, and construction methods, for others, by function, comfort, or adaptability. This section examines how design standards translate into everyday housing experiences, focusing on four interrelated themes: the standardisation of spaces and finishes, residents' understanding of housing quality, their ability to alter and personalise their homes, and the challenges of maintenance and repair.

Design Standards of Everyday Spaces

The differences in specifications and finishes expected across countries and offered by providers in different affordable housing are particularly evident in kitchen provision. Kitchens in Zurich come fully built-in and equipped with all appliances and storage. Residents expect quality appliances and finishes. In Barcelona, kitchens are provided fully functional, with essential appliances and fittings, but residents must install additional wall cabinets and sometimes upgrade their appliances to higher quality models. In England, kitchens vary by housing association and tenure – some provide fully equipped kitchens, while others offer only built-in furniture without appliances. In Santiago and Shenzhen, kitchens include only the basics: a water supply, sinks, and some countertop space (Figure 9.13). In Chile, for example, the minimum requirement is a countertop of 50 – 70 cm. Residents must complete the rest of the kitchen themselves, resulting in very varied and creative finishes.

In Amsterdam, kitchens are heavily standardised. Some residents described them as "nothing special", implying the rudimentary nature of the finishes, usually incorporating white cabinets. One resident in Amsterdam complained that the kitchen cabinets were so narrow that plates could barely fit inside them. Beyond size and appliance provision, cultural expectations also shape how kitchens are perceived. In London, May, who has also lived in Asia, pointed out that "the biggest difference in the kitchen in a Western setup is always [that] there's no window. . . here we rely on the extractor fan to take out the humidity".

(a) (b) (c) (d)

FIGURE 9.13 Kitchens in Zurich (a, b) and in Shenzhen (c, d).

Laundry spaces also vary significantly across countries, reflecting cultural differences. In Zurich, communal washing machines are very common and are beginning to appear in new developments in Amsterdam. In England, while many newly built affordable homes have a utility cupboard where washing machines can be placed, it is also not uncommon for laundry machines to be in the kitchen (Figure 9.14). There is also no designated space for drying clothes; therefore, many residents do so on the balcony in good weather or otherwise in the living room, taking up space in shared areas.

(a) (b)

FIGURE 9.14 Communal washing machines in Amsterdam (a) and a washing machine in a flat in London (b).

(a) (b) (c)

FIGURE 9.15 A private laundry area in a flat in Santiago (a); a washing machine on the balcony (b), and a common area for drying clothes (c) in Shenzhen.

In Chile, a laundry area, or loggia, with a minimum size of 2 m^2 is mandatory in flats, which typically includes a sink, washing machine, and sometimes a dryer. The Cuadro Normativo standards stipulate that access to the loggia must be through the kitchen, separated by a door that includes a window for ventilation and natural light. The loggia is commonly integrated into the building façade to ensure a homogenous appearance. Due to a lack of storage inside the home, the loggia often ends up as a storage space. Instead of a loggia in Shenzhen, residents have a small balcony with space for a washing machine and to air-dry their clothes. However, it is also common to have a large, shared space on the rooftop or elsewhere in the building for drying clothes as well (Figure 9.15). Both bathrooms and kitchens are naturally ventilated, with some bathrooms accessed through the balcony.

Defining High-Quality Homes

Housing quality can mean different things to different residents and is measured in various ways, reflecting their individual housing expectations. One important aspect is the architectural design and finishes of the buildings. Residents in Barcelona generally appreciated the innovative construction methods and non-traditional finishes used in their homes. For example, Cristina and Javier in Gavà noted that while the construction felt modern and different from traditional flats, they grew to like it over time. Isabel expressed her admiration for the same building's industrial aesthetic, enjoying the exposed concrete, visible pipes, and contrast between concrete and white plasterboard, as well as the spaciousness and natural light of her home. David in Cornellà was surprised to see wood being used in construction, something he had never witnessed before (Figure 9.16). David's building, Modulus Matrix by Peris + Toral Arquitectes, is an innovative modular timber-frame project consisting of 3.6 – 3.6-m modules and six storeys tall with no welded joints. Another Cornellà resident, Yeray, found the prefabrication process particularly striking, describing how "they came with a crane, , , like a puzzle. . . without putting in any wood, a nail, or anything. The assembly was super-fast". He also highlighted the high quality

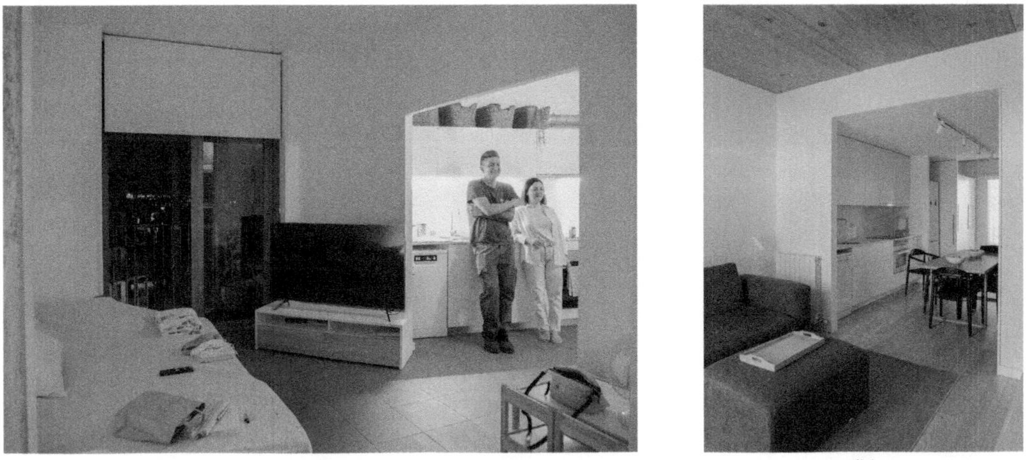

(a) (b)

FIGURE 9.16 Cristina and Javier's home (a) and David's home (b) in Barcelona.

of the wooden flooring in his home, appreciating its consistent design, which was even used in the kitchen.

Another critical aspect of how housing quality is experienced is thermal comfort, considering issues such as insulation, ventilation, and building orientation, which can influence indoor temperatures. For some, well-insulated homes provided excellent thermal regulation. Marielle in Amsterdam appreciated her home's insulation; even when outdoor temperatures reached 38°C, the inside of her home remained a comfortable 24°C. Similarly, May in London valued her home's efficiency, noting that they didn't need to turn on the heating even in the cool spring weather. For May and her cousin, June, thermal comfort is closely linked to sustainability, making them feel they were contributing positively to the environment.

In contrast, another London resident found her home uncomfortably warm year-round, with indoor temperatures reaching 27°C even in winter. In Barcelona, on the other hand, one resident spoke about how the design of her building enabled balanced thermal comfort, with heating rarely necessary in winter and air conditioning and fans seldom used in summer, thanks to the use of high-quality materials like wooden beams and flooring. Isabel highlighted how the provision of cross-ventilation improved comfort during hot summers in Barcelona by allowing air circulation and reducing the intensity of heat. Residents with dual-aspect homes echoed this, emphasising that dual-aspect design enhances both natural sunlight exposure and cross ventilation.

For some residents, poor housing quality was related to the developer's failure to consider minor design elements, which had a significant impact on their home's usability and overall quality. Emma in Eastleigh was not provided with curtain rails in her living room. While Andre in Zurich had curtain rails, they were placed exceptionally high, making it impossible to find standard curtains long enough to cover the window. Although Isabel in Barcelona generally perceived her home to be of high quality, she also expected it to come with roller shutters to help protect against the heat, as many flats in Spain do, but this was not the case (Figure 9.17).

The appearance of subsidised housing and the stigma this can create were also a significant concern for residents, against which they measured the quality of their homes. Many shared

FIGURE 9.17 Flats without external roller shutters, Barcelona.

their views on what social and affordable housing should look like and how design quality affected their wellbeing. They believed that their homes should be the same as private housing within the same development, both in appearance and quality. For Nergiz in London, living in a well-designed home contributed to a sense of dignity and equality, making her feel no different from those renting privately (Figure 9.18). She explained that because her home did not resemble typical council housing, "you value yourself more".

However, some residents felt that distinctions between social and private housing were still too visible, reinforcing inequality. Caroline, for example, noticed that the social housing in her Eastleigh estate was placed at the back of the development (Figure 9.19), right next to the motorway, while the more expensive homes were positioned more favourably. She felt this was a form of discrimination, reinforcing a social hierarchy within the community based on housing tenure rather than fostering inclusivity. In Santiago, Jennifer shared a similar view, noting that the DS49 flats for low-income households in her housing development were delivered without finishes. In contrast, DS19 flats were provided turnkey, which Cesar, her husband, found problematic. Cesar explained that some of the neighbours who obtained their home with the DS49 subsidy had to invest money and "do some extra work on the house" to complete them, for instance, fitting doors on their wardrobes and installing bathroom accessories.

At the same time, some residents believed that their social housing was of particularly high quality, contributing to a sense of pride. In Amsterdam, Marielle noted that the buildings in her development had a luxurious feel, "like in Barcelona and Madrid – those fancy, big apartment buildings", which she saw as unique for social housing (Figure 9.20). Improved construction standards were also noted as a necessary aspect of a good-quality home by some, especially

FIGURE 9.18 Nergiz's home (London).

FIGURE 9.19 Caroline's housing development (Eastleigh).

FIGURE 9.20 North Amsterdam social housing building.

those in Chile, moving from substandard, unsafe homes to formal housing built to seismic safety standards. Fernando highlighted the construction quality of his home, having observed the building process firsthand.

Adaptation and Personalisation

The ability to make changes to a home, whether structural or decorative, plays a significant role in determining how satisfied residents feel with their living space (Alonso Aranda & Jacoby, 2023). This ability enhances their housing satisfaction (Elsinga & Hoekstra, 2005) and supports the long-term utility of the dwellings (Carmona et al., 2010). Homeowners often make significant modifications as soon as they move in. In Santiago, residents fixed things to the walls, expanded their houses as much as possible, removed internal walls to create open-plan spaces, or even combined rooms for commercial purposes, such as creating an informal convenience shop. Participants living in houses could also make external modifications such as designing gardens, installing window protections, and building external paved areas for parking (Figure 9.21). Ownership allowed homeowners to shape their homes according to their needs and preferences.

In contrast, tenants often face restrictions on making even minor modifications. In England, many tenants are not permitted to paint walls, change appliances, or hang things on the walls, limiting their ability to personalise and use their space. Jennifer, who had previously lived in a flat share, emphasised how important it was to her to finally be able to decorate her home

(a) (b)

FIGURE 9.21 Soledad's flat adapted for a shop, with the removed wall still visible on the ceiling (a); Johana's modified front garden (b), Santiago.

as she liked, highlighting the emotional impact of having control over one's living space (Figure 9.22).

However, in places like Amsterdam, renters are expected to take on some home finishes and improvements themselves, such as painting walls or laying flooring. While this grants them more control over their space, it also incurs a financial cost. Babet described how unhappy residents were about having to cover these expenses, as the homes were designed for people with limited financial resources. She pointed out that a plain, smooth white wall should not be a "luxury", yet poor workmanship meant that she had to spend money on wallpaper to cover the walls (Figure 9.23).

(a) (b)

FIGURE 9.22 Undecorated living room interior in England (a) and Jennifer's home in Oxford (b).

(a) (b) (c)

FIGURE 9.23 Examples of finishes in Amsterdam flats (a and b) and wallpaper in Babet's home (c).

Similarly, in Chile, as inhabitants own their homes, they are expected to undertake some alterations themselves. However, the "level of completion" depends on the type of subsidy. The DS19 subsidy delivers turnkey homes with painted or wallpapered interior walls; bedrooms and living areas finished with either carpet or laminated flooring; bathrooms and kitchens fitted with ceramic tiles, and accessories such as towel racks and curtain rods. Households receiving the DS49 subsidy, by contrast, must complete their houses themselves. Technical requirements specify that the kitchen and bathroom ceilings are painted to prevent moisture damage to structural elements and that walls are tiled. However, all other walls, ceilings, and floors of DS49 homes are left unfinished without paint, plaster, or wallpaper.

Ultimately, the ability to make changes, whether structural or aesthetic, can create a stronger sense of belonging and housing satisfaction. While modifications can be expensive, they enable residents to tailor their homes to reflect their personal needs and lifestyles, thereby reinforcing the connection between autonomy and happiness in housing.

Maintenance and Long-Term Quality

Maintenance issues can significantly impact quality of life for residents, ranging from faulty installations to poor design. Across all cities, residents reported frustration with ongoing repairs, poor communication by housing providers, and unexpected maintenance burdens in newly built developments. Problems with maintenance play a key role in the perception of safety and, consequently, in neighbourhood satisfaction (Hur & Nasar, 2014).

In London, Maria compared housing standards to a car warranty, expecting new homes to function without major issues for at least two years. However, her negative experience with a new build left her stressed due to constant repairs, stating: "I don't think I will go to a new build ever again". Also in London, Jerry likewise faced persistent problems in his new building, with the housing provider taking three years to fix the incorrectly wired heating. Other London residents, such as May and June, felt unsafe due to a malfunctioning balcony door that could not be locked, while Jennifer in Oxford struggled with a front door that did not close properly, and Hannah in Liss having to replace faulty windows in her new home.

Basic design or maintenance problems also posed many practical challenges in daily use. For example, Candide in Zurich noted that residents could not clean their windows because the architects had not considered sufficient external access. Maria in London found that her kitchen lacked a splashback, leading to peeling paint and heat damage. May described fire alarms ringing for days before being switched off, while Michael, a wheelchair user, struggled when his intercom was broken for 13 weeks, preventing carers from accessing his home. Another London resident also reported a faulty fire alarm, stating that she could not use her kitchen appliances without setting it off and therefore had to use her air fryer on the balcony.

Another key concern was the lengthy response time from housing providers to complaints. In Amsterdam, Kerala expressed frustration with bureaucratic repair processes, emphasising that maintenance issues cannot always be resolved through "a flowchart". In both Zurich and Amsterdam, residents experienced ongoing problems with air vents. Babet in Amsterdam suffered significant health issues due to dust collecting around vents. At the same time, Andre in Zurich reported that his controlled air exchange system did not function properly, despite multiple repair attempts. Cristina in Santiago, experienced humidity issues in her bathroom, as the room had no window, and the extractor fan was too small. She asked the developers to fix the problem but was only told that "it was caused by a lack of ventilation and to open the bathroom door while showering". She also faced problems with her balcony after the first spell of rain, when plaster began peeling off. Although the developers advised her to file a warranty claim, they did not have a crane that could reach the fourth floor, and the issue was therefore also left unrepaired.

Sometimes creating an ideal home does not depend only on financial resources. Soledad in Santiago explained that it was difficult for her to carry out repairs or improvements to a satisfactory standard because she lacked both the necessary building skills and appropriate tools. A single mother, she compared her situation to that of a two-parent household in her neighbourhood, noting that they were able to furnish and improve their homes more easily because "those are families with a mother and a father, so they can do more stuff".

Generally, Chilean households are responsible for maintaining their homes, as they typically own them. Those living in housing complexes pay a monthly service charge for the upkeep of shared spaces. For instance, Karin paid approximately 20,000 CLP (£16) monthly, which covered the maintenance and cleaning of the common areas, as well as painting and gardening (Figure 9.24). This has historically been a concern in Chilean social housing, as low-income households often struggle to afford their homes and related expenses.

However, by contrast, some housing providers, like Institut Metropolità de Promoció de Sòl i Gestió Patrimonial (IMPSOL), take a proactive approach to maintenance. In Barcelona, residents were taught how to care for the wooden structures in their homes, and Yeray received a maintenance book detailing upkeep requirements, such as varnishing ceilings every five to seven years. In another development in Barcelona, architects briefed residents on energy-saving behaviour to discourage the installation of air conditioning units. However, these examples remain exceptions rather than the norm.

The experiences of residents across various contexts demonstrate that housing quality is not a fixed standard, but rather a negotiated outcome of design, regulation, cultural expectations, and everyday adaptation. The interplay between provision, personalisation, and long-term maintenance highlights that what makes a high-quality home is as much about usability and comfort as it is about technical compliance.

Housing, Community, and Wellbeing

Housing can significantly shape social dynamics, influencing relationships within families, between partners, and among neighbours. For many residents, moving to a new home has positively transformed their daily interactions and overall wellbeing. Nergiz, for example, experienced a positive change in her family life after moving into a larger home in London. Previously, space constraints made it difficult for her and her children to spend time together, and her

FIGURE 9.24 Common areas in Karin's housing development (Santiago).

daughter often stayed at her father's home due to the lack of having her own room. Now, with more space, they could cook and eat together, improving their relationship. Similarly, Emma recalled the difficulty of living in her brother's crowded home, where she and her son lacked personal space. Now, in her home in Eastleigh, she found everyday life much easier. In London, Jerry noticed a significant shift in his community's social atmosphere after it was relocated from a run-down estate to a better-quality development. "Since people have moved away from what was a depressing estate over to here, people have become much more friendly. It feels more of a community since we've moved".

For some, having a home that not only accommodates current needs but can allow for future changes is essential. Yeray and his partner intentionally bought a three-bedroom flat, knowing that if they decided to have a child, they would have enough space for the baby and also a separate workspace. "With two [bedrooms], it's a bit tight, but with three, it's better because you have a room for us, one for the child, and then another one for a studio", he said.

However, housing can equally affect social dynamics negatively. A lack of space can limit people's ability to form new relationships or adapt to changes in their family structure. In England, some single mothers felt their housing allocation assumed they would remain single indefinitely. One resident found it particularly challenging to even think of having a partner because she shared her bedroom with her daughter, while another struggled when her partner stayed over, as the space became uncomfortably tight. One single mother also highlighted how space limitations become more noticeable as children grow: "My oldest son is an adult and has a long-term girlfriend. You can barely swing a cat in his bedroom. When they're younger, you don't really think about space, but as they grow, you're like, the house is shrinking as well". Participants living in studio flats often complained that limited space affected their ability to share a home with others. While Anja found her small flat in Amsterdam cosy and easy to maintain, she described it as feeling "more like a hotel room" than "a place to live together" with her current partner. Similarly, Maartje believed that studios like hers in the same city were only suitable for one person and that living there meant having to "stay alone for the rest of your life".

Community and Neighbourhood

In addition to the physical, material aspects of the immediate home environment, residents also described how the local community and neighbourhood played a crucial role in their housing satisfaction, wellbeing, and sense of security. Living in large residential developments can be an overwhelming experience, as expressed by both Andre in Bülach and Cristina in Barcelona. Andre found that he had underestimated the scale of his building, feeling that 35 flats were too many for comfort. The sheer number of residents made the environment feel impersonal to him. Cristina, on the other hand, faced an even greater adjustment, moving into a development with 164 households. Having previously lived in a small neighbourhood with familiar long-term neighbours, she found the transition to a large community "a shock". She observed that in such a diverse environment, everyday habits and expectations vary widely, requiring residents to adapt and "learn to coexist". In this regard, David in Barcelona valued the interior garden in the building (Figure 9.25), believing that its design promoted contact between neighbours. Thus, while some struggled with the scale, others saw it as an opportunity to learn and adjust to a diverse range of people and experiences.

Integration with groups socially perceived as lower status or more vulnerable was often seen as a challenge. This was particularly the case in Amsterdam, with a new housing association scheme to rehouse vulnerable people, including formerly homeless individuals and those with substance abuse issues,in about one third of the development. This led to concerns about safety and negative interactions with neighbours. One resident described incidents of antisocial behaviour, including a stabbing, noting that while the neighbourhood in North Amsterdam felt safe, the building did not. Another initially supported the integration of vulnerable individuals but found herself unprepared for the level of aggression and conflict that followed, specifically

(a) (b)

FIGURE 9.25 The housing development where Andre lives in Bülach (a) and the garden in David's housing development in Barcelona (b).

highlighting discrimination on the community app, which she thereafter avoided. A third resident suggested that involving multiple charities rather than just one could have created a more balanced mix of residents. She pointed out that the aim of building a strong community was particularly disrupted by the COVID-19 pandemic, which halted planned engagement activities and efforts. While she believed that the system mostly worked, she acknowledged that the high concentration of people with psychiatric backgrounds had led to serious incidents, leaving some neighbours feeling unsafe.

In Chile, residents specifically expressed concerns about maintaining long-term community organisation and communication. For instance, Karin observed that some of her neighbours became less involved in community matters after they had acquired their homes: "to obtain something is not just about reaching it, the real challenge is maintaining it". She noted that lax enforcement of security measures, such as leaving access doors unlocked, undermined the safety of neighbours. For others in Santiago, the change from their original dwellings in informal settlements to their new homes was significant. Living in these gated housing developments necessitated adopting habits and norms alien to their previous residences. In this sense, Erica explained that the socio-economic mix impacted on coexistence within the community: "Social integration is extremely complicated … I don't know where they come from. They live poorly, they are rude, and they insult each other among neighbours".

Despite promoting social integration, projects funded by the DS19 subsidy in Chile face common social problems. According to Cristina, the developers deliberately separate residents by their socio-economic status into different buildings with their own entrances. While this design decision was intended to simplify maintenance, it actually social deepened divisions among residents. This clear separation by tenure is also still commonly found in other countries, such as England, whereas some developments in Barcelona have consciously tried to be completely tenure blind.

Good design can simultaneously enhance the sense of community. In their dual-aspect flat in London, Jake and Heather's kitchen faced the internal corridor. For them, this had been a positive experience, contributing to their sense of safety. They valued "seeing people walk past your window. . . because where we grew up in Liverpool everybody knew the neighbours". Nergiz in London also mentioned she now knew many of her former neighbours, whereas before relocating, "a neighbour will be living next to me for 20 years [that] I didn't even know about". Similarly, in Santiago, the DS49 projects developed through housing committees often fostered strong initial bonds among residents sharing a common interest. For example, Johana explained that families involved in the housing committee also participated in activities to build connections among future neighbours, such as organising events for children.

However, conflicts over how to use shared spaces were also common, as several examples from Santiago illustrate. Erica recounted that disagreements arose while arranging Christmas decorations, with safety concerns preventing neighbours from reaching a consensus. Soledad highlighted strict rules imposed on children, who had limited space to play and were often asked to "behave" or leave the housing complex. Carolinne found adapting to rules regarding noise and shared spaces was challenging to her family, as this was their first experience of living in a flat with communal spaces. Previously, when living in houses, they rarely needed to navigate neighbourhood dynamics or engage with their residential community to the same extent (Figure 9.26).

FIGURE 9.26 Common areas of four Chilean housing developments: Johana's (a), Erica's (b), Soledad's (c), and Carolinne's (d).

Safety and Privacy

The design of a home significantly impacts perceptions of privacy and safety, and varies across cultures and building typologies. Architectural features such as deck access, windows, and surveillance strongly shape residents' sense of security. In Santiago, located within a highly seismic area, the quality of construction and structure was considered especially important when discussing safety. Comparing their previous accommodation to their new homes, most residents praised the solid materials with which the latter were built.

Physical safety is often discussed in the context of building design and accessibility. For example, concerns about access to balconies were raised in several countries. Babet in Amsterdam and Nergiz in London both worried about how easily neighbours could climb onto their balconies. Likewise, Isabel, living on the first floor in Barcelona, was nervous because she felt her balcony could be easily accessed from the street. Residents in England described mixed feelings about different building types. Jake, for example, appreciated low-rise designs because they allow for visual connection with the street and neighbouring homes, creating a sense of community. By contrast, Maria preferred high-rise living for the unobstructed views and reduced sense of being watched (Figure 9.27).

For some, like Bart in Amsterdam, safety was defined by clean and quiet surroundings and friendly neighbours. He valued community interaction, noting how street parties with food,

(a) (b) (c)

FIGURE 9.27 Balconies: Isabel's in Barcelona (a) and Maria's (b) and Jake and Heather's (c) in London.

music, and local products for sale fostered a sense of belonging and wellbeing. Similarly, in some communities, residents connected through shared physical and virtual platforms such as community halls or WhatsApp groups, reinforcing emotional security through social relationships.

Privacy is also often closely linked to feelings of safety. Jennifer in Oxford avoided her balcony because it faced directly into other homes, illustrating how visibility and proximity affect whether people feel comfortable using their outdoor spaces. Javier and Cristina resolved their privacy concerns by frosting their hallway windows but maintained a social connection with their neighbours through balcony conversations. This contrast suggests that privacy needs are context-dependent and individualised, striking a balance between openness and personal comfort. In Chile, many residents reported feeling secure inside their housing complexes but unsafe in surrounding neighbourhoods, often citing issues such as proximity to informal settlements, inadequate street lighting, and limited police presence.

Other residents emphasised the importance of security measures such as CCTV, reinforced doors, concierge services, intercoms, and gated housing complexes, which increased their sense of safety. The ability to supervise shared areas from inside their homes – for example, watching children play – also gave many residents peace of mind. However, lack of maintenance in public or communal spaces was seen as a safety risk.

For others, financial and emotional stability was closely associated with safety. In Chile, owning a home has great social and economic value, often regarded as both a reward for personal effort and a source of long-term security. Johana described her strong emotional connection to her home, saying, "I love this home because we worked for it". Similarly, Karin contrasted her past experiences of living in temporary housing – whether in her father's or ex-partner's home – with the stability of ownership, saying, "It wasn't truly yours. . . In contrast, these spaces are yours: your tastes, your belongings. It's what you've achieved". Cristina also echoed this sense of empowerment, noting: "No one can tell you, for example, 'Get out of my house'. Because it's your house, they can't kick you out". In London, homeowners similarly felt greater stability and security, particularly when compared to the unpredictability of renting and the risk of rent increases. Emma, after years of instability, emphasised the peace of mind that came with owning her own home.

Accessibility also influenced how residents perceived safety. Michael, who lived in a first-floor flat in London, experienced anxiety when both lifts were out of order. In the event of a fire, he was advised to stay inside, raising serious concerns about the true inclusivity of his living conditions. In Chile, many developments are capped at five storeys to avoid the provision of lifts, which are expensive to install and maintain. Yet this can create barriers for residents with mobility needs.

As Karin explained, "Living here while wheelchair-bound is impossible. In fact, we're currently discussing with the management committee the possibility of installing a lift... it would be especially helpful for someone in a wheelchair". Designers are aware of these challenges, as architect Favio Salguero noted in an interview (personal communication, 28 March, 2023) the importance of reserving space for future lift installation in buildings of six or more storeys.

However, accessibility is not static – it changes as residents age or their needs evolve. Some worried, therefore, whether their current homes would allow them to age in place. In Zurich, Andre's priority was to live near healthcare facilities, but he recognised that his two-storey home might become impractical in the future. Similarly, Kerala in Amsterdam noted how her current layout forced her to "open one door before closing another door", reducing ease of use. She said that an entry where she could sit down to remove her shoes and greet guests would improve accessibility for her.

Overall, residents' accounts demonstrate that housing plays a central role in shaping social relationships, community life, and perceptions of safety and stability. Adequate space can strengthen family ties and enable future planning, while design and management influence whether neighbourhoods foster integration or reinforce divisions. At the same time, feelings of safety, privacy, and long-term security are closely tied to both the physical qualities of dwellings and the social dynamics of their surroundings.

Conclusion

This chapter argues that housing cannot be understood solely in terms of numerical standards. While metrics such as space per person, affordability ratios, or definitions of overcrowding provide a sense of structure and comparability, and can safeguard minimum standards, they can also obscure the lived realities of residents whose experiences are shaped equally or more by cultural expectations, family dynamics, and everyday practices than square metres or financial thresholds. Across ten cities and 37 households, residents demonstrated that what constitutes a "decent" or "good" home varies widely: some emphasised material conditions and finishes, while others valued privacy, adaptability, stability, or a sense of community. These findings highlight the inadequacy of universal frameworks and point to the importance of listening to residents' own definitions of housing quality.

The analysis also shows that housing standards are not neutral. They emerge from political agendas, economic priorities, and normative assumptions about family life, yet they often fail to anticipate how households evolve. Families with growing children, single parents sharing bedrooms, or couples negotiating life in small studios illustrate how rigid standards can constrain wellbeing and relationships. At the same time, participants also demonstrated resilience and creativity, adapting homes through decoration, alterations, or new routines to make spaces more liveable and suit their needs. These practices highlight the importance of autonomy in achieving greater housing satisfaction.

Community and neighbourhood dynamics further demonstrate how questions of quality are contextual and subjective. For some, moving into better-designed or regenerated developments fostered stronger social bonds, improved wellbeing, and inspired a feeling of pride. For others, large-scale housing schemes, tenure segregation, or poorly managed integration policies generated tensions, safety concerns, or feelings of exclusion. Such accounts reveal how the built environment interacts with social structures and governance, enabling or constraining collective life. The role of design is crucial here: elements such as balconies, dual-aspect layouts, shared gardens, and overlooked communal areas could either foster belonging and safety or amplify conflict and insecurity. The following are some suggestions based on conversations with the residents:

- **Rethink standards around capabilities.** Supplement minimum space requirements with performance-based criteria tied to everyday activities (e.g., study, leisure, caregiving, storage for seasonal items, ageing-in-place).
- **Flexibility and adaptability from the start.** Require layouts that permit multiple furniture configurations, easy partitioning, and future change (e.g., convertible rooms, generous door widths, double rooms).
- **Define design decisions that affect daily life.** Define practical details, such as adequate built-in storage, fixtures, laundry drying solutions, acoustic performance, and solar control, that are crucial to daily life but often overlooked.
- **Improve maintenance.** Handover homes with user guidance, transparent fault reporting, and time-bound repair obligations; define post-occupancy as part of quality, not an optional service.
- **Resident's opinions in design governance.** Utilise co-design, post-occupancy evaluation, and competition briefs (as seen in IMPSOL in Barcelona and housing cooperatives in Zurich) to translate social values, such as safety, inclusivity, and sustainability, into binding design requirements.
- **Contextualise affordability.** Assess costs beyond rent or mortgage and consider utilities, service charges, fit-out, and furniture.

Ultimately, the chapter emphasises the need to reassess housing standards and evaluative frameworks in a way that prioritises lived experience. Capabilities-based approaches offer one promising direction, shifting the focus from abstract metrics to what people are actually able to do and be in their homes. Recognising housing as more than shelter – as a site of identity, security, and wellbeing – requires balancing economic, objective, and subjective measures with attention to cultural diversity, household change, and residents' aspirations. By centring residents' voices, this study challenges the dominance of technocratic approaches and calls for a more inclusive and flexible understanding of housing quality, one that values both everyday practices and long-term possibilities.

Acknowledgements

We thank Dr. Raül Avilla-Royo (ETSAB Barcelona), Associate Professor Lu Wang (South China University of Technology), Gianna Bottema, and Salome Rohner (ETH Wohnforum) for their contributions and support in resident engagement. We are also grateful to the housing providers – ASIG, Baugenossenschaft Glattal Zürich, Clarion Housing Group, de Alliantie, AMB:IMPSOL, Peabody, and Ymere – for facilitating this study. Most importantly, we acknowledge the participants in England, Chile, China, Switzerland, Spain, and the Netherlands for their time and insights.

PART V
Conclusion

10

DECENT HOMES

Emerging Bodies of Evidence

Sam Jacoby

This book has examined how design governance – and the standardisation it often promotes – is a key driver of housing design, particularly in the subsidised sector, where homes are typically built to minimum legal and market standards. It traced the historical development of design governance in relation to key transformations in the socio-political and economic role of housing, showing how it has been shaped by emerging evidence and common practices in housing and its design. Although increasingly evidence-based, design regulations can be slow to adapt and often interpret evidence through established norms of family life and social order, as well as prevailing political agendas and economic priorities. As a result, existing norms tend to persist despite changing social practices and lived realities.

The book aimed to develop an integrated understanding of the relationship between housing policy and housing design, specifically how standards are defined and materialised, how architects and developers interpret and translate them and, ultimately, how residents experience them. Although architects perceive many of the factors that shape housing design outcomes, such as regulatory frameworks, design standards, and economic or procurement decisions, as external or separate from the design process, they are in fact integral to design governance processes. These interactions, however, remain insufficiently understood, particularly in regard to the reasoning and evidence that underpin design governance and housing norms as well as their impacts on everyday life.

At first concerned with the quality of construction and building materials, and subsequently with public health, design governance in countries like England evolved from a focus on technical requirements into more holistic considerations of housing quality that incorporate social value, family life, and wellbeing. Early regulatory interventions, such as the London Building Act 1667, were driven by the need to prevent large urban and socio-economic disasters like the Great Fire of London of 1666 and therefore focused on building and fire safety. But by the mid-twentieth century, design regulations informed by the seminal Parker Morris Report, *Homes for Today and Tomorrow* (Ministry of Housing and Local Government, 1961), were grounded in a diverse evidence base that included sociological research, household surveys, stakeholder consultations, and design studies of the modern home. Its recommendations consequently integrated a welfare-state ethos with the social and spatial functional requirements of modern living,

DOI: 10.4324/9781032679204-16

proposing housing layouts based on the analysis of the activities and needs of occupants rather than architectural conventions.

Over time, housing design governance has evolved to reflect changing technical standards, building and design practices, and social norms or biases, establishing a socio-technical framework for negotiating between functional performance requirements and cultural expectations, but also for translating these into built forms. Design governance can therefore be seen in tension between maintaining the status quo and promoting change. For example, the nuclear family model within housing design standards continues to dominate, despite demographic shifts toward ageing populations and an increase in single-person or shared households by unrelated adults, which create new social realities and practical design challenges.

To examine both the social and spatial realities of homes, the book compared current housing design standards, standardisation, and subsidised housing outcomes in England (London, Liss, Eastleigh, and Oxford), Chile (Santiago), China (Shenzhen), the Netherlands (Amsterdam), Spain (Barcelona), and Switzerland (Zurich). It collected first-hand evidence on how their differences are reflected in the everyday use and lived experiences of the homes they produce. The findings underscore that housing standards and expectations differ significantly across countries, shaped by historical events, policy trajectories, and context-specific housing practices, as well as housing-related social values and economies.

Design governance is therefore not simply a regulatory process informed by technical necessity and driven by technological advances, but also a socio-technical and socio-spatial framework rooted in social and cultural norms and experiential evidence. In this sense, housing design and its governance are socially constructed and politically informed practices that encode, institutionalise, and enforce values about what constitutes a "decent" home.

Under England's Decent Homes Standard – first introduced in 2000 as a minimum threshold for housing quality – a decent home is merely defined as "reasonable" in its repair, facilities, services, and thermal comfort – not as adequate or, in fact, decent. Both good design and maintenance are essential aspects of housing quality that were widely recognised by interviewed residents as positively influencing their wellbeing and housing satisfaction. However, many residents also expressed frustration with shortcomings in basic maintenance and repairs, even in newly built developments. As one participant highlighted, the challenge beyond an initially good design lies in the quality of construction, workmanship, and maintenance services: "A decent home standard? I think, when at least for two years you do not have to touch anything. [.. .] It's like when you get a new car, you have like, warranty. So, I think when you get into a house, it should be exactly the same thing".

Residents also emphasised the importance of user-centred design and meeting non-standard needs. One resident with limited mobility found that their supposedly "accessible" flat left them unable to use the kitchen or living room fully, as cabinet heights, furniture dimensions, and circulation spaces were inadequate. As they explained, genuine accessibility requires involving disabled people directly in the design process: "Put the disabled person in a chair in there, let them use the space, and then listen to them". This shows that standards alone cannot guarantee usability and reinforces the importance of resident consultation in the design process.

Although dwelling size is important, perceptions and experiences of a home are central to judging its quality and value. Yet design policy and practice often overlook these subjective aspects, as they can be difficult to capture and instrumentalise. Socio-cultural norms, individual life experiences, and personal circumstances profoundly shape housing expectations and perceptions of quality. Our home-use studies show how these factors interact with specific spatial preferences

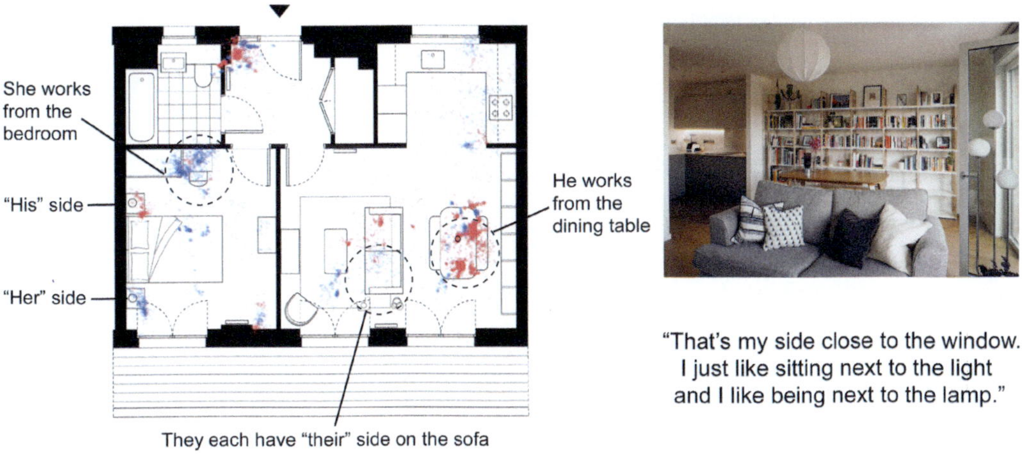

FIGURE 10.1 Spatial preferences and habits in a home in London.

and daily negotiations and choices within a home, influencing how different household members use available space (Figure 10.1). While the time spent in a space or using an area such as a kitchen or dining table does not necessarily indicate its social or functional value, an awareness of home use can improve spatio-temporal domestic relationships and use that might otherwise be difficult to understand. As one participant noted: "It's been insightful to observe how we use different areas of the house and how we might optimise our living space better".

Cross-national comparison further highlights how personal preferences interact with national housing norms. For example, kitchens, which are widely standardised, are fully built-in with appliances in Barcelona and Zurich, but only provide basic water, sinks, and worktops in Santiago and Shenzhen. In England, kitchens vary from fully equipped to offering just built-in furniture, depending on the housing provider and tenure (Figure 10.2). Similarly, storage design and provision – a design issue and common complaint in many subsidised homes – differs

FIGURE 10.2 Kitchen provisions in the studied homes.

Notes: 1: Santiago, 2: Amsterdam, 3: Barcelona, 4: Zurich, 5: London, 6: Shenzhen.

FIGURE 10.3 Differences in storage: Storage at common entrance in Amsterdam (a), fully equipped kitchen in Barcelona (b), lacking storage in Santiago (c), and bedroom with space for layout and storage variations (d).

significantly across countries: external basement or ground-floor storage rooms are common in Zurich and Amsterdam, while in Santiago internal storage is insufficient or almost entirely absent, greatly affecting how households can use and organise their homes (Figure 10.3). These differences in standards reflect national expectations about minimum provisions, available subsidies, and whose responsibility it is to make a home fully functional.

This book particularly focused on England and Chile, as both exemplify the entanglement of neoliberal logics, a quantification of housing values, and design standards. In England, decades of welfare-state regulation evolved into evidence-based but increasingly market-oriented standards that are inconsistently enforced and often subject to negotiation at local government levels. In Chile, the state institutionalised housing subsidies within a neoliberal framework, making ownership the sole path to affordability and pushing minimum dwelling standards to the threshold of adequacy. In both cases, the same instruments of design governance – standards, regulations, and subsidies – embody different political choices and institutional legacies. Comparing these contexts highlights that standards are not neutral or objective, but encode specific, local social expectations, showing that design governance is never only about technical thresholds but also about contested visions of housing as a social right, a market commodity, or both.

Building on these different cross-country comparisons, in particular in Chapters 5 and 6 on housing systems and standards, the in-depth housing case studies from six countries presented in Chapters 7, 8, and 9 further demonstrated how residents adapt their homes when spaces do not meet their needs. This is particularly evident in Santiago, where minimal space provisions, relaxed planning enforcement, and homeownership both necessitate and enable extensive adaptations. Furniture also often becomes a tool of flexibility, used in unconventional ways rather than according to the norms of space standards. One resident in a studio flat in Amsterdam constructed a movable screen to separate living and sleeping areas, describing how it restored their sense of dignity: "A bed in the living room is like being old, and it didn't feel very good. Before this thing was here, it felt like sleeping in the kitchen".

The extent to which making changes is possible often depends on tenure. In Santiago, owners frequently altered or extended their homes, especially houses, immediately after moving in, sometimes adding bedrooms, combining rooms, or creating informal commercial spaces for home-based work (Figure 10.4). In contrast, renters in England expressed deep frustration at restrictions preventing even minor changes, such as painting walls or hanging pictures, whereas tenants in Amsterdam are responsible for interior wall and floor finishes – which in some cases significantly impacted the quality of their life and housing satisfaction both negatively and positively (Figure 10.5). While this highlights the benefits of ownership, it also emphasises the need for secure tenure and sufficient renters' rights and support, enabling tenants both to afford necessary changes and to have the ability to make reasonable changes to their homes. In addition, the long-term maintenance challenge is not always sufficiently addressed. For example, in Chile, low-income groups as owners are responsible for the upkeep of their home, but are often unable to afford the necessary maintenance or carry it out to the required standards; approximately 40% of homes built from the 1980s to the 2000s require either demolition or extensive renovation due to poor construction quality (Secretaría

(a) (b)

FIGURE 10.4 Santiago: A convenience store in a former bedroom and an open-plan living area created by removing partitions (a) – with traces of the former wall still visible on the ceiling (b).

(a)

(b)

FIGURE 10.5 A living room in England, where residents are not permitted to make changes to the wall (a) and a studio flat in Amsterdam where wall and floor finishes are the responsibility of the tenant (b).

Técnica Presidencial, 2005). In social rent homes elsewhere, the lack of resident involvement in maintenance decisions and the timely repair or upgrade of homes is a common complaint.

Interviews with residents further highlight that perceptions of dwelling size or overcrowding do not always align with legal definitions or measurements. Some who lived in legally defined overcrowded housing conditions did not experience this as a problem, while others with "sufficient" space felt overcrowded (Figure 10.6). In larger households, especially, the need for more shared spaces and more visual and noise privacy are greater, emphasising that perceptions of overcrowding are contextual and directly linked to wellbeing. As one participant stated: "Sometimes the lack of size [. . .] a lack of privacy for the kids and myself, creates stress and then impacts my physical health".

Similarly, while affordable housing is commonly defined as accommodation costing no more than one-third of household income, residents' perceptions of affordability can vary and be subjective (Figure 10.7), shaped by how a home compares to others in the area and how well it meets their lifestyle needs, household requirements, or personal goals. One resident explained:

FIGURE 10.6 An overcrowded home in London occupied by a single parent with two children, one of whom is an adult.

FIGURE 10.7 The percentage of income spent on housing costs that study participants considered affordable.

"I maybe wouldn't say affordable, maybe 'affordable' is not the right word, but it's very reasonably priced compared to how the property market is".

Together, these findings highlight that housing quality is experienced spatially, socially, and financially, and that policies and regulations need to reflect these interconnected housing perceptions and realities. Common expectations of a decent home by participants therefore align less with the limited, technical Decent Homes Standard in England than the UN's rights-based definition of adequate housing and housing quality, which encompasses broader issues of tenure security, access to key public services, jobs, and infrastructures, affordability, habitability, accessibility, and cultural adequacy (UN-Habitat, 2010). A decent home standard must therefore recognise both the material and spatial qualities of housing but also the social and economic values of homes in supporting human dignity and wellbeing. This calls for design governance approaches that are socially and environmentally ambitious, viewing housing quality not merely as a temporary design problem but as a longer-term, intergenerational challenge and responsibility shared between those who inhabit, maintain, and own a home.

The Future of Housing Design Governance

Design governance must account for the knowledge and lived expertise of residents in both its processes and outcomes. However, empirical research into how residents use, experience, and perceive their homes shows a significant disconnect between housing regulations and housing realities, as everyday life often diverges from that envisioned by policymakers, developers, and designers. While direct observation and social science offer valuable insights into how people live, without a design research perspective that connects these to the spatial, material, and formal dimensions of a home, translating insights into actionable standards, policies, or design practices remains challenging. To effectively incorporate qualitative evidence into regulatory and housing design practices requires an interdisciplinary approach that integrates the social, spatial, material, and technical aspects of the home.

In negotiating housing policy objectives, technical standards, economic drivers, socio-cultural values, and historical precedents, design governance has continually reshaped housing quality and the ways in which homes are conceived, built, and inhabited, while adapting its processes, meanings, and outcomes to changing contexts. Housing quality, therefore, has no fixed or universal meaning and remains contested. While notions of "well-designed" homes are frequently invoked by policymakers, housing stakeholders, and the public, they often lack a clear definition, with housing quality often being assumed rather than substantiated and evidenced.

In addition, since design policies and regulations must be generalisable, they cannot easily account for individual and subjective experiences or needs. Instead, they prioritise measurable criteria, such as minimum room dimensions or thermal performance. This focus on quantifiable performance requirements overlooks the fact that housing quality depends not only on the size or materiality of homes but also on more nuanced, less tangible dimensions, including spatial arrangements and the perception of comfort, natural light, privacy, sociability, and adaptability to change. Rigid space standards, as in the case of Chile or England, particularly those prescribing minimum sizes or layouts for specific functions, can prevent residents from adapting their homes to changing needs and lifestyles. This reflects a fundamental dilemma in housing standards: they are designed to ensure efficiency through quantitative and functional minima, yet they are also expected to maximise flexibility of use and design. Thus, standards operate not only as instruments of efficiency but also as a means for translating minimum thresholds into an improved quality of use and, ultimately, quality of life. Designing for flexibility, therefore, requires considering how space can be used, combined, or reconfigured in the future, and understanding different spatial preferences and daily routines, which can be antithetical to the functionalist approach underpinning many design standards (Figure 10.8).

The spatial organisation of a home, including the layout of rooms and the distribution of space, is an important factor in how people experience and use their homes every day. While more space is often equated to greater flexibility, home use is also informed by common housing expectations around privacy, social interaction, or the function of key spaces. Thus, while bigger homes offer more options for adaptation, this does not necessarily translate into greater usability, which is subjective and varies with lifestyle preferences across households and countries.

FIGURE 10.8 A house in England with each room function-specific and sized accordingly (a), and a flat layout in Barcelona with more flexible, equally sized habitable rooms (b).

In fact, occupants ultimately judge whether they have enough space and whether it is usable for them based on how they actually intend to live in it, including the often non-standard furniture they own, personal routines, and whether they find the arrangement and use of space satisfactory. This can be, but does not necessarily have to be, measured in efficient or rational terms. While some prefer an additional small room instead of fewer large rooms, others favour open-plan living. Thus, flexibility is not only a problem of design or more space but also depends on cultural norms, social expectations, household routines, and individual preferences.

In England, homes are measured and valued according to the number of bedrooms rather than overall floor area, influencing what is considered adequate or flexible: a home with more bedrooms is often seen as most desirable, aligning with established expectations of social status, family life, and privacy. This preference has led to higher underoccupancy rates, currently at 69% in England (Office for National Statistics, 2023), meaning that even though English homes might historically have been smaller than in other European countries based on number of bedrooms, this does not necessarily mean that the space-per-person is lower (Ministry of the Interior and Kingdom Relations, 2010). In addition, current average home sizes in England are often more than 10% above those recommended by the Parker Morris standards in use until 1980 (Morgan & Cruickshank, 2014) and continue to grow in size, whereas in many countries new homes have become smaller (Kholodilin, 2025). For example, in Amsterdam, the size of homes has shrunk in the last 20 years from an average of 100 m^2 to 60 m^2 (Reniers & Loerakker, 2023). This shows that housing systems and design governance tend to tailor housing outcomes to shared, cultural housing preferences and respond to prevailing economic conditions.

Design governance also increasingly relies on standardisation to manage risks, control costs, and ensure regulatory compliance. This can result in homes that are designed more by regulations and standards, based on the use of standardised dwelling types and minimum performance requirements, than by architectural intentions. While this arguably produces more efficient and repeatable designs, it prioritises short-term economic returns over housing quality and meeting diverse housing needs.

However, for design governance to go beyond a regulatory culture of compliance and to make housing more equitable, it must be contextual and socially grounded, balancing regulation with design flexibility, standardisation with adaptability, and policy aims with lived realities. At the higher level, there are also at least three important social and environmental motivations that should drive housing design governance approaches and regulatory innovation: (1) recognising lived experience as evidence in housing design and policy; (2) addressing the climate crisis through sustainable and adaptable housing; and (3) using standardisation to promote equity and advance international sustainability goals.

As advocated by this book, there is a need to acknowledge lived experience as an important form of evidence in housing policy and design. This is essential for improving housing equity and quality by giving greater importance to the lifespan and lifecycles of a home that include the everyday reality of housing and needs, rather than focusing solely on the one-off planning and construction of new homes. As the collected evidence shows, everyday use and perceptions of homes are often less determined by efficiency or material characteristics than by individual preferences, socio-cultural expectations, spatial qualities, and past housing experiences. Thus, greater integration of lived experiences into policy and design decisions will particularly benefit populations most affected by poor housing access and dependent on subsidised housing, while disregarding them reinforces existing housing inequalities. This suggests rethinking design as not something that ends with the handover of a project but as a continuing process during the lifespan of a building.

This urgent need for a long-term perspective also extends to addressing the climate crisis. Current and proposed housing standards remain largely insufficient for tackling both the historic and future impacts of climate change, as well as the necessary reductions in resource consumption and both operational and embodied carbon emissions. Many participants in our study greatly supported this agenda and wanted housebuilders to provide energy-efficient homes to improve sustainability and reduce running costs. The sustainability challenge, however, affects not only the design of new homes but also requires the unprecedented retrofitting of existing housing stock and comprehensive lifecycle carbon assessments, raising questions about how maintenance and modernisation can be better integrated into new design processes. For example, although in the UK alone, 29 million homes will have to be retrofitted to meet the legally binding net-zero target by 2050 (UK Green Building Council, 2023), the Future Homes Standard for new housing is widely regarded as insufficient, aiming for only a 75–80% reduction in operational emissions and failing to address embodied carbon (Chartered Institute of Housing, 2020). If necessary policy changes and investment in these areas are delayed and lack ambition, the financial burden on the next generation will increase exponentially.

However, balancing housing quality and environmental concerns can be difficult. While building and designing more environmentally sustainable homes through lowering whole-life carbon emissions, better energy accounting, more efficient land use, and greater biodiversity has wide support across the housing sector, this can be at odds with popular concerns about dwelling size and housing density. For example, larger homes are often associated with improved housing quality and flexibility, but they also increase energy use, carbon emissions, and operational costs – raising questions once again about minimum space standards, albeit this time not from a functional, social, or economic perspective but predominantly from an environmental one. Similarly, while high-density housing can improve land and energy use, in some countries it has negative social connotations and contributes to heat-island effects and heat stress, making neighbourhoods less liveable.

A third key driver to consider in design governance is that housing standardisation has the potential to contribute to achieving UN Sustainable Development Goal 11, related to adequate, safe, and affordable housing and sustainable communities and cities. Standardisation can promote equity by ensuring minimum housing standards and quality, streamlining production, and enabling housing comparability across regions and housing sectors. However, as this book's findings underline, this potential can only be realised when standards and housing standardisation remain responsive to context, cultural differences, household composition, and local housing markets. The challenge lies less in establishing fixed, universal metrics – which often simply foster a culture of compliance with technical standards without necessarily improving long-term housing quality – and more in defining shared social and environmental ambitions that can be realised equitably in diverse housing systems.

At the same time, as the book's cross-national comparison of minimum space standards and housing perceptions shows, what is considered "adequate" or "good" housing is highly contextual, shaped not only by socio-cultural expectations and institutional priorities but also by the constraints of the housing market and economy, which strongly influence both housing satisfaction and perceptions of adequacy. In addition, there are clear differences in what residents, architects, developers, policymakers, and other stakeholders consider a "decent" home. This highlights the need for a more robust, evidence-based common ground and decision-making processes that consider a wider range of technical and social evidence, while also recognising the importance of debate and education in addressing the challenges of reconciling environmental imperatives and socio-economic pressures with diverse notions of housing adequacy and quality.

In both market- and policy-driven housing supply models, the voice of the public – as consumers or voters – holds great power, but requires clearer articulation of social and environmental demands and consensus, which can only be achieved through greater debate and education.

Together, these three highlighted motivations suggest that housing design governance must balance environmental responsibility, social justice, and contextual adaptability, requiring an integration of social and technical housing standards and greater public debate on the socio-environmental role of housing. Standards defined by techno-bureaucratic procedures and cost considerations, in disregarding more human-centred design aspects and ambitions, can undermine design ambitions and limit design quality. Yet the purpose of standards is not only to codify and safeguard minimum requirements but also to drive positive change and raise living standards.

Housing must be recognised as an essential part of broader social infrastructure, intrinsically linked to public health, education, climate action, and strategies for dealing with demographic change. Aligning housing design governance with urban planning and public services can ensure more equitable access to amenities, green spaces, transport, and social services, making homes central to community ecosystems. Well-defined standards can hereby stimulate innovation, experimentation, and improvements by embedding social values such as inclusivity, adaptability, and environmental sustainability into everyday housing practice, shaping expectations of what a "decent" home should be.

At a regulatory level, comprehensive yet flexible regulatory frameworks, such as the Wohnungs-Bewertungs-System (WBS) in Switzerland and, to some extent, the former Housing Quality Indicators (HQIs) in England, represent steps in this direction, though there remains considerable scope to more fully integrate social and environmental values into standard-making. At the institutional level, Peabody's *Design Guide: Strategic & Concept Design Requirements* (Peabody, 2025) is a good example of ambitious internal design standards and governance processes by a housing association. Similarly, the Institut Metropolità de Promoció de Sòl i Gestió Patrimonial's (IMPSOL) design briefs, developed in collaboration with local authorities through design competitions, exemplify good procurement and design practices that translate broad social and environmental priorities into concrete housing standards that can effectively guide practice while also encouraging creative architectural responses.

At the same time, it is important to recognise that the creation and implementation of design standards are inseparable from the housing system in which they operate, since political, institutional, social welfare, and economic agendas determine both the instruments, tools, and enforcement mechanisms in use as well as how standards are defined and who participates in the process. Whether a housing system is unitary or differentiated directly affects how space standards are applied and the resulting sectoral differences in design and housing quality. Housing outcomes are further influenced by how key terms, such as "affordability", are defined and measured: in the Netherlands, affordability is linked to income and translated into rent caps, producing subsidised homes that are genuinely affordable but sometimes too small for larger households; in England, affordability is largely measured against local market values, allowing for larger homes but often excluding low-income groups. Thus, housing design begins with the housing system and how policy terms and regulatory processes are formulated and implemented.

Design governance and regulatory cultures reflect policy and economic priorities that determine housing design outcomes, including their quality, tenure mix, and social integration. Whether stakeholders in a housing system prefer regulatory instruments that are mandatory, voluntary, or framed as best-practice guidance – each with different compliance mechanisms such as inspections, audits, incentives, or penalties – determines if design standards are simply met, exceeded, or ignored. Consequently, the way standards are implemented can matter as much as the formulation of standards themselves in determining their overall efficacy.

Mandatory standards, backed by enforceable regulations and effective monitoring, establish clear benchmarks that can raise overall housing quality if consistently applied. However, voluntary standards that rely on the willingness of stakeholders to adopt them, without offering incentives, are only implemented when they fully align with their institutional mission and objectives. Thus, the effectiveness of standards depends on the authority, capacity, and commitment of those enforcing or adopting them. Unsurprisingly, strong regulatory oversight, dedicated funding support, and aligned policies tend to produce higher-quality homes, whereas weak enforcement will undermine even well-designed standards. This highlights the importance of integrated design governance at both institutional and national levels.

As the book has argued, much subsidised housing is increasingly "designed" by regulations and standards, often with limited direct input from architects. In practice, many housebuilders make key decisions about housing design and quality themselves without directly consulting external design professionals, guided by internal design governance processes, past experiences, and, at times, individual preferences. Our study found that progressive and socially ambitious housebuilders – such as some Swiss housing cooperatives, housing associations like Peabody in England, or public agencies such as IMPSOL – play a central role in raising housing quality and driving design innovation in the social housing sector by providing practical examples and promoting ambitious design standards.

To strengthen design governance, procurement frameworks need to prioritise design quality, social value, and innovation over cost reduction, and support more small-scale and community-led developers. Architects and architectural education should also give greater importance to policymaking and regulatory oversight as an essential part of design expertise. In addition, robust enforcement is needed to uphold standards, particularly in affordable housing, ensuring socially and environmentally ambitious outcomes are not undermined by short-term cost pressures. The importance of these institutional processes and ambitions in determining housing quality and design outcomes is often overlooked by more traditional architectural studies, which tend to focus on designers and architects or history and theory. Equally important are policies that ensure equitable funding for subsidised housing, addressing funding shortfalls and improving the quality of subsidised housing. This should support mixed-tenure and tenure-blind models that improve social inclusion, provide long-term renters' rights, and offer tenure security, fostering community cohesion and long-term investment in homes.

This highlights the limits of relying solely on market mechanisms or voluntary standards to achieve high-quality housing. In market-driven housing systems, self-regulation is often both assumed as the best solution and lobbied for based on the argument that voluntary standards, encouraged by market competition, will deliver better housing outcomes than the lower mandatory limits needed to avoid discouraging private investment and supply. However, evidence suggests that this is not the case, as voluntary standards are typically only adopted if their uptake is financially incentivised. Minimum performance standards, whether voluntary or mandatory, tend to achieve only basic compliance, although when standards are sufficiently detailed yet allow at the same time design and user flexibility, they can also stimulate design innovation, as with the WBS in Switzerland. To ensure housing standards remain effective over time, regular review, testing against design innovation, longitudinal evaluations, and stakeholder input are essential, along with robust enforcement.

As Zurich's cooperative housing demonstrates, decoupling housing from short-term market pressures through subsidised land, cheaper loans, and long-term leases while taking into account diverse community needs and aspirations can result in larger and more varied unit designs and typologies. More broadly speaking, housing procurement and management – or localised housing governance – directly shape housing quality and typological diversity. In contexts like England, where large housing developers or housing associations rely on standardised house types, typological diversity is low. By contrast, in contexts such as Zurich and Spain, where housing projects are often the outcome of design competitions and supported by cooperative development, there is greater design diversity and innovation.

These differences also shape the typological association and social perception of particular housing forms. For example, in rural or suburban England, flats are associated with social housing and therefore frequently designed to resemble houses in order to reduce stigma and visually integrate them with the often-owner-occupied terraced houses in a development. Some of the interviewed residents living in social housing described feeling stigmatised and discriminated against where it was segregated or distinct from other tenures – for example, located on the least desirable sites and built from cheaper materials – thereby visibly reinforcing socio-economic divides.

In contrast, where social housing was fully integrated with other tenures, this was seen as significant for residents' wellbeing and sense of belonging, as it removed real and perceived differences in housing quality: "It feels like you going to a five star-hotel. You don't feel like this is a council housing association property [. . .]. You value yourself more. You say, you know what? You're not different from the other people that are renting" (Figure 10.9).

The strong interrelation between housing quality and the market is also evident in how local housing expectations and demand – the lowest housing standards that consumers will accept – are another key determinant of the quality of housing supply. At the same time, as the examples of market-driven housing systems such as those in England or Chile show, this tendency to provide only minimum acceptable housing quality necessitates extensive policy interventions and state subsidies to address basic, systemic market failures in housing supply or quality and improve affordability, while often still producing little or no social housing. This highlights the need for consumer education and pressure to raise awareness of and improve the various dimensions of housing quality.

(a) (b)

FIGURE 10.9 Tenure-blind developments. (a) Friary Park in London for Peabody by Chapman Taylor (2024). (b) Cornellà de Llobregat in Barcelona for IMPSOL by Peris + Toral Arquitectes (2021).

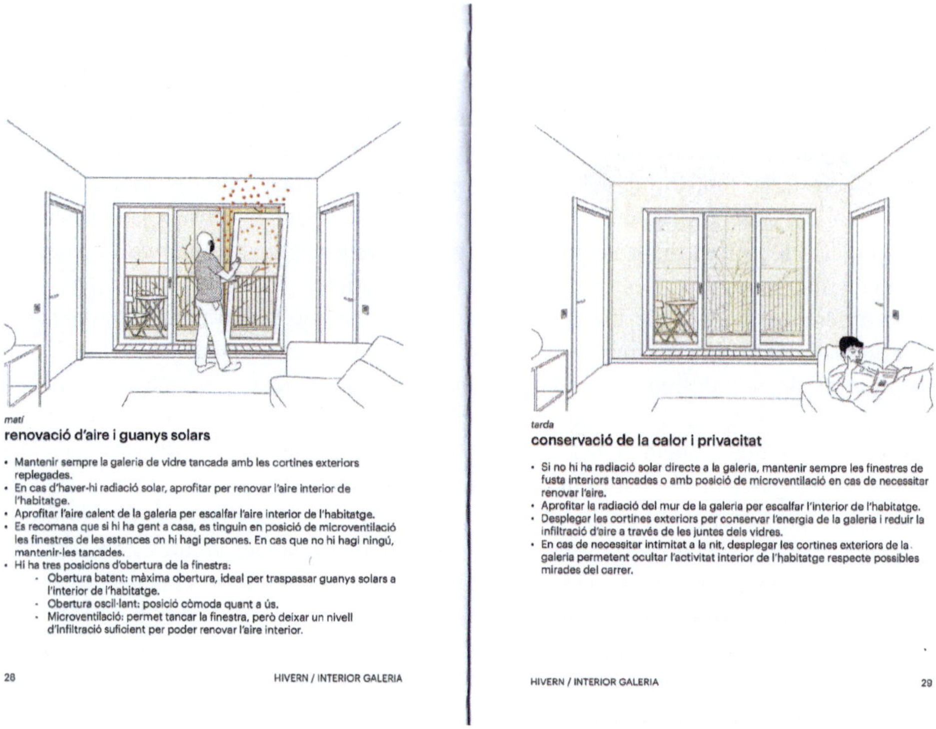

matí

renovació d'aire i guanys solars

- Mantenir sempre la galeria de vidre tancada amb les cortines exteriors replegades.
- En cas d'haver-hi radiació solar, aprofitar per renovar l'aire interior de l'habitatge.
- Aprofitar l'aire calent de la galeria per escalfar l'aire interior de l'habitatge.
- Es recomana que si hi ha gent a casa, es tinguin en posició de microventilació les finestres de les estances on hi hagi persones. En cas que no hi hagi ningú, mantenir-les tancades.
- Hi ha tres posicions d'obertura de la finestra:
  - Obertura batent: màxima obertura, ideal per traspassar guanys solars a l'interior de l'habitatge.
  - Obertura oscil·lant: posició còmoda quant a ús.
  - Microventilació: permet tancar la finestra, però deixar un nivell d'infiltració suficient per poder renovar l'aire interior.

28 HIVERN / INTERIOR GALERIA

tarda

conservació de la calor i privacitat

- Si no hi ha radiació solar directe a la galeria, mantenir sempre les finestres de fusta interiors tancades o amb posició de microventilació en cas de necessitar renovar l'aire.
- Aprofitar la radiació del mur de la galeria per escalfar l'interior de l'habitatge.
- Desplegar les cortines exteriors per conservar l'energia de la galeria i reduir la infiltració d'aire a través de les juntes dels vidres.
- En cas de necessitar intimitat a la nit, desplegar les cortines exteriors de la galeria permetent ocultar l'activitat interior de l'habitatge respecte possibles mirades del carrer.

HIVERN / INTERIOR GALERIA 29

FIGURE 10.10 Information on "air renewal and solar gains" (a) and "conservation of heat and privacy" (b) for a housing project in Montgat, Barcelona.

Source: DATAAE & AMB IMPSOL, *Efficient and sustainable housing user manual: 39 dwellings in Montgat, 18J* (2023).

Public engagement and education remain important to improve both the real and perceived quality of housing after a project is completed. For example, the social housing provider IMPSOL in Barcelona continues to work with residents and architects after the building is complete. Its projects are all tenure-blind and typically include informal assembly spaces and tenant guides (Figs. 10.10–10.11). This approach helps residents understand a building's design intentions and technical functions, fostering pride while also providing practical guidance on how to live in and care for their homes. In the Sant Just Desvern development by DATAAE and Xavier Vendrell Studio (2024), where air conditioning is prohibited, residents are shown how to use natural ventilation effectively. Similarly, in the Modulus Matrix housing project by Peris + Toral Arquitectes (2021), which uses a timber frame construction, residents are instructed on how to care for and maintain the wood (Figure 10.12).

Growing public pressure is critical to building support for social housing and ensuring the effective use of public funds. While demand-side subsidies have become the norm in market-driven housing policy contexts such as England (Gibb, 2024), supply-side subsidies deliver far greater financial and social returns. In England, private landlords receive more than six times the government's annual investment in new affordable housing through Universal Credit and Housing Benefit payments that subsidise tenants' rent (New Economics Foundation, 2024). Yet, despite this massive public investment in private renting rather than in new social housing, each

FIGURE 10.11 Assembly space in a social housing project by IMPSOL in Gáva, Barcelona, by HARQUITECTES (2022).

social home generates nearly three times the net economic and social value of a private rented home (Clifford et al., 2024; PricewaterhouseCoopers LLP, 2024).

Despite significant housing subsidies in the contexts studied, apart from the Netherlands, where 29% of the housing stock is classified as social housing, the proportion of both existing and new-built homes for social rent generally falls in the low single digits, pointing to the problematic undersupply of social or rent-controlled housing. This social housing crisis is often marginalised by a focus on the much wider housing affordability problem.

The persistent failures of market-driven housing systems that have dominated since the 1980s to deliver enough social or affordable housing underscores the need for an intergenerational housing perspective that recognises housing as a long-term and shared asset. A recognition of the systemic limitations of market-driven supply and a necessary return to social housing are slowly re-emerging, both in countries with a strong state-led housing welfare history, such as China, and in so-called neoliberal housing contexts like England. This suggests a need for change in housing design governance and a return to more rent-controlled homes to provide long-term affordable and socially equitable homes that are less susceptible to changes in housing markets.

A key challenge determining design governance approaches is the balance between the quantity and quality of housing supplied and maintained, often depending on the cost of building new homes, the scale of the housing deficit, available subsidies, and rent-generated income. It is therefore as much an economic as it is a socio-political problem – of how much a society is

(a) (b)

FIGURE 10.12 IMPSOL social housing developments in Sant Just Desvern by DATAAE and Xavier Vendrell Studio (2024, a) and Cornellà de Llobregat by Peris + Toral Arquitectes (2021, b), Barcelona.

invested in housing as supporting private wealth or public and collective social assets. Given the strong association of property ownership with financial and familial security, and thus with continuously increasing property values and investment, economic considerations have come to outweigh social concerns and ambitions. This has resulted in a focus on lower-cost – but not necessarily affordable – housing, with increasing public funding spent on subsidising private homeownership, supporting households entering the property ladder, and stimulating housing demand, rather than on building and maintaining public or collectively owned housing. Consequently, this has created a vicious cycle, driving up the cost of both private and subsidised homes, often without improving housing quality.

However, design governance and how standards are defined and negotiated can play a critical role in mediating the balance between a greater housing supply and greater housing quality, and can determine whether standards include quality measures that support positive change and ensure homes are both environmentally and socially sustainable. Consequently, housing quality tends to be a greater focus in less market-driven economies and in wealthier countries with a stable housing supply, where standards can more readily shape long-term social and design outcomes.

What emerges from the studies and analyses in the book is a call for a paradigm shift in how housing design governance is understood and practised. Rather than viewing it as a techno-bureaucratic constraint, it should be reimagined as a process that enables design ambitions while integrating social sustainability and intergenerational equity into housing delivery and maintenance. A decent home, therefore, is not merely about meeting a minimum standard but about actively creating and enhancing social, environmental, and communal wellbeing: a home capable of evolving with its inhabitants and their communities over time. Realising this ambition requires embedding community engagement and participatory governance into housing policy and design processes, ensuring residents' voices shape standards from inception to post-occupancy, in order for lived experience to become an integral part of design governance.

This calls for a redefinition of housing quality that not only recognises technical adequacy but also explicitly supports wellbeing, adaptability, inclusivity, and cultural relevance. Transitioning from prescriptive minimum standards to flexible, outcome- and performance-based criteria will allow housing to respond more dynamically to evolving household needs and life stages. This requires more adaptable and less function-specific design that can, for example, accommodate multi-generational living, ageing in place, and remote work. A shift away from nuclear-family-centric housing typologies towards context-sensitive and culturally inclusive housing models is critical for reflecting social diversity.

Building on the insights from the book and its study of design governance and subsidised housing, the following interrelated policy priorities and practical actions outline ways to support the creation of decent homes (Table 10.1). These aim to align design standards and governance more closely with lived experience, embed socio-cultural values, and strengthen environmental responsibility in the development of long-term, sustainable, and adaptable housing. At the same time, they encourage the strategic use of standardisation to foster housing equity and access without standardising everyday life.

TABLE 10.1 Policy and actions matrix

Policy priority	*Rationale*	*Practical actions*
Embedding participatory governance	Home-use and housing perception studies indicate a misalignment between technical housing standards and lived realities. Engaging residents in decision-making and review processes can improve the long-term relevance and quality of housing outcomes.	Mandate participatory processes at planning, design, and regulatory stages, including structured resident engagement, co-design workshops, and systematic POE feedback to inform policy and standard-setting. Ensure alignment of design governance at national and institutional levels.
Resident-centred design and quality redefinition	Evidence from home-use and lived experience studies shows that housing quality must be human-centred and address wellbeing, adaptability, inclusivity, access, cultural appropriateness, and rights-based definitions of adequate housing.	Implement flexible outcome- and performance-based approaches to design quality standards informed by POEs, ethnographic research, co-design workshops, and home-use studies to meet evolving household needs and daily practices.
Flexible and adaptable layouts	While standardisation supports basic housing quality, it can fail to accommodate evolving household structures and needs.	Promote flexibility in the use and distribution of space by deregulating room functions and accommodating socially and culturally diverse households, including ageing, multi-generational, and non-traditional family households.

(*Continued*)

TABLE 10.1 (Continued)

Policy priority	*Rationale*	*Practical actions*
Social, environmental, and cultural value integration	Housing quality extends beyond technical performance to include wellbeing, social and environmental sustainability, and cultural appropriateness, requiring long-term and intergenerational perspectives when assessing housing design and costs.	Integrate long-term usability, social values, spatial adaptability, and environmental performance into design standards, assessment, and enforcement, including strategies for energy efficiency, resource conservation, and climate adaptation strategies.
Context-sensitive governance	National standards cannot fully reflect local social, cultural, and spatial contexts. When procurement processes, funding, and tenure arrangements are not aligned with social and environmental priorities, they can undermine design quality, equity, and social inclusivity.	Enable local adaptation of standards based on site conditions, institutional legacies, and market realities. Embed procurement strategies that prioritise design quality, social value, and innovation, and support mixed-tenure housing, long-term leases, and equitable funding mechanisms.
Historical and comparative learning	Past housing standards and governance experiences provide valuable lessons for contemporary policy and design.	Draw on historical examples (e.g., Parker Morris standards) and cross-country comparisons to inform evidence-based updates to design governance frameworks.
Post-occupancy learning loop	Static standards risk overlooking how homes are actually used and experienced over time, limiting long-term housing quality standards and adaptability.	Establish iterative feedback loops through POEs, longitudinal studies, design innovation, and stakeholder input to continuously refine standards and maintain functional, adaptable, and socially valuable homes.
Integration with broader social agendas	Housing is a core component of public and social infrastructure, intersecting with health, education, ageing, and climate strategies.	Align housing design standards and governance with urban planning and public service strategies to ensure access to public infrastructure and amenities, and ensure funding and tenure policies promote inclusivity and social cohesion.

Acknowledgements

This conclusion builds on the work and chapters contributed to this book by my colleagues, Alvaro Arancibia, Lucia Alonso Aranda, Seyithan Özer, and Consuelo Albornoz Marambio. I am grateful for their valuable insights and feedback, which have informed the synthesis and arguments presented in this chapter.

REFERENCES

Aalbers, M. B. (2016). *The Financialization of Housing: A political economy approach*. Taylor & Francis.

Adams, D., Croudace, R., & Tiesdell, S. (2011). Design codes, opportunity space, and the marketability of new housing. *Environment and Planning B: Planning and Design, 38*(2), 289–306. https://doi.org/10.1068/b36055

AEDES. (2025, February 28). *Huurbeleid in 2025*. https://aedes.nl/huurbeleid-en-betaalbaarheid/huurbeleid-2025

Airey, J., Scruton, R., & Wales, R. (2018). *Building more, building beautiful: How design and style can unlock the housing crisis*. Policy Exchange. https://policyexchange.org.uk/wp-content/uploads/2018/09/Building-More-Building-Beautiful-for-print.pdf

Allen, J. G., & Macomber, J. D. (2020). *Healthy buildings: How indoor spaces drive performance and productivity*. Harvard University Press.

Alonso Aranda, L., & Jacoby, S. (2023). The impact of housing design and quality on wellbeing: Lived experiences of the home during COVID-19 in London. *Cities & Health, 7*(4), 615–627. https://doi.org/10.1080/23748834.2022.2103391

Alonso Aranda, L. (2024). The influence of space standards on housing typologies: The evolution of the nuclear family dwelling in England. *Urban Planning, 9*, 7758. https://doi.org/10.17645/up.7758

Alves, S. (2020). Divergence in planning for affordable housing: A comparative analysis of England and Portugal. *Progress in Planning, 156*, 100536. https://doi.org/10.1016/j.progress.2020.100536

Amati, M. (2022). *The city and the super-organism: A history of naturalism in urban planning*. Palgrave Macmillan.

Andreas, P., Jung, K., & Cachola Schmal, P. (Eds.). (2019). *Housing for all: Building catalogue*. DOM Publishers.

Anguita, A., & Becerra Ibañez, J. (2024). Estrategias e implementaciones habitacionales del Estado chileno. Revista de la Red de Intercátedras de Historia de América Latina Contemporánea, *11*(20), 1–20.

Appolloni, L., & D'Alessandro, D. (2021). Housing spaces in nine European countries: A comparison of dimensional requirements. *International Journal of Environmental Research and Public Health, 18*(8), 4278. https://doi.org/10.3390/ijerph18084278

Arancibia, A. (2024). The lifestyles of space standards: Concepts and design problems. *Urban Planning, 9*, 7800. https://doi.org/10.17645/up.7800

Arancibia Tagle, A. A. (2013). *The social housing centre: Type, urban form, policy-making, and standards in Santiago* (Master's thesis, Architectural Association School of Architecture, The Open University).

Arancibia Tagle, A. A. (2017). *The social re-signification of housing: A design guide for Santiago de Chile* (Doctoral thesis). Architectural Association School of Architecture, The Open University.

Aravena, A., & Iacobelli, A. (2012). *Elemental: Incremental housing and participatory design manual*. Hatje Cantz.

Arellano, J. P. (1985). Políticas sociales en Chile: una revisión histórica. CIEPLAN.

Arnold, J. E., Graesch, A. P., Ragazzini, E., & Ochs, E. (2017). *Life at home in the twenty-first century: 32 Families open their doors*. Cotsen Institute of Archaeology Press. https://escholarship.org/uc/item/1vq382j7.

Atria, F. (2013). The political theory of neoliberalism. In F. Atria, G. Larraín, J. M. Benavente, J. Couso, & A. Joignant (Eds.), *The other model: From the neoliberal order to the public regime* (pp. 15–61). Random House Mondadori.

Aydemir, A. Z., & Jacoby, S. (2022). Architectural design research: Drivers of practice. *The Design Journal*, *25*(4), 657–674. https://doi.org/10.1080/14606925.2022.2081303

Ball, M. (1983). *Housing policy and economic power: The political economy of owner occupation*. Routledge.

Barcelona Datastore. (2025) *Average household size [Data Set]* https://portaldades.ajuntament.barcelona.cat/en/statistics/yq3rps6n7t

Barenstein, J. D., Koch, P., Sanjines, D., Assandri, C., Matonte, C., Osorio, D., & Sarachu, G. (2022). Struggles for the decommodification of housing: The politics of housing cooperatives in Uruguay and Switzerland. *Housing Studies*, *37*(6), 955–974. https://doi.org/10.1080/02673037.2021.1966392

Barton, J. R., & Ramírez, M. I. (2019). The role of planning policies in promoting urban sprawl in intermediate cities: Evidence from Chile. *Sustainability*, *11*(24), 7165.

Beck, M. E., & Arnold, J. E. (2009). Gendered time use at home: An ethnographic examination of leisure time in middle-class families. *Leisure Studies*, *28*(2), 121–142. https://doi.org/10.1080/02614360902773888.

Beijing Municipal Commission of Housing and Urban–Rural Development. (2010). 关于印发〈北京市公共租赁住房建设技术导则(试行)〉的通知 [Notice on issuing the *Beijing technical guidelines for public rental housing construction (trial)*].

Bentley, D. (2017, February 6). *What role for council building? A market-focused solution is unlikely to deliver the homes we need*. Civitas. https://www.civitas.org.uk/2017/02/06/what-role-for-council-building-a-market-focused-solution-is-unlikely-to-deliver-the-homes-we-need/

Bentley-Gockmann, D. (2020). *RIBA health and safety guide* (2nd ed.). RIBA Publishing.

Beswick, J., Imilan, W., & Olivera, P. (2019). Access to housing in the neoliberal era: A new comparativist analysis of the neoliberalisation of access to housing in Santiago and London. *International Journal of Housing Policy*, *19*(3), 288–310.

Biblioteca del Congreso Nacional de Chile. (2014). *Sistemas de postulación y asignación de la vivienda social*. https://www.bcn.cl/obtienearchivo?id=repositorio/10221/37143/1/BCN__Sistema_de_postulacion_y_asignacion_de_la_vivienda_social__def.pdf

Bidwells. (2024). *The productivity engine*. https://www.bidwells.co.uk/insights-reports-events/productivity-engine-report/

Birkbeck, D. (1999, May 1). Top 50 homebuilders. *Building*. https://www.building.co.uk/top-50-home-builders/4025.article

Birkbeck, D., Kruczkowski, S., Collins, P., & Quinn, B. (2014). *Building for Life 12: The Sign of a Good Place to Live*. Building for Life Partnership.

Blackwell, T., & Bengtsson, B. (2021). The resilience of social rental housing in the United Kingdom, Sweden and Denmark. How institutions matter. *Housing Studies*, *38*(2), 269–289. https://doi.org/10.1080/02673037.2021.1879996

Blackwell, T., & Kohl, S. (2018). Historicizing housing typologies: Beyond welfare state regimes and varieties of residential capitalism. *Housing Studies*, *34*(2), 298–318. https://doi.org/10.1080/02673037.2018.1487037

Blanchar, C. (2020, April 18). Confinarse en Barcelona: 87 metros cuadrados de diferencia entre barrios ricos y pobres. El País. https://elpais.com/espana/catalunya/2020-04-18/confinarse-en-barcelona-87-metros-cuadrados-de-diferencia-entre-barrios-ricos-y-pobres.html

Blessing, A. (2015). Repackaging the poor? Conceptualising neoliberal reforms of social rental housing. *Housing Studies*, *31*(2), 149–172. https://doi.org/10.1080/02673037.2015.1070799

Booth, C. (1889). *Life and labour of the people in London*. Williams and Norgate.

Booth, P. (2003). *Planning by consent: The origins and nature of British development control*. Routledge. https://doi.org/10.4324/9780203402153

Bordass, B., & Leaman, A. (2005). Making feedback and post-occupancy evaluation routine 1: A portfolio of feedback techniques. *Building Research & Information*, *33*(4), 347–352. https://doi.org/10.1080/09613210500162016

Bouwbesluit 2012. (2012). Besluit van 27 november 2012 tot vaststelling van het Bouwbesluit 2012. Wetten.nl. https://wetten.overheid.nl/jci1.3:c:BWBR0030461

Boverket. (2019). *Boverket's building regulations – Mandatory provisions and general recommendations (BBR)*. Swedish National Board of Housing, Building and Planning. https://www.boverket.se/globalassets/publikationer/dokument/2019/bbr-2011-6-tom-2018-4-english-2.pdf

Bowley, M. (1947). *Housing and the State, 1919–1944*. G. Allen & Unwin.

Bramley, G. (2018). *Housing supply requirements across Great Britain*. Crisis and National Housing Federation. https://www.crisis.org.uk/media/239700/crisis_housing_supply_requirements_across_great_britain_2018.pdf

Bray, D. (2018). *Social space and governance in urban China*. Stanford University Press.

BRE Group. (2021). *The cost of poor housing in England*. https://files.bregroup.com/research/BRE_Report_the_cost_of_poor_housing_2021.pdf

British Columbia (BC) Housing. (2019). *Design guidelines and construction standards*. https://www.bchousing.org/publications/BCH-Design-Guidelines-Construction-Standards.pdf

Brown, F. E., & Steadman, J. P. (1987). The analysis and interpretation of small house plans: Some contemporary examples. *Environment and Planning B: Planning and Design*, *14*(4), 407–438. https://doi.org/10.1068/b140407

Brown, P., Armitage, R., Monchuk, L., Newton, D., & Robson, B. (2021). TEN: The COVID-19 lockdown and the impact of poor-quality housing on occupants in the UK. In B. Doucet, P. Filion, & R. van Melik (Eds.), *Volume 2: Housing and home* (pp. 109–119). Bristol University Press. https://doi.org/10.51952/9781529218985.ch010.

Bruey, A. (2014). *La "vivienda social" en Chile: Entre la cuestión social y la cuestión de Estado (1925–1973)*. LOM Ediciones.

Buckle, C., Williams, E., & Formston, D. (2024, November 14). *English Housing Supply Update Q3 2024*. Savills. https://www.savills.co.uk/research_articles/229130/369264-0

Building Better, Building Beautiful Commission. (2020). *Living with beauty: Promoting health, well-being and sustainable growth*. UK, Ministry of Housing, Communities & Local Government. https://assets.publishing.service.gov.uk/media/5e3191a9ed915d0938933263/Living_with_beauty_BBBBC_report.pdf

Bullock, N. (2002). *Building the post-war world: Modern architecture and reconstruction in Britain*. Routledge.

Bulmer, M. (2015). *The uses of social research: Social investigation in public policy-making*. Taylor & Francis.

Bundesamt für Statistik. (2024a). *Wohnungsgrösse*. https://www.bfs.admin.ch/bfs/de/home/statistiken/bau-wohnungswesen/wohnungen/groesse.html

Bundesamt für Statistik. (2024b). *Belegungsdichte nach Altersklassen der Haushaltsmitglieder, nach Kanton* [Data set]. https://www.bfs.admin.ch/bfs/de/home/statistiken/bau-wohnungswesen/wohnungen.assetdetail.32329691.html

Bundesamt für Statistik. (2025). *Rents, home ownership rate and owners of rented dwellings* [Data set]. https://www.bfs.admin.ch/news/en/2025-0573

Bundesamt für Wohnungswesen. (2015). *Wohnbauten planen, beurteilen und vergleichen: Wohnungs-Bewertungs-System (WBS), Ausgabe 2015*. https://backend.bwo.admin.ch/fileservice/sdweb-docs-prod-bwoadminch-files/files/2025/04/10/077d5b44-d479-4d85-8ff2-243455fa4e92.pdf

Burdon, T. (2017). *Modernising social policy: Unravelling new labour's welfare reforms*. Routledge.

Burnett, J. (1986). *A social history of housing: 1815–1985*. Routledge.

Burns, L. S., & Grebler, L. (1977). *The housing of nations: Analysis and policy in a comparative framework*. Palgrave Macmillan.

Caixa (2017). Programa Minha Casa Minha Vida - FAR/FDS Especificações Mínimas. https://www.google.com/url?q=https://autogestao.unmp.org.br/wp-content/uploads/2014/09/Espec_Min_CAIXA_UH_Fase3_-v07.pdf

Caldera Sánchez, A. (2012). *Building blocks for a better-functioning housing market in Chile* (OECD Economics Department Working Papers No. 943). OECD Publishing.

Campbell, C. (1715). *Vitruvius Britannicus, or, The British architect: Containing the plans, elevations, and sections of the regular buildings, both publick and private, in Great Britain; with variety of new designs*. [The author].

Carmona, M. (2001). *Housing design quality: Through policy, guidance and review*. Routledge.

Carmona, M. (2017). The formal and informal tools of design governance. *Journal of Urban Design*, *22*(1), 1–36. https://doi.org/10.1080/13574809.2016.1234338

Carmona, M., Bento, J., & Gabrieli,T. (2023). *Urban Design Governance: Soft Powers and the European Experience*. UCL Press. https://discovery.ucl.ac.uk/id/eprint/10166947/1/Urban-Design-Governance.pdf

Carmona, M., Gallent, N., & Sarkar, R. (2010). *Space standards: The benefits*. University College London.
Carrasco, S., & O'Brien, D. (2022). Re-thinking Elemental's incremental housing: Residential satisfaction and resident-driven adaptations in Villa Verde, Chile. *urbe. Revista Brasileira de Gestão Urbana, 14*, e20210171.
Castañeda, T., & Quiroz, J. (1986). Las políticas de vivienda en Chile y su impacto redistributivo. *Estudios Públicos*, *23*, 165–198.
Centraal Bureau voor de Statistiek. (2024). Voorraad woningen; eigendom, type verhuurder, bewoning, regio [Data set]. Retrieved September 2, 2025, from https://opendata.cbs.nl/statline/#/CBS/nl/dataset/82900NED/table?fromstatweb
Centraal Bureau voor de Statistiek. (2025). Voorraad woningen; gemiddeld oppervlak; woningtype, bouwjaarklasse, regio [Data set]. https://opendata.cbs.nl/statline/#/CBS/nl/dataset/82550NED/table?dl=AEC73
Central Housing Advisory Committee, Housing Manual Sub-committee. (1951). *Housing for special purposes: Supplement to the Housing Manual 1949*. H.M. Stationery Office.
Centre for Ageing Better. (2025). *The state of ageing 2025: Summary report*. https://ageing-better.org.uk/sites/default/files/2025-03/The-State-of-Ageing-2025-interactive-summary.pdf
Centro de Políticas Públicas UC. (2021). Evaluación de la integración social y territorial de proyectos DS19. https://politicaspublicas.uc.cl/web/content/uploads/2023/07/Informe-Cuantitativo-Evaluacion-de-la-Integracion-Social-y-Territorial-de-Poyectos-DS19_VF.pdf
Centro de Políticas Públicas UC. (2023). Informe evaluativo: Programa de Integración Social y Territorial DS19. https://politicaspublicas.uc.cl/web/content/uploads/2023/06/Informe-EVALUACION-DE-LA-INTEGRACION-SOCIAL-Y-TERRITORIAL-DE-PROYECTOS-D.S.19.pdf
Chadwick, E. (1842). *Report on the sanitary conditions of the labouring population of Great Britain: A supplementary report on the results of a special inquiry into the practice of interment in towns. Made at the request of Her Majesty's principal secretary of state for the Home department*. Her Majesty's Stationery Office. https://archive.org/details/reportonsanitary00chadrich
Chang, H.-J. (1997). The economics and politics of regulation. *Cambridge Journal of Economics*, *21*(6), 703–728. http://www.jstor.org/stable/23599768
Chartered Institute of Housing. (2020, February). *CIH response to the Future Homes Standard consultation*. https://www.cih.org/media/axtoql5o/cih-response-to-future-homes-consultation-feb20.pdf.
Chen, H. (2024). A study on Shenzhen's Public Housing Policy to address the brain drain problem: A sample of affordable rental housing. *Open Journal of Social Sciences*, *12*(1), 49–61. https://doi.org/10.4236/jss.2024.121005
Chey, K. (2017). *Multi-unit housing in urban cities: From 1800 to present day*. Routledge.
ChinaCensus.org. (2025, May 24). Shenzhen city population data and population census data and age pyramid. ChinaCensus.org. https://chinacensus.org/prefecture/shenzhen-city-population-data-and-population-census-data-and-age-pyramid
City of Vancouver. (2025). *Housing design and technical guidelines*. https://guidelines.vancouver.ca/guidelines-technical-housing-design.pdf
Clapham, D. (2019). *Remaking housing policy: An international study*. Routledge.
Clapham, D., Foye, C., & Christian, J. (2017). The concept of subjective well-being in housing research. *Housing, Theory and Society*, *35*(3), 261–280. https://doi.org/10.1080/14036096.2017.1348391.
Clapham, D., & Foye, C. (2019). *How should we evaluate housing outcomes?* UK Collaborative Centre for Housing Evidence. https://housingevidence.ac.uk/publications/how-should-we-evaluate-housing-outcomes/.
Clifford, B., & Ferm, J. (2021). Planning, regulation and space standards in England: From 'homes for heroes' to 'slums of the future'. *Town Planning Review*, *92*(5), 537–560. https://doi.org/10.3828/tpr.2021.11
Clifford, J., Hulbert, A., & Yeung, D. (2024). *The value of a social tenancy: Updating and developing the model in 2024*. Sonnet Advisory & Impact. https://sonnetimpact.co.uk/reports/the-value-of-a-social-tenancy-saves-78-billion-annually/
Code de la construction et de l'habitation. (2019). https://www.legifrance.gouv.fr/codes/section_lc/LEGITEXT000006074096/LEGISCTA000006177428/.
Commission for Architecture and the Built Environment. (2010). *Improving the design of new housing: What role for standards?. https://www.housinglin.org.uk/_assets/Resources/Housing/Support_materials/Other_reports_and_guidance/CABE_improving-the-design-of-new-housing.pdf*

Cooper, A., & Kurzer, P. (2023). Similar origins – Divergent paths: The politics of German and Dutch housing markets. *German Politics*, *32*(2), 341–360. https://doi.org/10.1080/09644008.2020.1764541

Cooper, M. A. (2010). Protecting our past: Political philosophy, regulation, and heritage management in England and Scotland. *The Historic Environment: Policy & Practice*, *1*(2), 143–159. https://doi.org/10.1179/175675010x12817059865961

Cooper, M. (2017). *Family values: Between neoliberalism and the new social conservatism*. Zone Books.

Cortés-Urra, V., Fuster-Farfán, R., & Monkkonen, P. (2023). Addressing housing deficits from a multi-dimensional perspective: A review of Chilean housing policy. *International Journal of Housing Policy*, *23*(5), 548–567.

Cousins, M. (2009). *Design quality in new housing: Learning from the Netherlands*. Taylor & Francis.

Crawford, D. (Ed.). (1975). *A decade of British housing, 1963–1973*. Architectural Press.

Cromarty, H., & Barton, C. (2022, December 20). *Housing conditions in the private rented sector (England)* (House of Commons Library Report No. 7328). https://researchbriefings.files.parliament.uk/documents/CBP-7328/CBP-7328.pdf

Croydon Council. (2008, June). *Room sizes in new housing developments: Findings and recommendations* [Scrutiny investigation report]. https://www.croydon.gov.uk/sites/default/files/articles/downloads/roomsizes.pdf

Cui, J., & Arundel, R. (2025). The changing social structure of housing tenures through China's successive urban housing reforms. *Housing Studies*, *40*(2), 279–301. https://doi.org/10.1080/02673037.2024.2329138

Czischke, D., & van Bortel, G. (2023). An exploration of concepts and polices on 'affordable housing' in England, Italy, Poland and The Netherlands. *Journal of Housing and the Built Environment*, *38*(1), 283–303. https://doi.org/10.1007/s10901-018-9598-1

DATAAE & AMB IMPSOL. (2023). *Efficient and sustainable housing user manual: 39 dwellings in Montgat, 18J*.

Davidovici, I. (2017). Renewable principles in Henry Astley Darbishire's Peabody Estates, 1864 to 1885. In P. Guillery & D. Kroll (Eds.), *Mobilising housing histories: Learning from London's past for a sustainable future* (pp. 57–73). RIBA Publishing.

Davies, C. (2005). *The prefabricated home*. Reaktion Books.

de Alliantie. (2017, December 21). *Functioneel en ruimtelijk programma van eisen deel uitmakend van het standaard programma van eisen voor de ontwikkeling van huurwoningen van de Alliantie*.

de Certeau, M. (1984). *The practice of everyday life* (S. Rendall, Trans.). University of California Press.

de Rijksoverheid. (2025). *Wat is het verschil tussen een sociale huurwoning, een middenhuurwoning en een huurwoning in de vrije sector?* Ministerie van Algemene Zaken. https://www.rijksoverheid.nl/onderwerpen/huurwoning-zoeken/vraag-en-antwoord/wat-is-het-verschil-tussen-een-sociale-huurwoning-een-middenhuurwoning-en-een-huurwoning-in-de-vrije-sector

Debrunner, G., & Hartmann, T. (2020). Strategic use of land policy instruments for affordable housing – Coping with social challenges under scarce land conditions in Swiss cities. *Land Use Policy*, *99*, 104993. https://doi.org/10.1016/j.landusepol.2020.104993

Decret 13/2010, de 2 de febrer, del Pla per al dret a l'habitatge 2009–2012, 13/2010 (Diari Oficial de la Generalitat de Catalunya, 11 Feb. 2010). https://portaljuridic.gencat.cat/ca/document-del-pjur/?documentId=537639.

Decret 141/2012, de 30 d'octubre, pel qual es regulen les condicions mínimes d'habitabilitat dels habitatges i la cèdula d'habitabilitat, 141/2012 (Diari Oficial de la Generalitat de Catalunya, 1 Nov. 2012). https://portaljuridic.gencat.cat/eli/es-ct/d/2012/10/30/141.

Decreto Supremo N° 49: Aprueba reglamento del programa fondo solidario de elección de Vivienda. (2012). https://www.bcn.cl/leychile/Navegar?idNorma=1039424

Decreto Supremo 19: Reglamenta programa de integración social y territorial, y modifica Ds N° 1, (v. Y U.), de 2011, reglamento del sistema integrado de subsidio habitacional. (2016). https://www.bcn.cl/leychile/navegar?idNorma=1092547

Demiddel, S. F., Torrent, H., Galeno, C., & Exss, U. (2023). La forma urbana de la CORMU: Proyecto urbano y tipología arquitectónica. In *ISUF-H 2023 International Seminar on Urban Form - Hispanic, VII Congreso ISUF-H Chile: Forma urbana para un buen vivir* (pp. 90–97). FADEU-PUC.

Department for Communities and Local Government. (2006a, June). *A decent home: Definition and guidance for implementation*. https://assets.publishing.service.gov.uk/media/5a7968b740f0b63d72fc5926/138355.pdf

Department for Communities and Local Government. (2006b). *The Code for Sustainable Homes: A step change in sustainable home building practice.*

Department for Communities and Local Government. (2007). *Building a greener future: Policy statement.*

Department for Communities and Local Government. (2015, March). *Technical housing standards – nationally described space standard.* https://www.gov.uk/government/publications/technical-housing-standards-nationally-described-space-standard

Department for Levelling Up, Housing & Communities. (2015). *Approved Document M: Access to and use of buildings – Volume 1: Dwellings.* https://assets.publishing.service.gov.uk/media/5a7f8a82ed915d74e622b17b/BR_PDF_AD_M1_2015_with_2016_amendments_V3.pdf

Department for Levelling Up, Housing & Communities. (2022a). *English Housing Survey: Private rented sector, 2020–21 (Private Rented Sector Report).* https://assets.publishing.service.gov.uk/media/68764f47352c290d20dcaea1/EHS_20-21_PRS_Report.pdf.

Department for Levelling Up, Housing & Communities. (2022b). *Live tables on affordable housing supply* [Data set]. Retrieved 16 August 2025, from https://www.gov.uk/government/statistical-data-sets/live-tables-on-affordable-housing-supply

Department for Levelling Up, Housing & Communities. (2023). *English Housing Survey 2022 to 2023: headline report.* https://www.gov.uk/government/collections/english-housing-survey-2022-to-2023-headline-report.

Department for Levelling Up, Housing and Communities. (2024a, November 21). *Affordable housing supply in England: 2023 to 2024.* https://www.gov.uk/government/statistics/affordable-housing-supply-in-england-2023-to-2024/affordable-housing-supply-in-england-2023-to-2024

Department for Levelling Up, Housing & Communities. (2024b). *Social housing lettings in England, tenancies: April 2022 to March 2023.* https://www.gov.uk/government/statistics/social-housing-lettings-in-england-april-2022-to-march-2023/social-housing-lettings-in-england-tenancies-april-2022-to-march-2023

Department for Levelling Up, Housing and Communities. (2025a). *Live tables on dwelling stock including vacants: Table 104 by tenure, England (historical series)* [Statistical data set]. Retrieved 4 September 2025, from https://www.gov.uk/government/statistical-data-sets/live-tables-on-dwelling-stock-including-vacants

Department for Levelling Up, Housing and Communities. (2025b). *Live table 244: Permanent dwellings started and completed, by tenure, England, historical calendar year series* [Data set]. Retrieved 4 September 2025, from https://assets.publishing.service.gov.uk/media/68541f0816eefd7361e989e3/LiveTable244.ods

Department for Work and Pensions. (2024, January 9). *Millions of renters better off with boost to housing support* [Press release]. https://www.gov.uk/government/news/millions-of-renters-better-off-with-boost-to-housing-support

Department of Housing, Planning and Local Government. (2018). *Sustainable urban housing: Design standards for new apartments: Guidelines for planning authorities.* https://www.gov.ie/en/department-of-housing-local-government-and-heritage/publications/design-standards-for-new-apartments-dsfna-2018/

Doling, J. (1997). *Comparative housing policy: Government and housing in advanced industrialized countries.* Red Globe Press.

Donzelot, J. (1997). *The policing of families.* Johns Hopkins University Press.

Dove, C. (2020). *Radical housing: Designing multi-generational and co-living housing for all.* RIBA Publishing.

Drury, A. (1998). *Standards and quality in development: A good practice guide.* National Housing Federation.

Drury, A. & Somers, E. (2010) *Room to swing a cat? A survey of dwelling sizes in London and the South East.* HATC Limited.

Dutta, A. (2014). Mammoths, Inc.: Nature, architecture, and the debt, part 2. *Aggregate*, *2*. https://doi.org/10.53965/asrh7672

Duyne Barenstein, J., & Koch, P. (2022, August 1). *How accessible and affordable are Swiss housing co-operatives? Insights and reflections on housing policies in Switzerland* (Working Paper 2020/03). ETH Wohforum – ETH CASE. https://doi.org/https://doi.org/10.3929/ethz-c-000783009

Eichler, W. (2025, February 18). *Average wait for council housing nearly at three years.* LocalGov. https://www.localgov.co.uk/Average-wait-for-council-housing-nearly-at-three-years/61958

Elsinga, M., & Hoekstra, J. (2005). Homeownership and housing satisfaction. *Journal of Housing and the Built Environment*, *20*(4), 401–424. https://doi.org/10.1007/s10901-005-9023-4.

Emmitt, S. (2013). *Architectural Technology: Research and Practice.* Wiley.

Eurostat. (2025a). *Average household size* [Data set]. https://doi.org/10.2908/ILC_LVPH01
Eurostat. (2025b). *Average size of dwelling by household composition and degree of urbanisation* [Data set]. https://doi.org/10.2908/ILC_LVHO31
Eurostat. (2025c). *Distribution of population by tenure status, type of household and income group* [Data set]. https://doi.org/10.2908/ILC_LVHO02
Evans, G. W., Wells, N. M., & Moch, A. (2003). Housing and mental health: A review of the evidence and a methodological and conceptual critique. *Journal of Social Issues*, *59*(3), 475–500. https://doi.org/10.1111/1540-4560.00074.
Evans, R. (1978). Figures doors passages. *Architectural Design*, *48*(4), 267–278.
Evans, R. (1997). *Translations from drawing to building and other essays*. Architectural Association.
Fang, Y., Liu, Z., & Chen, Y. (2020). Housing inequality in urban China: Theoretical debates, empirical evidences, and future directions. *Journal of Planning Literature*, *35*(1), 41–53. https://doi.org/10.1177/0885412219880898
Ferm, J., & Raco, M. (2020). Viability planning, value capture and the geographies of market-led planning reform in England. *Planning Theory & Practice*, *21*(2), 218–235. https://doi.org/10.1080/14649357.2020.1754446
Fletcher, B. (1871) *Model houses for the industrial classes*. Longmans, Green and Co.
Flynn, L. B., & Montalbano, G. (2024). Housing regime typologies and their discontents: A systematic literature review. *Housing, Theory and Society*, *41*(2), 127–146. https://doi.org/10.1080/14036096.2023.2265370
Forshaw, J. H., & Abercrombie, P. (1943). *County of London plan*. Macmillan and Co. Ltd.
Foucault, M. (2007). *Security, territory, population: Lectures at the Collège de France, 1977–78* (M. Senellart, Ed.; G. Burchell, Trans.). Palgrave Macmillan.
Friedman, B. (Ed.). (1938). *Flats: Municipal and private enterprise*. Ascot Gas Water Heaters Ltd.
Fuster-Farfán, X. (2019). Las políticas de vivienda social en Chile en un contexto de neoliberalismo híbrido. *EURE: Revista Latinoamericana de Estudios Urbanos y Regionales*, *45*(135), 5–26.
Gallent, N., Madeddu, M., & Mace, A. (2010). Internal housing space standards in Italy and England. *Progress in Planning*, *74*(1), 1–52. https://doi.org/10.1016/j.progress.2010.04.001
García, R. (2018). La vivienda popular en Chile urbano (1880–1930): Un estado de la cuestión interdisciplinario. *Historia*, *51*(1), 227–251.
Gaskell, S. M. (1986). *Model housing: From the great exhibition to the festival of Britain*. Mansell.
Generalitat de Catalunya. (n.d.). *Definició i característiques*. gencat.cat/. Retrieved 8 July 2025, from http://habitatge.gencat.cat/ca/ambits/Habitatge-proteccio-oficial/hpo/
Generalitat de Catalunya. (2010). *Decret 13/2010, de 2 de febrer, del Pla per al dret a l'habitatge del 2009–2012*. Diari Oficial de la Generalitat de Catalunya, núm. 5565, 11 de febrer de 2010. https://portaljuridic.gencat.cat/ca/document-del-pjur/?documentId=537639
Generalitat de Catalunya. (2012). *Decret 141/2012, de 30 d'octubre, pel qual es regulen les condicions mínimes d'habitabilitat dels habitatges i la cèdula d'habitabilitat*. Diari Oficial de la Generalitat de Catalunya, núm. 6245, 2 de novembre de 2012. https://portaljuridic.gencat.cat/ca/document-del-pjur/?documentId=619728
Gibb, K. (2024). *Housing subsidy's long-term shift from supply to demand and what might be done about it*. UK Collaborative Centre for Housing Evidence. https://housingevidence.ac.uk/wp-content/uploads/2024/06/Housing-subsidys-long-term-shift-from-supply-to-demand-and-what-might-be-done-about-it-v2.pdf
Gil, D. (2015). Right to Housing and Regulatory Minimalism in Chile. In *SELA 2015 Conference* (pp. 1–20). Yale Law School.
Gil, D. (2019). Law and inclusive urban development: Lessons from Chile's enabling markets housing policy regime. *American Journal of Comparative Law*, *67*(3), 587–636.
Gilbert, A. (2004). Helping the poor through housing subsidies: Lessons from Chile, Colombia and South Africa. *Habitat International*, *28*(1), 13–40.
Glasgow City Council (2019) The Glasgow Standard. https://www.glasgow.gov.uk/media/6184/The-Glasgow-Standard-A-Design-Schedule-for-Affordable-Warmth-Housing-in-Glasgow/pdf/The_Glasgow_Standard_200519.pdf
Goodchild, B. (2016). *Homes, cities and neighbourhoods: Planning and the residential landscapes of modern Britain*. Routledge.
Goodchild, B., & Furbey, R. (1986). Standards in housing design: A review of the main changes since the Parker Morris report (1961). *Land Development Studies*, *3*(2), 79–99. https://doi.org/10.1080/02640828608723903

Goodchild, B., & Karn, V. (1997). Standards, quality control and house building in the UK. In P. Williams (Ed.), *Directions in housing policy* (pp. 156–174). Paul Chapman.
Government of South Australia, Housing Authority. (2020). *Form of Housing: 1.1 House Design Guide: Design guidelines for sustainable housing & liveable neighbourhoods*. https://www.housing.sa.gov.au/__data/assets/pdf_file/0019/116290/1.1-House-Design-Guide_Rev-2020.pdf
Greater London Authority. (2010). *London Housing Design Guide. Interim Edition*. https://www.london.gov.uk/sites/default/files/interim_london_housing_design_guide.pdf.
Greater London Authority. (2023a, June). *Housing Design Standards LPG. London Plan Guidance*. https://www.london.gov.uk/sites/default/files/2023-06/Housing%20design%20standards%20LPG.pdf.
Greater London Authority (2023b). London Plan Guidance – Housing Design Standards. Greater London Authority. https://www.london.gov.uk/sites/default/files/2023-06/Housing%20design%20standards%20LPG.pdf
Greater London Council. (1977) *Preferred dwelling plans*. Architectural Press.
Greene, M. (2004). *The progressive housing program in Chile: 1990–2002*. Inter-American Development Bank.
Greenhalgh, P. (1990). *Modernism in design*. Reaktion Books.
Guillery, P., Donald, A., & Kendall, D. (2004). *The small house in eighteenth-century London: A social and architectural history*. Yale University Press.
Habinteg Housing Association. (2011). Lifetime homes design guide. IHS BRE Press.
Halfpenny, W. (1757). *The modern builder's assistant; or, a concise epitome of the whole system of architecture*. James Rivington and J. Fletcher; Robert Sayer.
Hansson, A. G., & Lundgren, B. (2018). Defining social housing: A discussion on the suitable criteria. *Housing, Theory and Society*, *36*(2), 149–166. https://doi.org/10.1080/14036096.2018.1459826
Harloe, M. (1995). *The people's home? Social rented housing in Europe & America*. Blackwell.
Harrison, J. (2017). The origin, development and decline of back-to-back houses in Leeds, 1787–1937. *Industrial Archaeology Review*, *39*(2), 101–116. https://doi.org/10.1080/03090728.2017.1398902
HATC. (2006). *Housing space standards*. Greater London Authority.
Heckmann, O., Schneider, F., & Zapel, E. (Eds.). (2017). *Floor plan manual housing* (5th rev. ed.). Birkhäuser.
Hegedüs, J., Lux, M., & Teller, N. (Eds.). (2012). *Social housing in transition countries*. Routledge. https://doi.org/10.4324/9780203095904
Heynen, H., & Baydar, G. (2005). *Negotiating domesticity: Spatial productions of gender in modern architecture*. Routledge.
Hidalgo, R. (2000). El papel de las leyes de fomento de la edificación obrera y la Caja de la Habitación en la política de vivienda social en Chile, 1931–1942. *Revista INVI*, *15*(39), 97–118.
Hidalgo, R. (2005). De la salubridad a la vivienda social: transformaciones del rol del Estado en el Santiago del siglo XX. *Revista INVI*, *20*(52), 85–112.
Hidalgo, R. (2019). *La vivienda social en Chile y la construcción del espacio urbano en Santiago del siglo XX* (2nd ed.). RIL Editores.
Hidalgo Dattwyler, R., Errázuriz Infante, T., & Booth Pinochet, R. (2005). Las viviendas de la beneficencia católica en Santiago: Instituciones constructoras y efectos urbanos (1890–1920). *Historia (Santiago)*, *38*(2), 327–366.
Hobhouse, H. (1994). Public housing in poplar: The inter-war years. In H. Hobhouse (Ed.), *Survey of London: Volumes 43 and 44, poplar, blackwall and isle of dogs* (pp. 23–37). London County Council. http://www.british-history.ac.uk/survey-london/vols43-4/pp23-37
Hochstenbach, C., & Ronald, R. (2020). The unlikely revival of private renting in Amsterdam: Re-regulating a regulated housing market. *Environment and Planning A: Economy and Space*, *52*(8), 1622–1642. https://doi.org/10.1177/0308518X20913015
Hoekstra, J. (2005). Is there a connection between welfare state regime and dwelling type? An exploratory statistical analysis. *Housing Studies*, *20*(3), 475–495. https://doi.org/10.1080/02673030500062509
Hoekstra, J. (2010). *Divergence in European welfare and housing systems*. Delft University Press.
Hofmann, F., & Ospina, P. (2010). *Housing finance in Chile: Instruments, actors, and policies* (IDB Working Paper No. 312). Inter-American Development Bank.
Hollow, M. (2014). The age of affluence revisited: Council estates and consumer society in Britain, 1950–1970. *Journal of Consumer Culture*, *16*(1), 279–296. https://doi.org/10.1177/1469540514521083
Hong Kong Housing Authority. (2015). 構件式單位設計 *Modular flat design*. Hong Kong: Housing Authority.

Hooper, A., & Nicol, C. (2000). Design practice and volume production in speculative housebuilding. *Construction Management and Economics*, *18*(3), 295–310. https://doi.org/10.1080/014461900370663
House of Lords Science and Technology Committee. (2005). *Building regulations* (2nd Report of Session 2005–06, HL Paper 21–I). https://publications.parliament.uk/pa/ld200506/ldselect/ldsctech/21/2102.htm
Housing, Communities and Local Government Committee. (2018). *Building more social housing* (HC 173). https://publications.parliament.uk/pa/cm5801/cmselect/cmcomloc/173/17308.htm
Housing Corporation. (1983). *Design and contract criteria*. London: Housing Corporation.
Housing Corporation. (1993). *Scheme development standards*. London: Housing Corporation.
Housing Corporation. (1999). *Housing quality indicators*. London: Housing Corporation.
Housing Corporation. (2007). *Design and quality standards*. London: Housing Corporation.
Housing Corporation. (2008, April). *721 Housing Quality Indicators (HQI) Form (Version 4) [PDF]*. London: Housing Corporation. Retrieved from https://assets.publishing.service.gov.uk/media/5a7d4f82e5274a2af0ae2d57/721_hqi_form_4_apr_08_update_20080820153028.pdf
Huang, R. (2022, April 28). 迈向"住有宜居", 深圳可探索哪些新路径? [Towards "livable housing": What new paths can Shenzhen explore?]. 综研观察. China Development Institute. Retrieved from http://www.cdi.com.cn/Article/Detail/17816
Hur, M., & Nasar, J. L. (2014). Physical upkeep, perceived upkeep, fear of crime and neighborhood satisfaction. *Journal of Environmental Psychology*, *38*, 186–194. https://doi.org/10.1016/j.jenvp.2014.02.001.
Huurcommissie. (n.d.). *Rent Check: Self-contained accommodation*. Retrieved July 28, 2025, from https://huurprijscheck.huurcommissie.nl/en/self-contained-accommodation
Iglesias, R., Porter, L., & Hidalgo, R. (2014). Understanding density in an uneven city: Contradictions of densification in Santiago de Chile. *Sustainability*, *6*(9), 5876–5899.
Imrie, R. (2006). *Accessible housing: Quality, disability and design*. Routledge.
Imrie, R., & Street, E. (2009). Risk, regulation and the practices of architects. *Urban Studies*, *46*(12), 2555–2576. https://doi.org/10.1177/0042098009344231
Inside Housing. (2022, October 5). *How much does Section 106 really contribute to affordable housing supply?* https://www.insidehousing.co.uk/insight/how-much-does-section-106-really-contribute-to-affordable-housing-supply-78091
Institut Català del Sòl [INCASOL] (2019). *Estàndards d'habitatge social: Criteris de disseny i programes funcionals*. https://incasol.gencat.cat/web/.content/01_home_continguts/actualitat/190521_estandarsHabitatge.pdf
Instituto Nacional de Estadísticas. (1952). *XII Censo General de Población y I de Vivienda*.
Instituto Nacional de Estadísticas. (1960). *VII Censo de Población y II de Vivienda*.
Instituto Nacional de Estadísticas. (1970). *VIII Censo de Población y III de Vivienda*.
Instituto Nacional de Estadísticas. (1971). Estadísticas de edificación y vivienda en Chile.
Instituto Nacional de Estadistica. (2023). Viviendas familiares principales convencionales según régimen de tenencia (capitales de provincia y municipios de más de 50.000 habitantes) [Data set]. https://www.ine.es/jaxi/Tabla.htm?tpx=59529&L=0
Inter-American Development Bank. (2004). *Reforming Latin American housing markets: A guide for policy analysis* (IDB Publications No. 312). Inter-American Development Bank.
IPA. (2023, June 21). *New IPA TouchPoints 2023 data*. https://ipa.co.uk/news/touchpoints-2023
Islam, A. (2022). Work-from/at/for-home: CoVID-19 and the future of work – A critical review. *Geoforum*, *128*, 33–36. https://doi.org/10.1016/j.geoforum.2021.11.018.
Jacoby, S. (2020). Urban design and spatialised governmentality: Collective forms in China. In S. Jacoby & J. Cheng (Eds.), *The socio-spatial design of community and governance: Interdisciplinary urban design in China* (pp. 3–15). Springer.
Jacoby, S. & Cheng, J. (Eds.). (2020). *The socio-spatial design of community and governance: Interdisciplinary urban design in China*. Springer.
Jacoby, S., & Alonso Aranda, L. (2022). Home use and experience during COVID-19 in London: Problems of housing quality and design. *Sustainability*, *14*(9), 5355. https://doi.org/10.3390/su14095355
Jacoby, S., Arancibia, A., & Alonso Aranda, L. (2022). Space standards and housing design: typological experimentation in England and Chile. *The Journal of Architecture*, *27*(1), 94–126. https://doi.org/10.1080/13602365.2022.2045340
Jacoby, S., & Özer, S. (2024). Housing norms and standards: The design of everyday life. *Urban Planning*, *9*, Article 8339. https://doi.org/10.17645/up.8339

Jenkins, P., & Smith, H. (2001). An institutional approach to analysis of state capacity in housing systems in the developing world: Case studies in South Africa and Costa Rica. *Housing Studies*, *16*(4), 485–507. https://doi.org/10.1080/02673030120066563

Kadi, J., & Lilius, J. (2024). The remarkable stability of social housing in Vienna and Helsinki: A multidimensional analysis. *Housing Studies*, *39*(7), 1607–1631. https://doi.org/10.1080/02673037.2022.2135170

Karakusevic, P., & Batchelor, A. (2017). *Social housing: Definitions and design exemplars*. RIBA Publishing.

Karn, V., & Sheridan, L. (1994). *New homes in the 1990s: A study of design, space and amenity in housing association and private sector production*. University of Manchester.

Karn, V., & Nystrom, L. (1998). The control and promotion of quality in new housing design: The context of European integration. In M. Kleinman, W. Matznetter, & M. Stephens (Eds.), *European Integration and Housing Policy*. Routledge.

Kast, F. (2009). *Housing Assistance and Student Achievement in Low-Income Households in Chile*. Harvard University Joint Center for Housing Studies. https://www.jchs.harvard.edu/sites/default/files/w09-8_kast.pdf

Kearns, A. (2022). Housing space and occupancy standards: Developing evidence for policy from a health and wellbeing perspective in the UK context. *Building Research & Information*, *50*(7), 722–737. https://doi.org/10.1080/09613218.2021.2024756

Kemeny, J. (1995). *From public housing to the social market: Rental policy strategies in comparative perspective*. Routledge.

Kholodilin, K. A. (2025, August 8). *The end of the era of increasing home sizes*. RPubs. https://rpubs.com/Konstantin_Xo/Decline.

Koch, P. (2021, May 20). *Working Paper 3.1: The Role of Housing Cooperatives in Switzerland*. ZHAW. https://digitalcollection.zhaw.ch/server/api/core/bitstreams/a447dad1-167d-40ea-b661-0c75e929defa/content

Koppelman, C. M. (2018). *"Property Owners and Not Proletarians": Housing Policy and the Contested Production of Neoliberal Subjects in Chile and Brazil* (Doctoral dissertation, University of California, Berkeley).

Kraniotis, L., & de Jong, W. (2021, April 24). Sociale huurwoning? In zeker een kwart van de gemeenten wacht je meer dan 7 jaar. *NOS*. https://nos.nl/op3/artikel/2377995

Kusnetzoff, D. (1974). *Exposición del Ministro de Vivienda y Urbanización* (Act 143a, p. 1). Biblioteca del Congreso Nacional, Chile.

Labour Party. (2024). *Kickstart economic growth*. https://labour.org.uk/change/kickstart-economic-growth/

Langley, B. (1740). *The city and country builder's and workman's treasury of designs: Or, the art of drawing and working the ornamental parts of architecture. Illustrated by upwards of four hundred grand designs*. Printed by J. Ilive for Thomas Langley.

Langley, B. (1790). *The builder's complete assistant: Or, a library of arts and sciences, absolutely necessary to be understood by builders and workmen in general*. I. and J. Taylor.

Larkin, J., & Hughes, P. (Eds.). (1973). *Stuart Royal Proclamations: Royal Proclamations of King James I, 1603–1625*. Oxford University Press.

Lawner, M. (2023). La vivienda como acto revolucionario: Testimonio de la Unidad Popular. Revista de Arquitectura y Urbanismo, *45*(2), 15–32.

Lawrence, R. J. (1983). The comparative analyses of homes: Research method and application. *Social Science Information*, *22*(3), 461–485. https://doi.org/10.1177/053901883022003006

Lawrence, R. J. (1985). Design by legislation: The ideological nature of house planning in the United Kingdom, 1918–1961. *Habitat International*, *9*(2), 123–140. https://doi.org/10.1016/0197-3975(85)90014-1

Le Corbusier. (1927). *Towards a new architecture* (F. Etchells, Trans.). Architectural Press. (Original work published 1923).

Leoni, G. (Ed.). (1715). *The architecture of A. Palladio in four books: Containing a short treatise of the five orders, and the most necessary observations concerning all sorts of building: As also the different construction of private and publick houses, high-ways, bridges, market-places, xystes, and temples, with their plans, sections, and uprights*. London: Printed by John Watts.

Leopold, E., & Bishop, D. (1983). Design philosophy and practice in speculative housebuilding: Part 1. *Construction Management and Economics*, *1*(2), 119–144. https://doi.org/10.1080/01446198300000010

Levitt, D., & McCafferty, J. (2018). *The housing design handbook: A guide to good practice* (2nd ed.). Routledge.

Ley, A. J. (1990). *Building control: its development and application 1840–1936* [MPhil thesis, The Open University].
Ley, A. J. (2000). *A history of building control in England and Wales 1840–1990*. RICS Books.
LGBl. Nr. 11/1930 zuletzt geändert durch LGBl. Nr. 37/2023 [Bauordnung für Wien] (2023). https://www.ris.bka.gv.at/eli/lgbl/WI/1930/11/P119/LWI40016463
Local Government Association. (2022). *Improving health and wellbeing through housing: A high impact change model*. Local Government Association.
Local Government Board. (1919). *Manual on the preparation of state-aided housing schemes*. H.M. Stationery Office.
Local Government Boards for England and Wales, and Scotland. (1918). *Report of the committee appointed by the President of the Local Government Board and the Secretary for Scotland to consider questions of building construction in connection with the provision of dwellings for the working classes in England and Wales, and Scotland, and report upon methods of securing economy and despatch in the provision of such dwellings* [Tudor Walters Report] (Cmd. 9191). HMSO. https://books.google.co.uk/books?id=0Hw3AQAAMAAJ
London County Council. (1956). *Housing type plans*. London County Council Architect's Department.
López, M., & Correa, C. (2007). Las nuevas periferias metropolitanas de la vivienda social en Chile. *EURE, Revista Latinoamericana de Estudios Urbano Regionales*, *33*(98), 5–23.
Lucas, R. (1997). The tax on bricks and tiles, 1784–1850: Its application to the country at large and, in particular, to the County of Norfolk. *Construction History*, *13*, 29–55.
Lund, B. (2017). *Understanding housing policy*. Policy Press.
Lynch, G. (2010). *The history of gauged brickwork*. Taylor & Francis.
M'Sirdi, N., Namaane, A., Howlett, R. J., & Jain, L. C. (Eds.). (2012). *Sustainability in Energy and Buildings. Proceedings of the 3rd International Conference on Sustainability in Energy and Buildings (SEB'11)* (Smart Innovation, Systems and Technologies, 12). Springer.
Madigan, R., & Milner, J. (1999). Access for all: Housing design and the Disability Discrimination Act 1995. *Critical Social Policy*, *19*(3), 396–409. https://doi.org/10.1177/026101839901900307
Malpass, P., & Murie, A. (1987). *Housing policy and practice*. Macmillan.
Manoochehri, J. (2012). *The politics of social housing in Britain*. Peter Lang.
Marmot, M. (2020). *Health equity in England: The Marmot Review 10 years on*. UCL Institute of Health Equity & The Health Foundation.
Marrs, C. (2015, January 26). Third of biggest housebuilders don't employ own architects. *Architects Journal*. https://www.architectsjournal.co.uk/archive/third-of-biggest-housebuilders-dont-employ-own-architects
Marsh, A., Gordon, D., Heslop, P., & Pantazis, C. (2000). Housing deprivation and health: A longitudinal analysis. *Housing Studies*, *15*(3), 411–428. https://doi.org/10.1080/02673030050009258
Marshall, D., Worthing, D., Heath, R., & Dann, N. (2013). *Understanding housing defects*. Taylor & Francis.
Matthews, J. (1774). *An abstract of the Act of Parliament made in the fourteenth year of his present Majesty King George III*. W. Strahan and M. Woodfall.
McCabe, J. (2020, July 17). *Top 50 Biggest Builders 2020*. Inside Housing. https://www.insidehousing.co.uk/insight/top-50-biggest-builders-2020-67141
McIntosh, I., & Wright, S. (2018). Exploring what the notion of 'lived experience' offers for social policy analysis. *Journal of Social Policy*, *48*(3), 449–467. https://doi.org/10.1017/S0047279418000570
McMullan, L., Osborne, H., Blight, G., & Duncan, P. (2021, March 31). UK housing crisis: How did owning a home become unaffordable? *The Guardian*. https://www.theguardian.com/business/ng-interactive/2021/mar/31/uk-housing-crisis-how-did-owning-a-home-become-unaffordable
McNelis, S. (2016). Researching housing in a global context: New directions in some critical issues. *Housing, Theory and Society*, *33*(4), 1–21. https://doi.org/10.1080/14036096.2016.1167121
Merrett, S. (1979). *State housing in Britain*. Routledge.
Ministerio de Desarrollo Social. (2018). *CASEN 2017: Síntesis de resultados*. Ministerio de Desarrollo Social.
Ministerio de Desarrollo Social. (2023). *CASEN 2022*. https://observatorio.ministeriodesarrollosocial.gob.cl/encuesta-casen-2022
Ministerio de Desarrollo Social & El Centro de Estudios de Ciudad y Territorio. (2025). *Resultados Vivienda Censos 2024, 2017 y 2002*. Ministerio de Desarrollo Social.

Ministerio de Obras Públicas. (1959, septiembre 5). Reglamento Especial de Viviendas Económicas (Decreto Supremo No. 1.608). Biblioteca del Congreso Nacional de Chile.

Ministerio de Transportes, Movilidad y Agenda Urbana, Dirección General de Vivienda y Suelo. (2020). Boletín Especial Vivienda Social 2020. https://www.mivau.gob.es/urbanismo-y-suelo/suelo/observatorio-de-vivienda-y-suelo

Ministerio de Vivienda y Urbanismo. (1984). Memoria 1984.

Ministerio de Vivienda y Urbanismo. (2004). Chile, un siglo de política en vivienda y barrio: Elementos para una política de vivienda social.

Ministerio de Vivienda y Urbanismo. (2005). Historia de la vivienda social en Chile: 1906–2006.

Ministerio de Vivienda y Urbanismo. (2012). *Decreto Supremo N° 49, de 2012, que aprueba el reglamento del programa Fondo Solidario de Elección de Vivienda. Biblioteca del Congreso Nacional de Chile.* https://www.bcn.cl/leychile/navegar?idNorma=1039424

Ministerio de Vivienda y Urbanismo. (2013). Política habitacional: Avances y desafíos.

Ministerio de Vivienda y Urbanismo. (2014). Plan de regeneración de conjuntos habitacionales.

Ministerio de Vivienda y Urbanismo. (2016). Decreto Supremo N° 19 (V. y U.), de 2016, que reglamenta el Programa de Integración Social y Territorial y modifica el DS N° 1 (V. y U.), de 2011, Reglamento del Sistema Integrado de Subsidio Habitacional. Biblioteca del Congreso Nacional de Chile. https://www.minvu.gob.cl/wp-content/uploads/2020/07/DS-19-de-2016_Integracion-Social-y-Territorial_23jul20.pdf

Ministerio de Vivienda y Urbanismo. (2017). Cuadro normativo y tabla de espacios y usos mínimos para el mobiliario. (Versión 2017). https://www.minvu.gob.cl/wp-content/uploads/2019/05/Res_7712-16062017-Cuadro-Normativo.pdf

Ministerio de Vivienda y Urbanismo. (2023). *Déficit habitacional cuantitativo y cualitativo según Casen 2022* [Datos oficiales]. Centro de Estudios MINVU.

Ministerio de Vivienda y Urbanismo – Centro de Estudios Ciudad y Territorio. (2023). Historia y patrimonio del MINVU*: 1970–1973.*

Ministerio de Vivienda y Urbanismo de Chile. (2005). Reglamento Fondo Solidario de Vivienda: Cuadro normativo D.S. 174.

Ministerio de Vivienda y Urbanismo de Chile. (2012). Tabla de espacios y usos mínimos para el mobiliario del DS N°1 e itemizado técnico para proyectos del título I del DS N°1.

Ministry of Health. (1939). *Houses we live in*. HMSO.

Ministry of Health. (1949). *Housing manual 1949*. H.M. Stationery Office.

Ministry of Health, & Great Britain. Ministry of Public Building and Works. (1944). *Housing manual 1944*. H.M. Stationery Office.

Ministry of Housing. (1952). *Houses: Second supplement to the Housing manual 1949*. H.M. Stationery Office.

Ministry of Housing. (1953). *Houses: Third supplement to the Housing manual 1949*. H.M. Stationery Office.

Ministry of Housing and Local Government. (1944). *Design of dwellings: Report of the Design of dwellings subcommittee of the Central housing advisory committee appointed by the minister of health and Report of a study group of the Ministry of town and country planning on site planning and layout in relation to housing* [Dudley Report]. HMSO. https://wellcomecollection.org/works/ks3vhaaa

Ministry of Housing and Local Government. (1951). *Housing manual 1949: Technical appendices*. H.M. Stationery Office.

Ministry of Housing and Local Government. (1958). *Flats and houses 1958: Design and economy*. H.M. Stationery Office.

Ministry of Housing and Local Government. (1961). *Homes for today and tomorrow* [Parker Morris Report]. HMSO. https://archive.org/details/op1266209-1001/page/n7/mode/2up

Ministry of Housing and Local Government. (1963). *Design Bulletin 8: Dimensions and components for housing: with special reference to industrialised building*. HMSO.

Ministry of Housing and Local Government. (1966). *Design bulletin 11: Old people's flatlets at Stevenage: An account of the project with an appraisal*. HMSO.

Ministry of Housing and Local Government. (1968a). *Design bulletin 6: Space in the home (metric edition)*. HMSO.

Ministry of Housing and Local Government. (1968b). *Design bulletin 2: Grouped flats for old people: A sociological study – Metric edition*. HMSO.

Ministry of Housing and Local Government. (1968c). *Design bulletin 14: House planning: A guide to user needs*. H.M. HMSO.

Ministry of Housing and Local Government. (1969). *Design bulletin 17: The family at home – A study of households in Sheffield*. HMSO.

Ministry of Housing, Communities and Local Government. (2017). *The role of international evidence in housing policy: A report from the Ministry of Housing, Communities and Local Government to the Public Accounts Committee*.

Ministry of Housing, Communities and Local Government. (2020a). *English Housing Survey 2018: size of English homes - fact sheet*. https://www.gov.uk/government/statistics/english-housing-survey-2018-size-of-english-homes-fact-sheet

Ministry of Housing, Communities and Local Government. (2020b). *Planning for the future: White Paper*. https://assets.publishing.service.gov.uk/media/601bce418fa8f53fc149bc7d/MHCLG-Planning-Consultation.pdf

Ministry of Housing, Communities and Local Government. (2024a, November 21). *Affordable housing supply in England: 2023 to 2024*. https://www.gov.uk/government/statistics/affordable-housing-supply-in-england-2023-to-2024/affordable-housing-supply-in-england-2023-to-2024

Ministry of Housing, Communities and Local Government. (2024b, December 12). *National Planning Policy Framework*. https://assets.publishing.service.gov.uk/media/67aafe8f3b41f783cca46251/NPPF_December_2024.pdf

Ministry of Housing, Communities and Local Government. (2025, December 4). Chapter 1: Profile of *Households* and *Dwellings* (English Housing Survey 2024–25: Headline findings on demographics and household resilience). GOV.UK. https://www.gov.uk/government/statistics/chapters-for-english-housing-survey-2024-to-2025-headline-findings-on-demographics-and-household-resilience/chapter-1-profile-of-households-and-dwellings

Ministry for Housing, Communities and Local Government, Department for Levelling Up, Housing & Communities, & Regulator of Social Housing. (2022, December 14). *Policy statement on rents for social housing*. https://www.gov.uk/government/publications/direction-on-the-rent-standard-from-1-april-2020/policy-statement-on-rents-for-social-housing

Ministry of the Interior and Kingdom Relations. (2010). *Housing statistics in the European Union 2010*. http://www.iut.nu/wp-content/uploads/2017/07/Housing-Affordability-Housing-Statistics.pdf.

Mitchell, S. (1988). *Victorian Britain, an Encyclopedia*. Garland Science.

Molina, C., Kent, M., Hall, I., & Jones, B. (2020). A data analysis of the Chilean housing stock and the development of modelling archetypes. *Energy and Buildings*, *206*, 109568. https://doi.org/10.1016/j.enbuild.2019.109568

Montealegre, P., Rodríguez, F., & López, C. (2023). Tipologías habitacionales en el Chile moderno: vivienda serializada y racionalización constructiva en los años 60. *Cuadernos de Historia de la Vivienda*, *2*(2), 45–68.

Montgomery, H. (2022). Lessons from Chile's 'enabling markets' housing policy regime. *Housing Studies*, *37*(5), 731–752.

Morales, C., Gutiérrez, P., Henríquez, D., Campos, P., & Wilde, N. (2024). Evaluación de una política de integración social a partir de las percepciones de los involucrados: un caso de estudio en el norte de Chile. *Economía y Política*, *11*(1), 5–35.

Morgan, M., & Cruickshank, H. (2014). Quantifying the extent of space shortages: English dwellings. *Building Research & Information*, *42*(6), 710–724. https://doi.org/10.1080/09613218.2014.922271.

Mullins, D. & Murie, A. (2006). *Housing policy in the UK*. Palgrave Macmillan.

Muñoz, T. L. (2011). Evolución del espacio doméstico en 'blocks' de vivienda social: autoconstrucción y vulnerabilidad en conjuntos de vivienda básica. Revista CIS – Un Techo para Chile, *4*, 1–18.

Murray, C., & Clapham, D. (2015). Housing policies in Latin America: Overview of the four largest economies. *International Journal of Housing Policy*, *15*(3), 347–364. https://doi.org/10.1080/14616718.2015.1055090.

Muthesius, S. (1982). *The English terraced house*. Yale University Press.

National Building Agency. (1965). *Generic Plans: Two and Three Storey Houses*.

National Bureau of Statistics of China. (2020). *China population census yearbook – 2020 (Seventh National Population Census)*. National Bureau of Statistics of China. https://www.stats.gov.cn/sj/pcsj/rkpc/7rp/indexch.htm

National Housing Federation. (n.d.). *About social housing*. Retrieved September 12, 2025, from https://www.housing.org.uk/about-housing-associations/about-social-housing/

Navarro, M. (2005). Housing finance policy in Chile: The last 30 years. *Land Lines*, *17*(3), 12–14.
Netwerk Conceptueel Bouwen & Aedes. (2024, March). De woonstandaard: Leidraad voor het conceptueel uitvragen aan conceptaanbieders middels product-marktcombinaties (Versie 3.1). https://www.conceptueelbouwen.nl/_files/ugd/b56e43_f7b4c04498b1458dba0cdd2ad0dc53ab.pdf
Neufert, E. (1926). *Bauentwurfslehre* [Architect's Data]. Bauwelt-Verlag.
New Economics Foundation. (2024, January 31). *Government subsidising private landlords £70 billion over next five years*. https://neweconomics.org/2024/01/government-subsidising-private-landlords-70bn-over-next-five-years
New York City Department of Buildings. (2022). *2022 NYC building code, Chapter 12: Interior environment*. https://codes.iccsafe.org/content/NYNYCBC2022P1/chapter-12-interior-environment
Nicholson, P. (1812–1819). *An architectural dictionary: Containing a correct nomenclature and derivation of the terms employed by architects, builders, and workmen; exhibiting, in a perspicuous point of view, the theory and practice of the various branches of architecture, in carpentry, joinery, masonry, bricklaying, and their dependence on each other; the science necessary to understand; and the lives of the principal architects. The whole forming a complete guide to the science of architecture and the art of building*. J. Barfield.
Nicholson, P. (1823). *The new practical builder and workman's companion: Containing a full display and elucidation of the most recent and skilful methods pursued by architects and artificers in the various departments of carpentry, joinery, bricklaying, masonry, slating, plumbing, painting, glazing, plastering, etc.; including also new treatises on geometry, theoretical and practical, trigonometry, conic sections, perspective, shadows, and elevations; a summary of the art of building; copious accounts of building materials, strength of timber, cements, etc.; a description of the tools used by the different workmen; an extensive glossary of the technical terms peculiar to each department; and the theory and practice of the five orders, as employed in decorative architecture*. Thomas Kelly.
Nicholson, P. (1834). *The builder's and workman's new director*. J. Taylor.
Nicholson, P. (1852). *Practical carpentry joinery and cabinet making; being a new and complete system of lines for the use of workmen founded on accurate geometrical and mechanical principles with their application in carpentry - to roofs domes centring etc.; in joinery - to stairs hand-rails soffits niches etc.; in cabinet-making to furniture both plain and ornamental fully and clearly explained*. (Thomas Tredgold, Rev.). Thomas Kelly.
Nicol, C., & Hooper, A. (1999). Contemporary change and the housebuilding industry: Concentration and standardisation in production. *Housing Studies*, *14*(1), 57–76. https://doi.org/10.1080/02673039983000
Numbeo. (2024). *Cost of living*. https://www.numbeo.com/cost-of-living/
Nussbaum, M. C. (2011). *Creating capabilities*. Harvard University Press.
OECD. (2021). *PH3.1 Public spending on housing allowances*. https://www.oecd.org/content/dam/oecd/en/data/datasets/affordable-housing-database/ph3-1-public-spending-on-housing-allowances.pdf
OECD. (2023). Public spending on financial support and subsidies for home-buyers and home-owners (Indicator PH2.1). In *OECD Affordable Housing Database*. https://www.oecd.org/en/data/datasets/oecd-affordable-housing-database.html.
Office for National Statistics. (2022, June 28). *Population and household estimates, England and Wales: Census 2021* [Statistical bulletin]. https://www.ons.gov.uk/peoplepopulationandcommunity/populationandmigration/populationestimates/bulletins/populationandhouseholdestimatesenglandandwales/census2021
Office for National Statistics. (2023, 25 August). *Overcrowding and under-occupancy by household characteristics, England and Wales: Census 2021*. https://www.ons.gov.uk/peoplepopulationandcommunity/housing/articles/overcrowdingandunderoccupancybyhouseholdcharacteristicsenglandandwales/census2021.
Office for National Statistics. (2024a). *Housing affordability in England and Wales: 2023*. https://www.ons.gov.uk/peoplepopulationandcommunity/housing/bulletins/housingaffordabilityinenglandandwales/2023
Office for National Statistics. (2024b). *Private rental affordability, England and Wales: 2023*. https://www.ons.gov.uk/peoplepopulationandcommunity/housing/bulletins/privaterentalaffordabilityengland/2023
Office for National Statistics. (2025a). *Households by household size, regions of England and Great Britain constituent countries*. https://www.ons.gov.uk/peoplepopulationandcommunity/birthsdeathsandmarriages/families/datasets/householdsbyhouseholdsizeregionsofenglandandgbconstituentcountries
Office for National Statistics. (2025b, August 1). *Subnational estimates of dwellings and households by tenure, England: 2023*. https://www.ons.gov.uk/peoplepopulationandcommunity/housing/articles/researchoutputssubnationaldwellingstockbytenureestimatesengland2012to2015/2023

Office of the Leading Group of the State Council for the Seventh National Population Census. (2021). *中国人口普查年鉴-2020* (No. Table 9-4) [Data set]. https://www.stats.gov.cn/sj/pcsj/rkpc/7rp/zk/indexch.htm

Ozaki, R. (2002). Housing as a reflection of culture: Privatised living and privacy in England and Japan. *Housing Studies*, *17*(2), 209–227. https://doi.org/10.1080/02673030220123199

Özer, S., & Jacoby, S. (2022). The design of subsidized housing: Towards an interdisciplinary and cross-national research agenda. *Housing Studies*, *39*(1), 297–322. https://doi.org/10.1080/02673037.2022.2045005

Özer, S., & Jones, A. (2022). Changing socio-spatial definitions of sufficiency of home: Evidence from London (UK) before and during the Covid-19 stay-at-home restrictions. *International Journal of Housing Policy*, *24*(2), 290–315. https://doi.org/10.1080/19491247.2022.2147354

Özer, S., & Jacoby, S. (2023). Space standards in affordable housing in England. *Building Research & Information*, *52*(6), 611–626. https://doi.org/10.1080/09613218.2023.2253337

Pain, W. (1793). *Pain's British Palladio, or, The builder's general assistant: Demonstrating in the most easy and practical method, all the principal rules of architecture, from the ground plan to the ornamental finish*. I. and J. Taylor.

Palate, S. (2022). *Homes for Today and Tomorrow*: Britain's Parker Morris Standards and the West Ham Experimental Scheme. *Architecture and Culture*, *10*(3), 457–482. https://doi.org/10.1080/20507828.2022.2198299

Park, J. (2017). *One hundred years of housing space standards: What now?* Levitt Bernstein. housingspacestandards.co.uk

Payne, S. (2013). Pioneers, pragmatists and sceptics: speculative housebuilders and brownfield development in the early twenty-first century. *Town Planning Review*, *84*(1), 37–62. https://doi.org/10.3828/tpr.2013.3

Peabody. (2025, February). *Design Guide: Strategic & concept design requirements* [Draft sample]. https://ehq-production-europe.s3.eu-west-1.amazonaws.com/30b760fd8ffbe7a804be4bcf3aa58e896fb5b8b4/original/1741878175/af9025653829af84d81f88ffecf4bb85_2310_Peabody-DesignGuide_V5_DraftSample.pdf?X-Amz-Algorithm=AWS4-HMAC-SHA256&X-Amz-Credential=AKIA4KKNQAKIJHZMYNPA%2F20251003%2Feu-west-1%2Fs3%2Faws4_request&X-Amz-Date=20251003T061707Z&X-Amz-Expires=300&X-Amz-SignedHeaders=host&X-Amz-Signature=0ce1721e9c56f9ecf81405e306e4b7676a1ca5c5b992f912b05a294512678d5f

Pedro, J. A. C. B. D. O., & Boueri, J. J. (2011). Affordable housing in Portugal and Sao Paulo municipality: Comparison of space standards and socio-economic indicators. In *COBRA 2011. Proceedings of RICS Construction and Property Conference* (pp. 287–305). RICS & University of Salford.

Perrot, M. (2018). *The bedroom: An intimate history* (L. Elkin, Trans.). Yale University Press. (Original work published 2009).

Pfeifer, G., & Brauneck, P. (2007). *Courtyard houses: A housing typology*. Birkhäuser.

Place Alliance. (2020). *A housing design audit for England*. https://discovery.ucl.ac.uk/id/eprint/10106239/

Porter, T. M. (1996). *Trust in numbers: The pursuit of objectivity in science and public life*. Princeton University Press, p. 8.

PricewaterhouseCoopers LLP. (2024, March 19). *Economic contribution of the private rented sector: Focusing on landlords with fewer than 15 properties in England and Wales*. https://www.paragonbank.co.uk/resources/paragonblogs/mortgageblogs/economic-contribution-of-the-private-rented-sector

Pugh, C., Trivelli, P., Jacobs, M., & Savedoff, W. (1970). *The Long Road to Housing Reform: Lessons from the Chilean Experience*. Inter-American Development Bank.

Punter, J., & Carmona, M. (1997). *The Design Dimension of Planning: Theory, Content and Best Practice for Design Policies*. Routledge.

Queensland Department of Housing. (2024). *Social Housing Design Guideline Toolkit: Technical summary sheets*. Queensland Government. https://www.housing.qld.gov.au/__data/assets/pdf_file/0011/19100/technical-summary-sheets-march-2024.pdf

Quintana, Francisco. (2014). Urbanizando con tiza. *ARQ (Santiago)*, (86), 30–43. https://dx.doi.org/10.4067/S0717-69962014000100005

Rabinow, P., & Rose, N. (2006). Biopower today. *BioSocieties*, *1*(2), 195–217. https://doi.org/10.1017/S1745855206040014

Ramsey, C. G., & Sleeper, H. R. (1932). *Architectural graphic standards for architects, engineers, decorators, builders and draftsmen*. John Wiley & Sons.

Raposo, A. (1999). La vivienda social de la CORVI: un otro patrimonio. *Revista INVI*, *14*(37), 41–73.

Rasmussen, S. E. (1967). *London: The unique city*. MIT Press.

Ratcliff, R. U. (1952). Housing standards and housing research. *Land Economics*, *28*(4), 328–332. https://doi.org/10.2307/3159481

Ravetz, A. (1974). From working-class tenement to modern flat: Local authorities and multi-storey housing between the wars. In A. Sutcliffe (Ed.), *Multi-storey living: The British working-class experience* (pp. 133–147). Croom Helm.

Ravetz, A., & Turkington, R. (1995). *The place of home: English domestic environments, 1914–2000*. Routledge.

Rebolledo, M. (2023, July). *Supervised models for the detection of subsidized housing complexes in Chile* [Conference paper]. 64th ISI World Statistics Congress, Ottawa, Canada. https://www.bis.org/ifc/events/ifc_230716_20_agenda/IPS243PaperRebolledo.pdf

Regulator of Social Housing. (2019, October 10). *Statistical Data Return shows majority of social housing stock owned by large providers*. GOV.UK. https://www.gov.uk/government/news/statistical-data-return-shows-majority-of-social-housing-stock-owned-by-large-providers

Reniers, M., & Loerakker, J. (2023). *Formats for living*. Architectura & Natura Press.

Reynolds, L., & Robinson, N. (2005). *Full house? How overcrowded housing affects families*. Shelter. https://assets.ctfassets.net/6sxvmndnpn0s/6dU8FFbZ6RnSk6DbnDOMHb/61e30884aff47a789891b2dce54fcbc7/Full_house_overcrowding_effects.pdf

Riley, H. T. (1863). Additions to the chronicles: Assize of buildings (Richard I). In H. T. Riley (Ed.), *Chronicles of the Mayors and Sheriffs of London 1188–1274* (pp. 179–187). Trübner and Co. http://www.british-history.ac.uk/no-series/london-mayors-sheriffs/1188-1274/pp179-187

Roberts, H. (1850). *The dwellings of the labouring classes, their arrangement and construction: With the essentials of a healthy dwelling; illustrated by references to the model houses of the Society for Improving the Condition of the Labouring Classes; with plans and elevations of dwellings adapted to towns and to rural districts*. The Society for Improving the Condition of the Labouring Classes.

Rodger, R. (1995). *Housing in Urban Britain 1780–1914* (New Studies in Economic and Social History, Series Number 8). Cambridge University Press.

Rodríguez, A., & Sugranyes, A. (Eds.). (2005). *Los con techo: Un desafío para la política de vivienda social*. Ediciones SUR.

Rojas, E. (1999). *The long road to housing reform: Lessons from the Chilean experience* (Sustainable Development Dept. Best Practices Series No. SOC-113). Inter-American Development Bank.

Rojas, F. (2012). La Ley de Habitaciones Obreras de 1906 y la vivienda popular en Chile. *Revista INVI*, *27*(74), 23–45.

Ross, J., & Pelletiere, D. (2014). Chile's new rental housing subsidy and its relevance to U.S. housing choice voucher program reform. *Cityscape*, *16*(2), 289–298.

Royal Institute of British Architects. (2011). *The Case for Space: The size of England's new homes*. https://www.architecture.com/knowledge-and-resources/resources-landing-page/space-standards-for-homes

Royal Institute of British Architects. (2018, June 21). *Finding ways to design for the public good*. https://www.architecture.com/knowledge-and-resources/knowledge-landing-page/finding-ways-to-design-for-the-public-good

Royal Institute of British Architects. (2020). *Social value toolkit for architecture*. https://www.architecture.com/knowledge-and-resources/resources-landing-page/social-value-toolkit-for-architecture

Royal Institute of British Architects. (2025, March 21). *Foundations for the future: A new delivery model for social housing*. https://www.architecture.com/knowledge-and-resources/resources-landing-page/riba-social-housing-report-summary

Rudofsky, B. (1964). *Architecture without architects: An introduction to non-pedigreed architecture*. Museum of Modern Art. https://www.moma.org/documents/moma_catalogue_3459_300062280.pdf

Sal Moslehian, A., Warner, E., & Andrews, F. (2023). The impacts of kitchen and dining spatial design on cooking and eating experience in residential buildings: A scoping review. *Journal of Housing and the Built Environment*, *38*(3), 1983–2003. https://doi.org/10.1007/s10901-023-10027-z.

Salvi del Pero, A. (2016). *A case study on two housing programmes for low-income households: Chile's Fondo Solidario and DS1 subsidy schemes*. OECD Publishing.

Samuel, F. (2018). *Promoting design value in public rented housing: An English perspective* (CaCHE Social Housing Policy Working Group Report). UK Collaborative Centre for Housing Evidence (CaCHE). https://housingevidence.ac.uk/wp-content/uploads/2024/03/R2018_SHPWG_01_Promoting_Design_Value.pdf

Sayce, S., Crosby, N., Garside, P., Harris, R., & Parsa, A. (2017). *Viability and the Planning System: The Relationship between Economic Viability Testing, Land Values and Affordable Housing in London.* Royal Agricultural University, Cirencester.

Scanlon, K., Whitehead, C., & Fernández Arrigoitia, M. (Eds.). (2014). *Social housing in Europe*. John Wiley & Sons.

Schiilder, F., & Scherpenisse, R. (2018). *Policy and practice: Affordable housing in the Netherlands*. PBL Netherlands.

Scottish Government. (2017). *Building standards technical handbooks: Domestic buildings*. https://www.gov.scot/publications/building-standards-2017-domestic/

Secretaría Técnica Presidencial. (2005). Informe diagnóstico de la política habitacional en Chile.

Sen, A. (2009). *The idea of justice*. Harvard University Press.

Sendi, R. (2013). The low housing standard in Slovenia: Low purchasing power as an eternal excuse. *Urbani Izziv*, *24*(1), 107–124. https://doi.org/10.5379/urbani-izziv-en-2013-24-01-002.

Shanghai Municipal Planning and Land Resources Bureau. (2010). 关于印发〈上海市保障性住房建设导则(试行)〉的通知 [Notice on issuing the *Shanghai Affordable Housing Design Guidelines* (trial)].

Shaw M. (2004). Housing and public health. *Annual Review of Public Health*, *25*, 397–418. https://doi.org/10.1146/annurev.publhealth.25.101802.123036

Shelter. (2021, Oct 13). *Health of one in five renters harmed by their home*. https://england.shelter.org.uk/media/press_release/health_of_one_in_five_renters_harmed_by_their_home

Shenzhen Housing and Construction Bureau & Shenzhen Municipal Development and Reform Commission. (2021, August 15). *公共住房建设标准 [Public Housing Design Standard].* https://zjj.sz.gov.cn/attachment/1/1533/1533953/9023096.pdf.

Silva, C., & Vergara-Perucich, F. (2021). Determinants of urban sprawl in Latin America: Evidence from Santiago de Chile. *SN Social Sciences*, *1*(202), 1–22.

Society of Architects. (1779). *The builder's magazine: Or, a universal dictionary for architects*. Francis Newbery.

Spink, B. (2005). What has the state ever done for us? A review of the state's role in influencing the UK's housing market 1800 to 2003. In P. Somerville & N. Sprigings (Eds.), *Housing and social policy: Contemporary themes and critical perspectives* (pp. 14–42). Routledge.

Stadt Zurich. (2025). *Wohnungsbestand* [Data set]. https://www.stadt-zuerich.ch/de/politik-und-verwaltung/statistik-und-daten/daten/bauen-und-wohnen/wohnungen/wohnungsbestand.html

Steffel, R. V. (1976). The Boundary Street Estate: An example of urban redevelopment by the London County Council, 1889–1914. *The Town Planning Review*, *47*(2), 161–173. http://www.jstor.org/stable/40103181

Stephens, M. (2020). How housing systems are changing and why: A critique of Kemeny's theory of housing regimes. *Housing, Theory and Society*, *37*(5), 1–27. https://doi.org/10.1080/14036096.2020.1814404

Stephens, M., & Norris, M. (Eds.). (2014). *Meaning and measurement in comparative housing research*. Routledge.

Stephens, M., Perry, J., Williams, P., & Young, G. (2024). *UK Housing Review Autumn Briefing Paper 2024*. Chartered Institute of Housing. https://www.cih.org/media/ox2gxc55/ukhr-autumn-briefing-2024.pdf

Stevenson, F. (2019). *Housing fit for purpose: Performance, feedback and learning*. RIBA Publishing.

Stewart, J., & Lynch, Z. (2018). *Environmental health and housing: Issues for public health* (2nd ed.). Routledge.

Stewart, R. (2009). *The town house in Georgian London*. Paul Mellon.

Summerson, J. (1945). *Georgian London*. Pleiades.

Susanto, D., Nuraeny, E., & Widyarta, M. N. (2020). Rethinking the minimum space standard in Indonesia: Tracing the social, culture and political view through public housing policies. *Journal of Housing and the Built Environment*, *35*(3), 983–1000. https://doi.org/10.1007/s10901-020-09770-4

Swenarton, M. (2008). *Building the new Jerusalem: Architecture, housing and politics 1900–1930*. IHS BRE Press.

Swenarton, M., Avermaete, T., & van den Heuvel, D. (Eds.). (2014). *Architecture and the welfare state*. Routledge.

Tallon, A. (2020). *Urban Regeneration in the UK*. Routledge.

Tarn, J. N. (1973). *Five per cent philanthropy: An account of housing in urban areas between 1840 and 1914*. Cambridge University Press.

Taylor, F. (1911). *Principles of scientific management*. Harper & Brothers.

Teige, K. (2002). *The minimum dwelling* (E. Ehrenburg, Trans.; G. K. Kulhánek, Ed.). MIT Press. (Original work published 1932).

The State Council. (2022, January 11). *China to build more subsidized rental homes to meet housing needs*. English.Gov.Cn. https://english.www.gov.cn/statecouncil/ministries/202201/11/content_WS61dd4b28c6d09c94e48a3733.html

Thiesen, C. (2020). Switzerland. In C. Baiges, M. Ferreri, & L. Vidal (Eds.), *International policies to promote cooperative housing* (pp. 104–111). La Dinamo Fundació. https://ladinamofundacio.org/wp-content/uploads/2020/04/La-Dinamo-International-policies-1.pdf

Thom, C. (2017). Miles of Silly Little Dirty Houses: Lessons of Victorian Battersea. In P. Guillery & D. Kroll (Eds.), *Mobilising housing histories: Learning from London's past for a sustainable future*. RIBA Publishing.

Till, J., & Schneider, T. (2007). *Flexible housing*. Architectural Press.

Turner, C. (2015). *Homes through the decades: The making of modern housing*. NHBC Foundation.

UK Green Building Council. (2023). *Home retrofit: Accelerating the UK's journey to net zero*. https://ukgbc.org/our-work/home-retrofit/.

United Nations. (2018). *Report of the Special Rapporteur on adequate housing as a component of the right to an adequate standard of living* (A/HRC/37/53/Add.1).

United Nations. (2022). *UN Procurement Practitioners Handbook*. https://www.ungm.org/Shared/KnowledgeCenter/Document?widgetId=3518&documentId=1294233

UN-Habitat. (2010). *The right to adequate housing: Fact Sheet No. 21 (Rev. 1)*. https://unhabitat.org/the-right-to-adequate-housing-fact-sheet-no-21rev1.

UN-Habitat. (2019). *Monitoring SDG indicator 11.1.1: Global monitoring of slums remains a key concern for achieving the right to adequate housing* (Urban SDG Monitoring Series, Issue 1). United Nations Human Settlements Programme. https://unhabitat.org/sites/default/files/2020/06/the_urban_sdg_monitoring_series_monitoring_sdg_indicator_11.1.1.pdf

UN-Habitat. (2023). *Rescuing SDG 11 for a resilient urban planet: SDG 11 synthesis report 2023 – Executive summary*. United Nations Human Settlements Programme. https://unhabitat.org/sites/default/files/2023/11/sdg_11_synthesis_report_2023_executive_summary_2023.pdf

Urban, F. (2011). *Tower and slab: Histories of global mass housing*. Routledge.

Urbistat. (2023). *Family trends in the Municipality of Amsterdam*. https://ugeo.urbistat.com/AdminStat/en/nl/demografia/famiglie/amsterdam/23055764/4

van der Molen, F. (2025, July 5). *Amsterdamse corporaties*. NUL20. https://www.nul20.nl/dossiers/dashboard-amsterdamse-woningcorporaties

van Gent, W., & Hochstenbach, C. (2020). The neo-liberal politics and socio-spatial implications of Dutch post-crisis social housing policies. *International Journal of Housing Policy*, *20*(1), 156–172. https://doi.org/10.1080/19491247.2019.1682234

Vargas, J. R. (2006). Housing subsidies and residential segregation in Santiago: Is there a causal relationship? *Journal of Urban Affairs*, *28*(5), 437–457.

Veenstra, J., Koolma, H. M., & Allers, M. A. (2017). Scale, mergers and efficiency: The case of Dutch housing corporations. *Journal of Housing and the Built Environment*, *32*(2), 313–337. https://doi.org/10.1007/s10901-016-9515-4

Vega, D. M., & Liñán, L. J. (2024). Handbook, standard, room: The prescription of residential room types in Sweden between 1942 and 2023. *Urban Planning*, *9*. https://doi.org/10.17645/up.7846

Vergara, J. E., Álvarez, D., Dintrans, D., & Asenjo, D. (2021). CORVI, tipologías de viviendas racionalizadas: un ejercicio de estandarización. *Arquitecturas del Sur*, *39*(59), 119–138.

Verrest, H., & Post, J. (2007). Home-based economic activities, livelihoods and space in Paramaribo, Suriname. *International Development Planning Review*, *29*(2), 161–184. https://doi.org/10.3828/idpr.29.2.2.

Wagemann, E., Maynard, V., & Simons, B. (2024). Housing and home-based work: Considerations for development and humanitarian contexts. *Cities*, *147*, 104833. https://doi.org/10.1016/j.cities.2024.104833.

Wakeman, R. (2016). *Practicing Utopia: An intellectual history of the new town movement*. University of Chicago Press.

Wall, C. (2016). *An architecture of parts: Architects, building workers and industrialisation in Britain 1940–1970*. Routledge.

Wang, L., Cheng, J. C., Mazan, W., & Jacoby, S. (2024). Standard block and modular dwelling designs in Hong Kong's public housing. *Architecture*, *4*(1), 89–111. https://doi.org/10.3390/architecture4010007

Wang, L., & Jacoby, S. (2023). Housing experimentation and design guides: Affordable housing in Guangzhou since 2006. *Architecture*, *3*(4), 692–712. https://doi.org/10.3390/architecture3040038

Wang, Y. P., & Murie, A. (2011). The new affordable and social housing provision system in China: Implications for comparative housing studies. *International Journal of Housing Policy*, *11*(3), 237–254. https://doi.org/10.1080/14616718.2011.599130

Ware, I. (1756). *A complete body of architecture: Adorned with plans and elevations, from original designs. In which are interspersed some designs of Inigo Jones, never before published.* Printed for T. Osborne and J. Shipton.

Watling, S., & Breach, A. (2023, February 22). *The housebuilding crisis: The UK's 4 million missing homes.* Centre for Cities. https://www.centreforcities.org/reader/the-housebuilding-crisis/executive-summary/

Wetzstein, S. (2018). Comparative housing, urban crisis and political economy: An ethnographically based 'long view' from Auckland, Singapore and Berlin. *Housing Studies*, *34*(2), 1–26. https://doi.org/10.1080/02673037.2018.1487038

White, J. T., Kenny, T., Samuel, F., Foye, C., James, G., & Serin, B. (2020). *Delivering design value: The housing design quality conundrum.* UK Collaborative Centre for Housing Evidence (CaCHE). https://housingevidence.ac.uk/wp-content/uploads/2024/04/12506_CaCHE_Delivering_Design_Main_Report_IA-1.pdf

White, J. T., Kenny, T., Samuel, F., Foye, C., James, G., & Serin, B. (2024). Are well-designed places possible? A model of design governance intervention in the planning, design and development of new neighbourhoods. *Journal of Urban Design*, *29*(5), 495–516. https://doi.org/10.1080/13574809.2023.2296885

Wilcox, A., Mota, N., Haffner, M., & Elsinga, M. (2024). Compact housing for incremental growth: The K206 RDP Project in Alexandra, Johannesburg. *Urban Planning*, *9*. https://www.cogitatiopress.com/urbanplanning/article/view/7736

Williams, K. (2009). Space per person in the UK: A review of densities, trends, experiences and optimum levels. *Land Use Policy*, *26*, S83–S92. https://doi.org/10.1016/j.landusepol.2009.08.024.

Wohnbaugenossenschaften Schweiz. (2022, May). Marktanteil des gemeinnützigen Wohnungsbaus. https://www.wbg-schweiz.ch/data/wbg-infopool-marktanteil-2022_3520.pdf

Woodman, E., & Greeves, E. (2008). *Home/Away: Five British architects build housing in Europe: The development of housing in Britain 1870–2008.* Visual Arts Publications.

World Health Organization. (2013). *Combined or multiple exposure to health stressors in indoor built environments.* https://iris.who.int/bitstream/handle/10665/350495/WHO-EURO-2014-4523-44286-62555-eng.pdf?sequence=1&isAllowed=y

Yates, L., & Warde, A. (2017). Eating together and eating alone: Meal arrangements in British households. *The British Journal of Sociology*, *68*(1), 97–118. https://doi.org/10.1111/1468-4446.12231.

Ympäristöministeriön asetus asuin-, majoitus- ja työtiloista 1008/2017 (2017). https://www.finlex.fi/fi/lainsaadanto/saadoskokoelma/2017/1008

Yuan, Q. (2015). Guang zhou bao zhang xing zhu fang she qu jian she liang li. *Beijing Planning Review*, *4*, 174–177.

Zheng, N. (2023, February 24). 600 million buildings isn't too many for China, expert says. Yicai Global. https://www.yicaiglobal.com/news/600-million-buildings-isnt-too-many-for-china-expert-says.

INDEX

Note: Page references in *italics* denote figures and in **bold** tables.